KAFFE FASSETT'S
Quilts on an English Farm

featuring
Liza Prior Lucy

location photography
Debbie Patterson

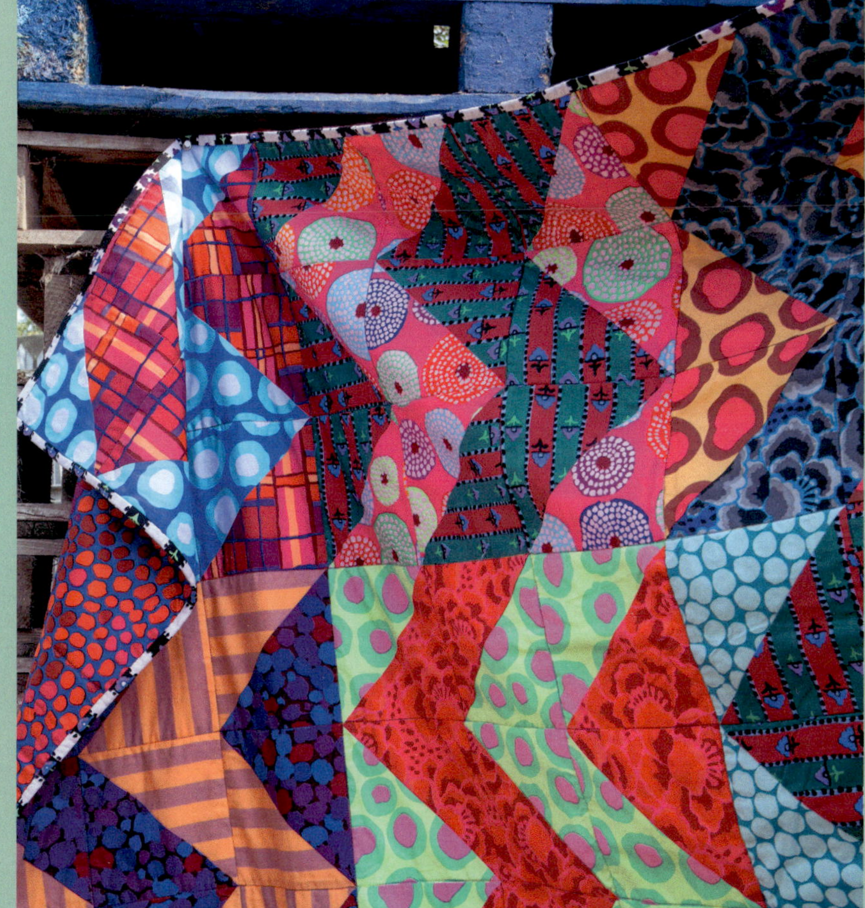

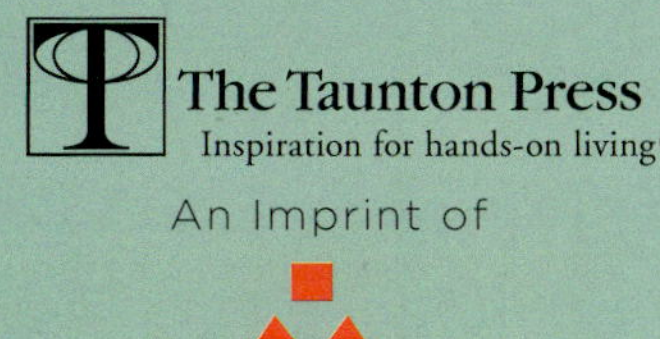
The Taunton Press
Inspiration for hands-on living®

An Imprint of

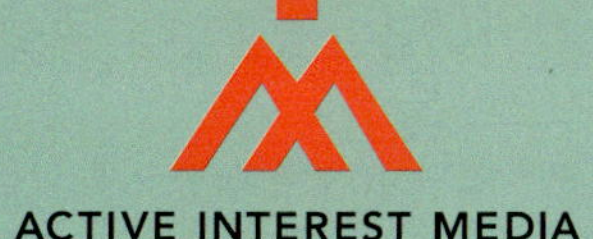
ACTIVE INTEREST MEDIA

First published in the USA in 2024

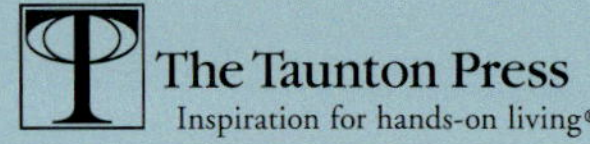

The Taunton Press
Inspiration for hands-on living®

An Imprint of

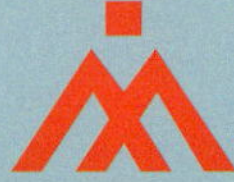

ACTIVE INTEREST MEDIA

2143 Grand Ave, Des Moines, IA 50312

Patchwork designs	Kaffe Fassett Liza Prior Lucy
Quilt making coordination	Heart Space Studios (UK) Liza Prior Lucy (US)
Technical editor	Bundle Backhouse
Designer Art direction/styling	Anne Wilson Kaffe Fassett
Location photography Additional photography	Debbie Patterson Brandon Mably (pp 4; 6; 7C, CR, BL; 8TL, C 3rd from left, BR)
Stills photography	Steven Wooster
Quilt illustrations	Heart Space Studios
Publishing consultant	Susan Berry (Berry & Co)

Library of Congress Cataloging-in-Publication Data
in progress

ISBN 978-1-64155-222-6

Colour reproduction	Pixywalls Ltd, London
Printed in China	

Page 1: A detail of my bold *Lightning Strike* quilt with its strong
graphic structure.
Right: Subtle shifts of tone and pattern in my *Leafy Circles* quilt
echo the mossy background.

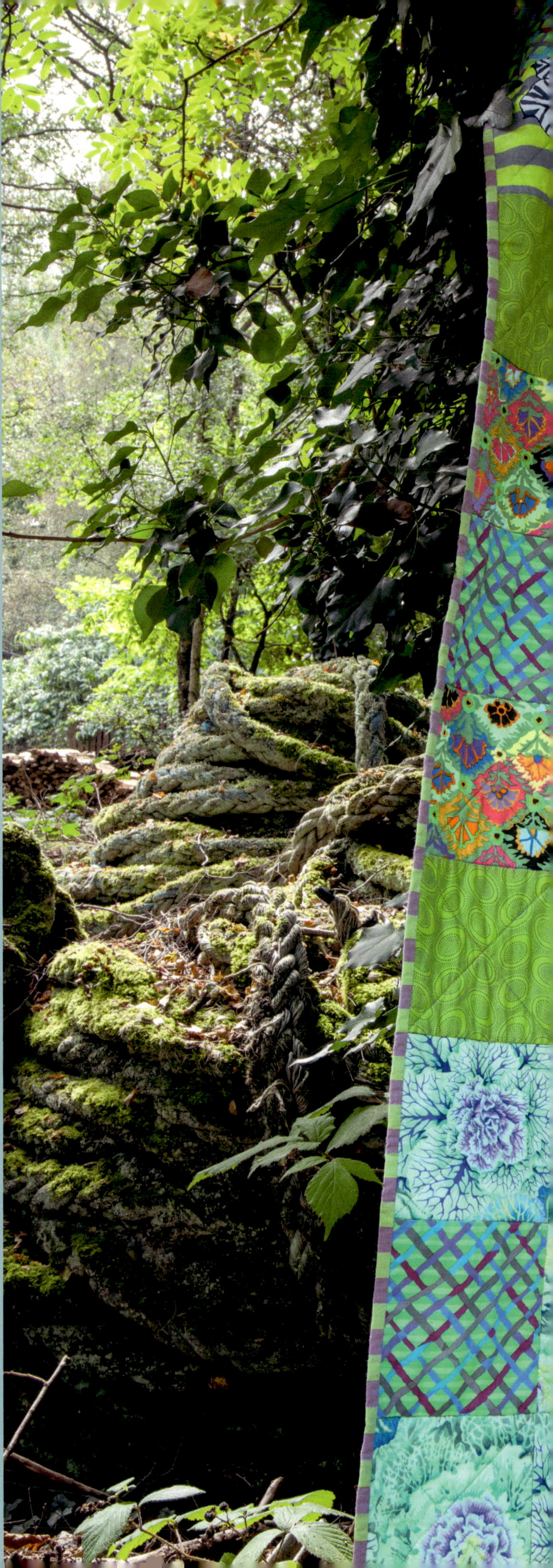

Contents

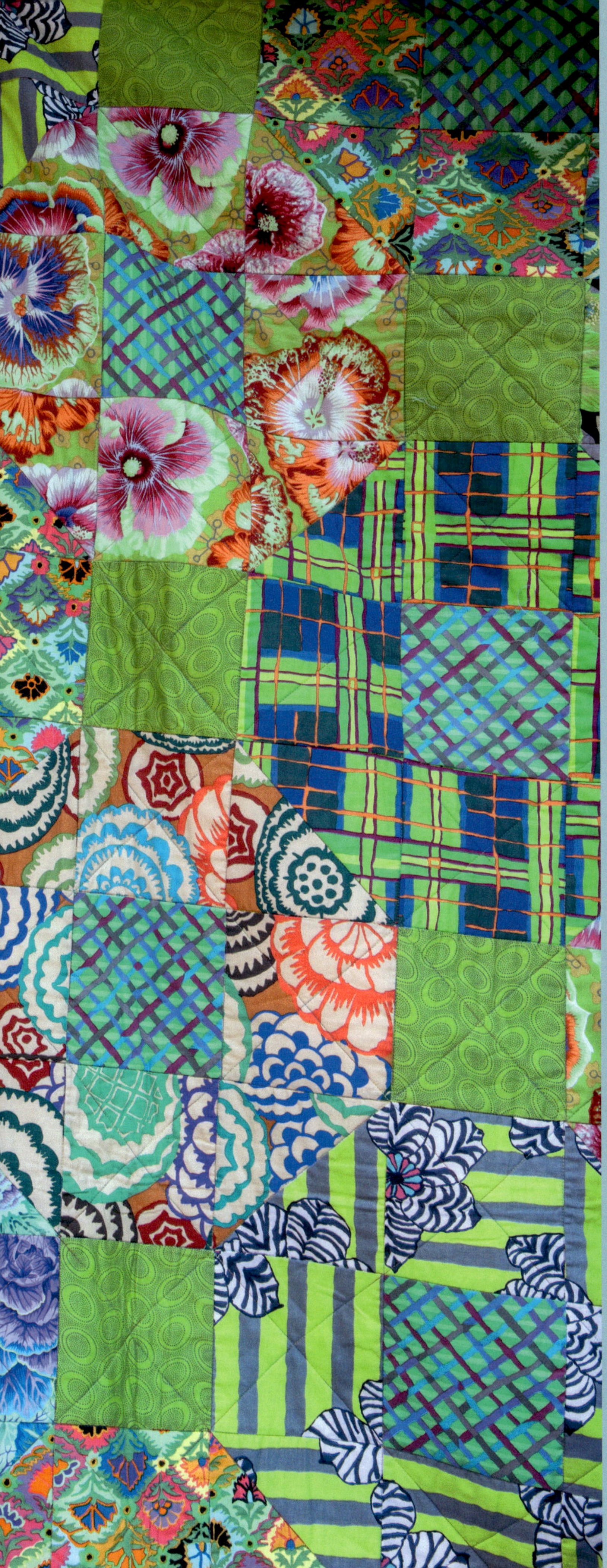

introduction

What a stimulating experience this shoot was! To spend time in a good working environment, where everything has a use and everyone knows the jobs they have to do to keep it all going, took me back to my childhood years when we were building and running our family restaurant business in Big Sur in California.

Earlier in the year, Brandon and I had set our hearts on a farm setting for our next book. Brandon's sister, Belinda, who does our social media, made it her job to find us a good location. She and her mother use a farm shop in Kent for their fruit and vegetables, so she scouted round the grounds on her next visit and sent me some great shots of the working quarters of the farm. When we visited the place ourselves, we were equally struck by all the other interesting elements of the farm, including tractors and ivy-covered walls that we hadn't seen in the photos.

Because the background colours in our location were going to be predominantly weathered wood, old brickwork and rusty

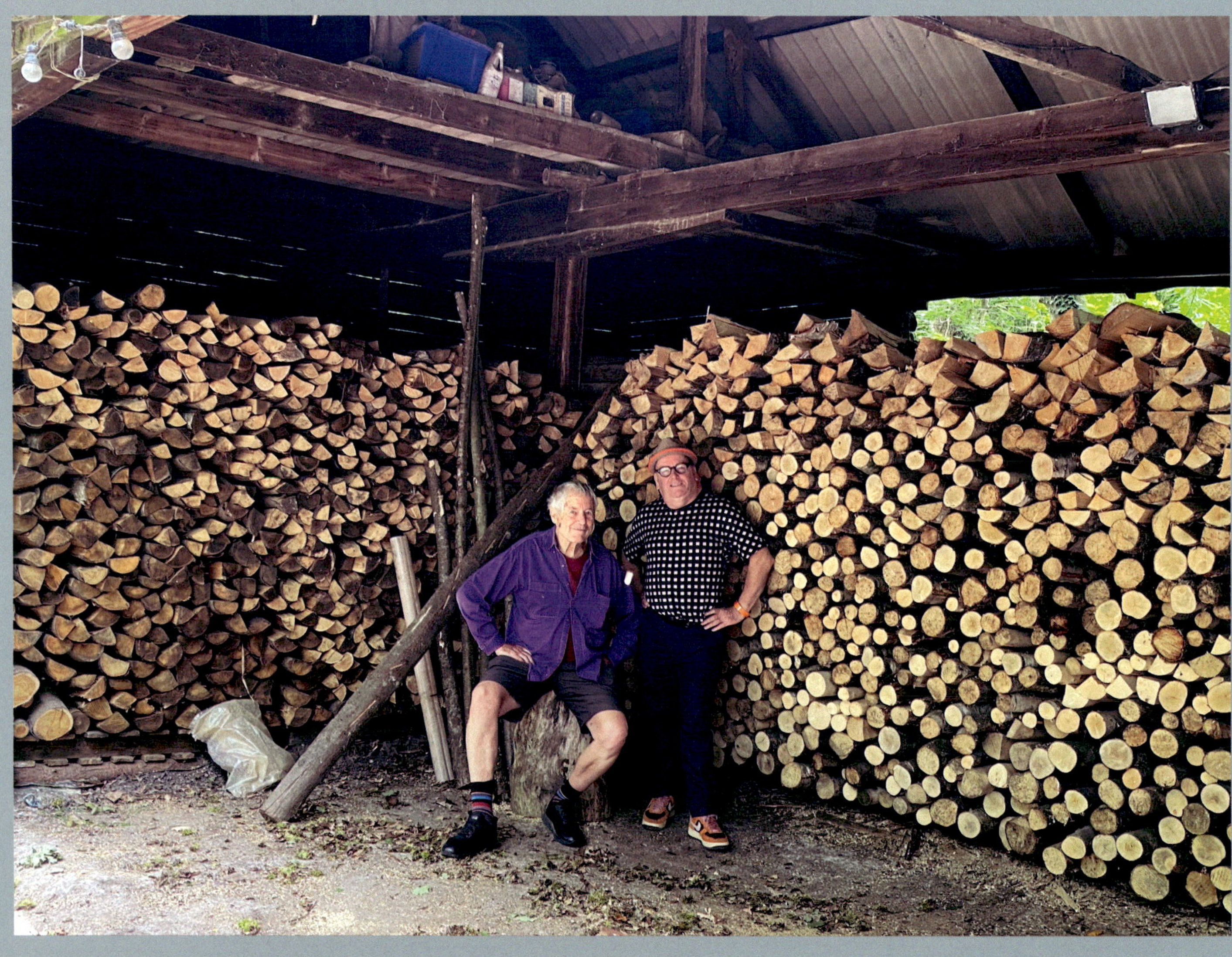

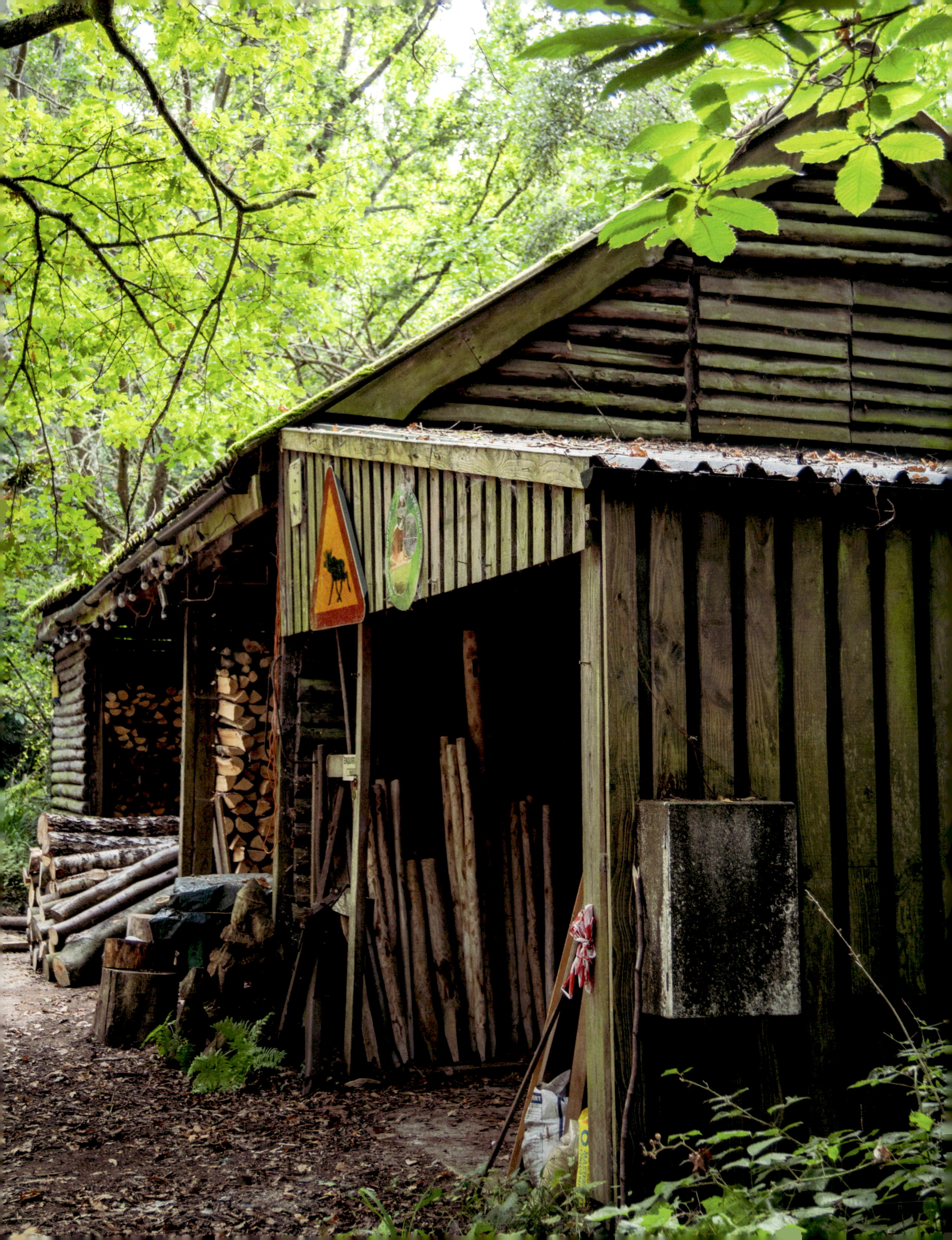

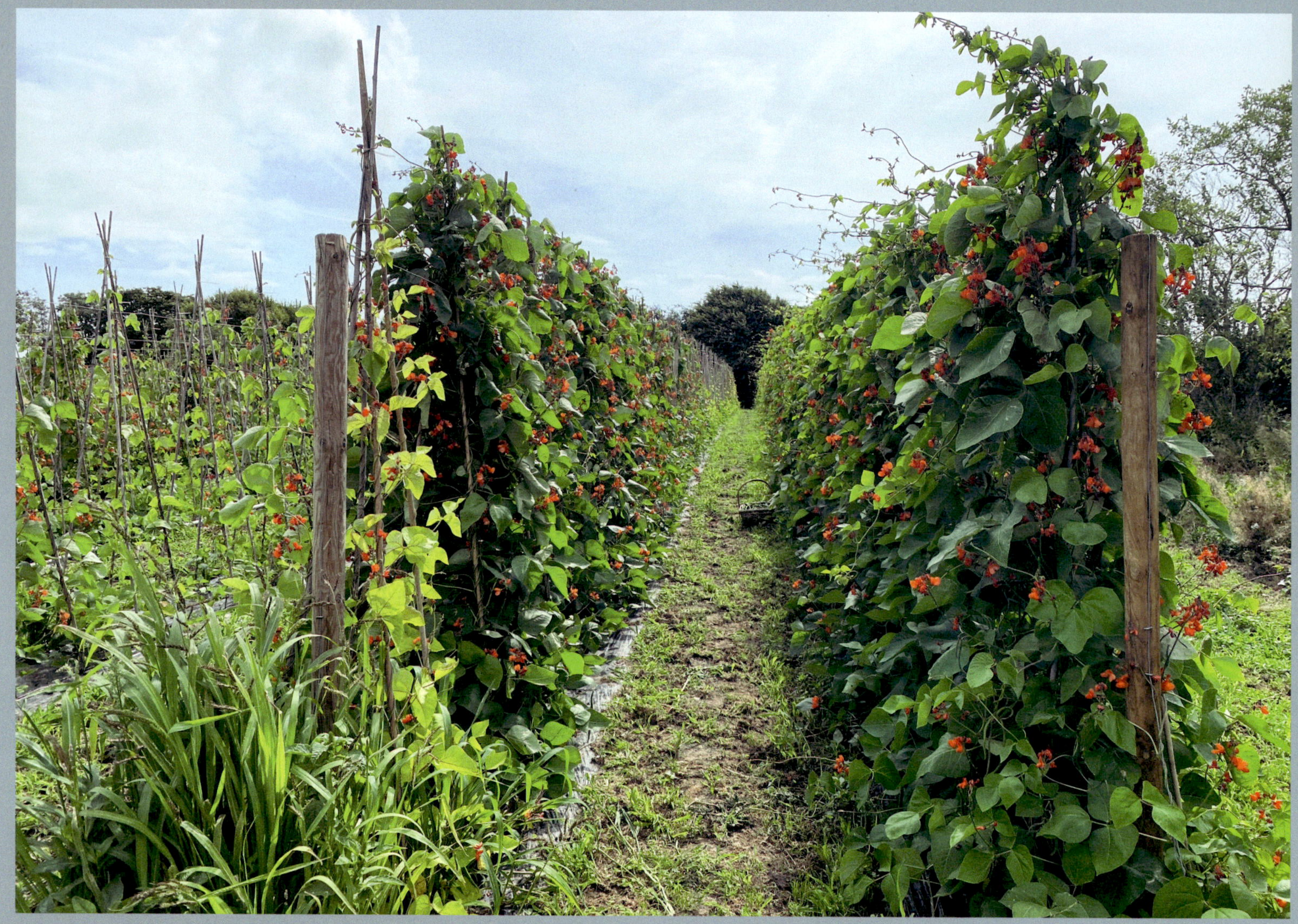

metal, I made sure most of the quilts reflected that muted aesthetic. Belinda had also found a woodland setting with some handsome stacks of wood and a gorgeous pile of mossy old ropes. The cut rounds of ochre wood prompted me to do a new version of my favourite quilt block: the snowball. I chose all the deep woody tones in our collection to create my *Country Snowballs* quilt. Other quilts were designed to go with corrugated metal walls and silvered stacks of wooden stakes. Even a plastic barrel in duck-egg blue served to pick up a colour in one quilt.

In fact, there was not a corner of this wonderful working environment that did not have its own intrinsic beauty, from the vintage tractors to the stalks of pick-your-own beans left in the field. We delighted in one handsome setting for our quilt collection after another. The farm shop itself was ablaze with colour: it was so good to be able to celebrate the eternal beauty of seasonal fruit and vegetables.

As we beavered away, hanging our quilts, photographing them and folding them away into the boot of our car, we could hear a farmer repairing a metal fence, to the accompaniment of a Cat Stevens' song on his transistor radio. An old apple tree in the sun-dappled yard of the farmhouse gave us a lush setting for the

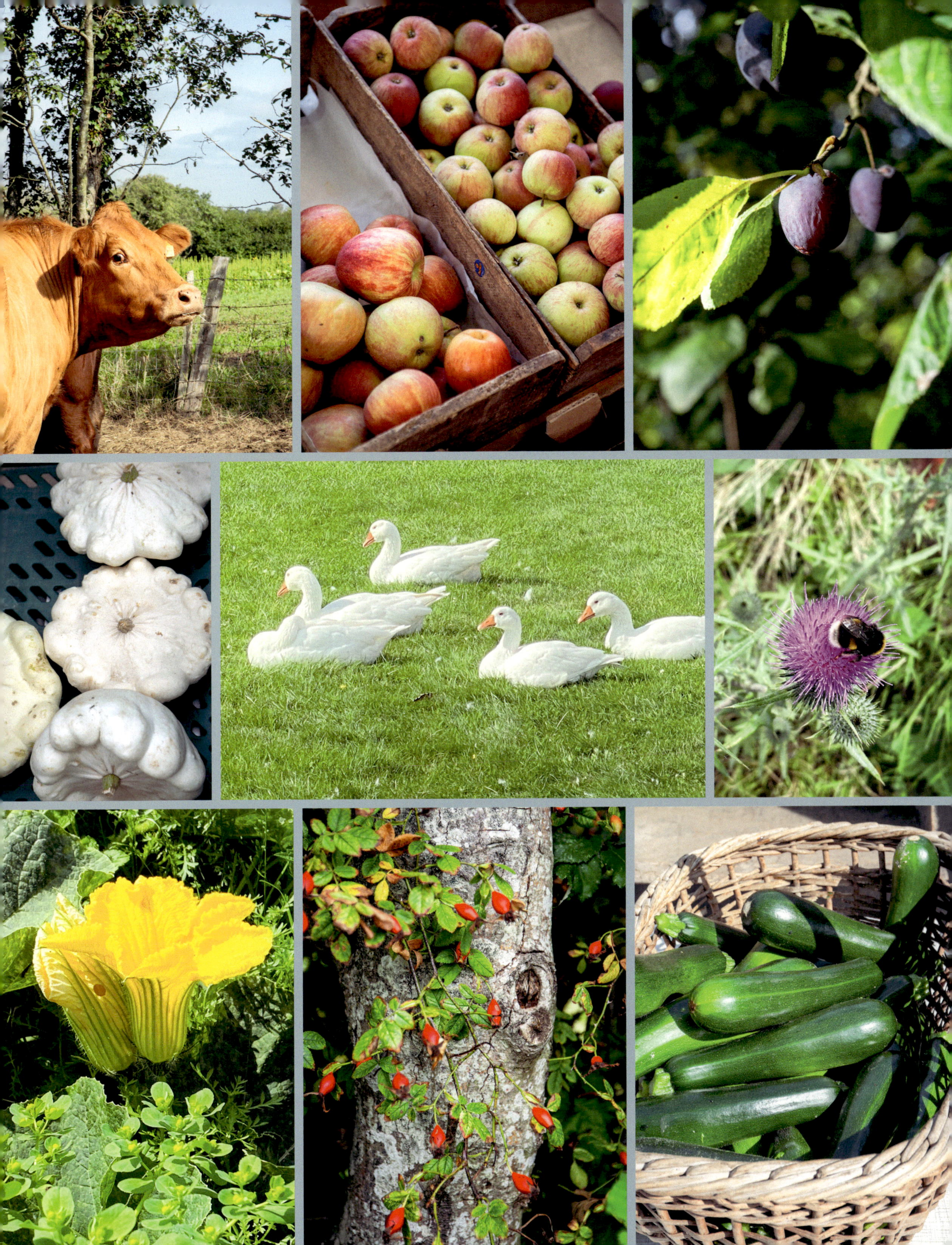

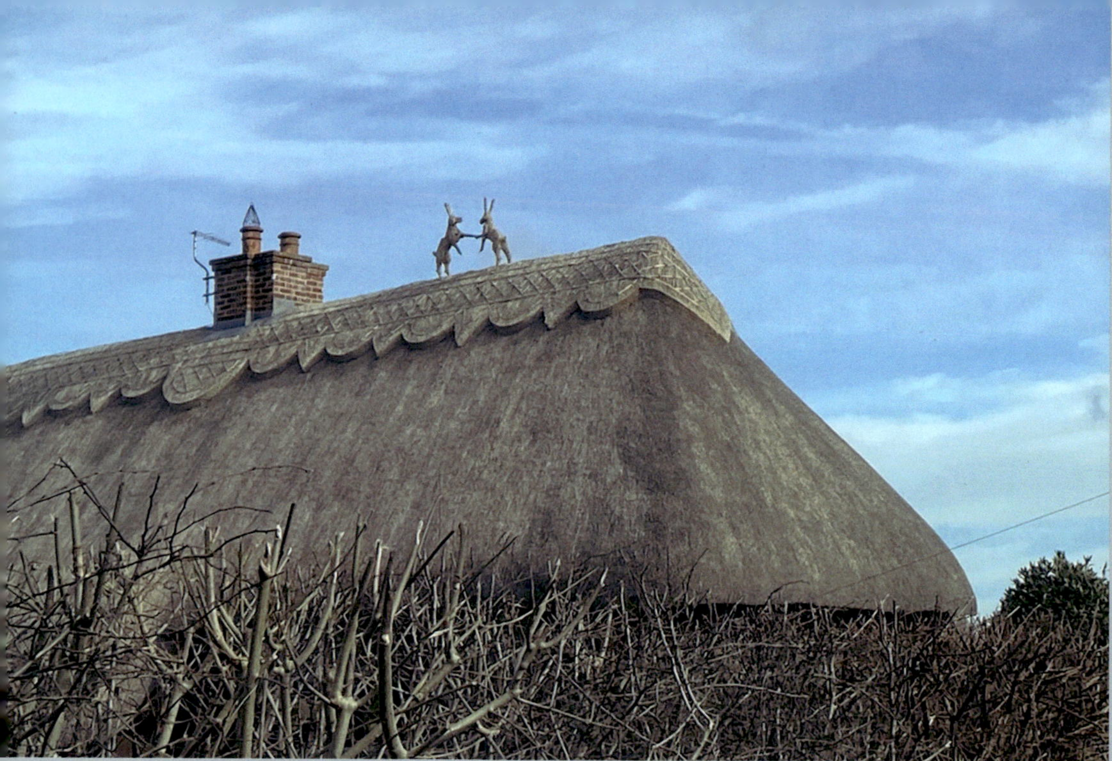

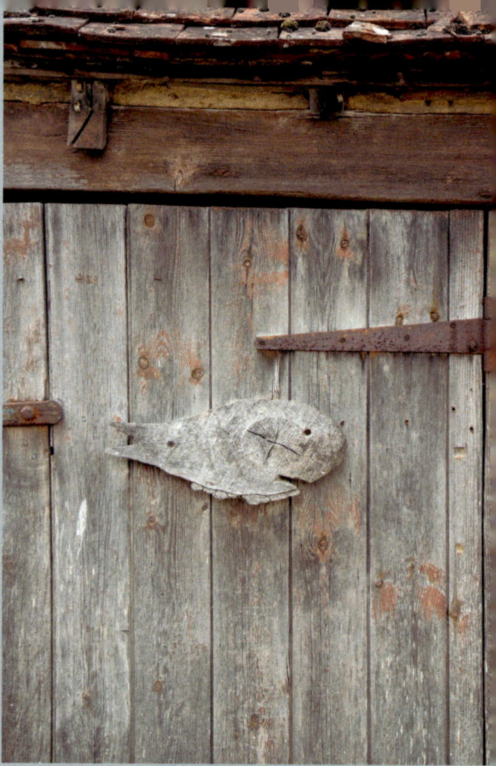

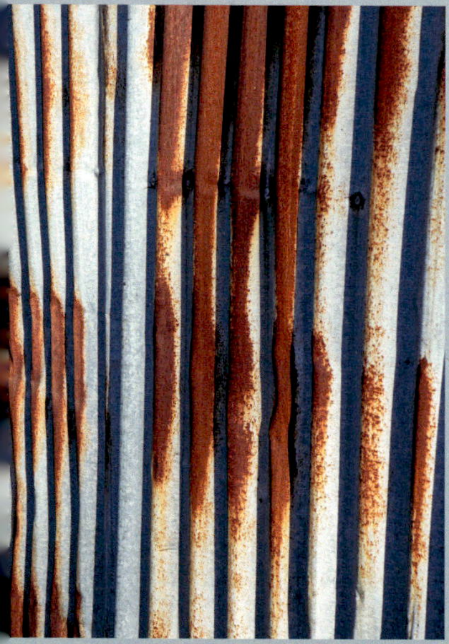

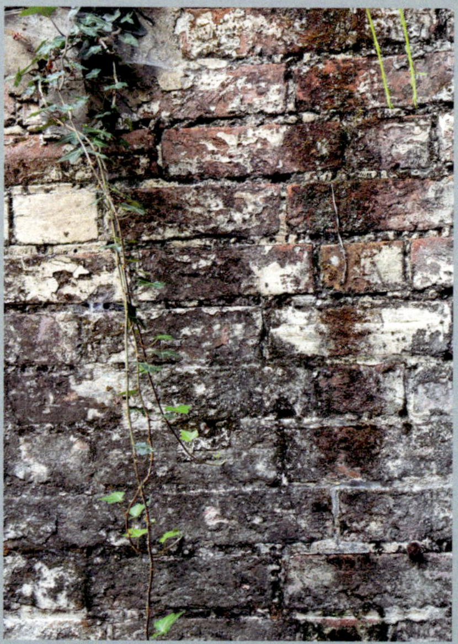

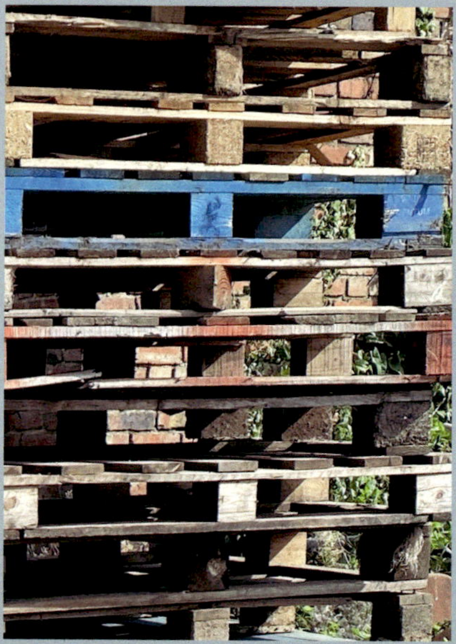

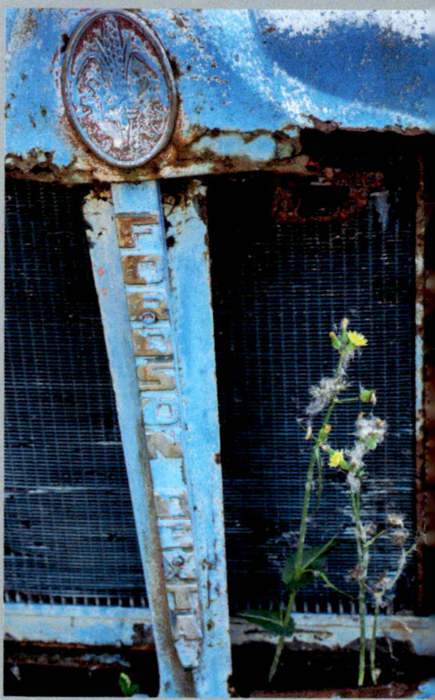

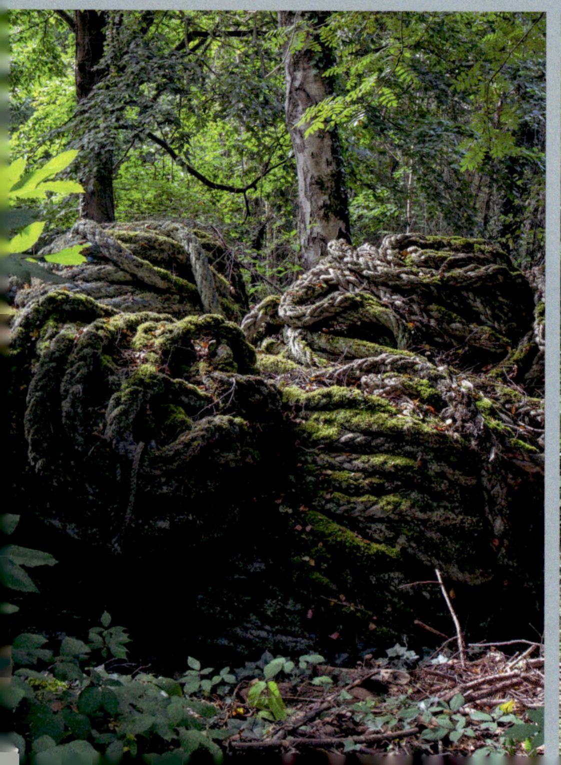
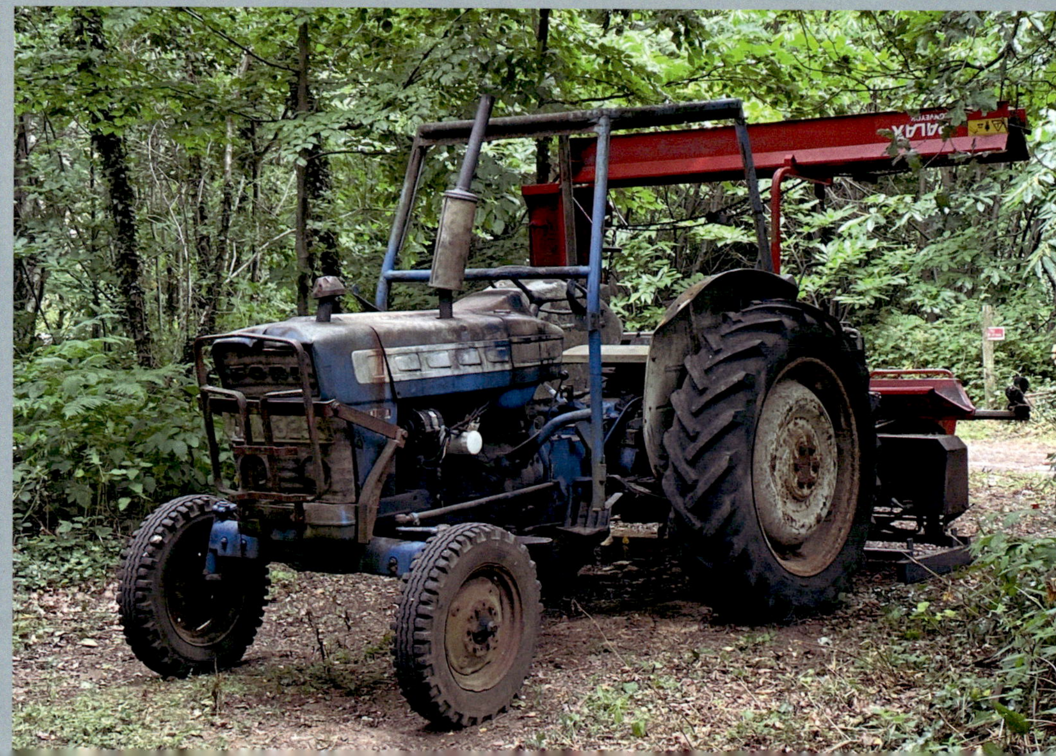
PALAX
CONVEYOR

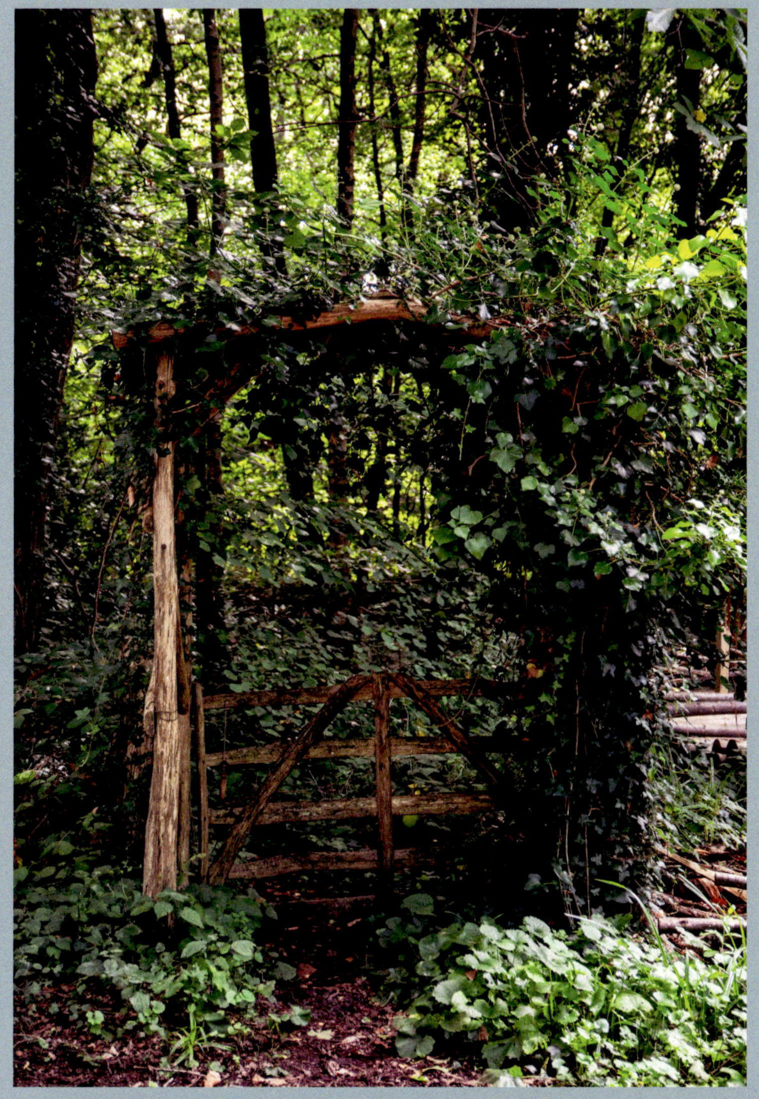 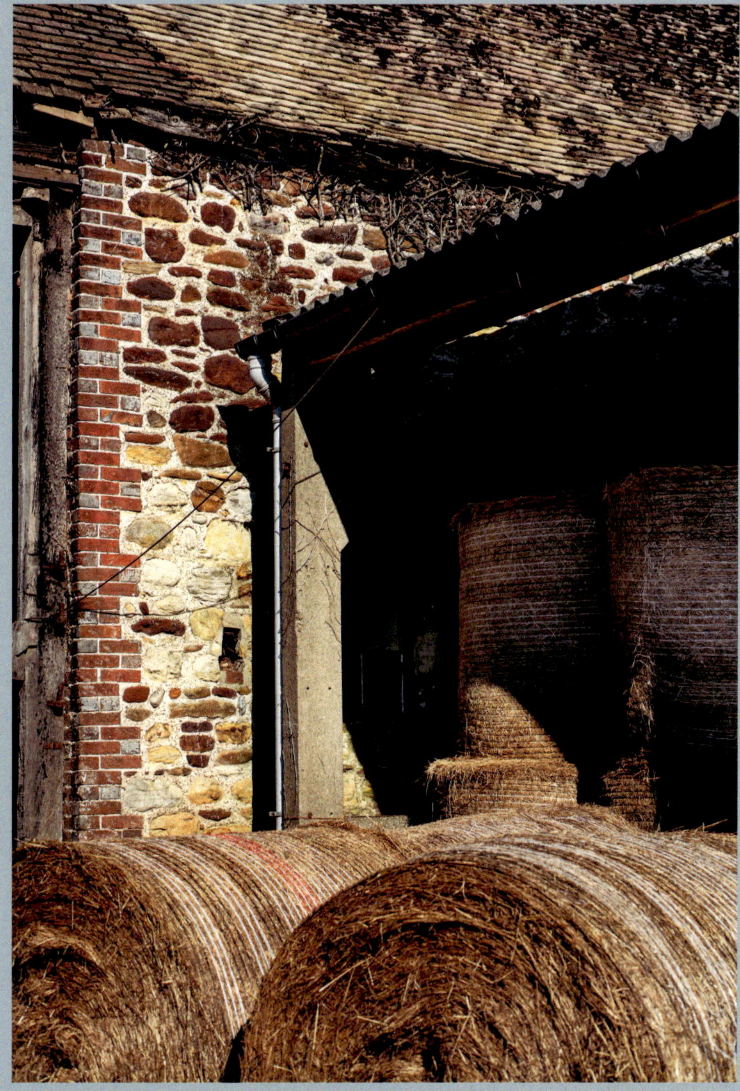

green *Bean Stalk*s quilt. Even a stack of coloured pallets was put to good use as a gritty backdrop for our bold *Lightning Strike* quilt.

Debbie, our faithful photographer, was particularly delighted when she came across the pen of chestnut-coloured cows enthusiastically munching their mid-morning meal. These, and other beautiful little details of farm life, help to bring our introduction pages to life.

At a time when we are all having to think more deeply about the environment and the food we consume, it felt good spending time on a thriving farm with their gorgeous harvest of produce, including the russet-coloured apples and handsome deep-green courgettes, among other life-enhancing products.

I am so grateful to Belinda and her mother, not only for introducing us to the perfect location for our quilts but also for providing us with delicious meals made from some of the produce. It was the perfect way to keep our energies up for the intensive roller-coaster of our photo shoot.

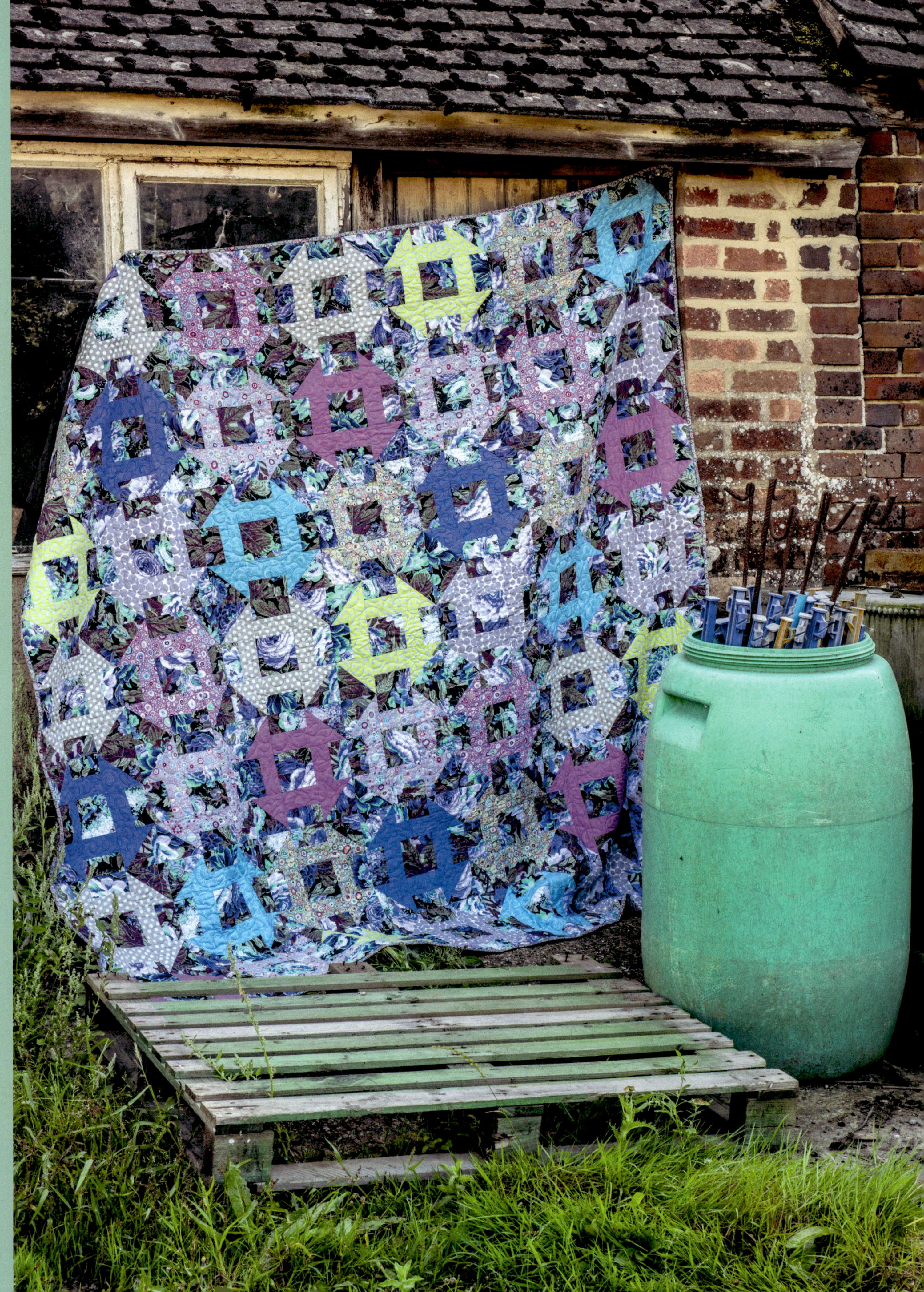

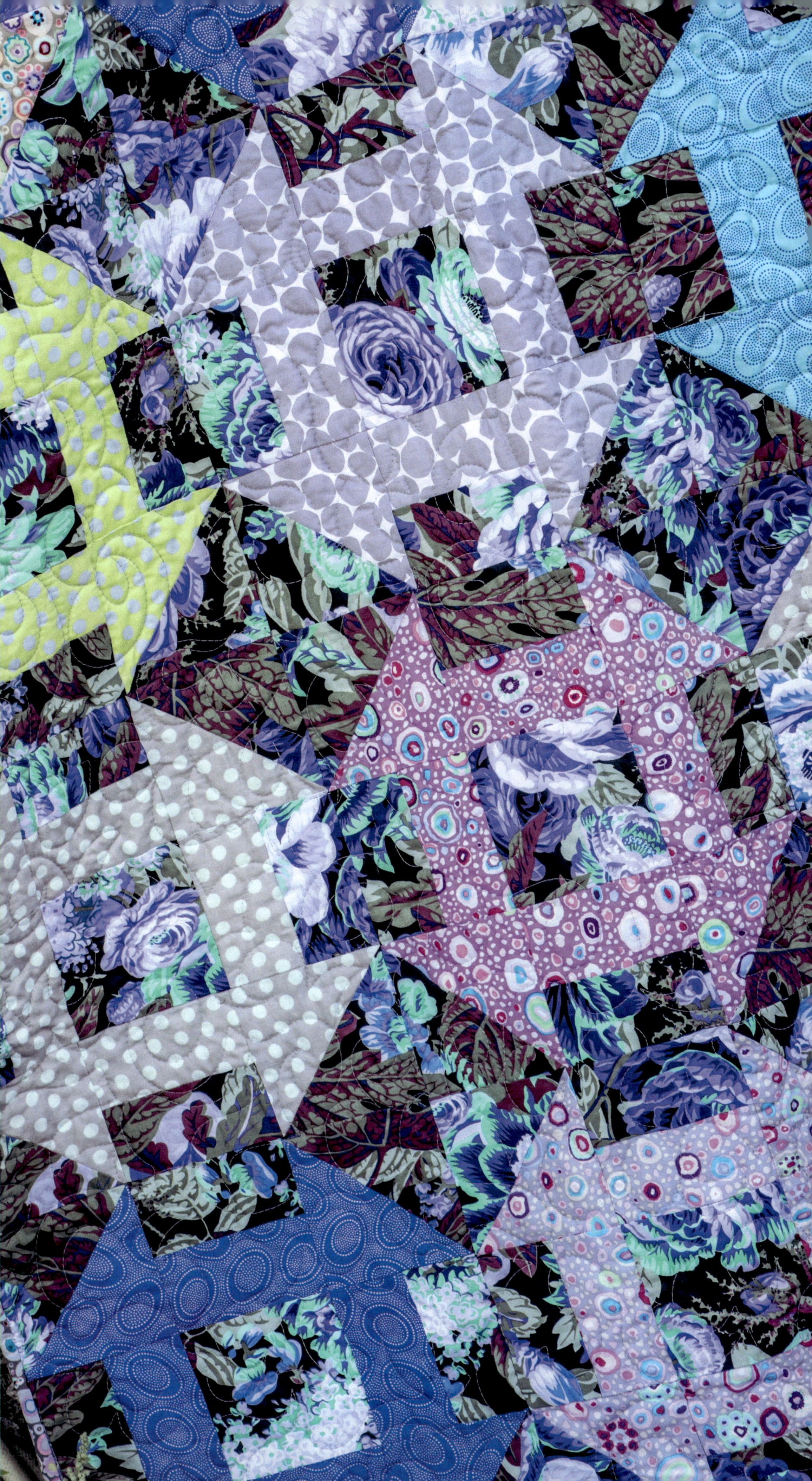

Barn Doors
by Liza Prior Lucy

Liza created this lively quilt
which looks right at home
with that glowing, duck-egg
blue barrel and the faded
wooden slats.

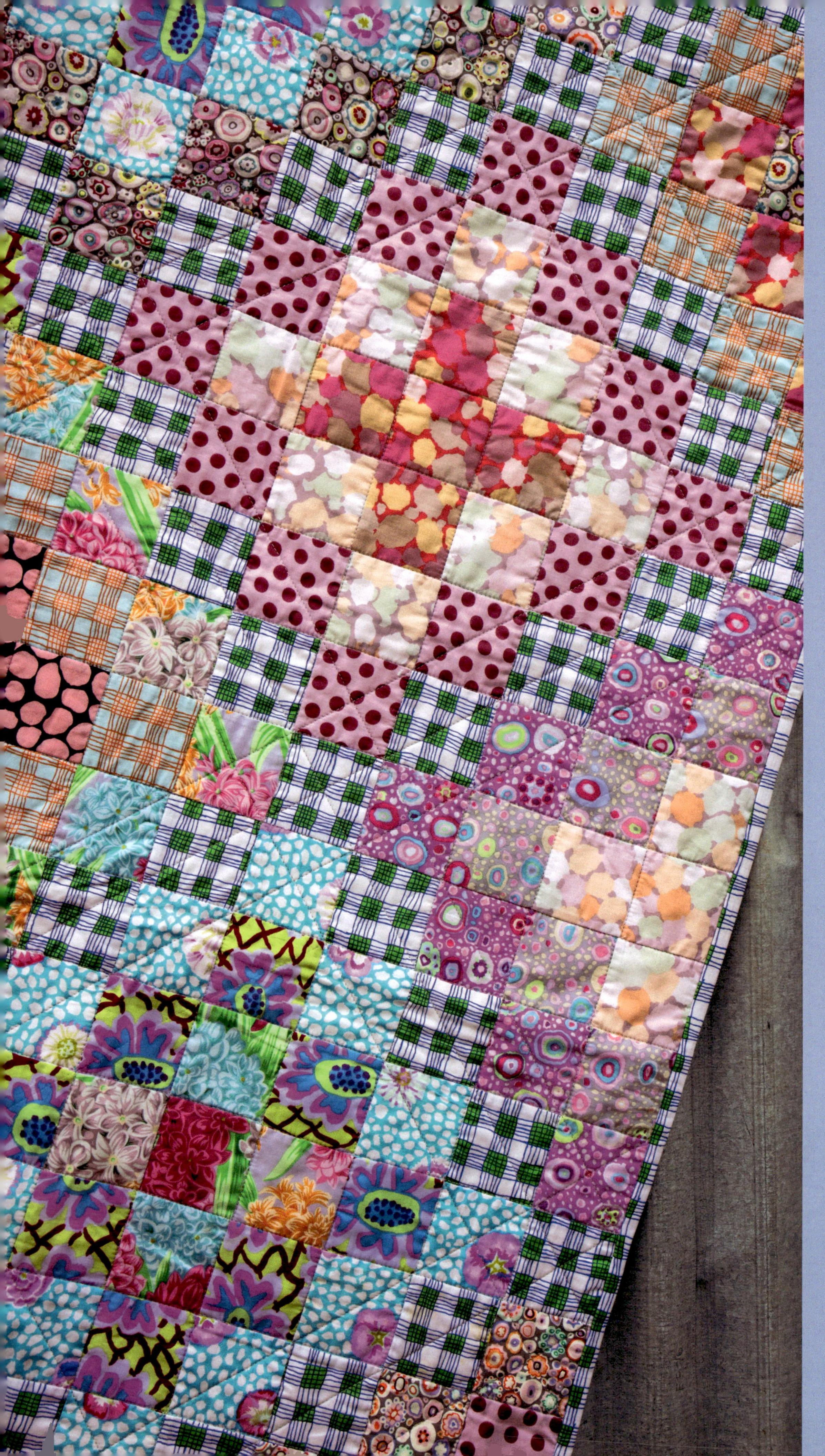

Gingham Lattice
by Kaffe Fassett

Another simple-to-construct quilt, in this case from squares. The dusty palette is delicately framed by Brandon's new Gingham print. This quilt would be perfect for a 'shabby chic' bedroom.

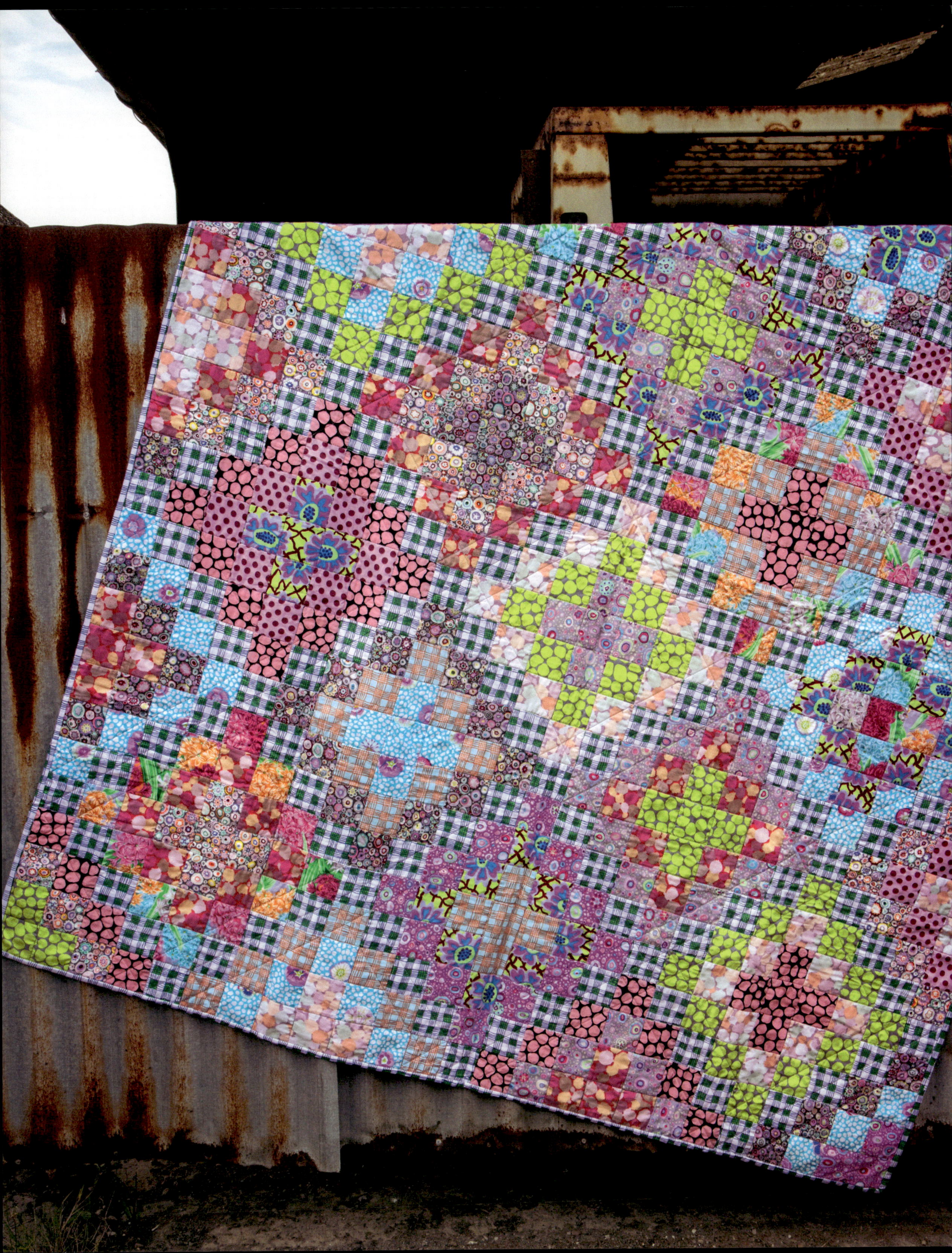

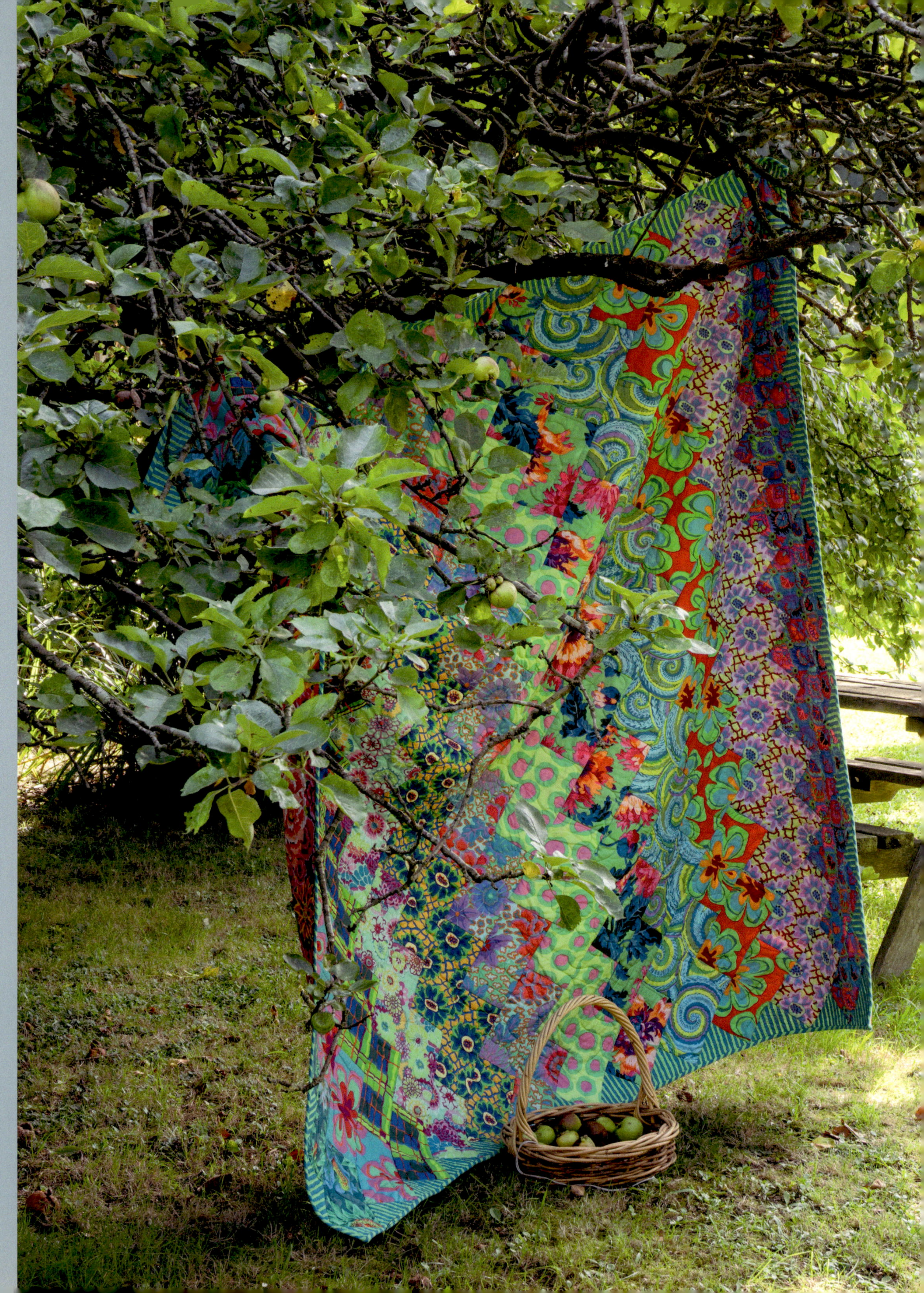

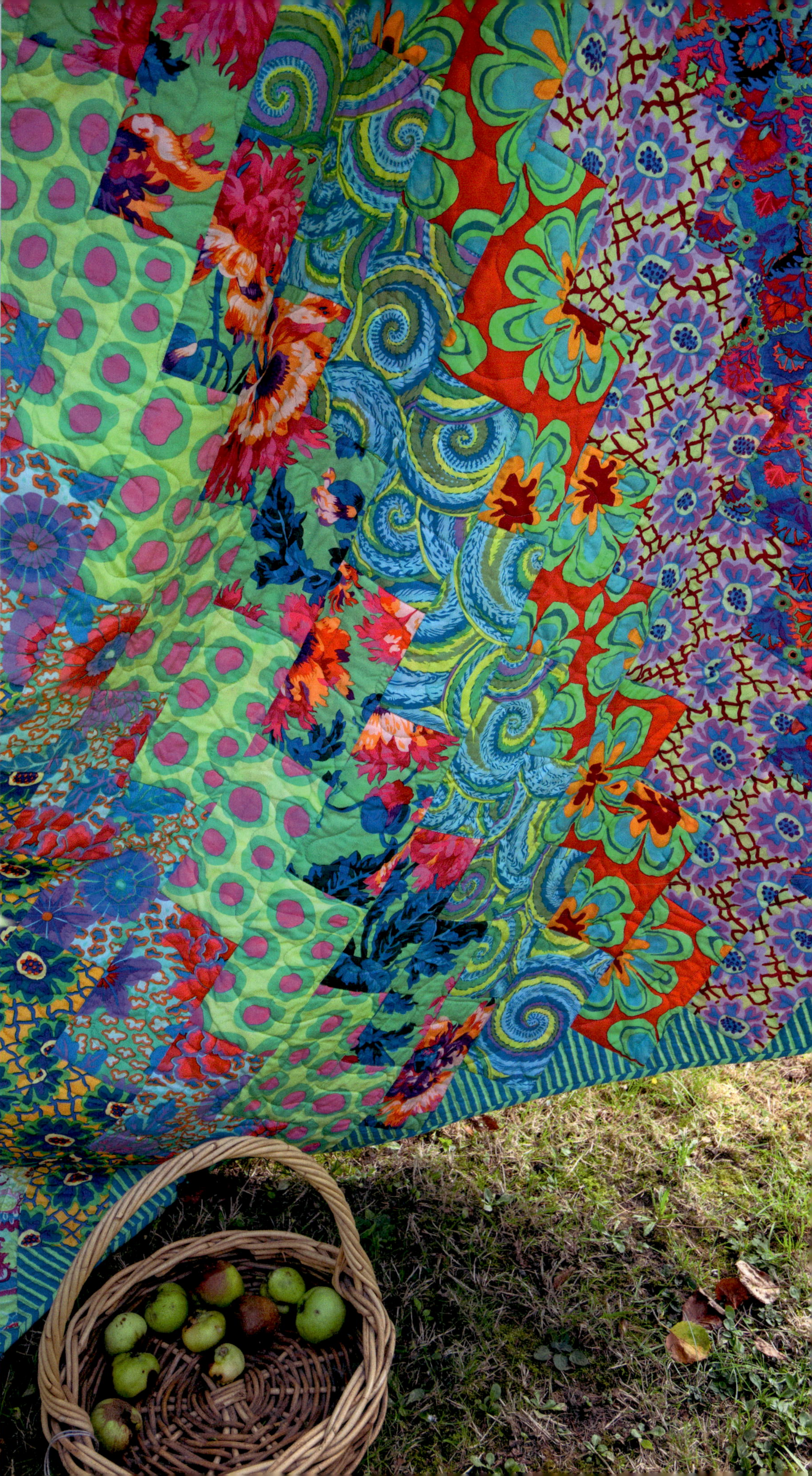

Bean Stalks
by Kaffe Fassett

This quilt is named after
the field of bean stalks
we saw on the farm, but
it looked more at home in
this lovely old apple tree.
The setting stirs my own
childhood memories. One
of the reasons why I like
the simple brick structure
of this quilt is that it lends
itself to so many different
colour schemes.

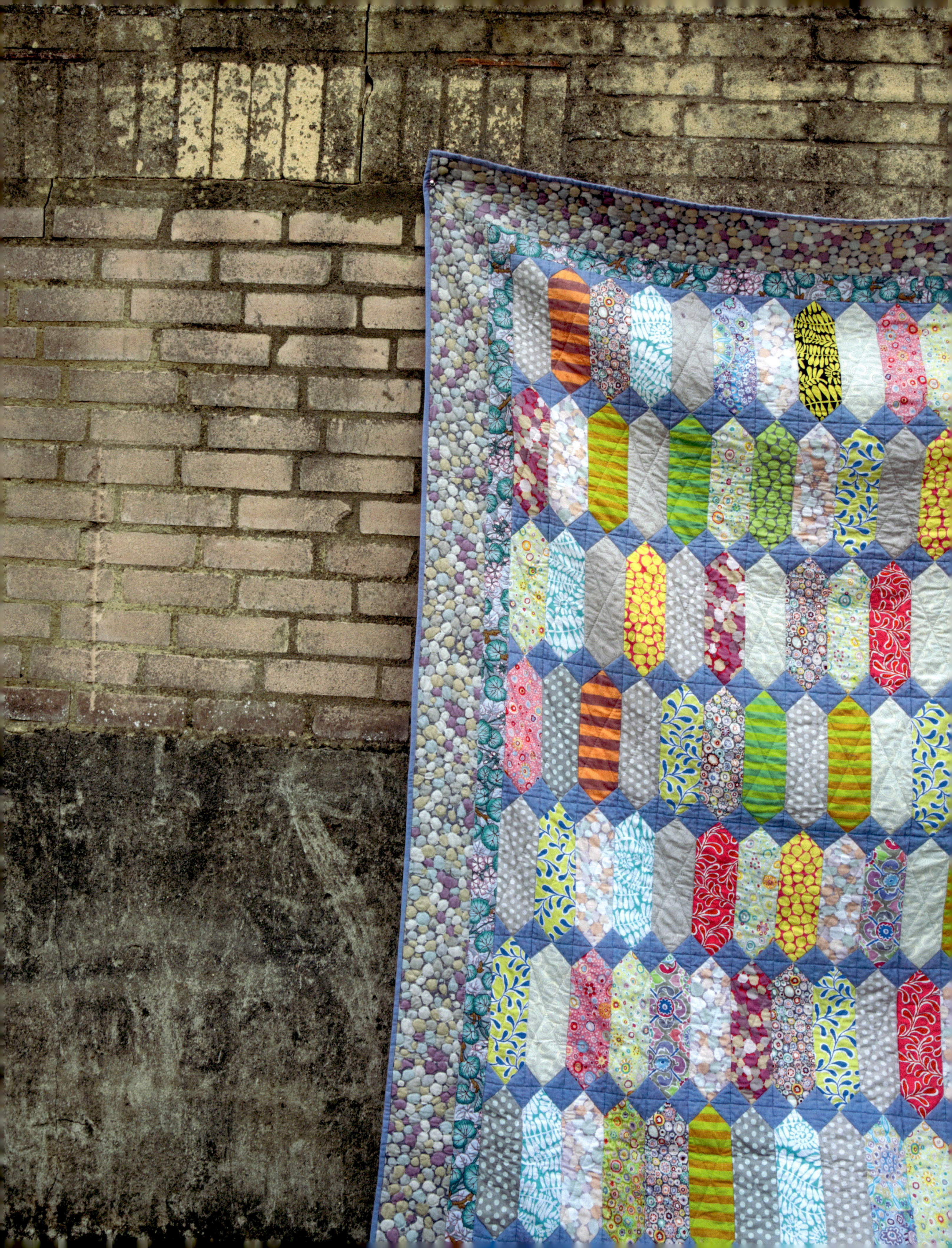

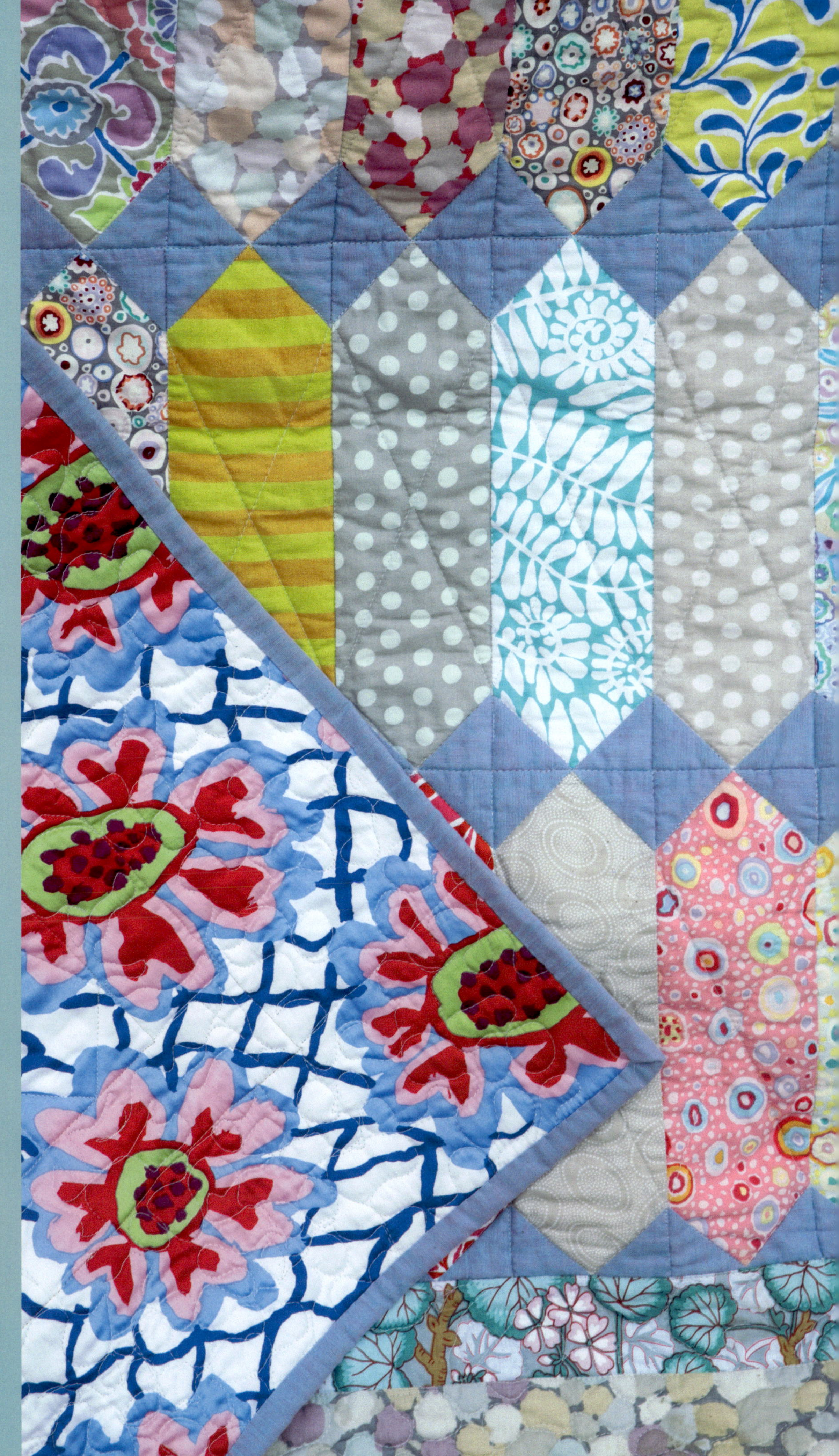

Faded Shuttles
by Kaffe Fassett

The layout of this quilt was inspired by the great African artist El Anatsui, who uses bottle tops to create his rippling, repeating patterns. Using my smaller prints and classics, I created my own version of one of Anatsui's glorious hangings in this quilt, for which Brandon's Reflections fabric makes the perfect border.

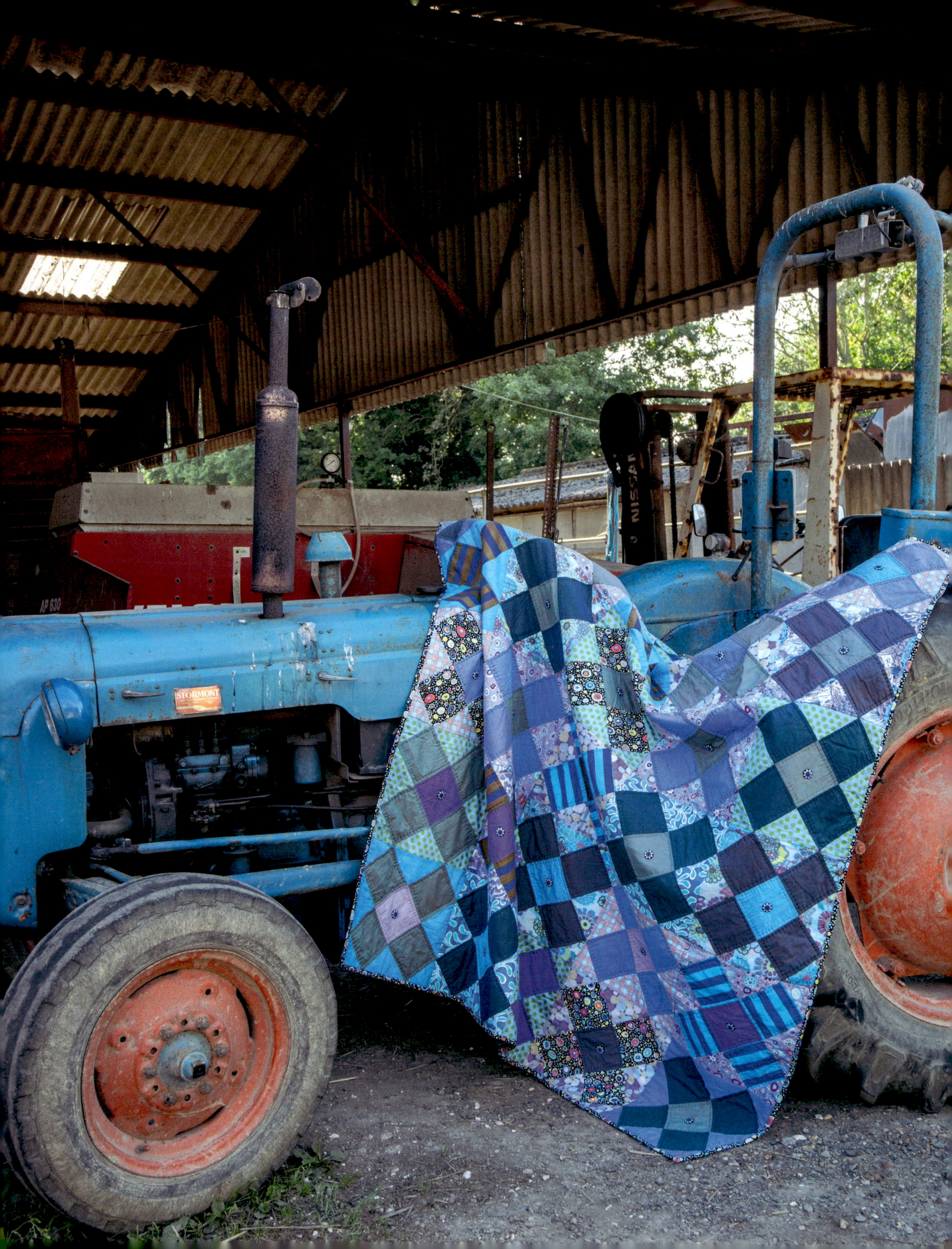

Criss Cross
by Kaffe Fassett

This jaunty blue tractor was the perfect setting for my grey
and blue quilt. I like the simple boldness of this layout in
such a smoky palette. I used some of my Dill buttons to add
a spicy touch to the quilt. You can see that Brandon, sporting
his flowery shirt, enjoyed the tractor!

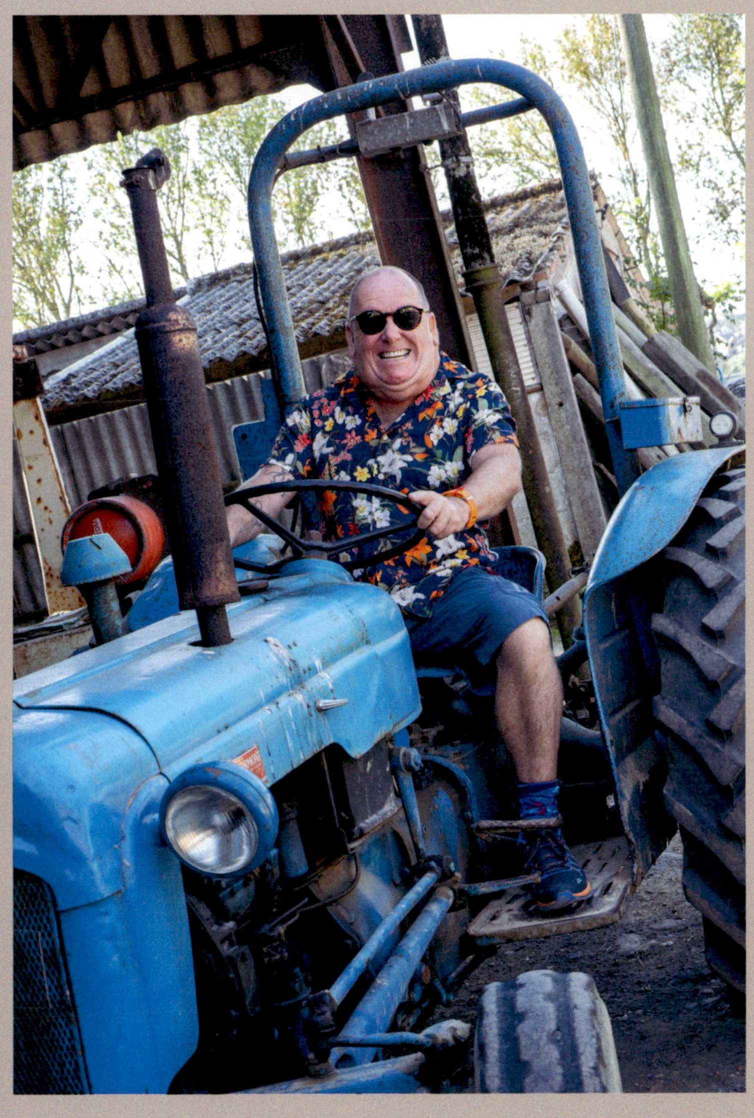

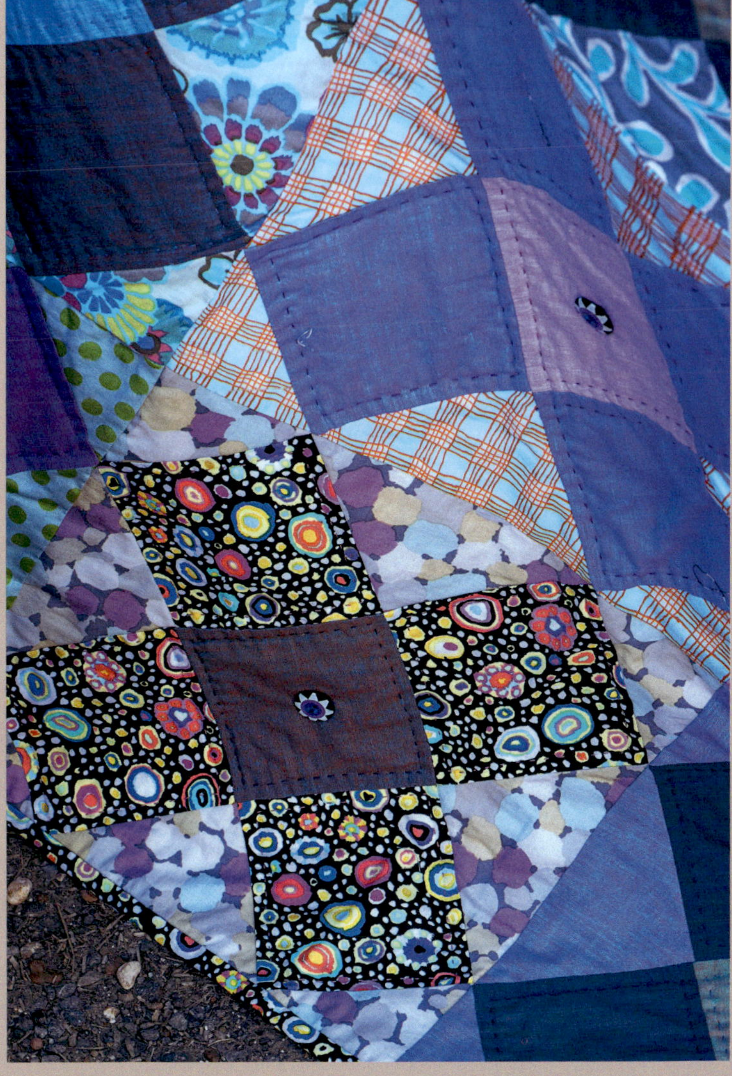

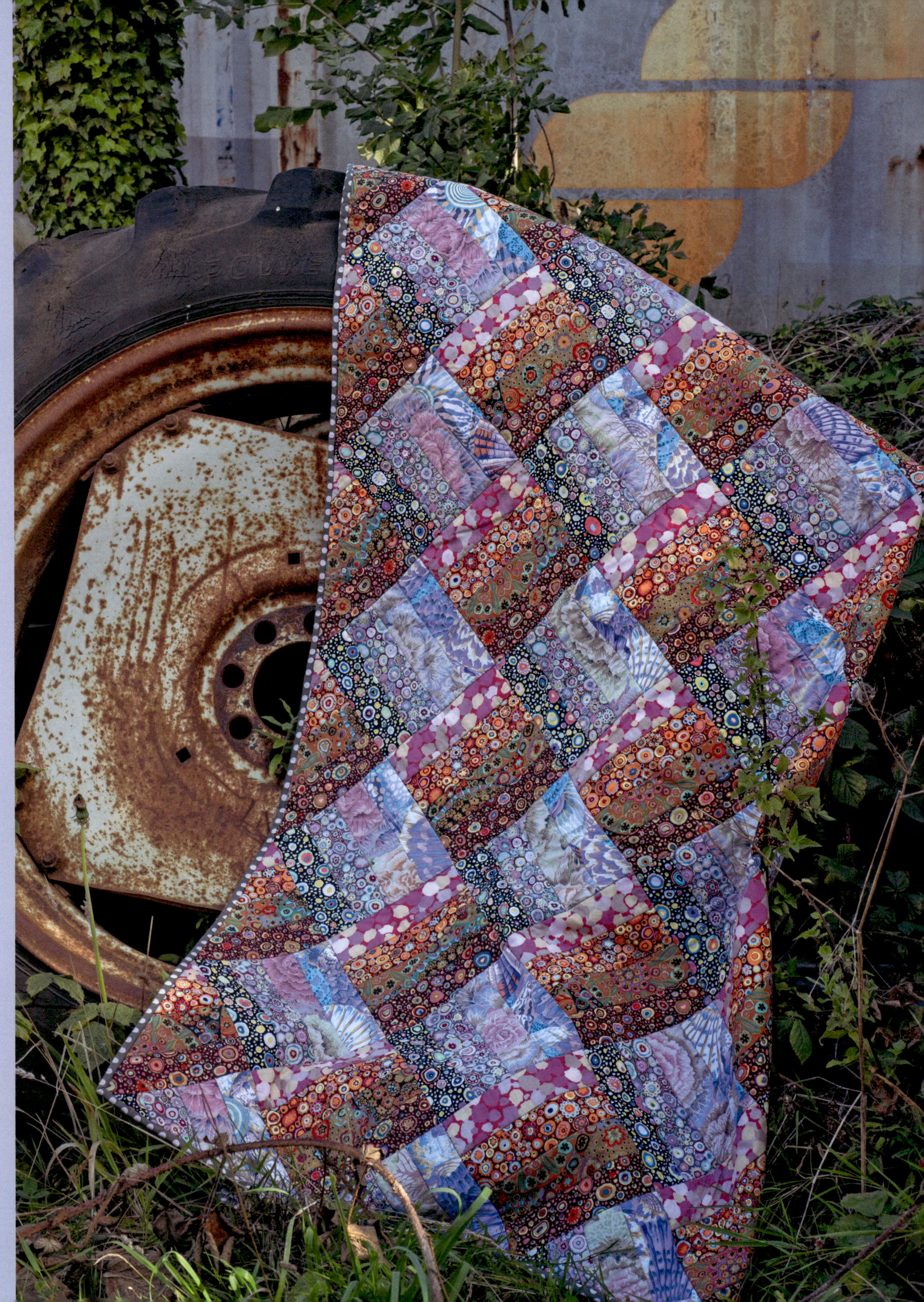

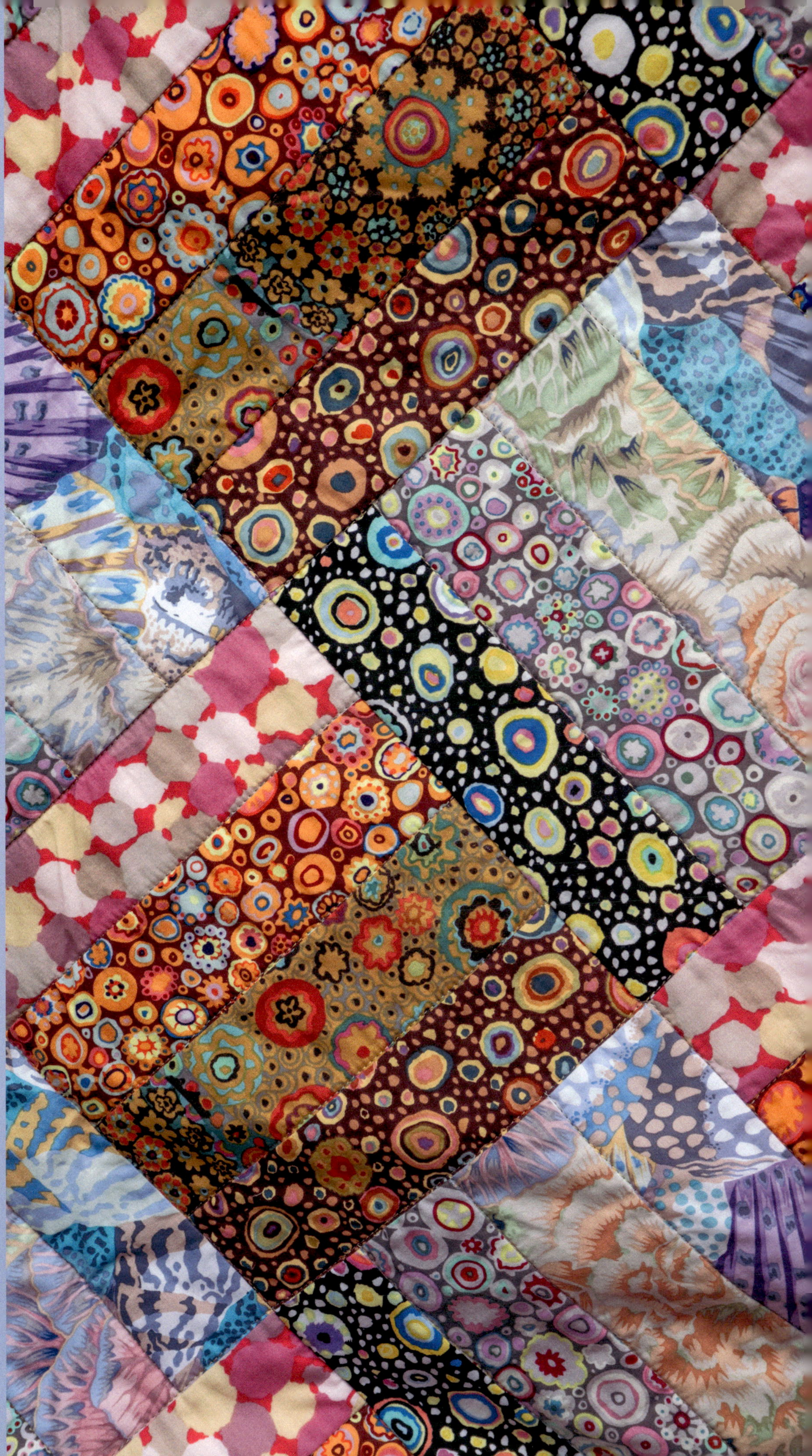

A huge rusty old tractor tyre provides just the right texture to complement the subtle colouring of this simple-to-make quilt, while the fizzy dottiness of the prints responds to the shifts of tone in its corroded metal.

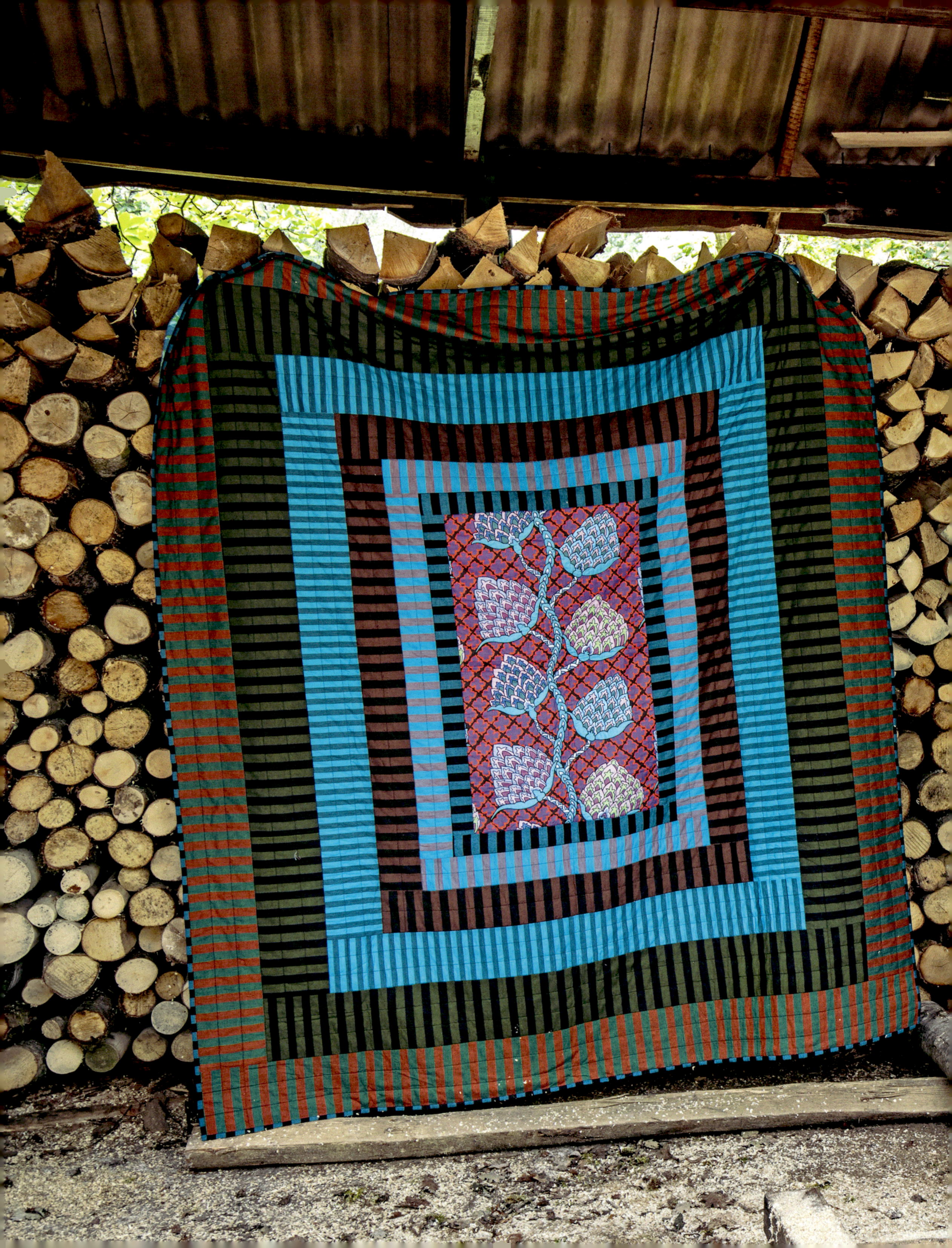

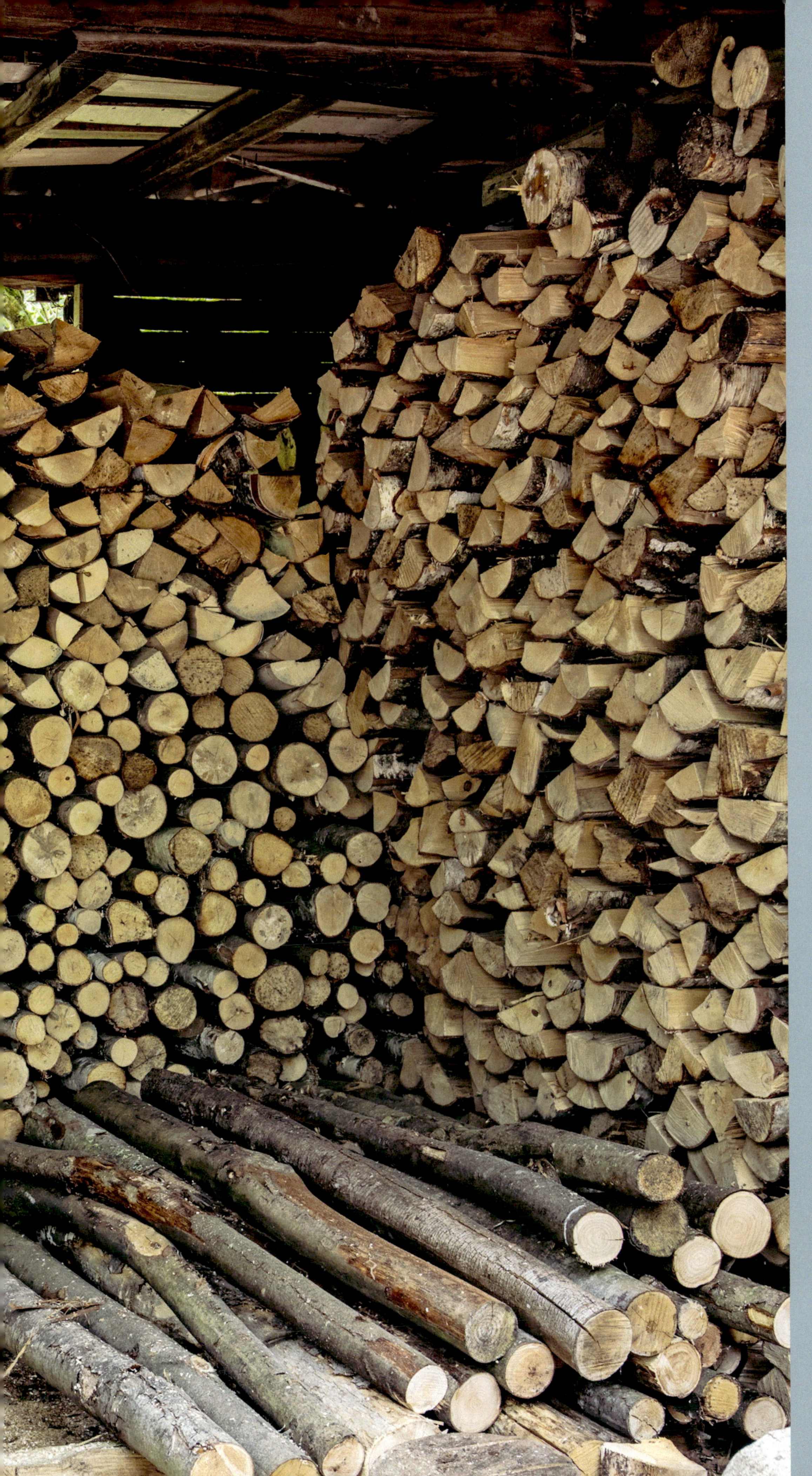

Gentleman's Relish
by Kaffe Fassett

I used the darkest of our
Woven Stripe fabrics and
my big Paisley Flower
print to create this simple,
striking layout. It sings
out against the different
tones and textures of the
sawn logs and the rusty
metal roof.

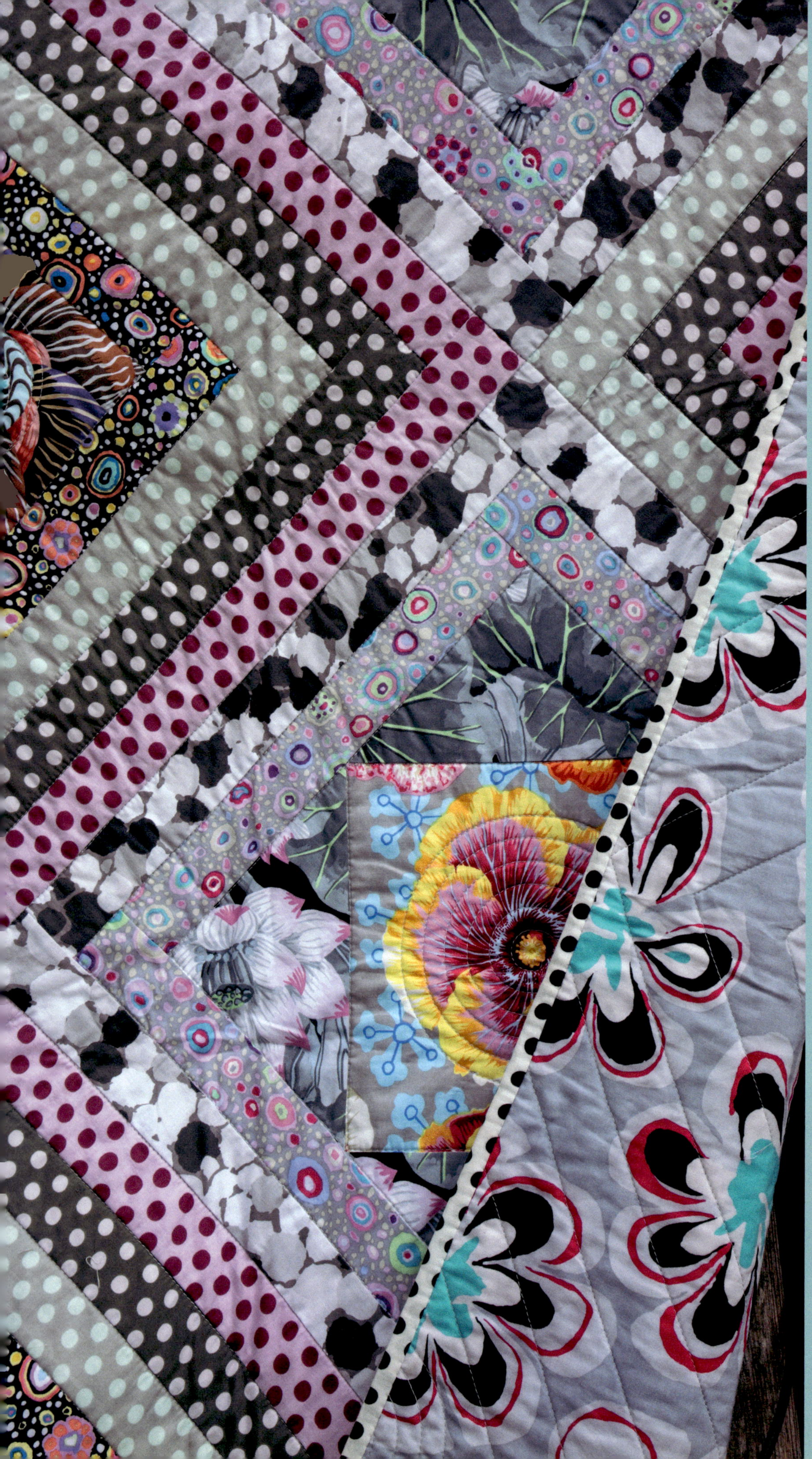

Pearly Dream
by Kaffe Fassett

When I designed this quilt, I had just such a setting in mind – silvery wood and weathered brickwork. It shows just how elegant grey can be as a base colour for a quilt.

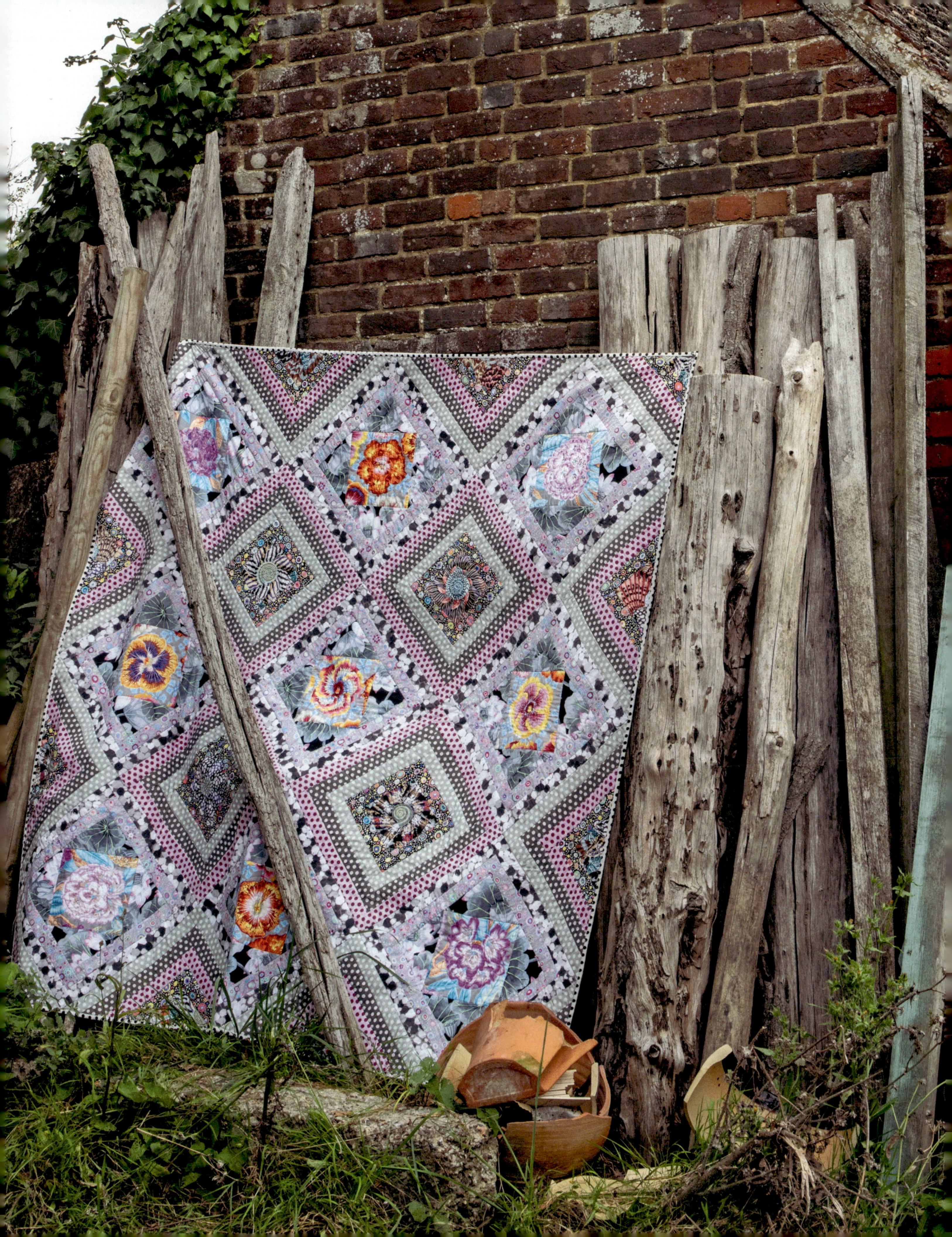

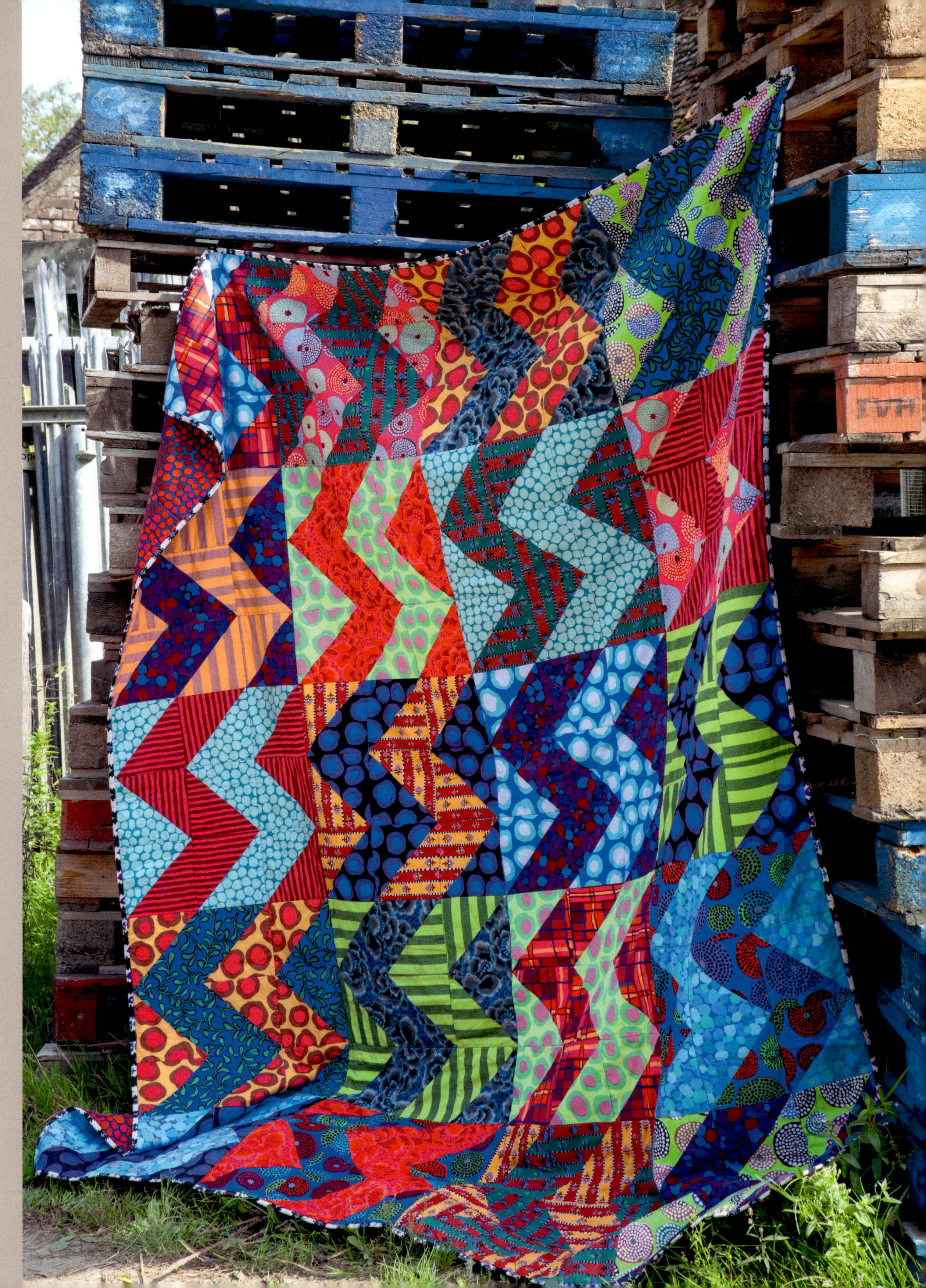

Lightning Strike
by Kaffe Fassett

The powerful use of colour in a quilt that uses the
boldest of geometric patterns is complemented by the
informal geometry of a huge stack of pallets. It creates
a really confident effect.

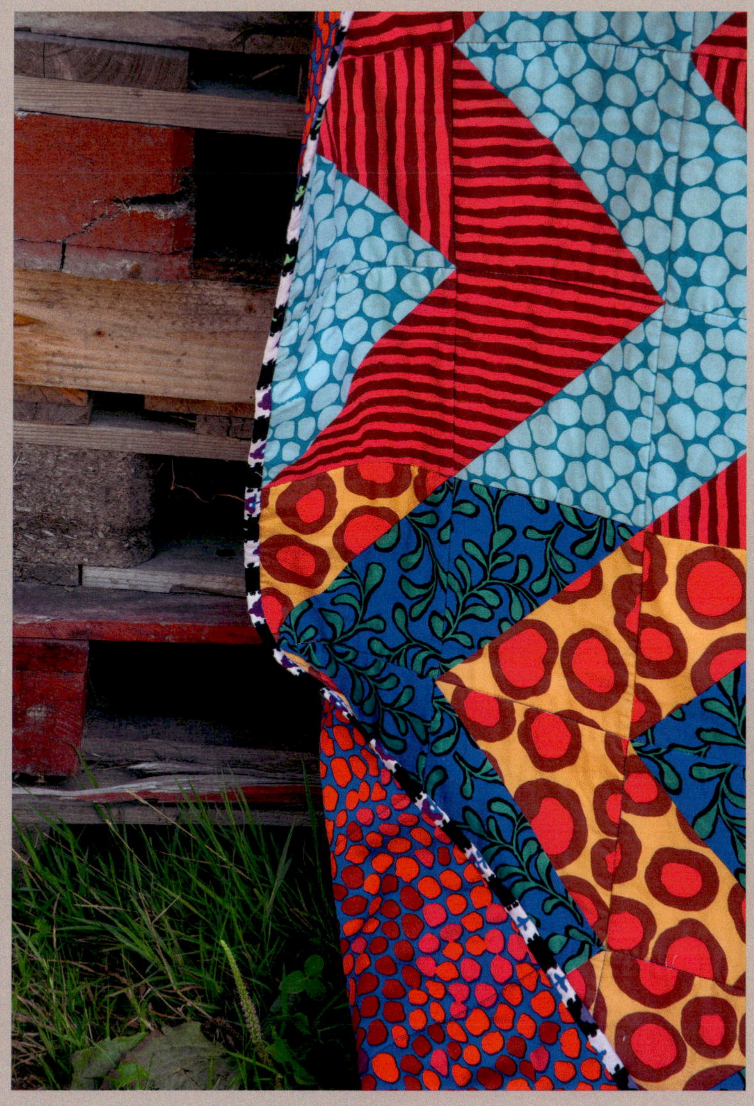

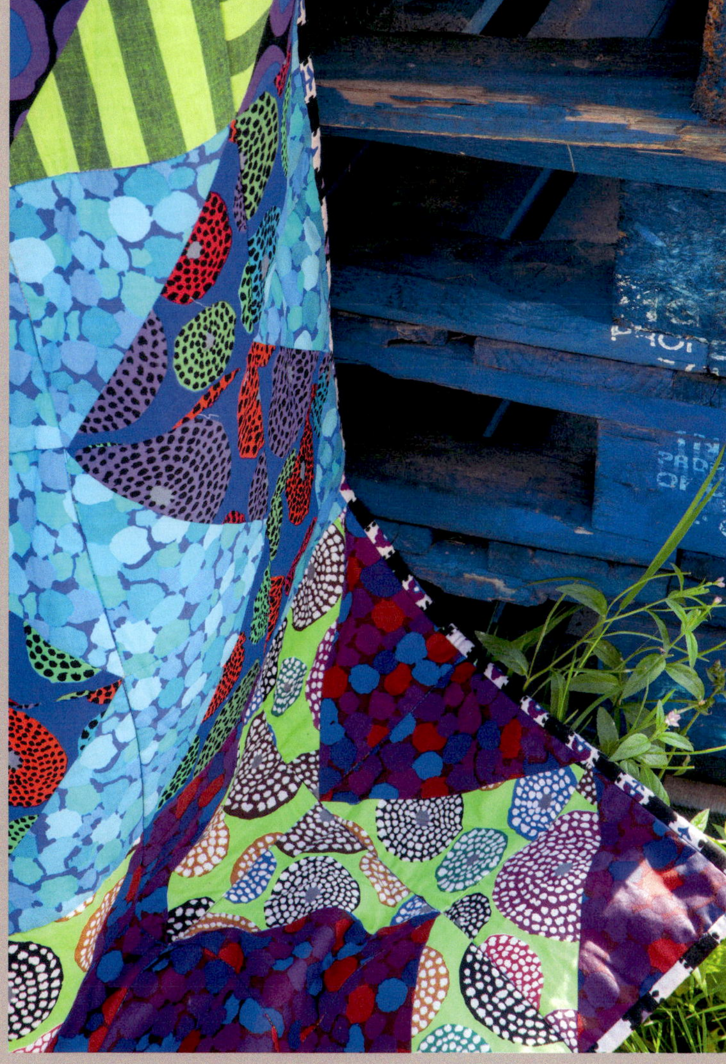

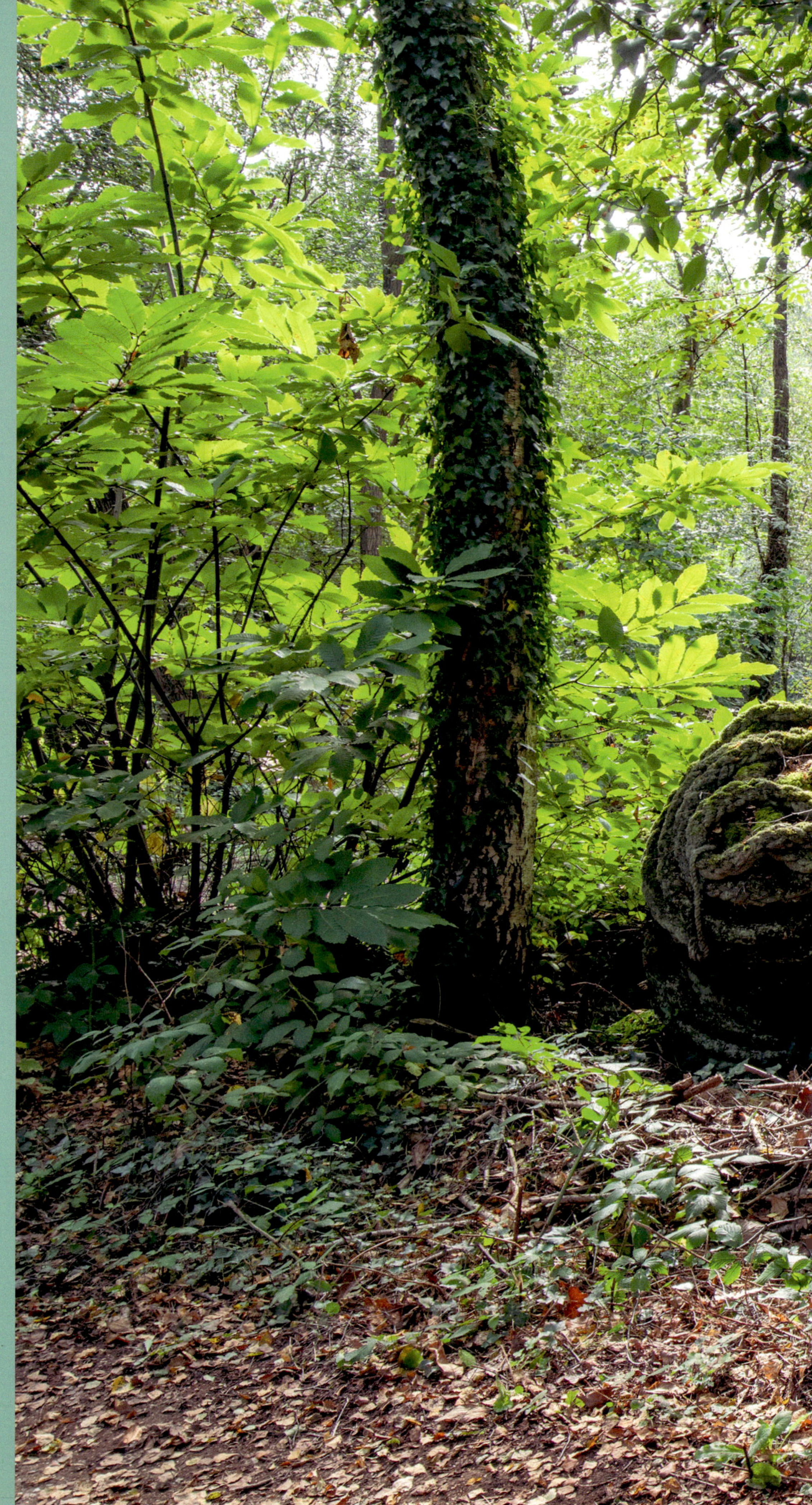

Leafy Circles
by Kaffe Fassett

Imagine my delight when
I came across this lyrical
woodland scene to show off
our green quilt and realized
how beautifully the mossy
ropes echoed the circular
shapes within it.

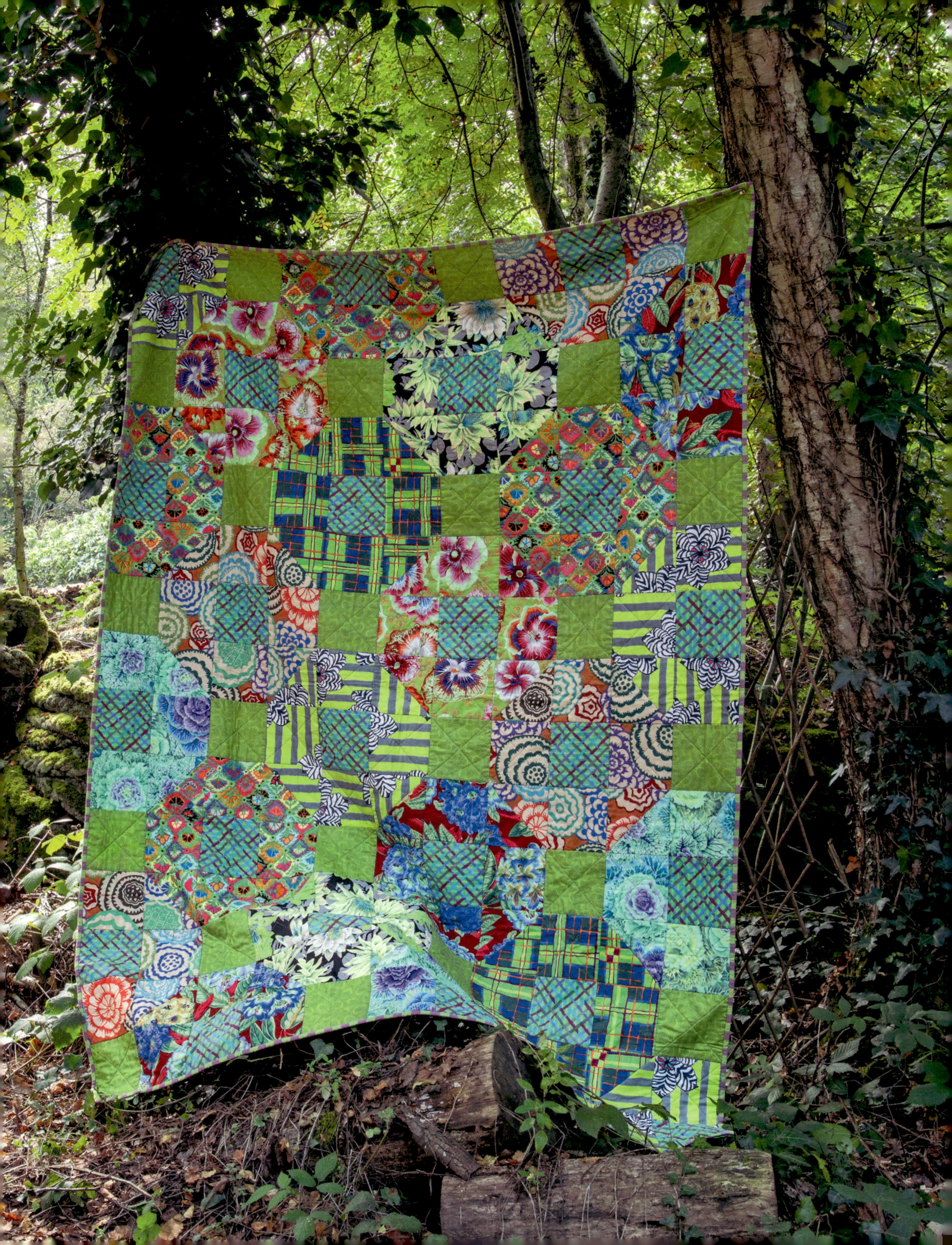

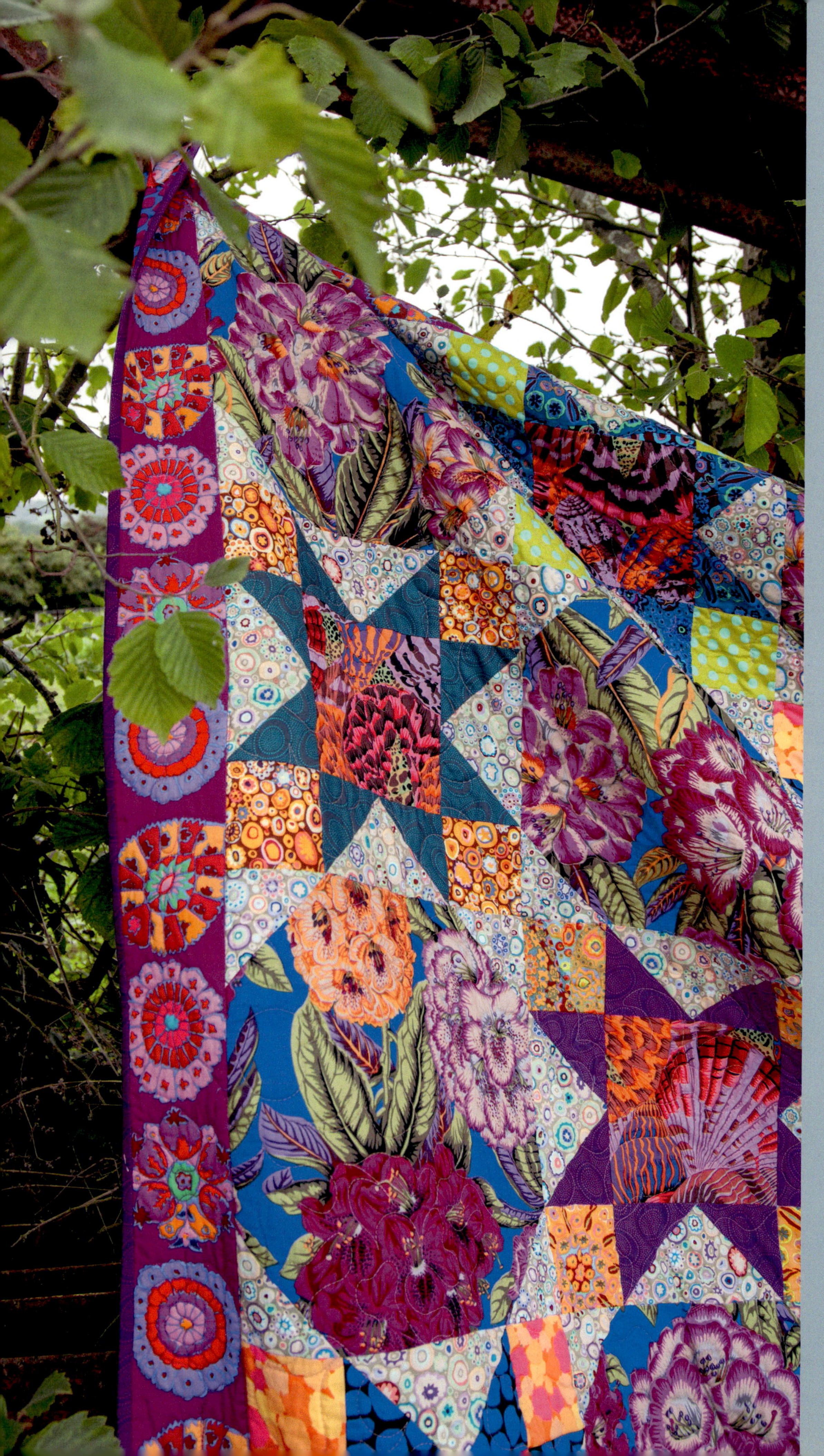

Rhododendron Stars
by Liza Prior Lucy

You can see how much fun Liza had making this colourful starry quilt. She used the leftovers from the Carpet Cookies fabric border to create a gorgeous bolster in hexagon shapes. (See page 143 for details of how to obtain the free downloadable bolster pattern).

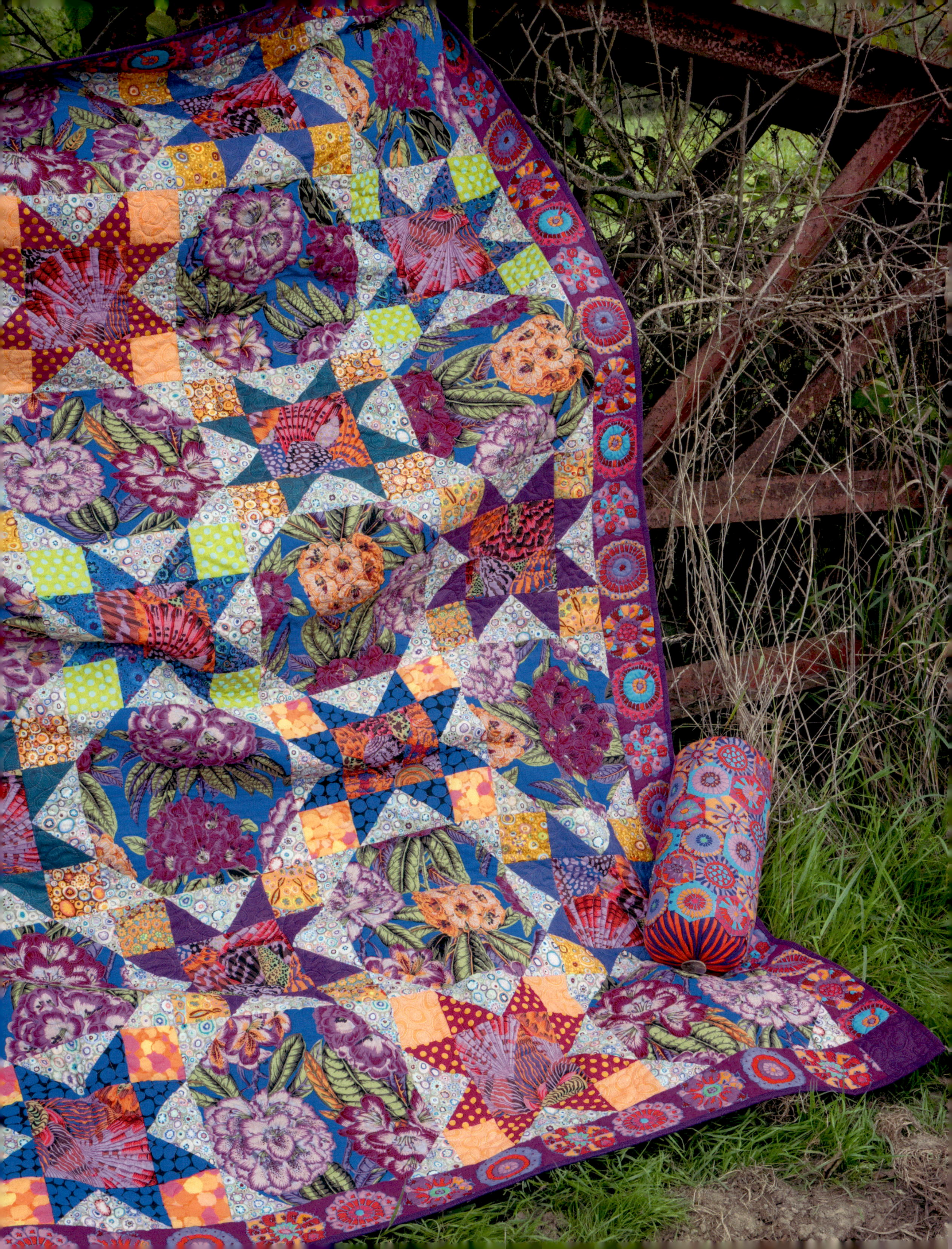

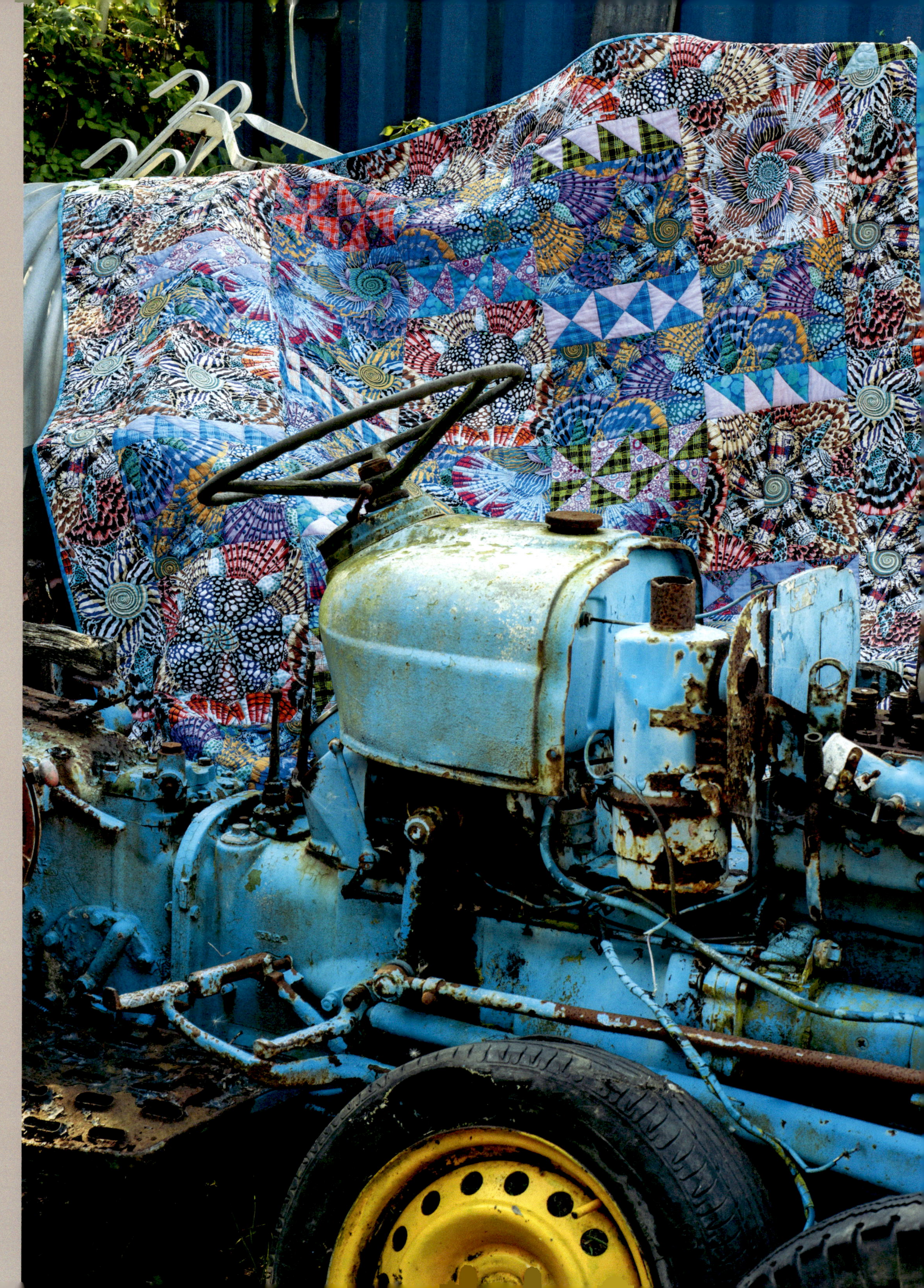

Sailor's Gift
by Kaffe Fassett

What is it about old, corroded machinery that looks so exciting? I love the contrast between the milky blues and rust colours that sets off this quirky quilt beautifully. Using Philip Jacobs' new Sailor Valentine print, I placed random geometric fabrics across this quilt, but you could use any lively print of your choice for the base to get a similar effect.

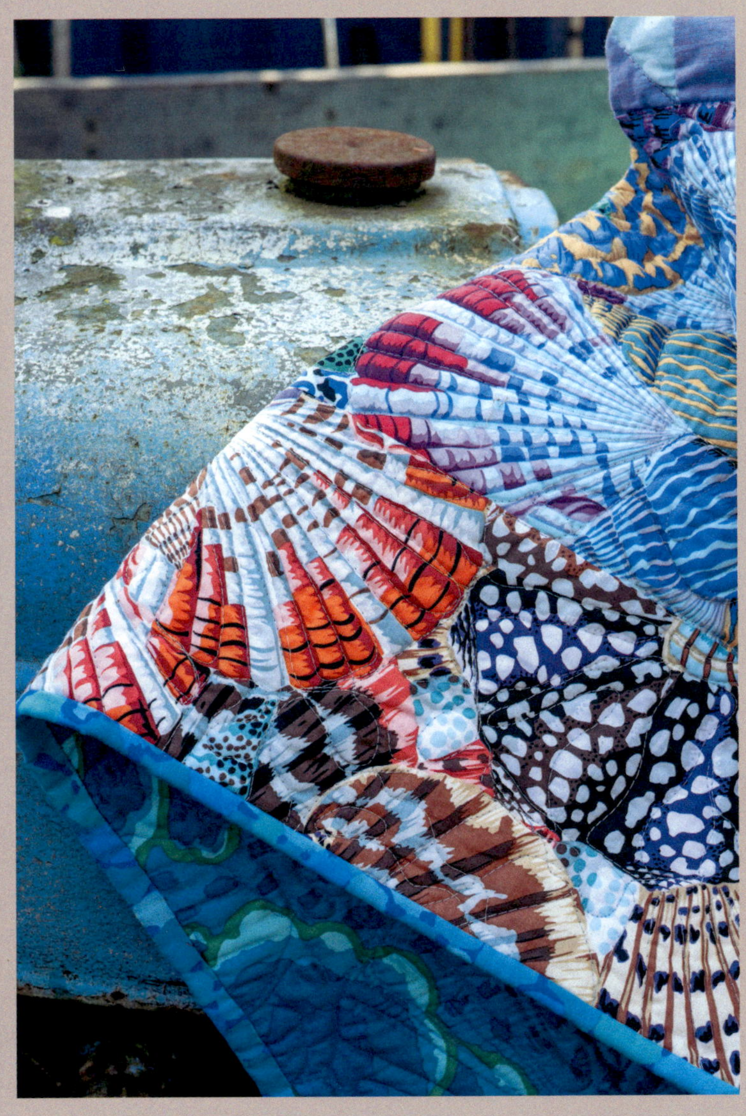

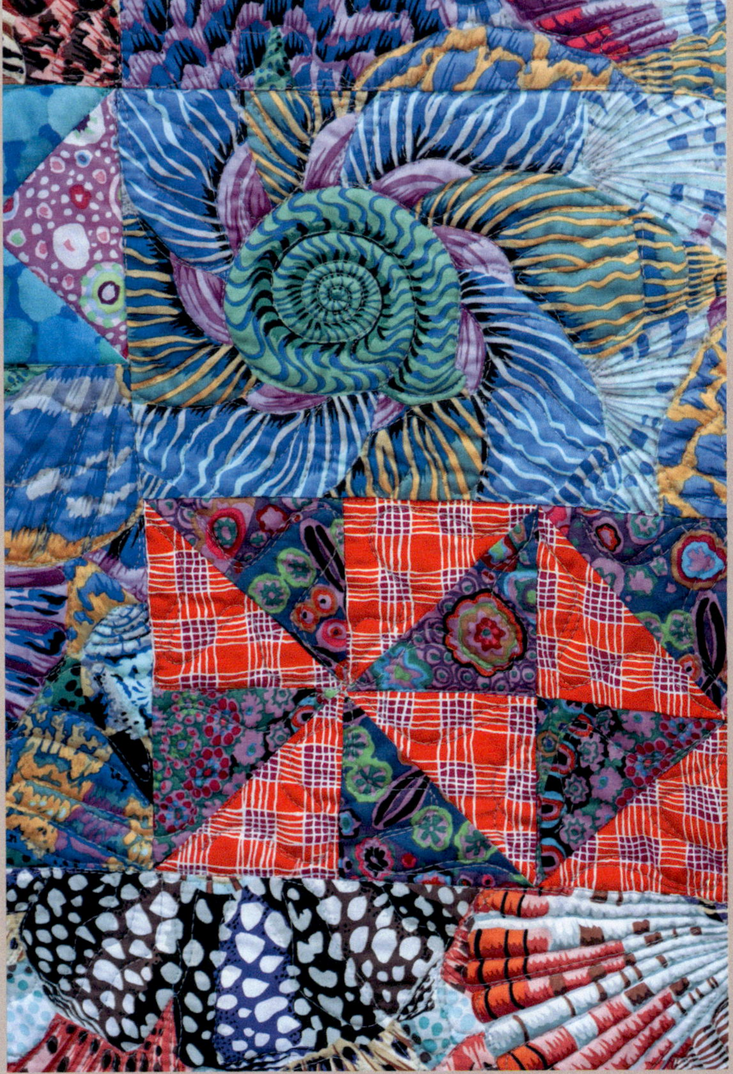

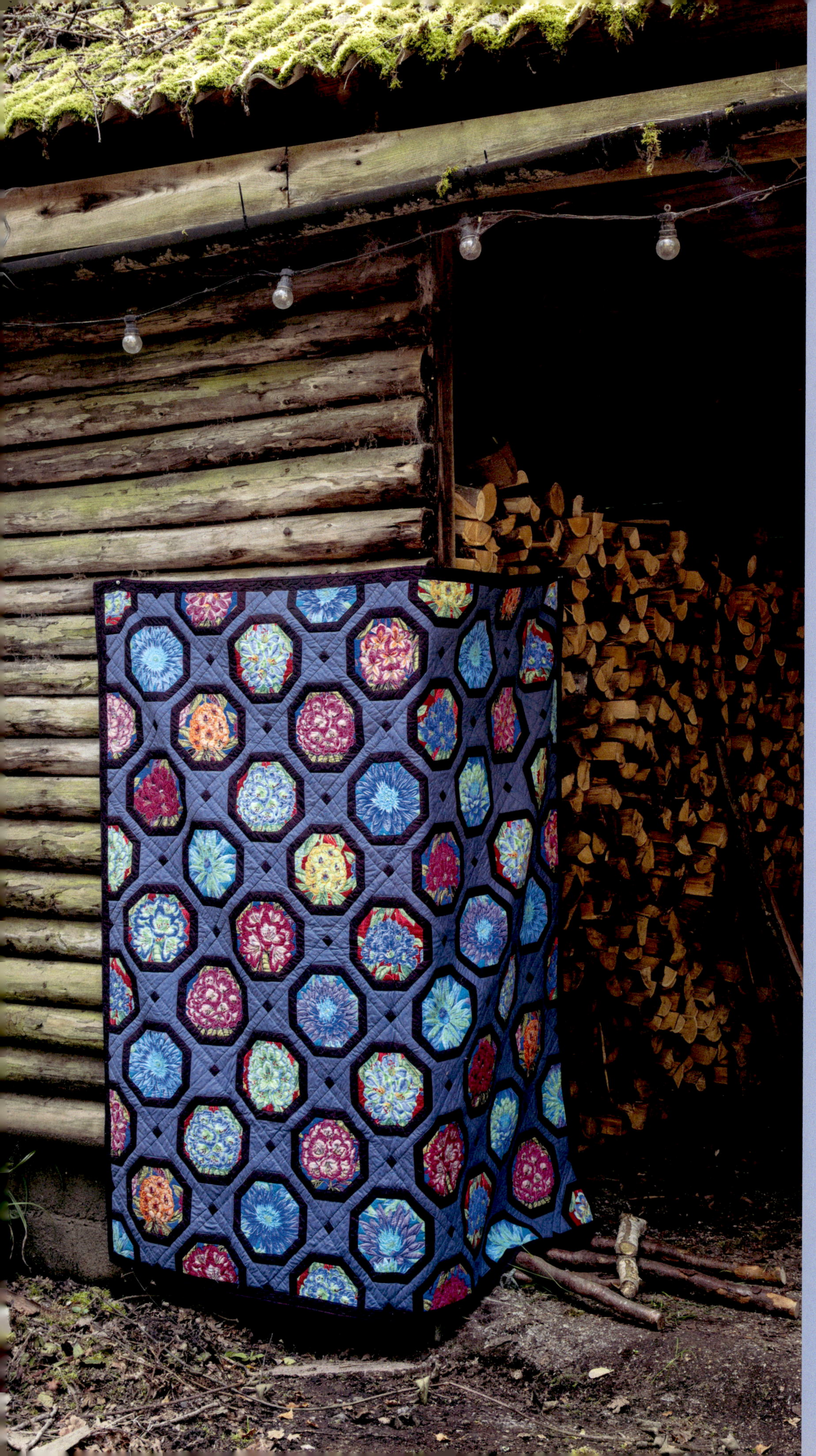

Blooming Octagons Dark
by Kaffe Fassett

Framing our darker floral prints with black borders against a purple-grey makes them really glow in this powerful arrangement. The old wood stacks in the log barn set it all off perfectly.

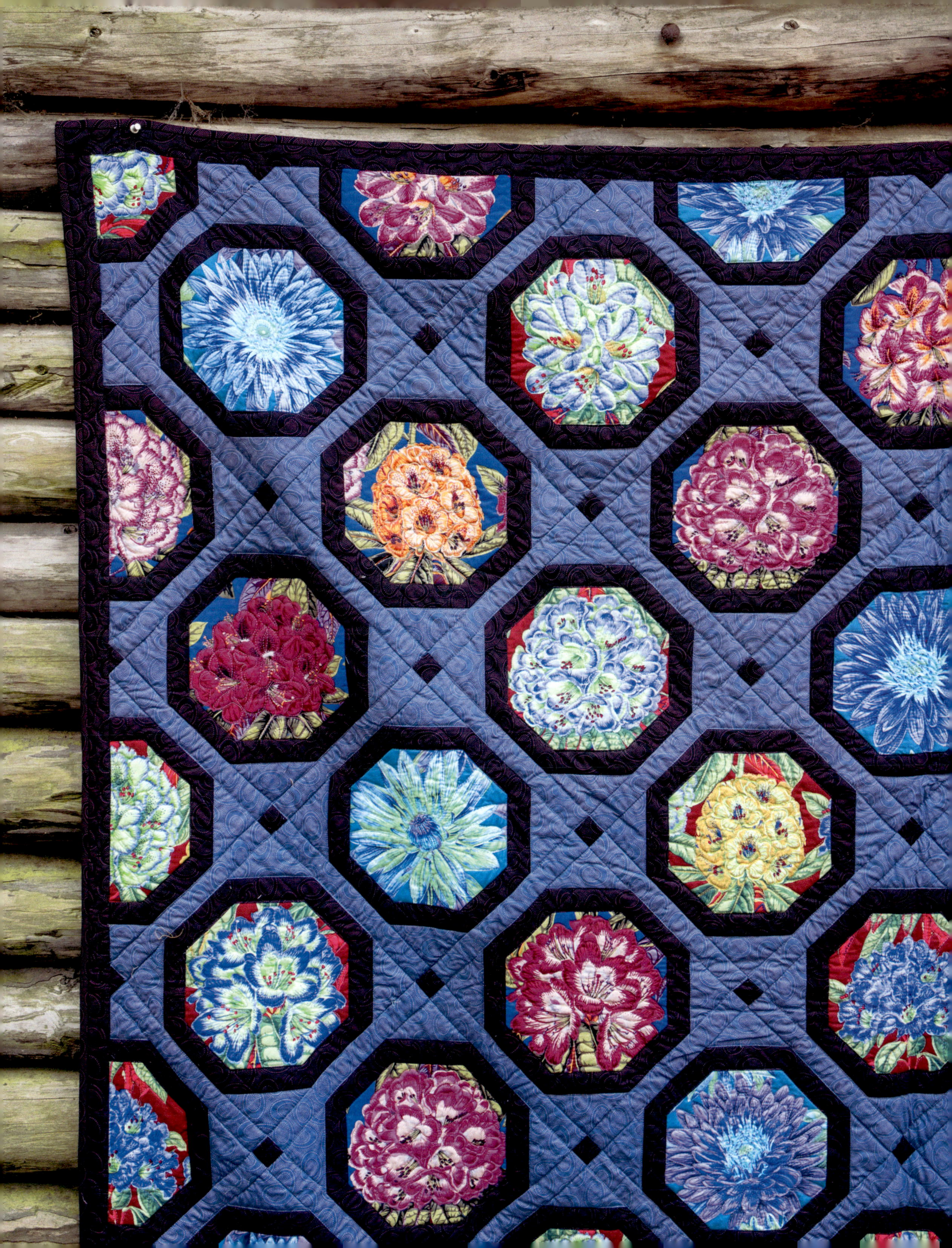

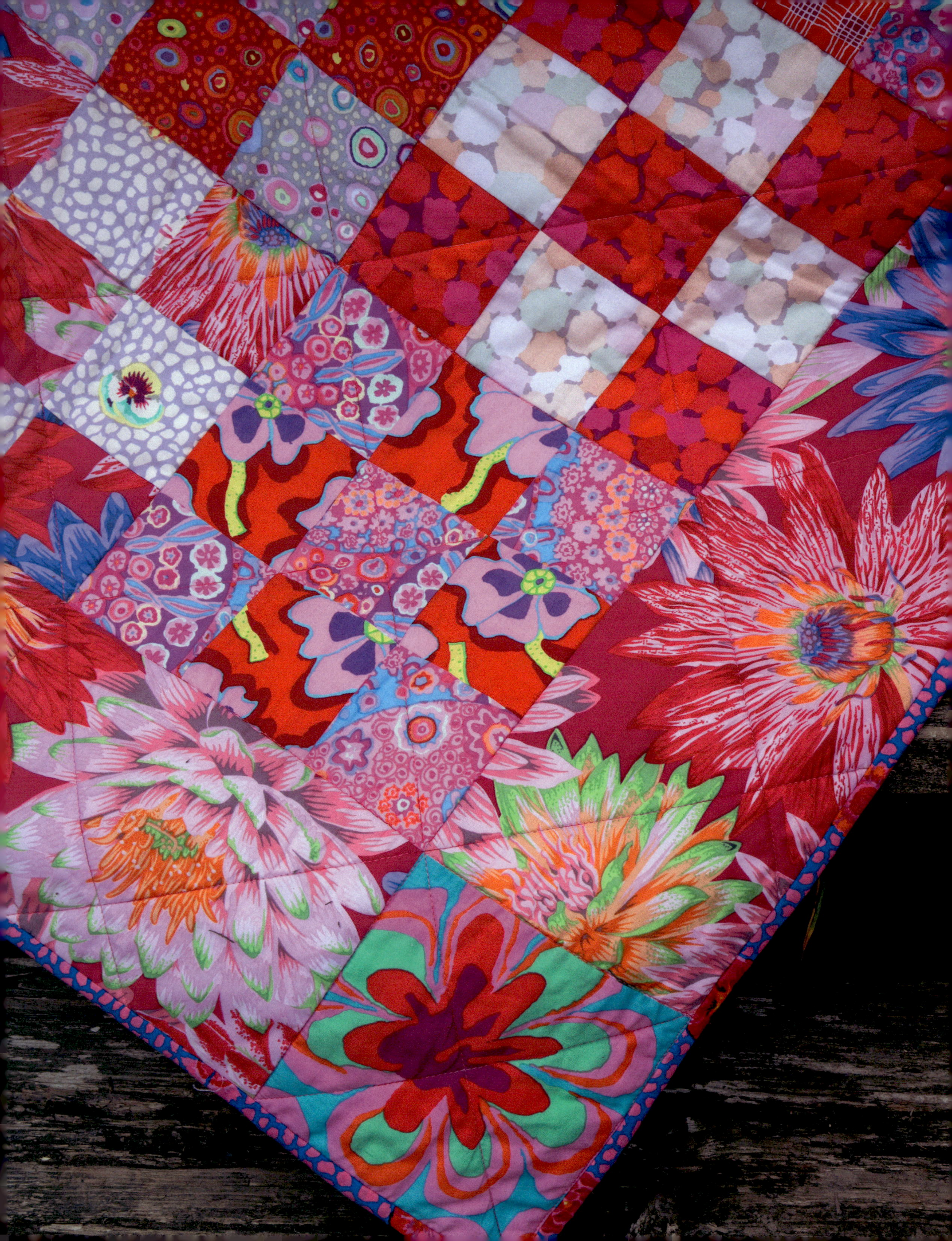

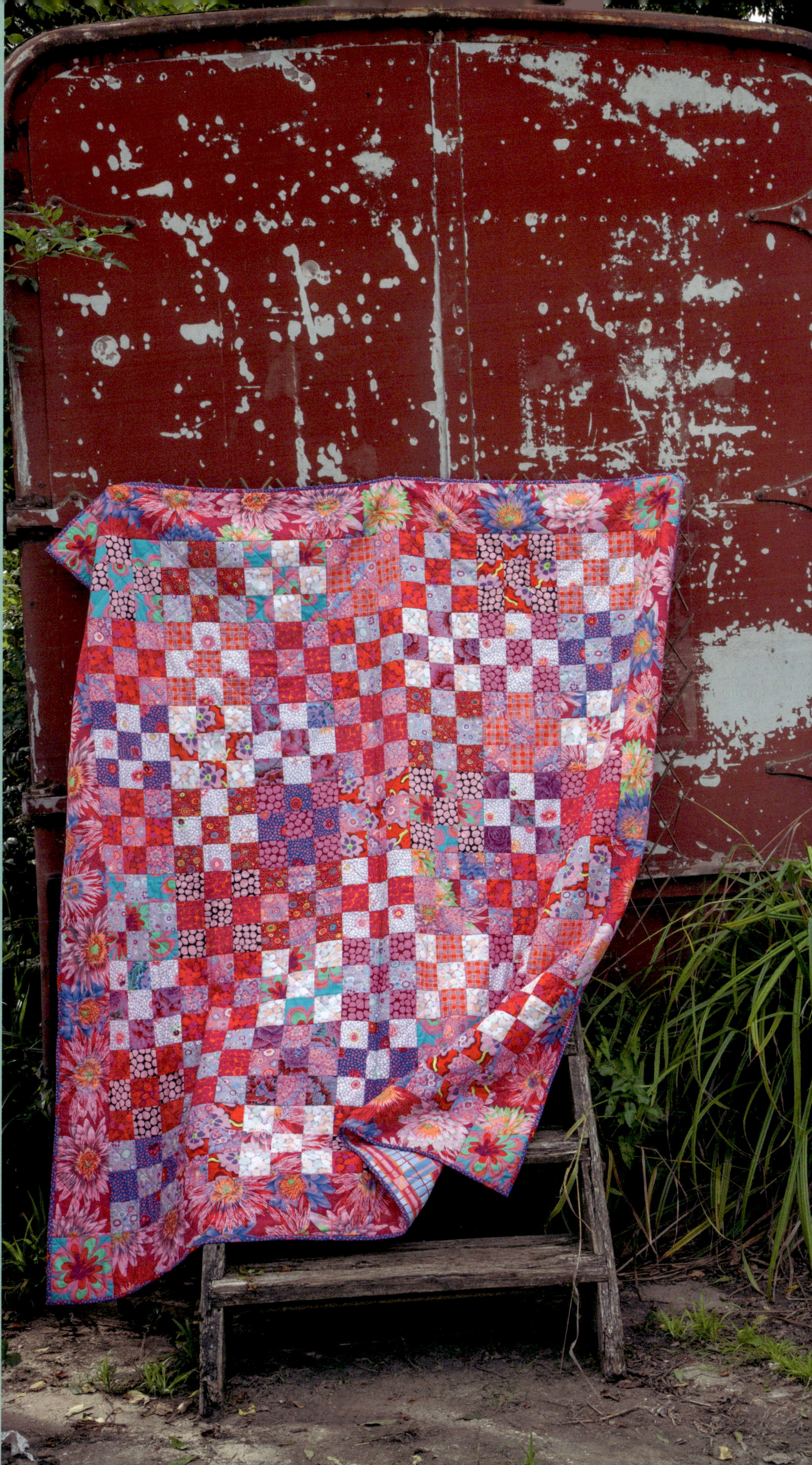

Blushing Nine-Patch
by Kaffe Fassett

The old peeling red wall really complements our *Blushing Nine-Patch*. I like the way the upscale Tropical Water Lilies border almost disappears in the dancing squares. Brandon's Checkmate backing fabric is just right for it as well.

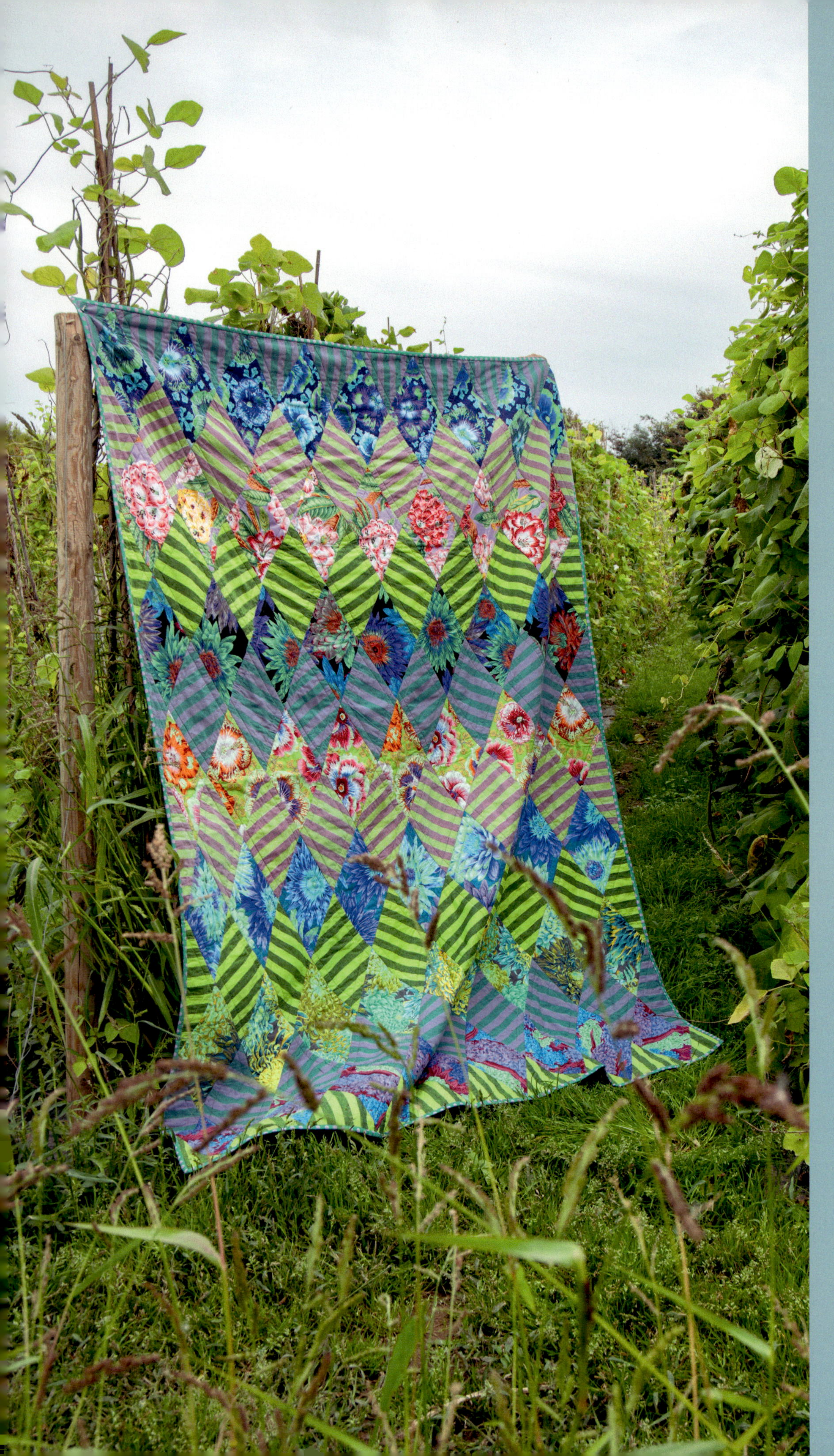

Flowers and Fences
by Kaffe Fassett

This bold diamond quilt looked totally at home in the field of bean stalks on the farm. The stripes and big florals help to make the arrangement really dance.

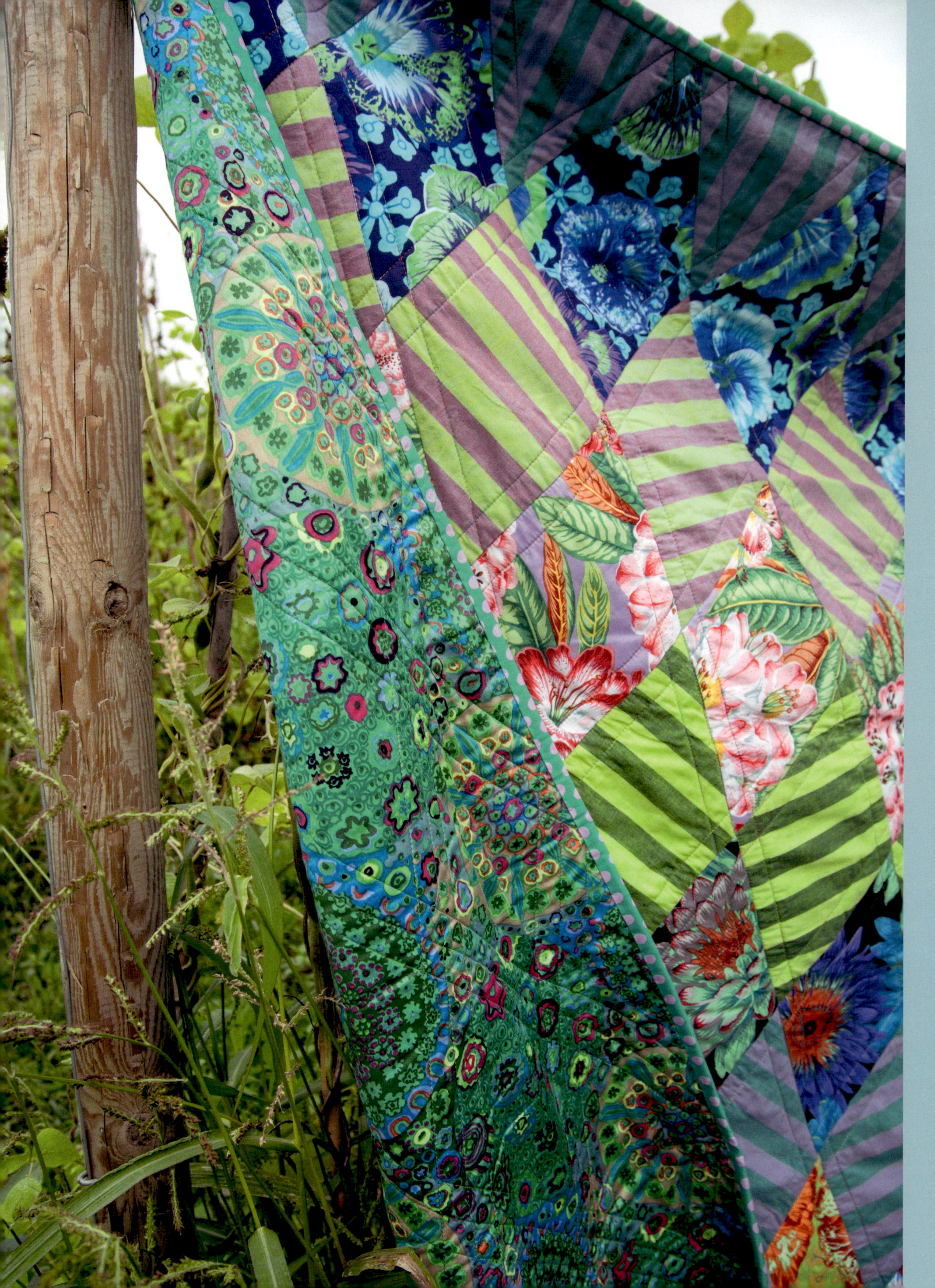

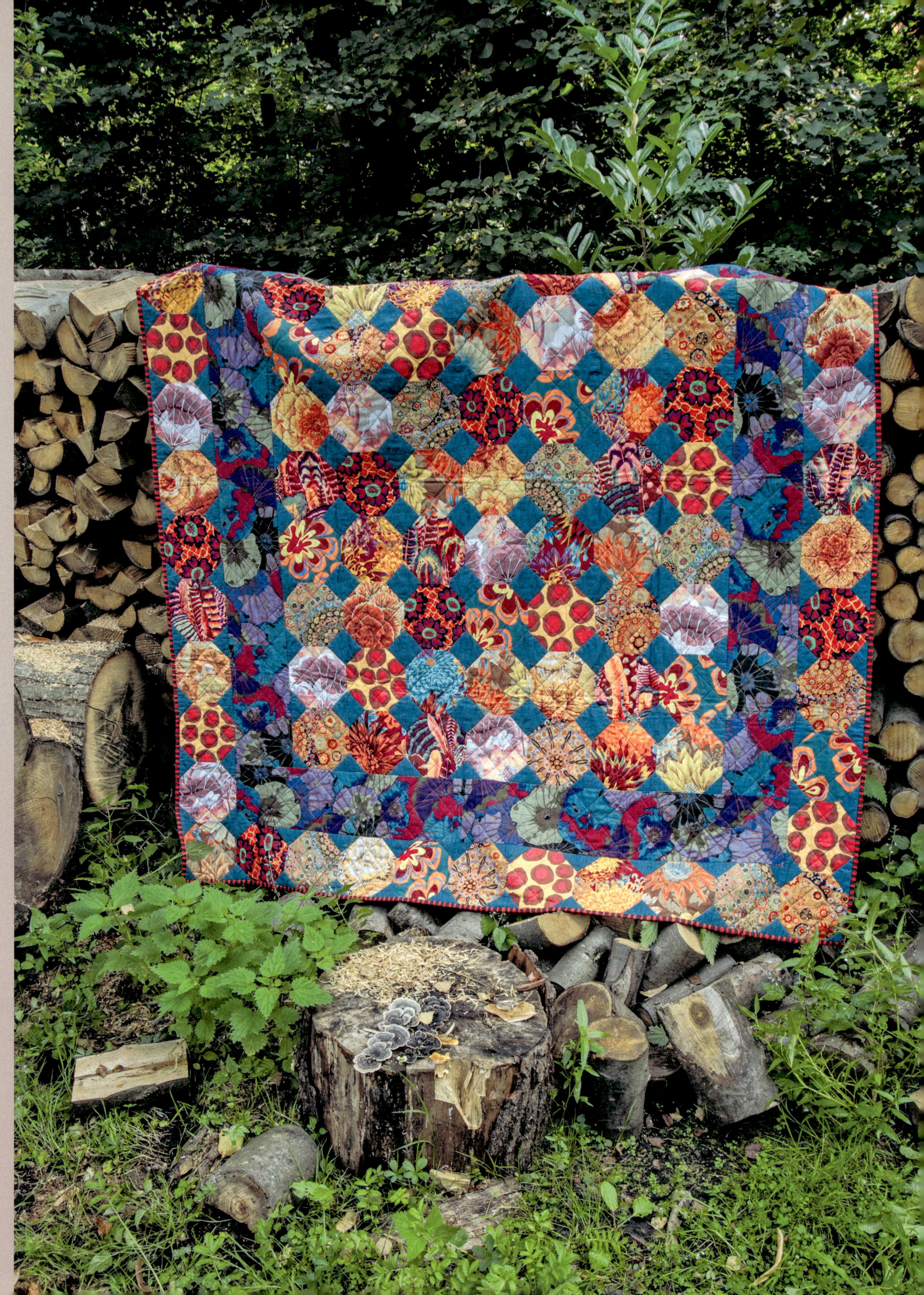

Country Snowballs
by Kaffe Fassett

Since I have a particular fondness for wood stacks,
I designed this quilt to echo the round log ends. Once
on location, we were delighted to find the visual bonus
of the round fungus on the old log in the foreground.

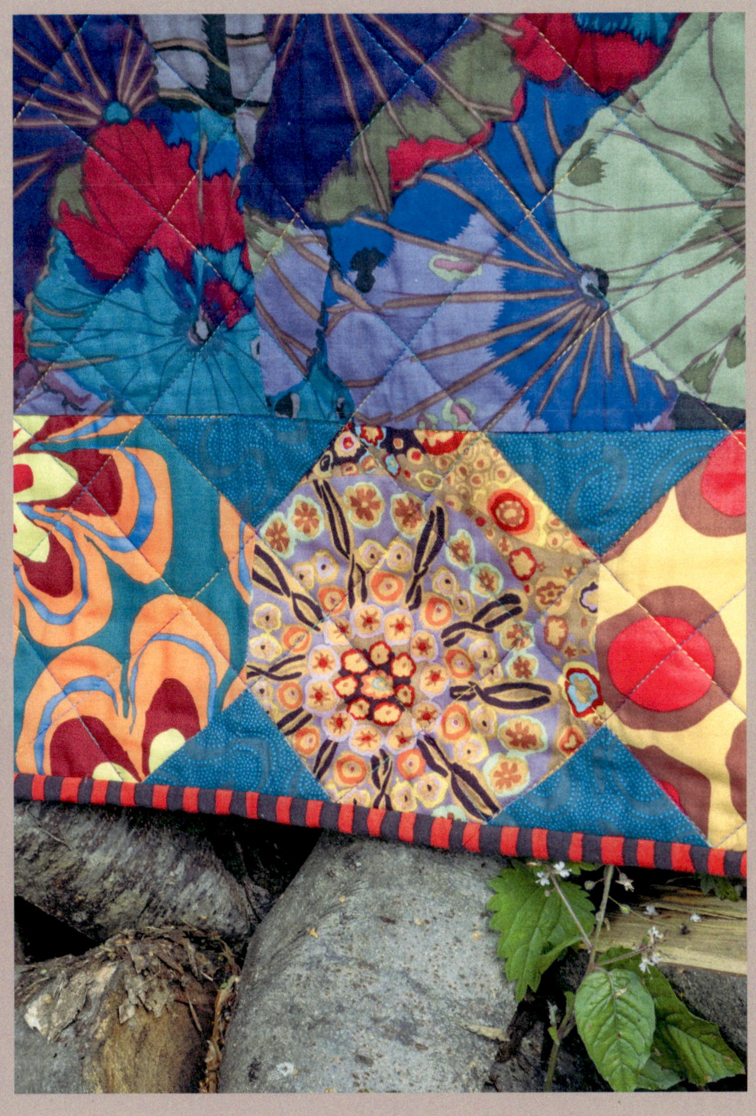

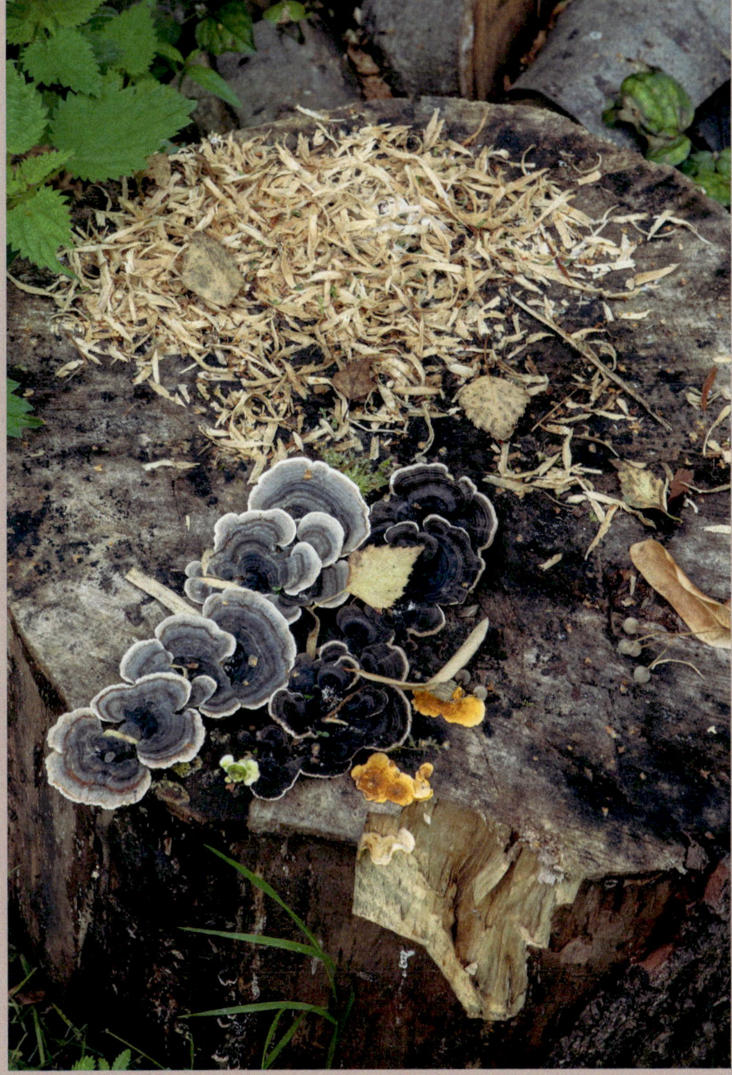

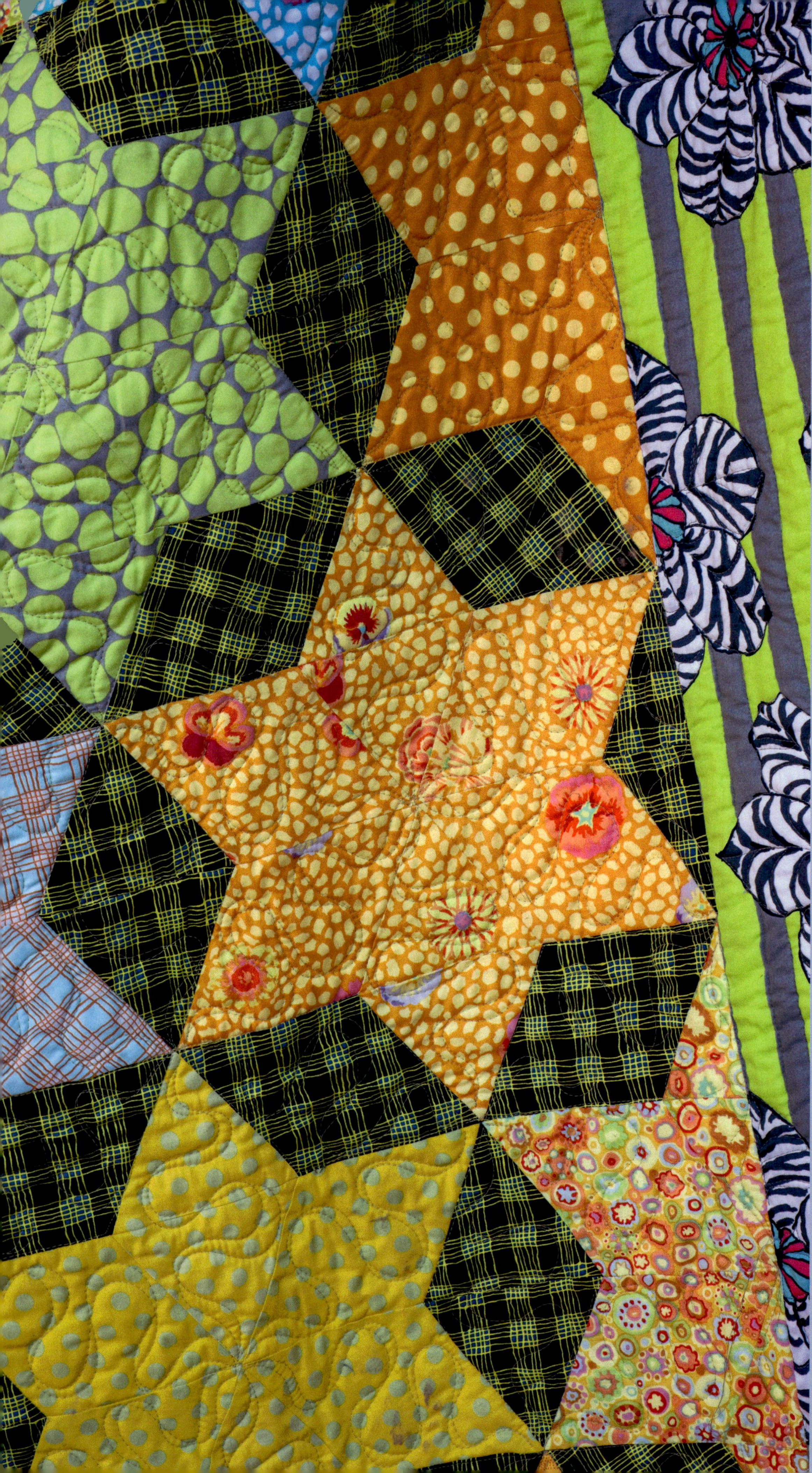

Golden Stars
by Kaffe Fassett

Because so many elements
of the farm were in strong
yellows, I designed this
bold star quilt in the
brightest of our yellow,
lime and blue fabrics. The
monumental bales of hay
make a powerful setting
for it.

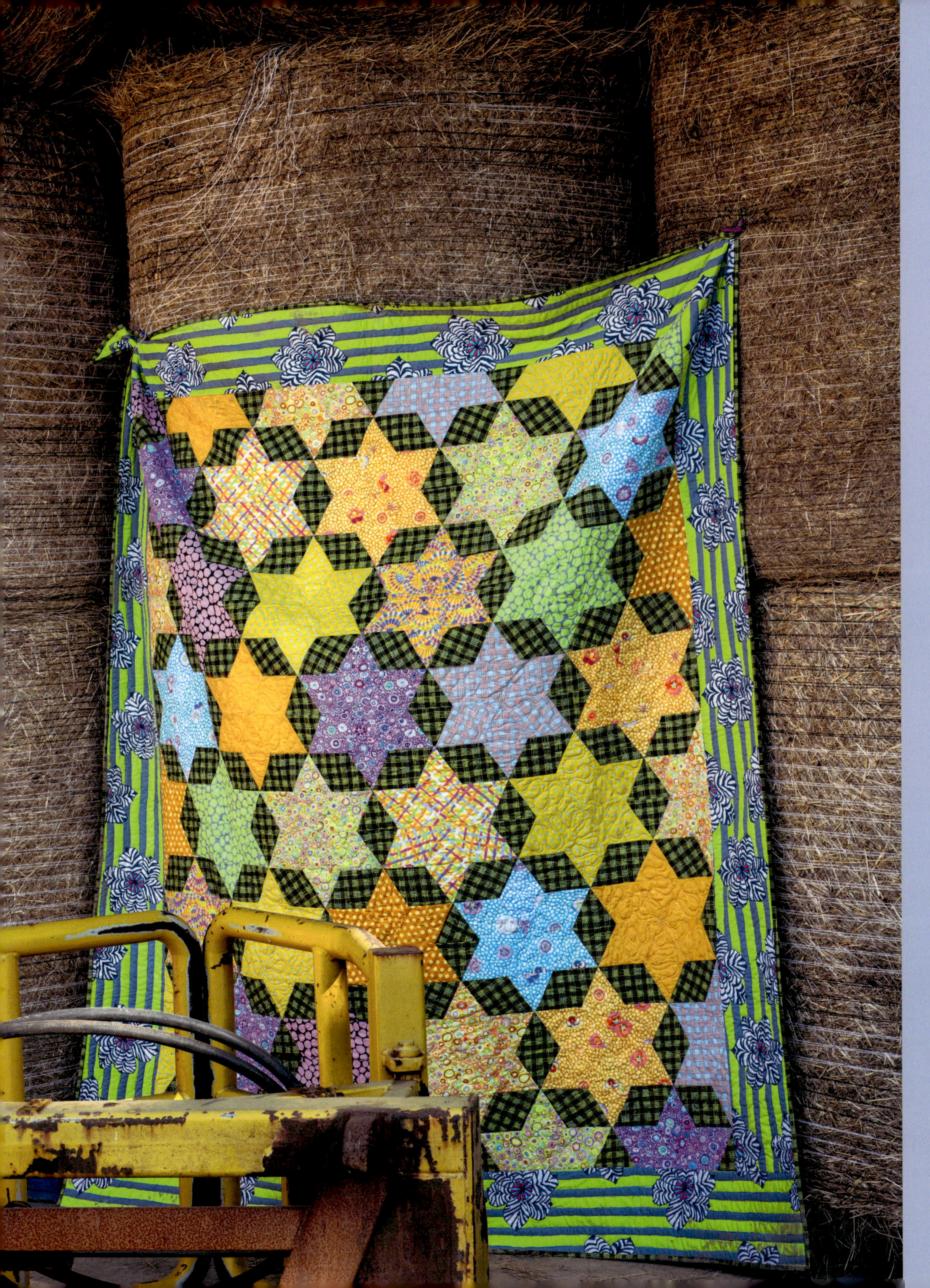

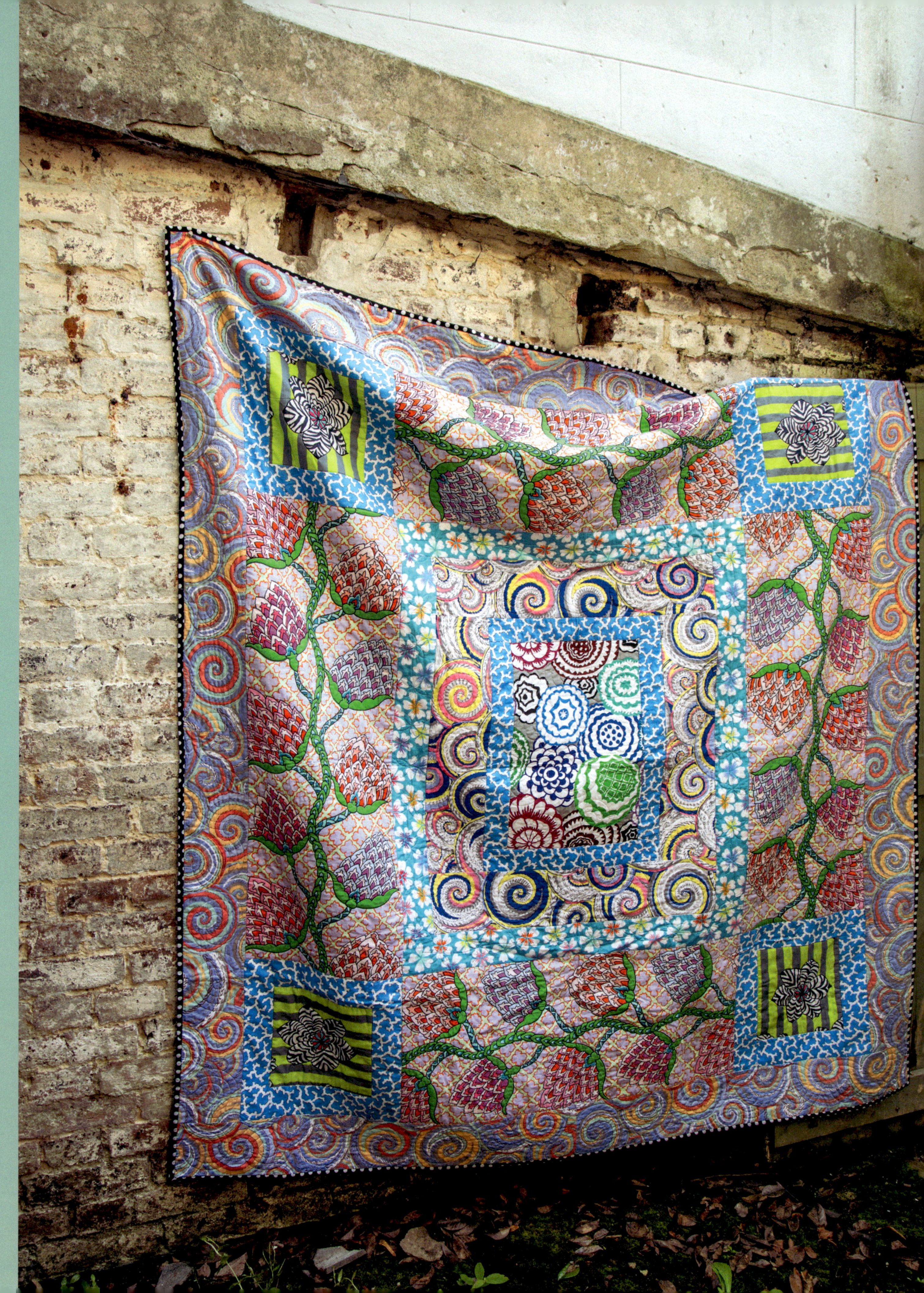

Deco Floral
by Kaffe Fassett

The soft hues of an old painted brick wall were just right to show off the subtle palette of this quilt. The bold shapes are softened by the subdued colours in this easy-to-make quilt.

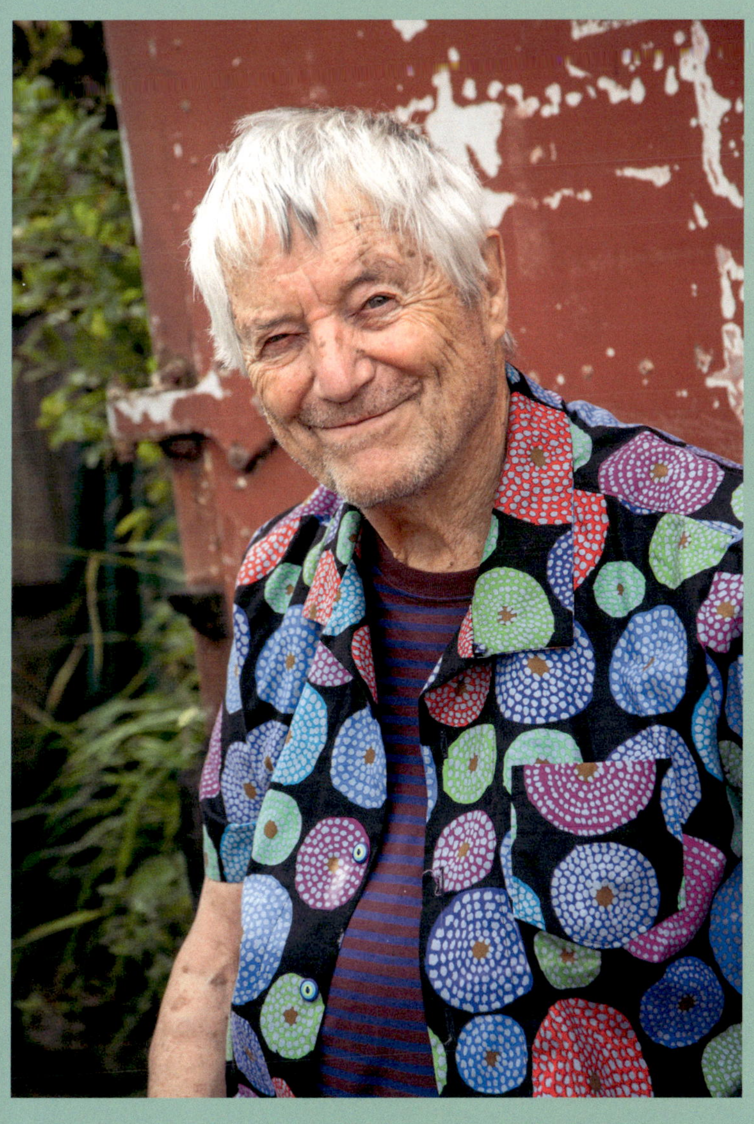

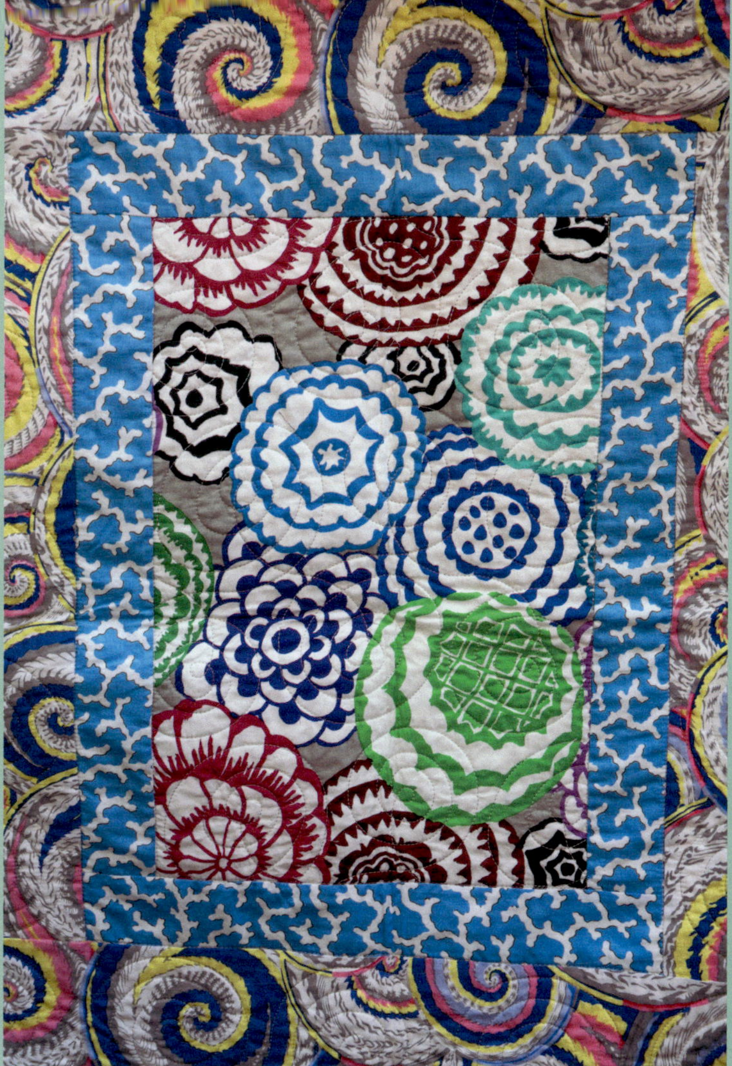

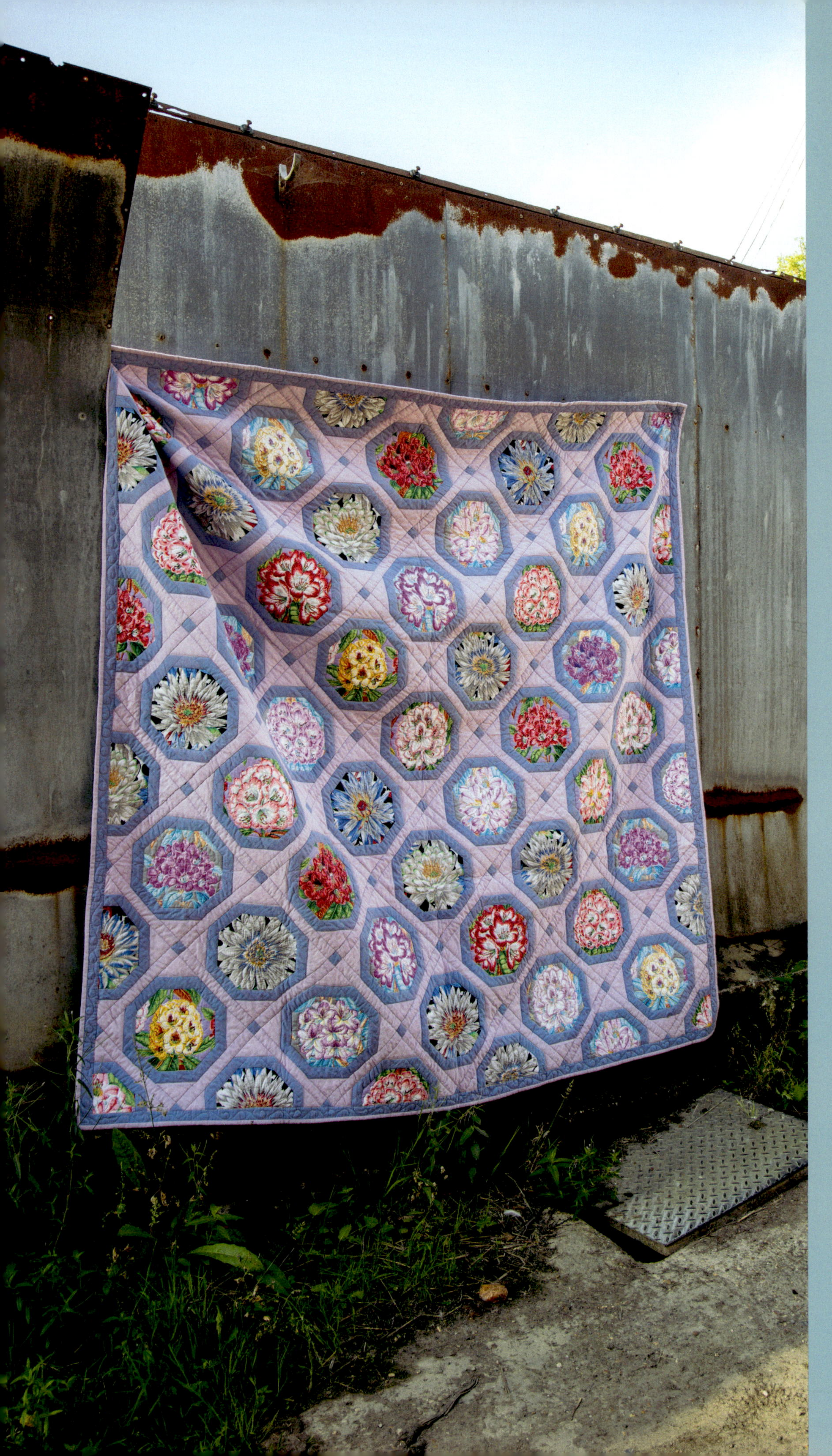

Blooming Octagons Pastel
by Kaffe Fassett

I am intrigued by how much the colour choice can affect a quilt layout. Here we have the same strong arrangement as in its sister quilt, but in this one the softest of lavenders makes such a good setting for the pastel florals, which glow against the silver grey.

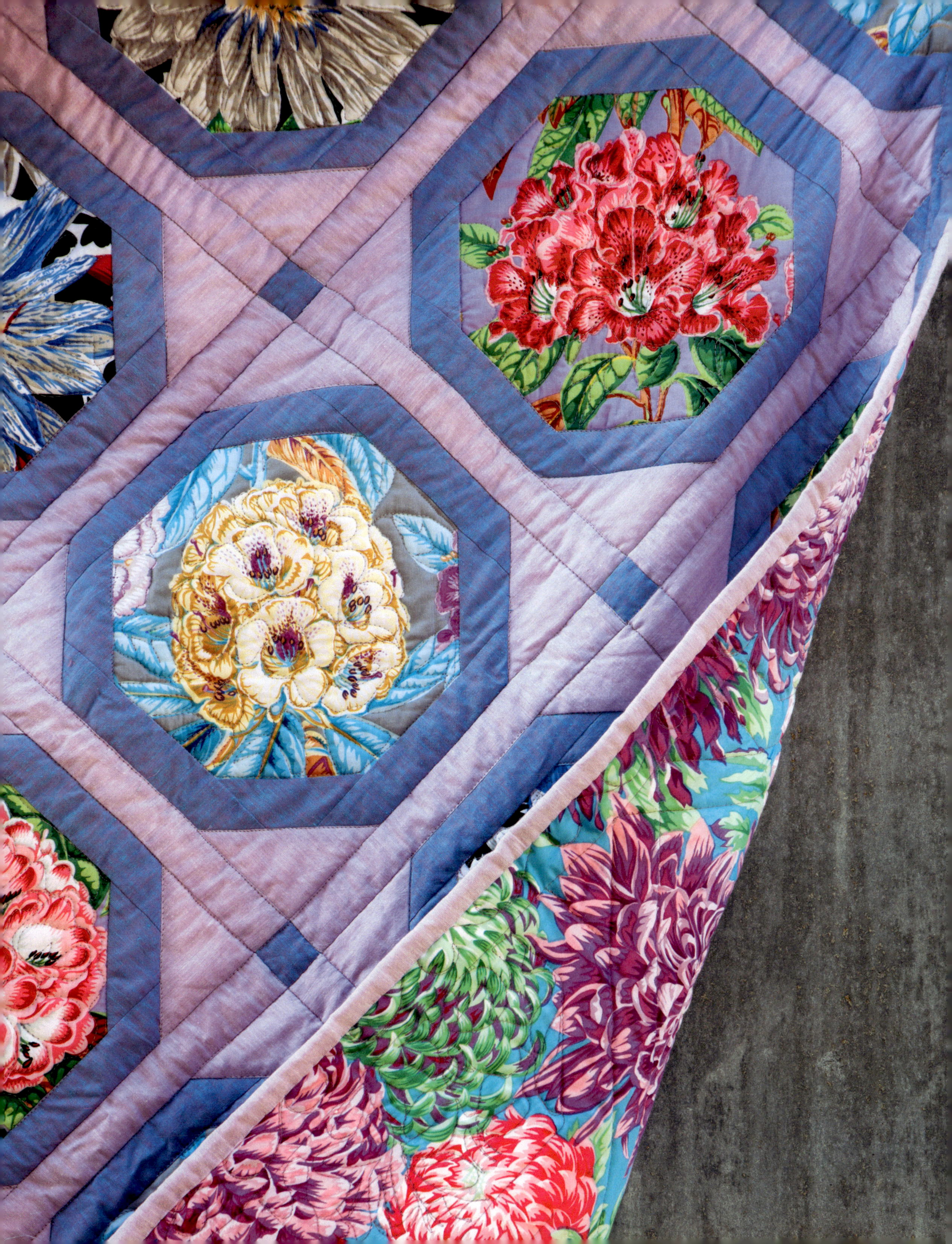

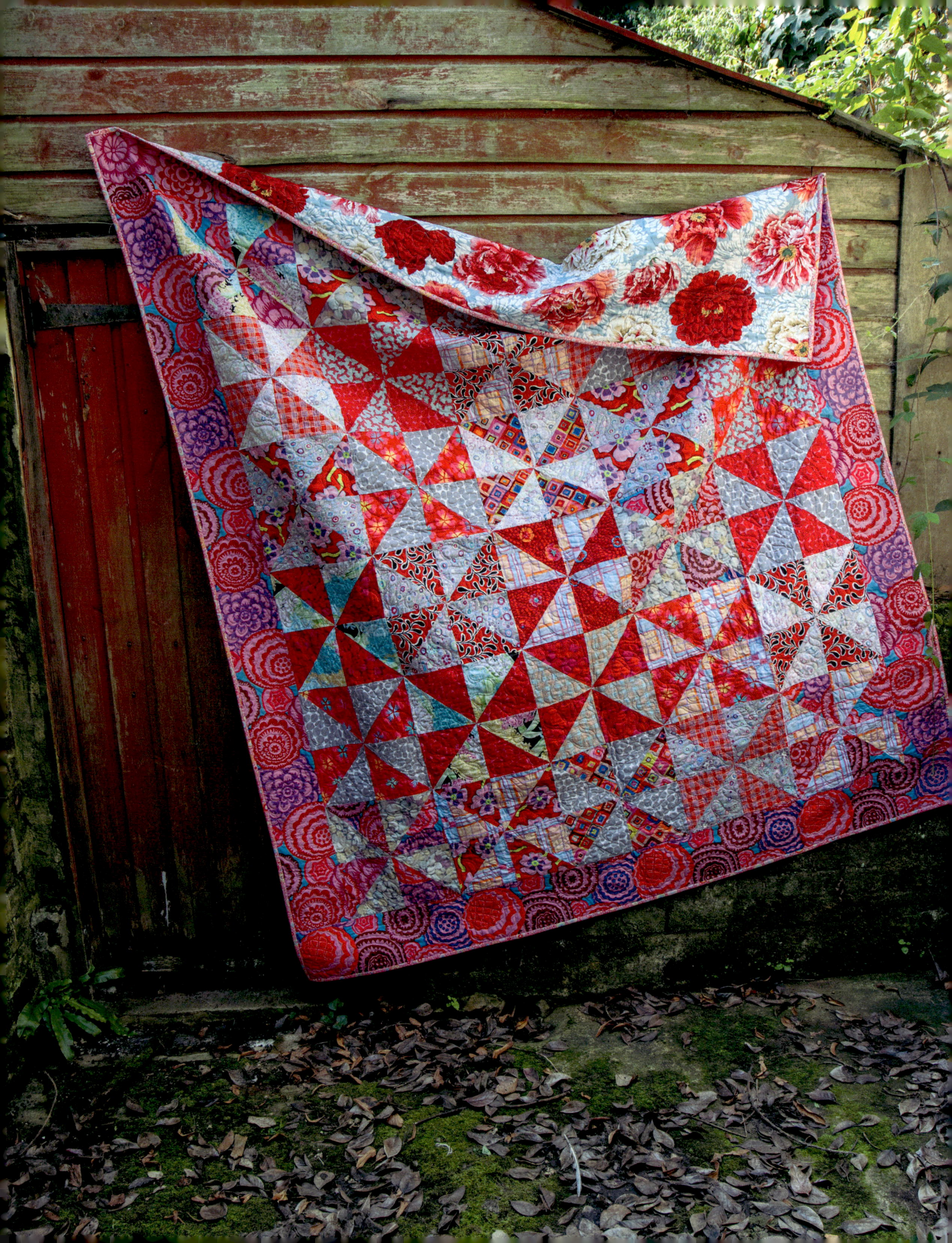

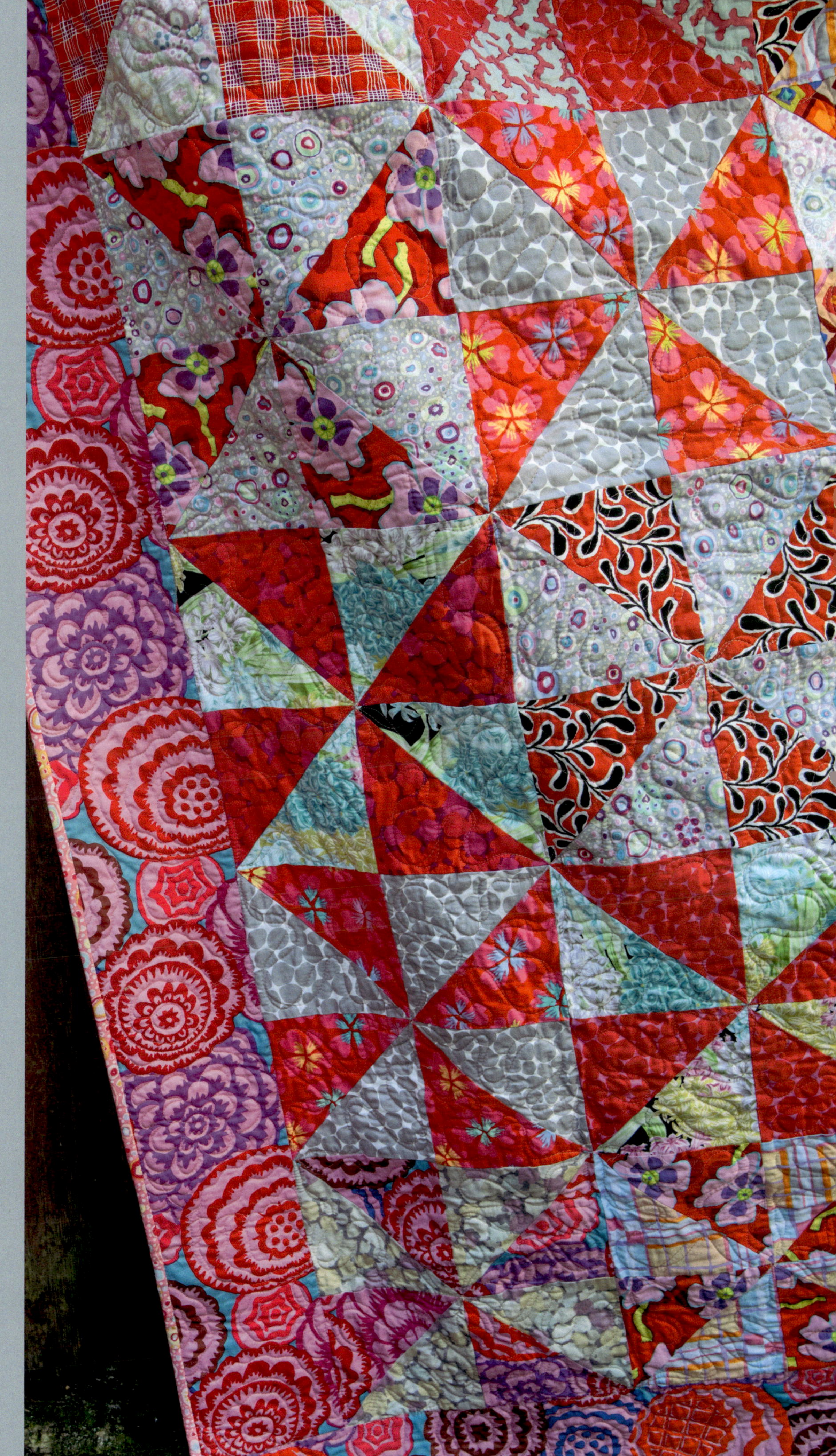

Windmills
by Kaffe Fassett

A simple pinwheel layout
in bright contrasts always
gets my attention. I think
the Brocade Peony backing
fabric and the floral Deco
fabric for the border work
so well in this happy union
of prints.

barn doors **

Liza Prior Lucy

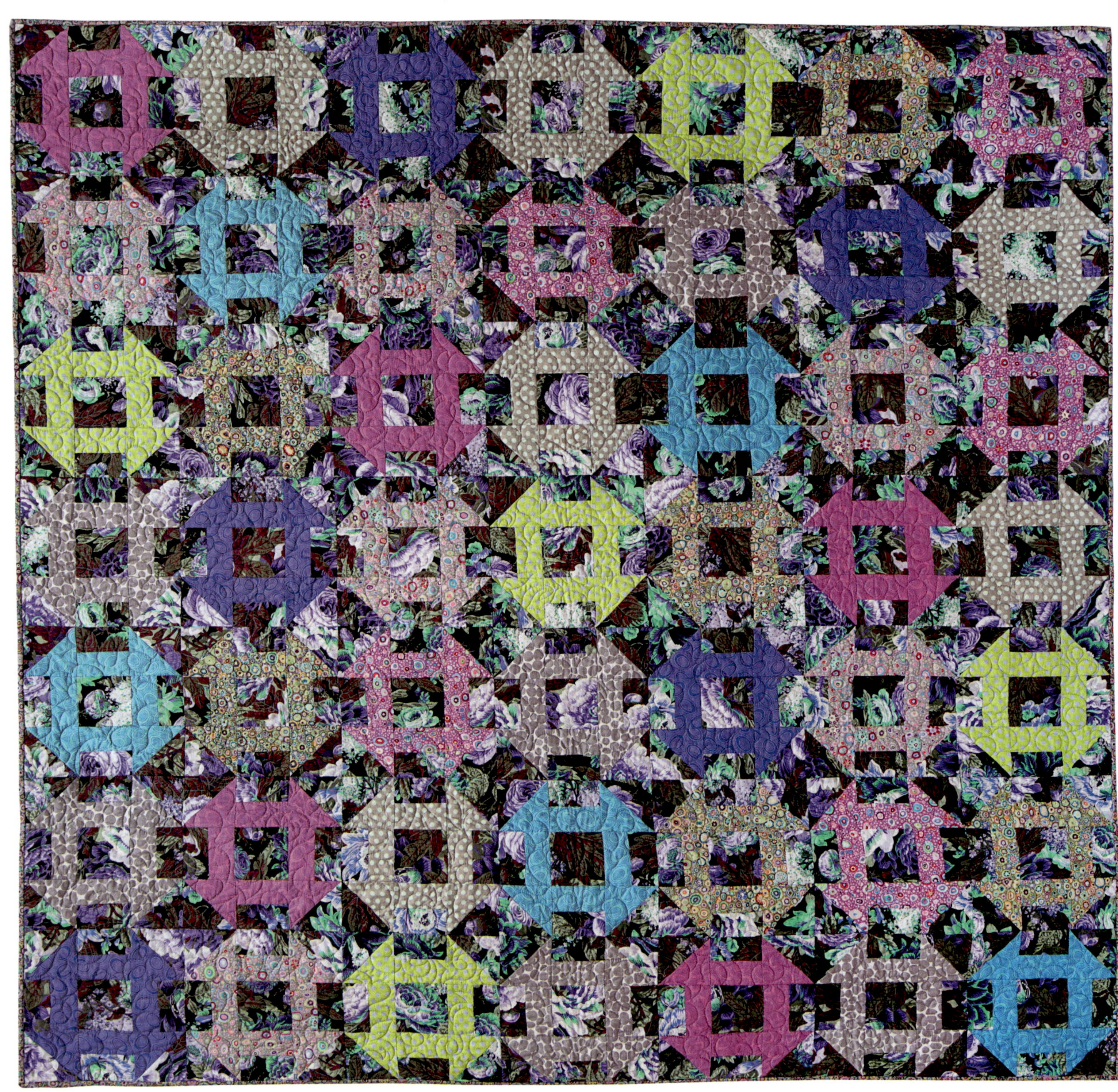

Liza's cool, calm quilt uses the traditional 'Churn Dash' block which features a new colourway of Philip Jacobs' Floral Burst fabric.

SIZE OF FINISHED QUILT
84in x 84in (213cm x 213cm)

FABRICS
Fabrics have been calculated at a maximum width of 40in (102cm). Fabrics have been given a number – see the Fabric Swatch Diagram for details.

Patchwork Fabrics
FLORAL BURST
Fabric 1	Purple	4½yd (4.2m)

ABORIGINAL DOT
Fabric 2	Iris	⅝yd (60cm)
Fabric 3	Turquoise	⅝yd (60cm)
Fabric 4	Wisteria	⅝yd (60cm)

ROMAN GLASS
Fabric 5	Grey	⅝yd (60cm)
Fabric 6	Lavender	⅝yd (60cm)

SPOT
Fabric 7	Apple	⅝yd (60cm)
Fabric 8	Steel	⅝yd (60cm)

PAPERWEIGHT
Fabric 9	Sludge	⅝yd (60cm)

JUMBLE
Fabric 10	Grey	⅝yd (60cm)

Backing and Binding Fabrics
TREE FUNGI extra-wide backing
Fabric 11	Contrast	2¾yd (2.6m)

PAPERWEIGHT
Fabric 12	Grey	¾yd (70cm)

Batting
94in x 94in (239cm x 239cm)

PATCHES
Each 9-square block uses 4 half-square triangles (HSTs) each of a feature fabric and an accent fabric, 4 rectangles each of a feature fabric and an accent fabric, and 1 square of a feature fabric. Patches are sewn together to form squares that in turn form 9-square blocks finished at 12in (30.5cm). There are 49 blocks, 6 blocks using each of the grey accent fabrics (Fabrics 5, 8, 9 and 10) and 5 blocks using each of the coloured accent fabrics (Fabrics 2, 3, 4, 6 and 7). Blocks are set in 7 rows of 7.

FABRIC SWATCH DIAGRAM

Patchwork Fabrics

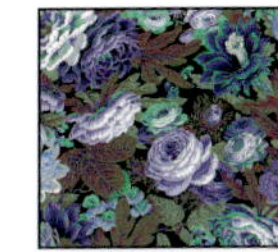
Fabric 1
FLORAL BURST
Purple
PJ29PU

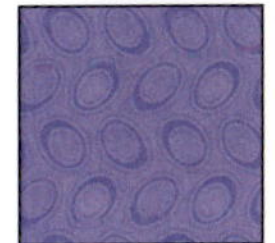
Fabric 2
ABORIGINAL DOT
Iris
GP71IR

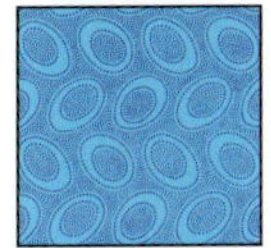
Fabric 3
ABORIGINAL DOT
Turquoise
GP71TQ

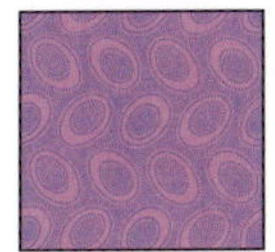
Fabric 4
ABORIGINAL DOT
Wisteria
GP71WS

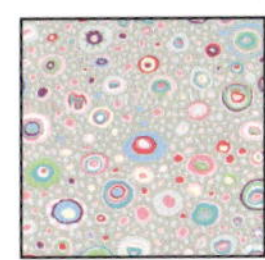
Fabric 5
ROMAN GLASS
Grey
GP01GY

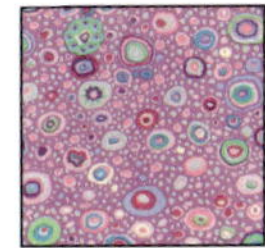
Fabric 6
ROMAN GLASS
Lavender
GP01LV

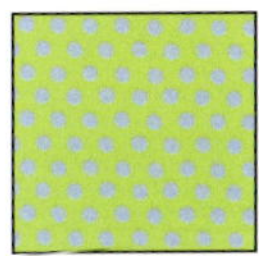
Fabric 7
SPOT
Apple
GP70AL

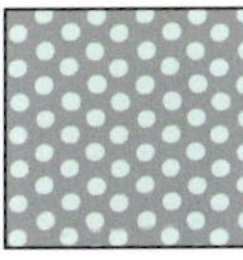
Fabric 8
SPOT
Steel
GP70ST

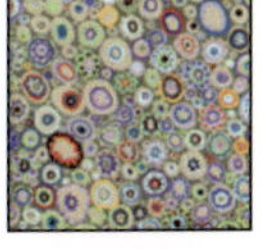
Fabric 9
PAPERWEIGHT
Sludge
GP20SL

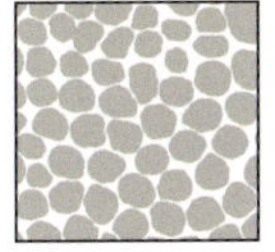
Fabric 10
JUMBLE
Grey
BM53GY

Backing and Binding Fabrics

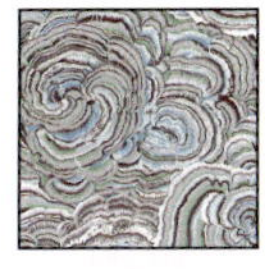
Fabric 11
TREE FUNGI
Contrast
QJ01CN

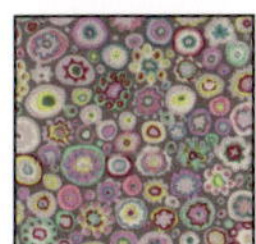
Fabric 12
PAPERWEIGHT
Grey
GP20GY

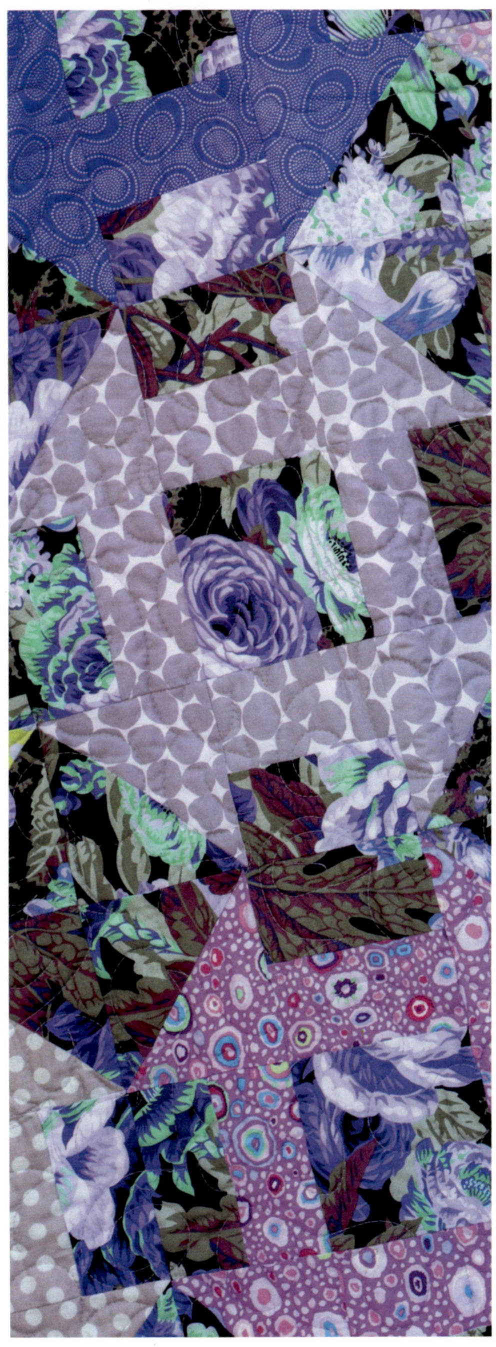

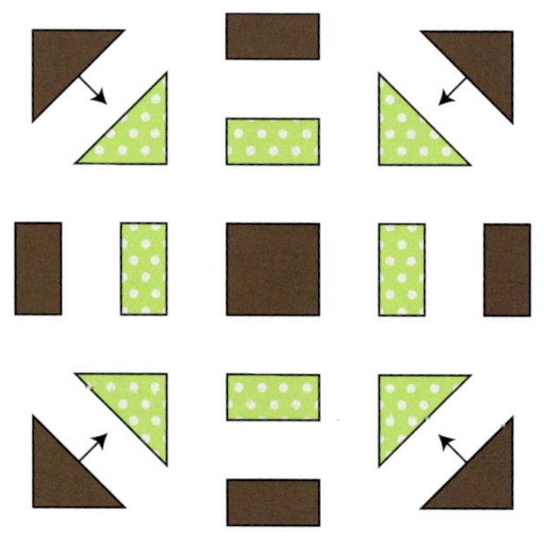

a

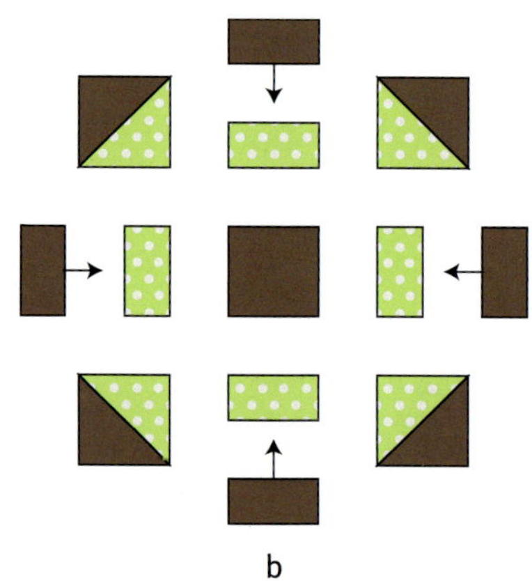

b

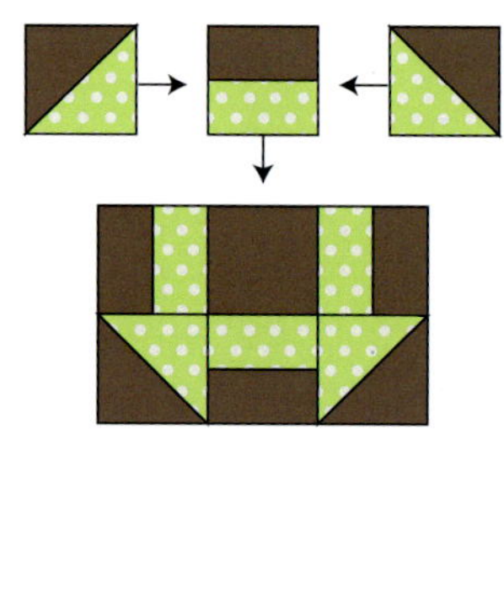

c

CUTTING OUT
Fabric is cut across the width unless otherwise stated. When cutting different pieces from the same fabric, always cut the larger pieces first.

Feature Fabrics
Triangles: From Fabric 1 cut 13 strips 4⅞in (12.4cm) wide and cross cut squares at 4⅞in (12.4cm). Each strip will yield 8 squares. Cut a total of 98 squares. Cut each square in half diagonally to form 2HSTs. Cut 196 triangles in total.
Rectangles: From Fabric 1 cut 13 strips 4½in (11.4cm) wide and cross cut rectangles 2½in x 4½in (6.4cm x 11.4cm). Each strip will yield 16 rectangles. Cut 196 rectangles in total.
Squares: From Fabric 1 cut 7 strips 4½in (11.4cm) wide and cross cut squares at 4½in (11.4cm). Each strip will yield 8 squares. Cut 49 triangles in total.

Accent Fabrics
Triangles: Cut 2 strips 4⅞in (12.4cm) wide and cross cut squares at 4⅞in (12.4cm). Each strip will yield 8 squares. Cut each square in half diagonally to form 2 HSTs. Cut 196 triangles in total, from fabrics as follows:
Cut 10 squares – 20 triangles from each of Fabric 2, 3, 4, 6 and 7.
Cut 12 squares – 24 triangles from each of Fabric 5, 8, 9 and 10.
Rectangles: Trim the remaining strips from the triangles down to 4½in (11.4cm) wide and cut an additional strip from each fabric 4½in (11.4cm) wide. Cross cut rectangles 2½in x 4½in (6.4cm x 11.4cm). Each full strip will yield 16 rectangles. Cut 196 rectangles in total, from fabrics as follows:
Cut 20 rectangles from each of Fabric 2, 3, 4, 6 and Fabric 7.
Cut 24 rectangles from each of Fabric 5, 8, 9 and 10.

Backing
Trim Fabric 11 to 94in x 94in (239cm x 239cm).

Binding
From Fabric 12 cut 9 strips 2½in (6.4cm) wide. Remove selvedges and sew end to end with 45° seams (see page 141).

MAKING THE QUILT
Using a design wall will help to place patches in the required layout.
Use ¼in (6mm) seams throughout.

Making the Blocks
Each block has 4 HSTs of feature fabric paired with 4 half-square triangles from an accent fabric, and 4 rectangles of feature fabric paired with 4 rectangles of an accent fabric plus 1 large square of feature fabric. Referring to the Block Assembly Diagram, sew pairs of triangles together for the corners (a), then sew pairs of rectangles together for the sides (b) and then sew the 3 rows together to complete the block (c). Make 49 blocks in total.

Centre
Lay out the blocks in 7 rows of 7, referring to the Quilt Assembly Diagram and quilt photograph. Sew together one row at a time, aligning crossing seams and pressing seams in opposite directions on alternate rows – odd rows to the left, even rows to the right – to allow the finished seams to lie flat. Sew the 7 rows together, taking care to align crossing seams.

FINISHING THE QUILT
Press the quilt top. Layer the quilt top, batting and backing, and baste together (see page 140).
Quilt as desired.
Trim the quilt edges and attach the binding (see page 141).

Fabric 1   Fabric 3   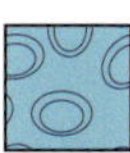 Fabric 5   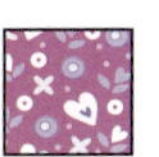 Fabric 7   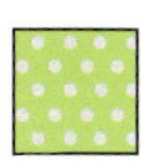 Fabric 9 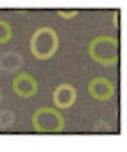

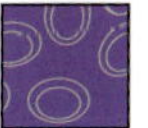 Fabric 2   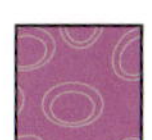 Fabric 4   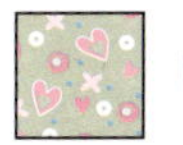 Fabric 6   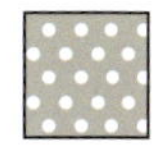 Fabric 8   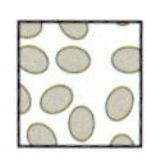 Fabric 10

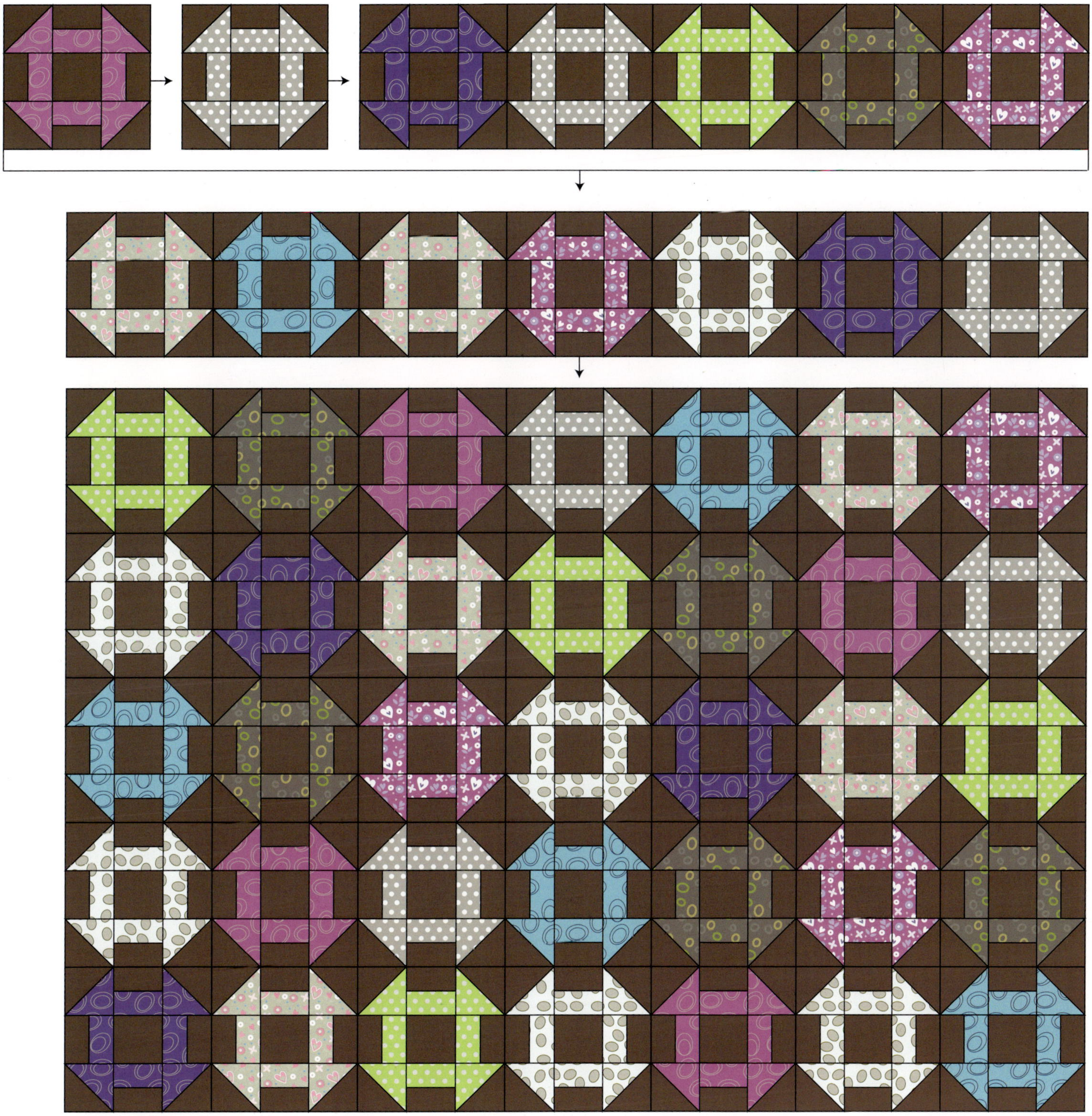

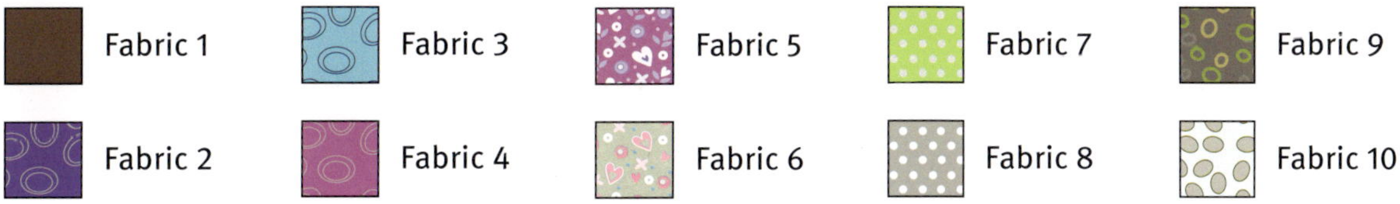

rhododendron stars **

Liza Prior Lucy

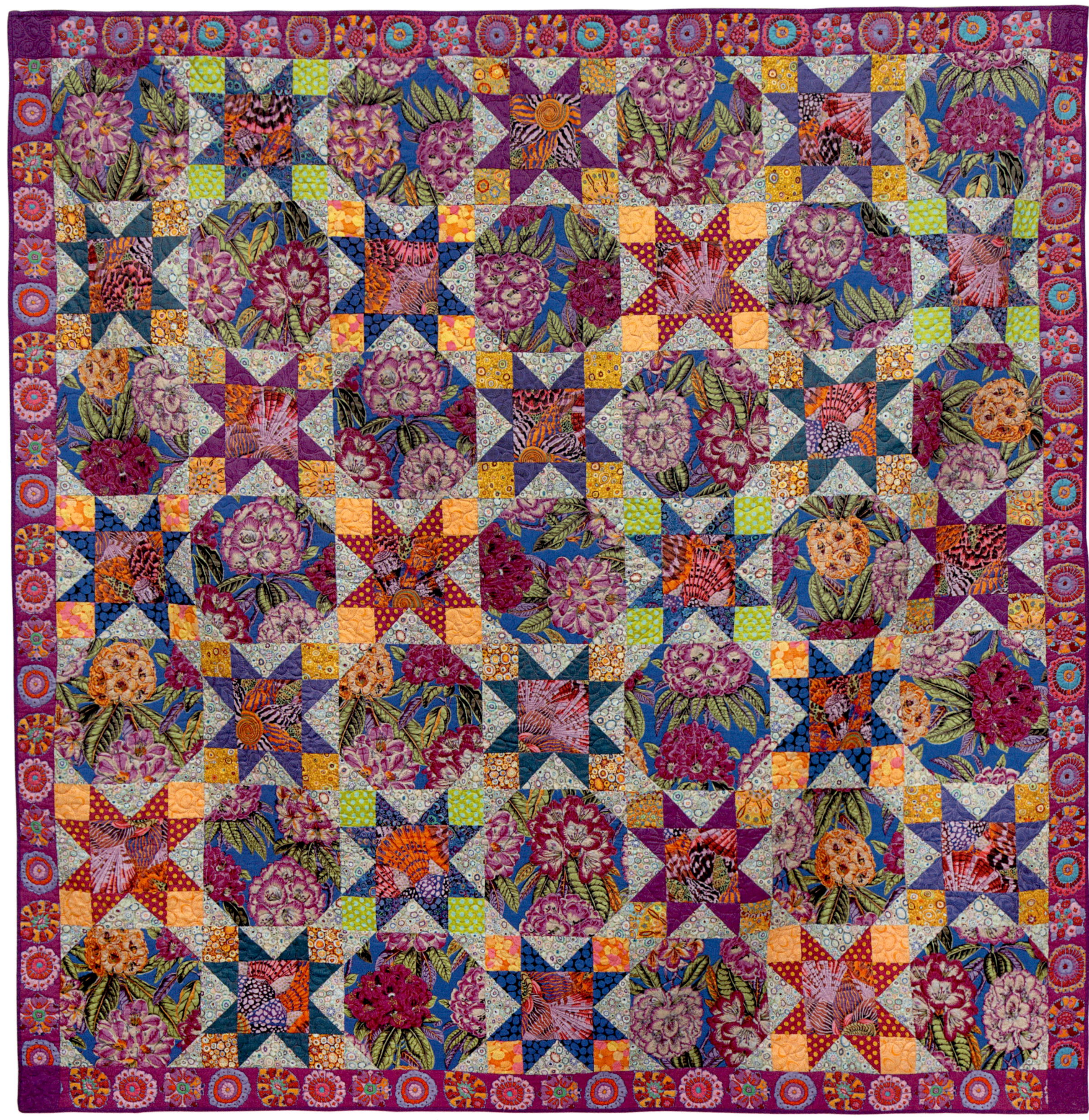

Liza's combination of large feature snowball blocks and star blocks looks particularly striking set against my softly coloured Paperweight fabric background, set off with a border of Carpet Cookies fabric motifs.

SIZE OF FINISHED QUILT
91in x 91in (231cm x 231cm)

FABRICS
Fabrics have been calculated at a maximum width of 40in (102cm). Fabrics have been given a number – see the Fabric Swatch Diagram for details.

Patchwork Fabrics
RHODODENDRONS
Fabric 1	Magenta	3¼yd (3m)

SAILOR VALENTINE
Fabric 2	Red	¾yd (70cm)

PAPERWEIGHT
Fabric 3	Sludge	2yd (1.9m)
Fabric 4	Pumpkin	⅜yd (40cm)

REFLECTIONS
Fabric 5	Orange	¼yd (25cm)

MILLEFIORE
Fabric 6	Blue	⅜yd (40cm)
Fabric 7	Orange	¼yd (25cm)

ROMAN GLASS
Fabric 8	Gold	¼yd (25cm)

SPOT
Fabric 9	Pond	¼yd (25cm)
Fabric 10	Magenta	⅜yd (40cm)

JUMBLE
Fabric 11	Blue	⅜yd (40cm)

ABORIGINAL DOT
Fabric 12	Cantaloupe	¼yd (25cm)
Fabric 13	Periwinkle	⅜yd (40cm)
Fabric 14	Plum	½yd (50cm)
* see also Binding Fabric		
Fabric 15	Charcoal	¼yd (25cm)

CARPET COOKIES
Fabric 16	Magenta	2½yd (2.3m)

Backing and Binding Fabrics
PEBBLE MOSAIC extra-wide backing
Fabric 17	Prune	3yd (2.8m)

ABORIGINAL DOT
Fabric 14	Plum	¾yd (70cm)
* see also Patchwork Fabrics		

Batting
102in x 102in (259cm x 259cm)

FABRIC SWATCH DIAGRAM

Patchwork Fabrics

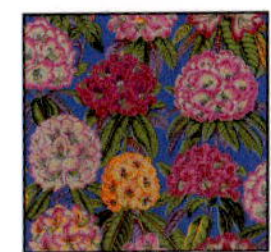
Fabric 1
RHODODENDRONS
Magenta
PJ124MG

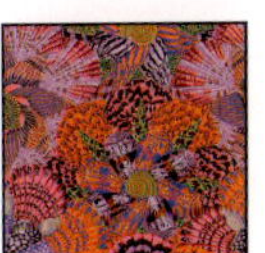
Fabric 2
SAILOR VALENTINE
Red
PJ121RD

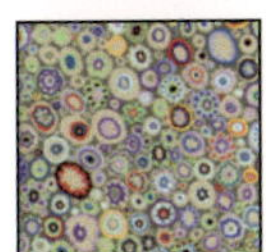
Fabric 3
PAPERWEIGHT
Sludge
GP20SL

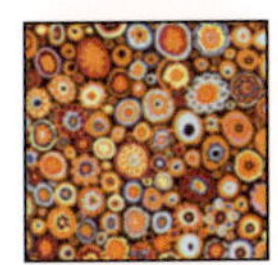
Fabric 4
PAPERWEIGHT
Pumpkin
GP20PN

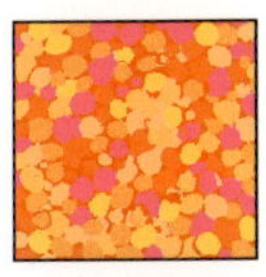
Fabric 5
REFLECTIONS
Orange
BM87OR

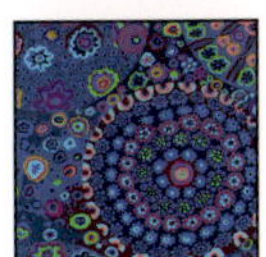
Fabric 6
MILLEFIORE
Blue
GP92BL

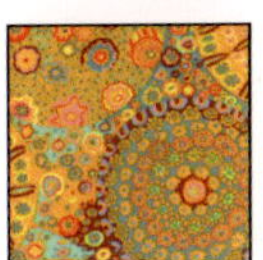
Fabric 7
MILLEFIORE
Orange
GP92OR

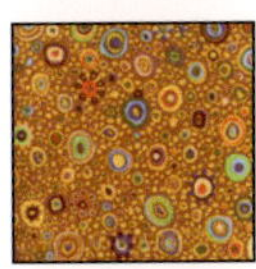
Fabric 8
ROMAN GLASS
Gold
GP01GD

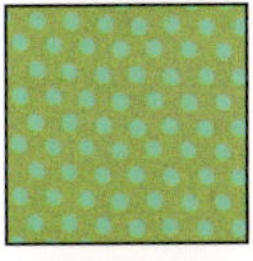
Fabric 9
SPOT
Pond
GP77OPO

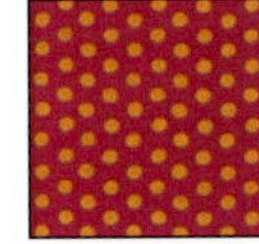
Fabric 10
SPOT
Magenta
GP70MG

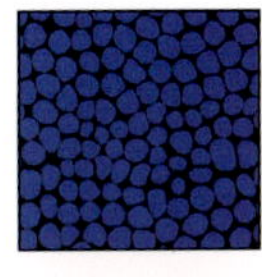
Fabric 11
JUMBLE
Blue
BM53BL

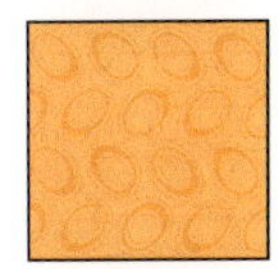
Fabric 12
ABORIGINAL DOT
Cantaloupe
GP71CA

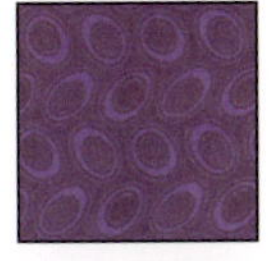
Fabric 13
ABORIGINAL DOT
Periwinkle
GP71PE

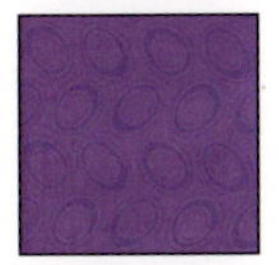
Fabric 14
ABORIGINAL DOT
Plum
GP71PL

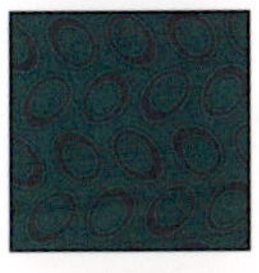
Fabric 15
ABORIGINAL DOT
Charcoal
GP71CC

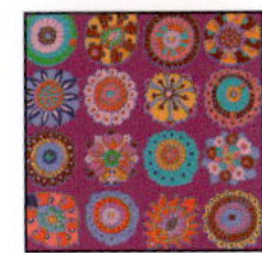
Fabric 16
CARPET COOKIES
Magenta
GP192MG

Backing and Binding Fabrics

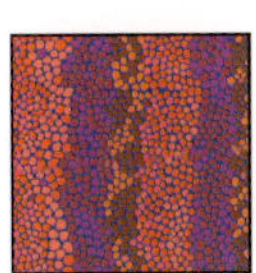
Fabric 17
PEBBLE MOSAIC
Prune
QM04PV

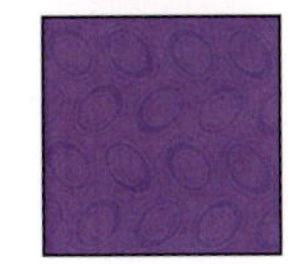
Fabric 14
ABORIGINAL DOT
Plum
GP71PL

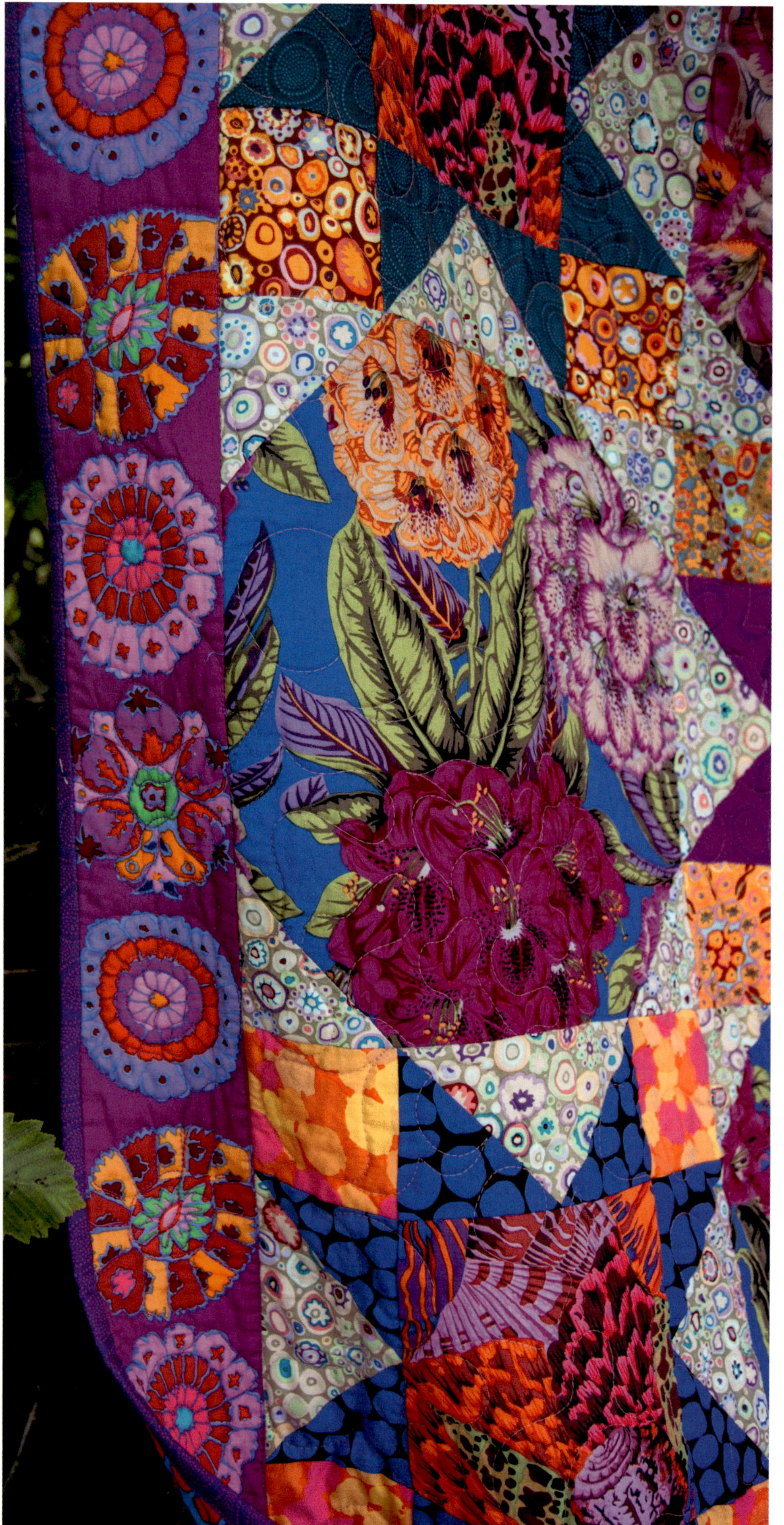

PATCHES

This quilt comprises 25 snowball blocks and 24 star blocks.

Each snowball block has 1 large square from Fabric 1 and 4 small squares from Fabric 3.

Each star block has 1 large centre square from Fabric 2 and 4 background quarter-square triangles (QSTs) from Fabric 3, with 4 corner squares (from one of Fabrics 4 to 9) plus 8 small star-point, half-square triangles (HSTs) (from 1 of Fabrics 10 to 15).

Snowball and star blocks alternate in 7 rows of 7 blocks.

CUTTING OUT

Fabric is cut across the width unless otherwise stated. When cutting different pieces from the same fabric, always cut the larger pieces first.

Star Blocks

Centre squares: From Fabric 2 cut 4 strips 6½in (15.5cm) wide and cross cut 24 squares at 6½in (15.5cm).

Background triangles: From Fabric 3 cut 5 strips 7¼in (18.4cm) wide and cross cut 24 squares at 7¼in (18.4cm). Each strip will yield 5 squares. Cross cut each square twice diagonally to yield 4 QSTs from each square. Cut 96 in total.

Corner squares: From each of Fabrics 5, 7, 8, 9, 12 and 15 cut 2 strips 3½in (8.9cm) wide and cross cut 16 squares at 3½in (8.9cm) from each fabric. Each strip will yield 11 squares.

Star-point triangles: From each of Fabrics 4, 6, 10, 11, 13 and 14 cut 3 strips 3⅞in (9.8cm) wide and cross cut 16 squares at 3⅞in (9.8cm). Cross cut each square once diagonally to yield 2 HSTs from each square. Cut 32 from each fabric.

Snowball Blocks

From Fabric 1 cut 9 strips 12½in (31.8cm) wide and cross cut 25 squares at 12½in (31.8cm). Each strip will yield 3 squares.

From Fabric 3 cut 9 strips 3½in (8.9cm) wide and cross cut 99 squares at 3½in (8.9cm). Each strip will yield 11 squares. One more square is needed; cut it from the remainder of star blocks Fabric 3. Cut a total of 100 squares.

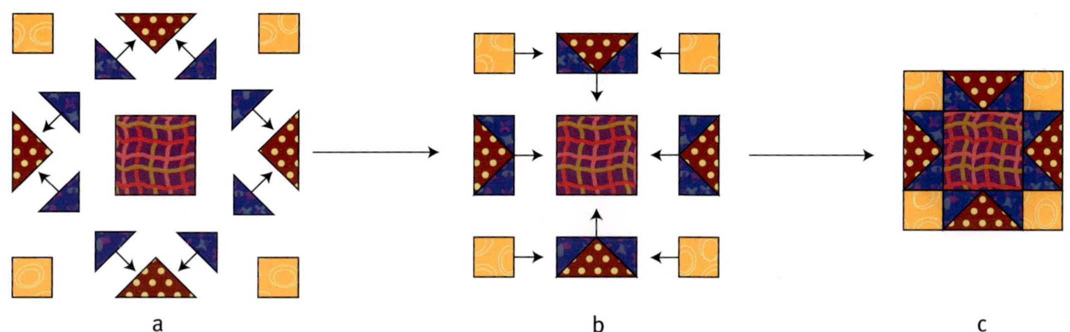

STAR BLOCK ASSEMBLY DIAGRAM

a   b   c

Border

From Fabric 16 fussy cut **down the length of the fabric,** centering the 'cookies' within each strip. In order to get 4 of these borders, it will be necessary to skip columns of 'cookies' between each border length. Cut 4 strips 84½in x 4in (214.6cm x 10.2cm).

Note: The excess fabric would be perfect to use in a small paper-piecing project.

Corner Squares

From the remaining Fabric 14 cut half a strip 4in (10.2cm) wide and cross cut 4 squares at 4in (10.2cm).

Backing

Trim Fabric 17 to 102in x 102in (259cm x 259cm).

Binding

From Fabric 14 cut 10 strips 2½in (6.4cm) wide. Remove selvedges and sew end to end using 45° seams (see page 141).

MAKING THE QUILT

Using a design wall will help to place patches in the required layout. Use ¼in (6mm) seams throughout.

Star Blocks

Referring to the Star Block Assembly Diagram, make 24 star blocks, all with Fabric 2 centre squares and Fabric 3 background triangles. Make 4 blocks with each of the following fabric combinations for corner squares and star points respectively:
Fabric 12 and 10; 5 and 11; 15 and 4; 8 and 13; 7 and 14; and 9 and 6.

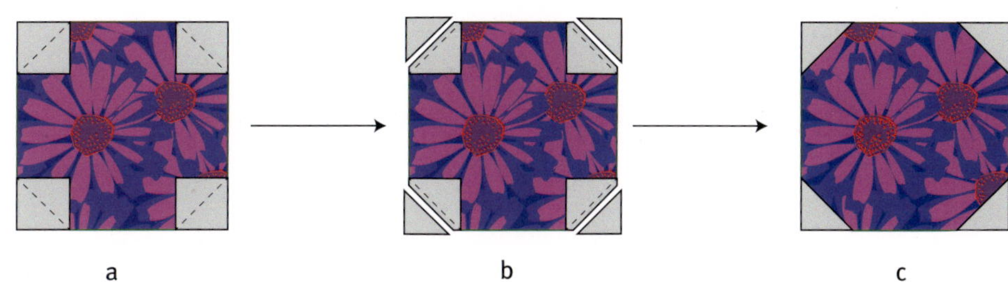

SNOWBALL BLOCK ASSEMBLY DIAGRAM

a   b   c

Sew 2 star-point triangles to each of the 4 background triangles (a). Sew a corner square to each side of the top and bottom triangle sections. Sew the side triangle sections to each side of the centre square (b), then sew the 3 rows together to form each star (c).

Snowball Blocks

Referring to the Snowball Block Assembly Diagram, take a large Fabric 1 square and 4 of Fabric 2 small squares. With right sides together, position a small square on each corner of the large square and sew diagonally (a). Trim off the excess leaving a ¼in (6mm) seam allowance (b). Press seams towards the corners to finish the block (c). Make 25 blocks.

Centre

Referring to the Quilt Assembly Diagram on page 58 and quilt photograph, lay out the blocks, alternating between the snowball and star blocks, and positioning snowball blocks in all 4 corners. Stand back and check the layout is well-balanced before sewing together one row at a time, pressing seams in opposite directions on alternate rows – odd rows to the left, even rows to the right – to allow the finished seams to lie flat. Sew the rows together, taking care to align crossing seams.

Border

Pin (to prevent stretching the borders), then sew a Fabric 16 border strip to each side of the quilt. Sew a Fabric 14 corner square to each end of the remaining 2 border strips, then pin and sew the top and bottom borders to the centre to complete the quilt top.

FINISHING THE QUILT

Press the quilt top. Layer the quilt top, batting and backing, and baste together (see page 140).
Quilt as desired.
Trim the quilt edges and attach the binding (see page 141).

QUILT ASSEMBLY DIAGRAM

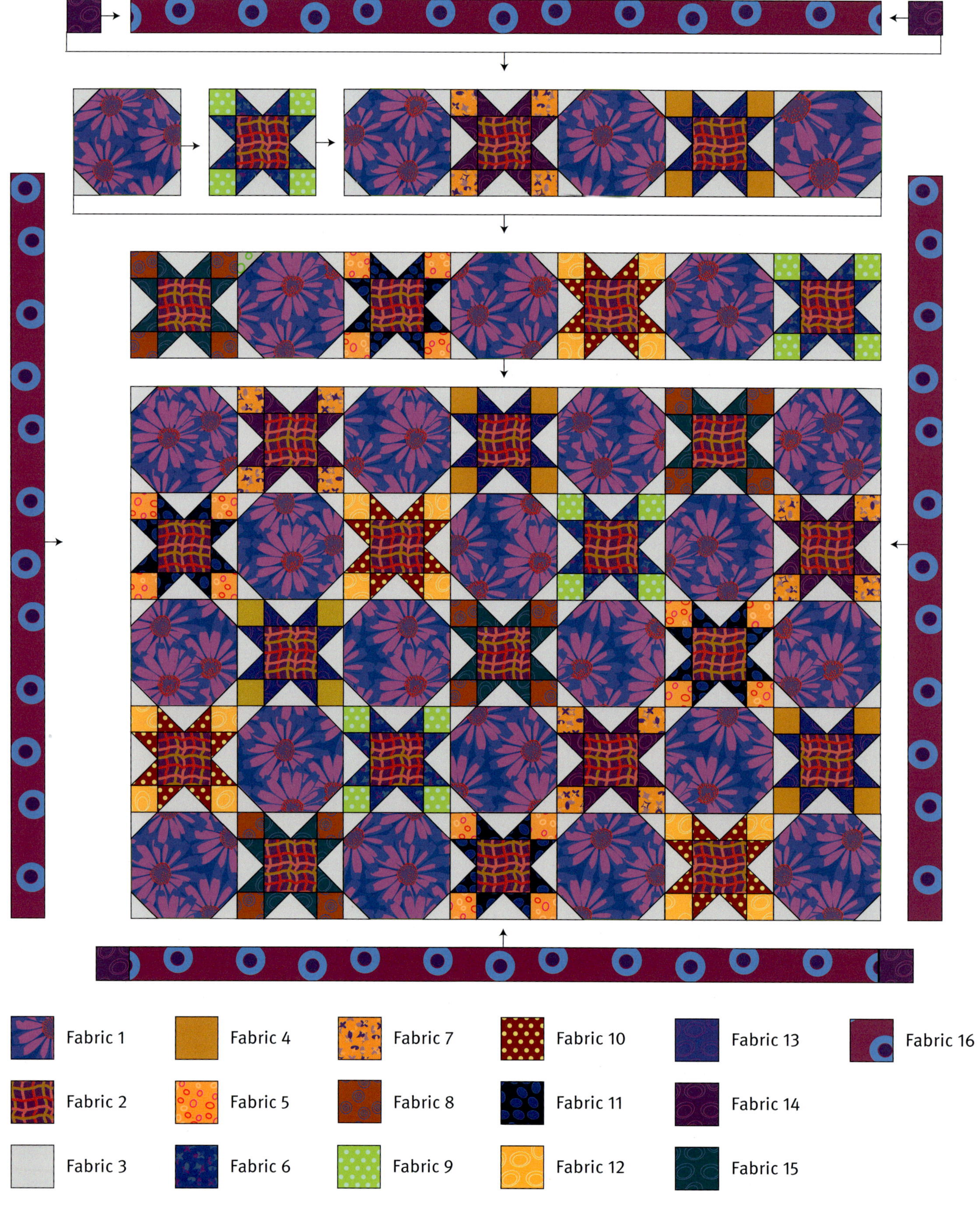

sailor's gift **

Kaffe Fassett

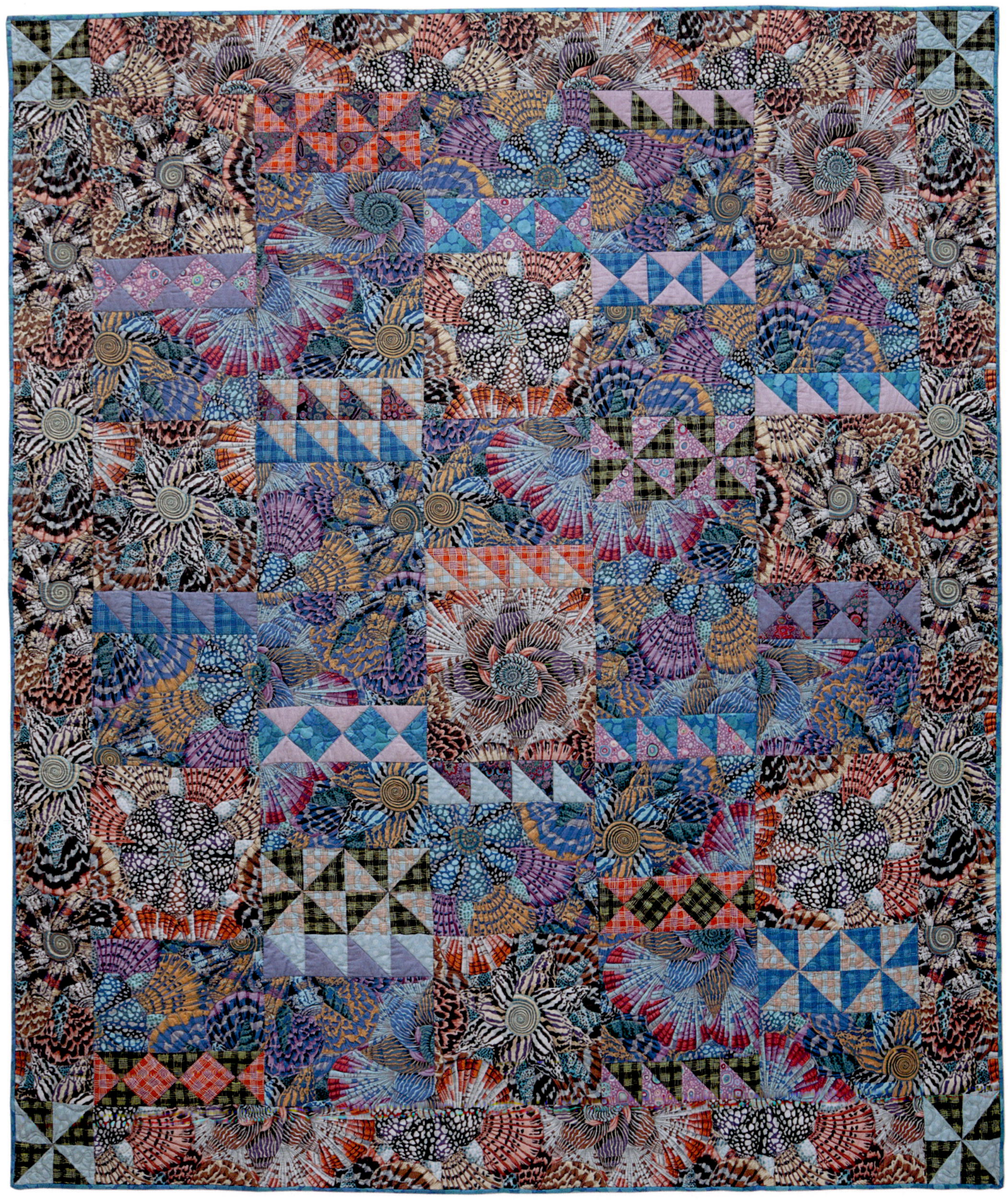

For this quilt I used two colourways of Philip Jacobs' seashell-inspired Sailor Valentine fabric to really show it off, combined in some blocks with sections of sawtooth, hourglass and pinwheel blocks emerging from the seashells. It looks more complicated than it is. It is made from 12in (30.5cm) blocks, some cut entirely from the feature fabric, others combined with the pieced strips.

SIZE OF FINISHED QUILT
84in x 72in (213cm x 183cm)

FABRICS
Fabrics have been calculated at a maximum width of 40in (102cm). Fabrics have been given a number – see the Fabric Swatch Diagram for details.

Patchwork Fabrics
SAILOR VALENTINE

| Fabric 1 | Contrast | 4yd (3.7m) |
| Fabric 2 | Cool | 2yd (1.9m) |

ROMAN GLASS

| Fabric 3 | Lavender | ⅜yd (40cm) |

GINGHAM

Fabric 4	Black	½yd (50cm)
Fabric 5	Blue	⅜yd (40cm)
Fabric 6	Grey	¼yd (25cm)
Fabric 7	Red	⅜yd (40cm)

SPOT

| Fabric 8 | Duck Egg | ¼yd (25cm) |

SHOT COTTON

| Fabric 9 | Dawn | ¼yd (25cm) |
| Fabric 10 | Opal | ¼yd (25cm) |

REFLECTIONS

| Fabric 11 | Teal | ¼yd (25cm) |

* see also Binding Fabric

MILLEFIORE

| Fabric 12 | Dusty | ⅜yd (40cm) |

Backing and Binding Fabrics
TONAL FLORAL extra-wide backing

| Fabric 13 | Turquoise | 2⅝yd (2.45m) |

REFLECTIONS

| Fabric 11 | Teal | ¾yd (70cm) |

* see also Patchwork Fabrics

Batting
94in x 82in (239cm x 208cm)

PATCHES
Blocks are 12in (30.5cm) finished. Some are fussy cut from a single Fabric 1 feature square while others include sections of either sawtooth, hourglass or pinwheel blocks. All patches are half-square or quarter-square triangles sewn into squares that are then pieced in sections. Sawtooth sections are made with 3in (6.6cm) squares, hourglass sections are made with 4in (10.2cm) squares and pinwheel sections are made with 6in (15.2cm) squares, all completed with Fabric 2 rectangles. Blocks are arranged in 6 rows of 5.

CUTTING OUT
Fabric is cut across the width unless otherwise stated. When cutting different pieces from the same fabric, always cut the larger pieces first.

Fabric 1 is used as the border and also for fussy-cut feature blocks. To make the best use of the fabric, border strips are cut **down the length** on each side of the fabric, leaving a panel down the middle of the fabric from which to fussy cut some of the required blocks, as shown in the Fabric 1 Cutting Diagram.

Border
Referring to the Fabric 1 Cutting Diagram, from Fabric 1 cut a length 72½in (184.2cm) long across the width of the fabric. Remove selvedges and from one side cut two side borders 6½in (16.5cm) wide and 72½in (184.2cm) long. From the opposite side cut 2 more lengths 6½in (16.5cm) wide and trim them to 60½in (153.7cm) long for the top and bottom borders.

Square Feature Blocks
From the remaining centre panel of Fabric 1 from above, fussy cut 5 feature squares at 12½in x 12½in (31.8cm x 31.8cm), each square approximately centring a shell arrangement.
From the remaining full-width piece of Fabric 1 fussy cut a further 4 feature squares at 12½in x 12½in (31.8cm x 31.8cm) using the shell arrangements to each side of the centre. Cut 9 feature squares in total.

Partial Feature Blocks
From Fabric 2 cut 5 strips 12½in (31.8cm) wide and cross cut the following rectangles, cutting the larger rectangles first:

10 rectangles 9½in x 12½in (24.1cm x 31.8cm);
7 rectangles 8½in x 12½in (21.6cm x 31.8cm);
4 rectangles 6½in x 12½in (16.5cm x 31.8cm).

Hourglass Blocks
Cut a strip 5¼in (13.2cm) wide and cross cut squares at 5¼in (13.2cm). Cut each square twice diagonally to yield 4 quarter-square triangles (QSTs) from each square. Cut a total of 84 QSTs from fabrics as follows:

Fabric 3 3 squares – 12 triangles;
Fabric 4 3 squares – 12 triangles;
Fabric 5 2 squares – 6 triangles;
Fabric 7 3 squares – 12 triangles;
Fabric 9 3 squares – 12 triangles;
Fabric 10 3 squares – 12 triangles;
Fabric 11 3 squares – 12 triangles;
Fabric 12 2 squares – 6 triangles.

Sawtooth and Pinwheel Blocks
Sawtooth and pinwheel blocks are made from the same-sized triangles so cut together as follows. Trim the remaining strips from the hourglass blocks above to 3⅞in (9.8cm) wide, if required, and cut additional strips 3⅞in (9.8cm) wide. Cross cut squares at 3⅞in (9.8cm). Each full strip will yield 10 squares. Cross cut each square once diagonally to yield 2 half-square triangles (HSTs) from each square. Cut a total of 176 HSTs from fabrics as follows:
Fabric 3 (1 strip) 8 squares – 16 triangles;
Fabric 4 (2 strips) 20 squares – 40 triangles;
Fabric 5 (1 strip) 8 squares – 16 triangles;
Fabric 6 (1 strip) 14 squares – 28 triangles;
Fabric 7 (1 strip) 6 squares – 12 triangles;
Fabric 8 (1 strip) 12 squares – 24 triangles;
Fabric 9 4 squares – 8 triangles;
Fabric 10 4 squares – 8 triangles;
Fabric 11 4 squares – 8 triangles;
Fabric 12 (1 strip) 8 squares – 16 triangles.

Backing
Trim Fabric 13 to 94in x 82in (239cm x 208cm).

Binding
From Fabric 11 cut 9 strips 2½in (6.4cm) wide. Remove selvedges and sew end to end with 45° seams (see page 141).

Patchwork Fabrics

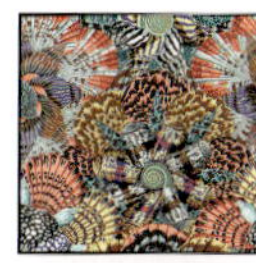

Fabric 1
SAILOR VALENTINE
Contrast
PJ121CN

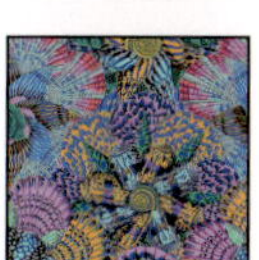

Fabric 2
SAILOR VALENTINE
Cool
PJ121BL

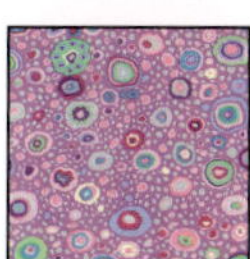

Fabric 3
ROMAN GLASS
Lavender
GP01LV

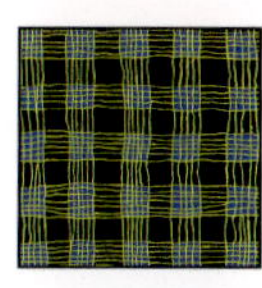

Fabric 4
GINGHAM
Black
BM89BK

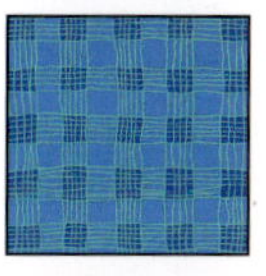

Fabric 5
GINGHAM
Blue
BM89BL

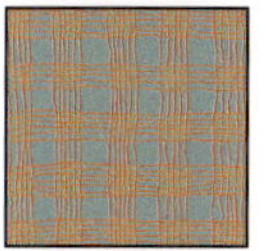

Fabric 6
GINGHAM
Grey
BM89GY

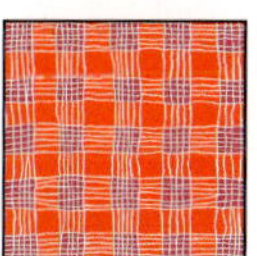

Fabric 7
GINGHAM
Red
BM89RD

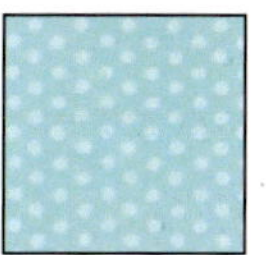

Fabric 8
SPOT
Duck Egg
GP70DE

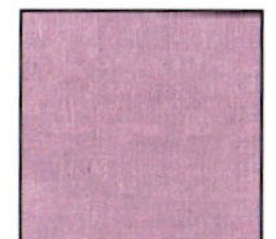

Fabric 9
SHOT COTTON
Dawn
SC122DN

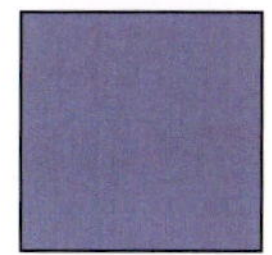

Fabric 10
SHOT COTTON
Opal
SC114OP

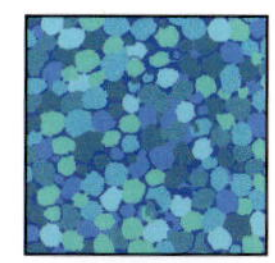

Fabric 11
REFLECTIONS
Teal
BM87TE

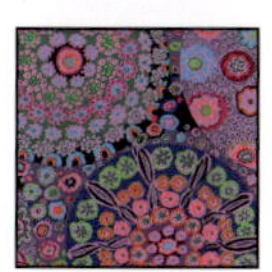

Fabric 12
MILLEFIORE
Dusty
GP92DY

Backing and Binding Fabrics

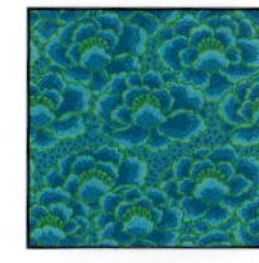

Fabric 13
TONAL FLORAL
Turquoise
QB09TQ

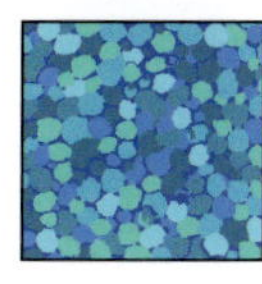

Fabric 11
REFLECTIONS
Teal
BM87TE

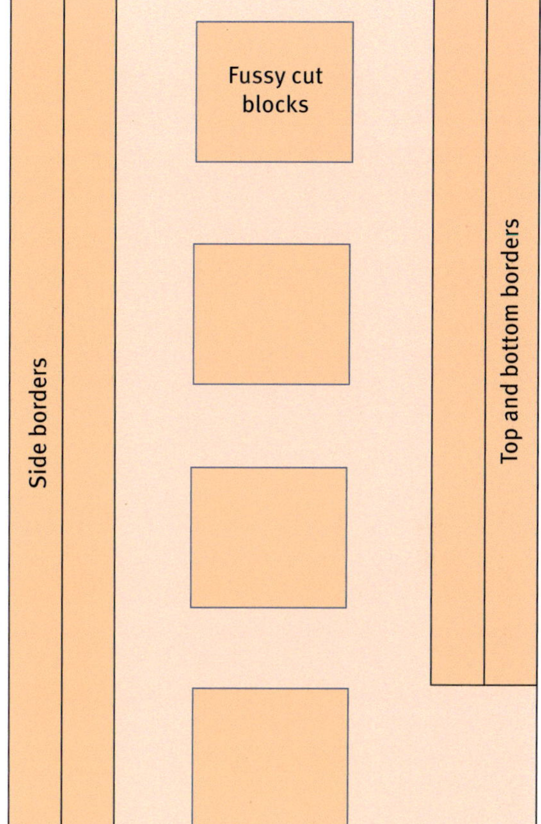

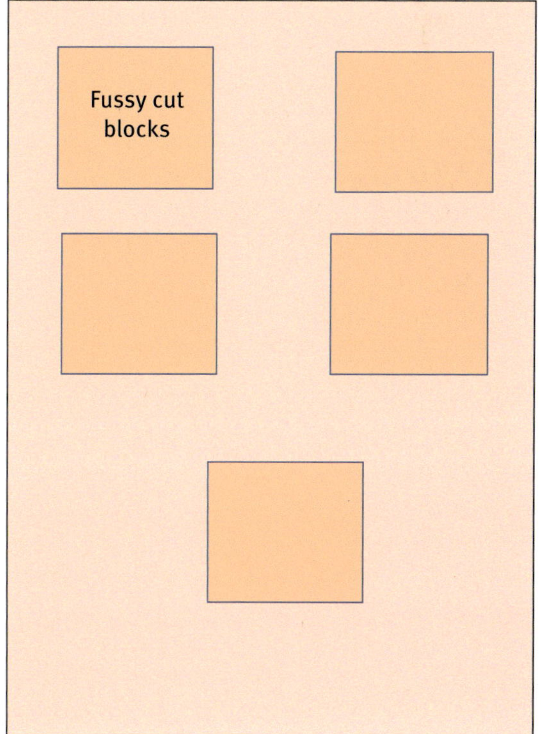

MAKING THE QUILT

Using a design wall will help to place patches in the required layout.
Use ¼in (6mm) seams throughout.

Hourglass Blocks

Referring to the Hourglass Block Assembly Diagram, and fabric combinations listed below, sew triangles together in pairs, dark triangles to light (a), press seams towards the darker triangles and then sew the two pairs of triangles together (b). Lightly press seams to one side of the finished block (c).

Join 3 hourglass blocks to form an hourglass section. Some sections are sewn together with alternating dark and light triangles. Others are sewn together matching triangles together, as shown in the Hourglass Sections Diagram. Referring to the quilt photograph for patch placements, make 7 sections from the following fabric combinations, each with 3 hourglass blocks:
1 x Fabric 3 and Fabric 11
1 x Fabric 3 and Fabric 10
2 x Fabric 4 and Fabric 7
1 x Fabric 5 and Fabric 9
1 x Fabric 9 and Fabric 11
1 x Fabric 10 and Fabric 12

Complete the 7 blocks by sewing each section to a Fabric 2 rectangle at 8½in x 12½in (21.6cm x 31.8cm).

Sawtooth and Pinwheel Blocks

Sew pairs of triangles together along their long sides to form squares, lightly pressing seams towards the darker fabrics. In order to speed up machine piecing, pairs of triangles can be sewn continually by feeding each new pair under the machine's feed dogs once the previous pair has passed under the needle. Sew pairs of triangles together in the following fabric combinations:

For the sawtooth sections:
4 x Fabric 3 and Fabric 4
4 x Fabric 3 and Fabric 11
4 x Fabric 4 and Fabric 9
4 x Fabric 5 and Fabric 6
4 x Fabric 5 and Fabric 10
4 x Fabric 6 and Fabric 7
4 x Fabric 6 and Fabric 12
4 x Fabric 8 and Fabric 10

4 x Fabric 8 and Fabric 12
4 x Fabric 9 and Fabric 11
Referring to the Quilt Assembly Diagram and quilt photograph, sew the sawtooth patches into sections of 4, checking the orientation before sewing. Complete the 10 sawtooth blocks by sewing each section to a Fabric 2 rectangle 9½in x 12½in (24.1cm x 31.8cm).

For the pinwheel sections:
8 x Fabric 3 and Fabric 4
8 x Fabric 4 and Fabric 6
16 x Fabric 4 and Fabric 8
8 x Fabric 5 and Fabric 6
8 x Fabric 7 and Fabric 12
Referring to the Pinwheel Block Assembly Diagram, sew the pinwheel patches forming pinwheel squares, checking the orientation before sewing. Sew 2 complete pinwheels together to form each section and retain the 4 corner pinwheels for the border.

Complete the 4 pinwheel blocks by sewing each section to a Fabric 2 rectangle 6½in x 12½in (16.5cm x 31.8cm).

Centre

Referring to the Quilt Assembly Diagram and quilt photograph, lay out the feature blocks and pieced blocks in 6 rows of 5. Once happy with the layout, sew the blocks together one row at a time, pressing seams in opposite directions on alternate rows – odd rows to the left, even rows to the right – to allow the finished seams to lie flat. Sew the rows together, taking care to align crossing seams.

Borders and Corner Squares

Pin (to prevent stretching the borders) then sew the longer Fabric 1 borders to each side of the centre. Sew a corner pinwheel block to each end of the top and bottom borders, then pin and sew the top and bottom borders to the centre to complete the quilt top.

FINISHING THE QUILT

Press the quilt top. Layer the quilt top, batting and backing, and baste together (see page 140).
Quilt as desired.
Trim the quilt edges and attach the binding (see page 141).

HOURGLASS BLOCK ASSEMBLY DIAGRAM

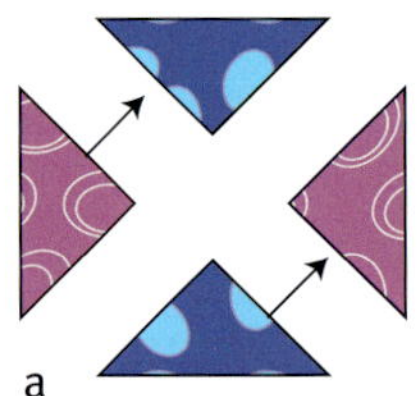
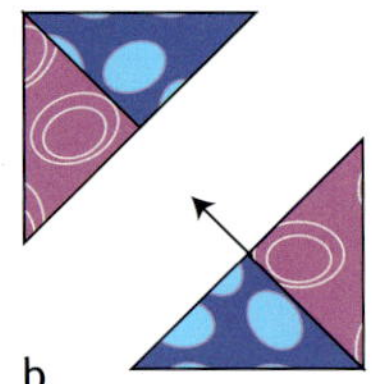
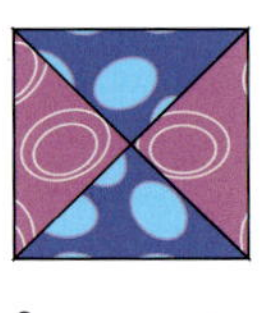

a   b   c

HOURGLASS SECTIONS DIAGRAM

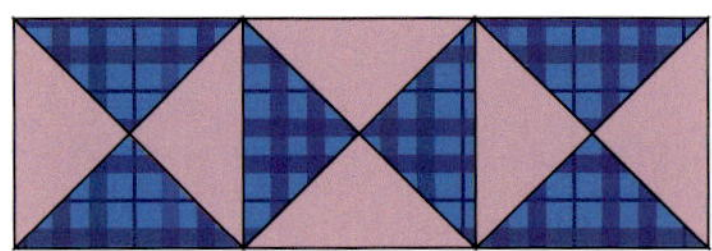

Alternating dark and light triangles

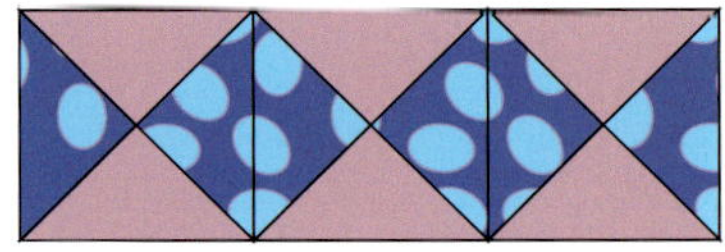

Matching triangles together

PINWHEEL BLOCK ASSEMBLY DIAGRAM

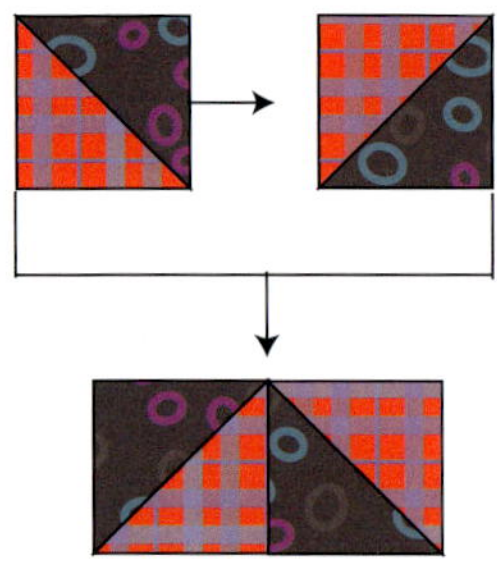
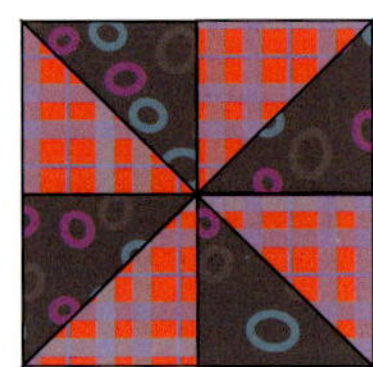

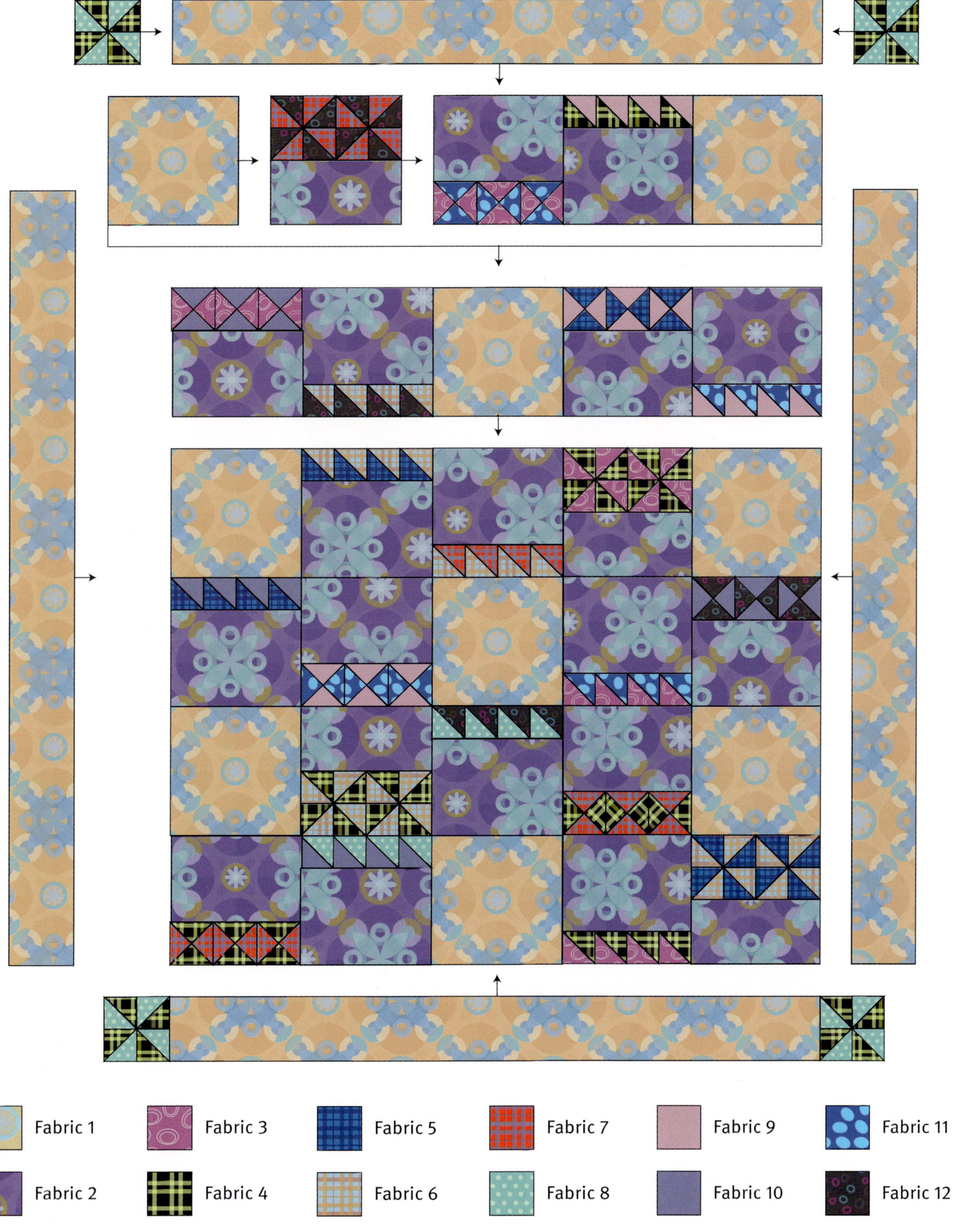

Fabric 1
Fabric 3
Fabric 5
Fabric 7
Fabric 9
Fabric 11
Fabric 2
Fabric 4
Fabric 6
Fabric 8
Fabric 10
Fabric 12

pearly dream **

Kaffe Fassett

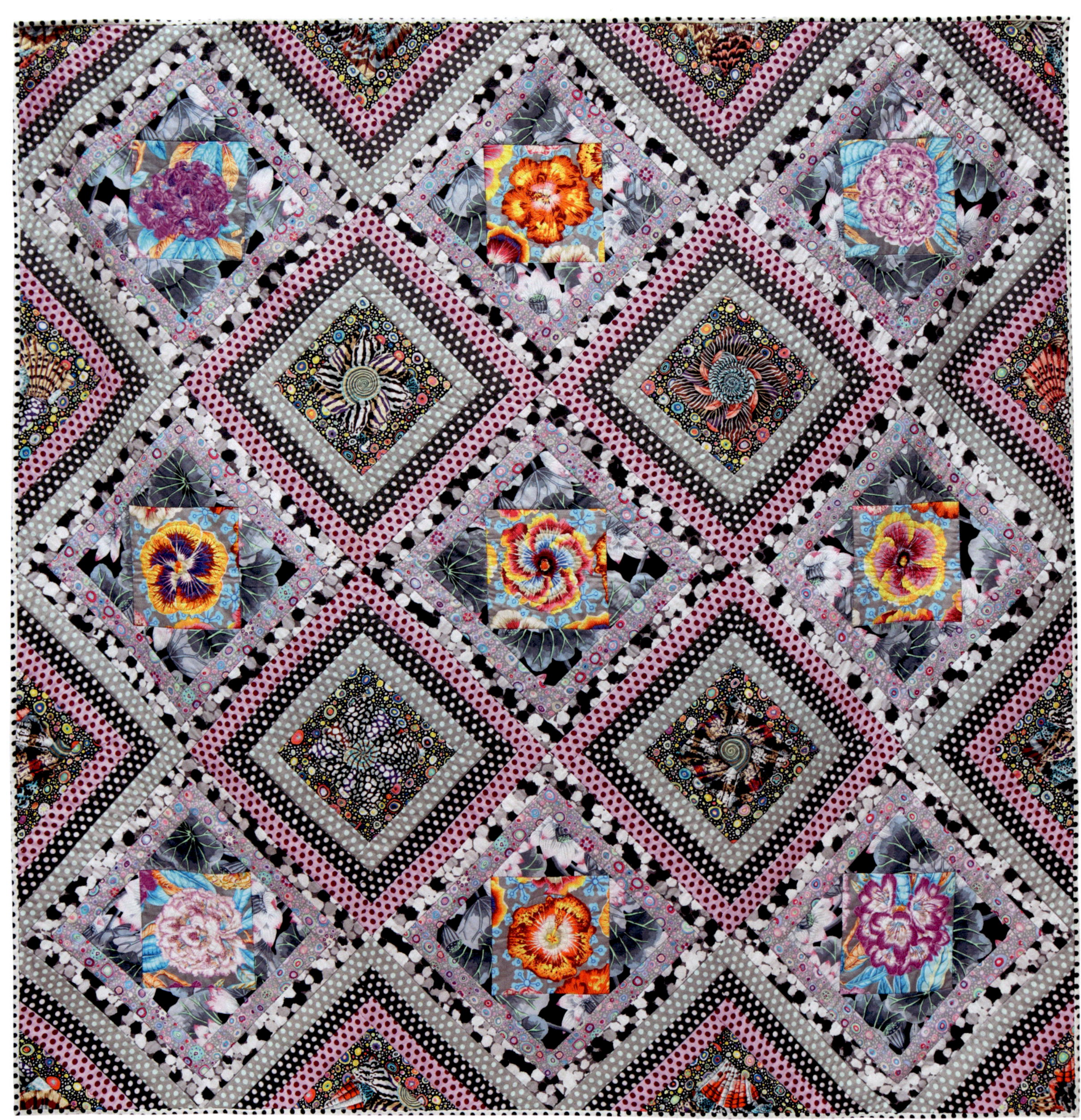

Philip Jacobs' latest floral- and shell-inspired fabrics feature in this cool combination of two different 'log cabin' blocks – one with a small fussy-cut shell centre, the other with a larger floral on-point square-in-square centre that is also fussy cut.

SIZE OF FINISHED QUILT
77in x 77in (196cm x 196cm)

FABRICS
Fabrics have been calculated at a maximum width of 40in (102cm). Fabrics have been given a number – see the Fabric Swatch Diagram for details.

Patchwork Fabrics
FLOATING HIBISCUS
Fabric 1   Grey   ⅝yd (60cm)
RHODODENDRONS
Fabric 2   Grey   ⅝yd (60cm)
LAKE BLOSSOMS
Fabric 3   Contrast   ⅞yd (85cm)
SAILOR VALENTINE
Fabric 4   Contrast   ⅝yd (60cm)
ROMAN GLASS
Fabric 5   Grey   ⅞yd (85cm)
Fabric 6   Contrast   ⅝yd (60cm)
SPOT
Fabric 7   Steel   1yd (95cm)
Fabric 8   Charcoal   ⅞yd (85cm)
Fabric 9   Mauve   1yd (95cm)
REFLECTIONS
Fabric 10   Contrast   1yd (95cm)

Backing and Binding Fabrics
FUNKY FLORA
Fabric 11   Grey   5½yd (5.1m)
SPOT
Fabric 12   White   ¾yd (70cm)

Batting
86in x 86in (218cm x 218cm)

PATCHES
There are two types of log cabin square blocks both measuring 18in (45.7cm) finished. One is a flower block made as a square-in-square with 2 narrow borders (9 blocks in all) and the other is a shell block made of a central square with 4 narrow borders (4 blocks in all). The blocks are set on point and squared up using 8 side-setting half blocks and 4 corner-setting quarter blocks.

Patchwork Fabrics

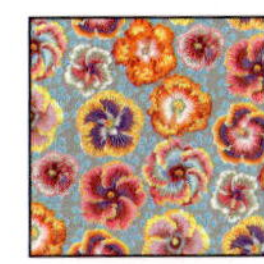

Fabric 1
FLOATING HIBISCUS
Grey
PJ122GY

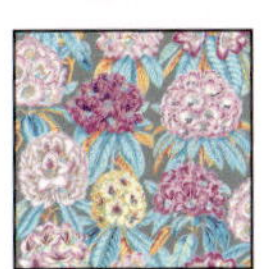

Fabric 2
RHODODENDRONS
Grey
PJ124GY

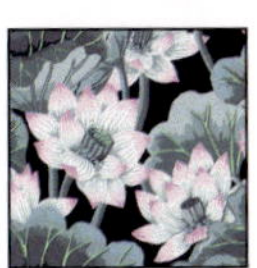

Fabric 3
LAKE BLOSSOMS
Contrast
GP93CN

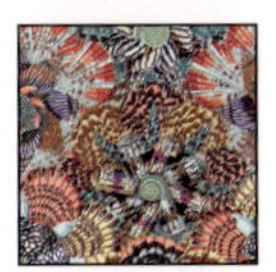

Fabric 4
SAILOR VALENTINE
Contrast
PJ121CN

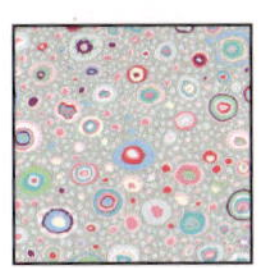

Fabric 5
ROMAN GLASS
Grey
GP01GY

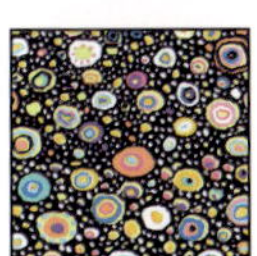

Fabric 6
ROMAN GLASS
Contrast
GP01CN

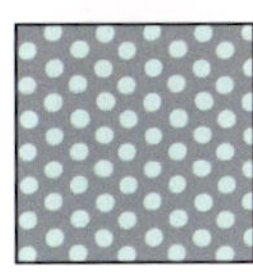

Fabric 7
SPOT
Steel
GP70ST

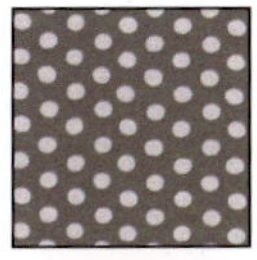

Fabric 8
SPOT
Charcoal
GP70CC

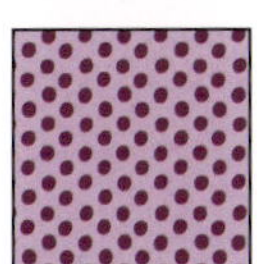

Fabric 9
SPOT
Mauve
GP70MV

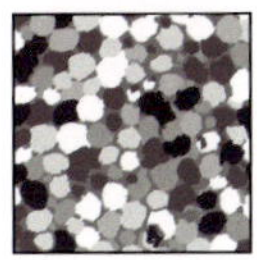

Fabric 10
REFLECTIONS
Contrast
BM87CN

Backing and Binding Fabrics

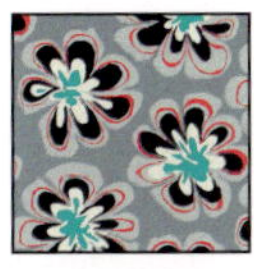

Fabric 11
FUNKY FLORA
Grey
BM11GY

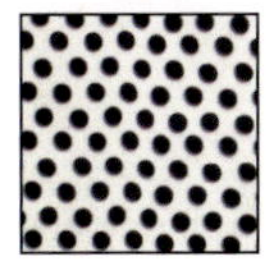

Fabric 12
SPOT
White
GP70WH

The half blocks and quarter blocks are constructed in the same way as the square shell blocks but are slightly larger with a different sequence of borders. They are then cut diagonally to make setting triangles.

CUTTING OUT
Fabric is cut across the width unless otherwise stated. When cutting different pieces from the same fabric, always cut the larger pieces first.
As there are different-sized strips for different blocks, label and keep the pieces for the different blocks separate to avoid confusion.

Flower Blocks
From Fabric 1 fussy cut 5 squares 9in x 9in (22.9cm x 22.9cm). Extra fabric has been allowed for this purpose.
From Fabric 2 fussy cut 4 squares 9in x 9in (22.9cm x 22.9cm). Extra fabric has been allowed for this purpose.
From Fabric 3 cut 4 strips 6⅞in (17.5cm) wide and cross cut 18 squares at 6⅞in (17.5cm). Each strip will yield 5 squares. Cross cut each square once diagonally to yield 36 triangles.
From Fabric 5 cut a strip 15½in (39.4cm) wide and cross cut 18 pieces 15½in x 2in (39.4cm x 5.1cm). Also from Fabric 5 cut a strip 12½in (31.8cm) wide and cross cut 18 pieces 12½in x 2in (31.8cm x 5.1cm).

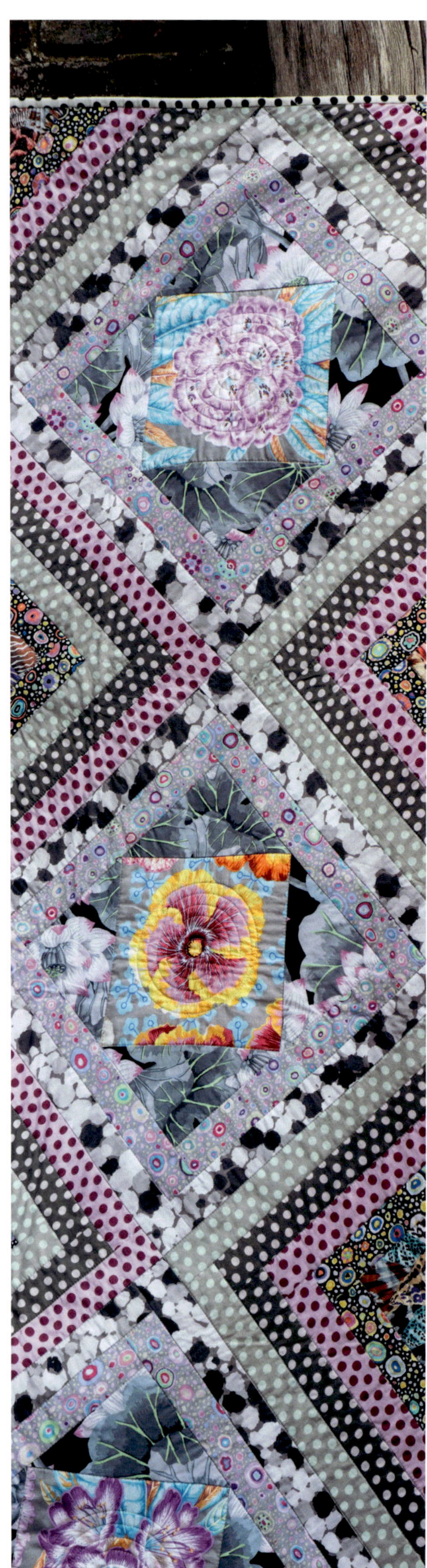

From Fabric 10 cut a strip 18½in (47cm) wide and cross cut 18 pieces 18½in x 2in (47cm x 5.1cm). Also from Fabric 10 cut a strip 15½in (39.4cm) wide and cross cut 18 pieces 15½in x 2in (39.4cm x 5.1cm).

Shell Blocks and Setting Blocks
From Fabric 4 fussy cut 4 squares at 6½in (16.5cm). Extra fabric has been allowed for this purpose.
From the remaining Fabric 4 cut 1 square at 7¾in (19.7cm) for the corner-setting triangles and 4 squares at 7⅜in (18.7cm) for the setting blocks. There is no need for these squares to be fussy cut.

From Fabric 6 cut a strip 10¾in (27.3cm) wide and cut pieces as follows, trimming the strip down after cutting each different size:
2 pieces 10¾in x 2in (27.3cm x 5.1cm);
8 pieces 10⅜in x 2in (26.4cm x 5.1cm);
8 pieces 9½in x 2in (24.1cm x 5.1cm).
Cut a strip 7¾in (19.7cm) wide and cross cut pieces as follows:
2 pieces 7¾in x 2in (19.7cm x 5.1cm);
8 pieces 7⅜in x 2in (18.7cm x 5.1cm);
8 pieces 6½in x 2in (16.5cm x 5.1cm).

From Fabric 7 cut a strip 19¾in (32.3cm) wide and cut pieces as follows, trimming the strip down after cutting each different size:
2 pieces 19¾in x 2in (50.2cm x 5.1cm);
8 pieces 19⅜in x 2in (49.2cm x 5.1cm);
2 pieces 16¾in x 2in (42.5cm x 5.1cm);
8 pieces 16⅜in x 2in (41.6cm x 5.1cm).
Cut a strip 12½in (31.8cm) wide and cross cut pieces as follows:
8 pieces 12½in x 2in (31.8cm x 5.1cm);
8 pieces 9½in x 2in (24.1cm x 5.1cm).

From Fabric 8 cut a strip 16¾in (42.5cm) wide and cut pieces as follows, trimming the strip down after cutting each different size:
2 pieces 16¾in x 2in (42.5cm x 5.1cm);
8 pieces 16⅜in x 2in (41.6cm x 5.1cm);
8 pieces 15½in x 2in (39.4cm x 5.1cm).
Cut a strip 13¾in (34.9cm) wide and cross cut pieces as follows:
2 pieces 13¾in x 2in (34.9cm x 5.1cm);
8 pieces 13⅜in x 2in (34cm x 5.1cm);
8 pieces 12½in x 2in (31.8cm x 5.1cm).

From Fabric 9 cut a strip 8½in (47cm) wide and cut pieces as follows, trimming the strip down after cutting each different size:
8 pieces 18½in x 2in (47cm x 5.1cm);
8 pieces 15½in x 2in (39.4cm x 5.1cm);
2 pieces 13¾in x 2in (34.9cm x 5.1cm).
Cut a strip 13⅜in (34cm) wide and cross cut pieces as follows:
8 pieces 13⅜in x 2in (34cm x 5.1cm);
2 pieces 10¾in x 2in (27.3cm x 5.1cm);
8 pieces 10⅜in x 2In (26.4cm x 5.1cm).

Backing
From Fabric 11 cut 2 pieces 86in x 40in (218cm x 102cm) and 1 piece 22in x 40in (55.9cm x 102cm). Cross cut the short section into 4 equal pieces 22in x 10in (55.9cm x 25.4cm).

Binding
From Fabric 12 cut 9 strips 2½in (6.4cm) wide. Remove selvedges and sew end to end with 45° seams (see page 141).

MAKING THE QUILT
Using a design wall will help to place patches in the required layout.
Use ¼in (6mm) seams throughout.

Flower Blocks
Referring to the Flower Block Assembly Diagram, sew the long edge of a Fabric 3 triangle to opposite sides of a Fabric 1 fussy-cut square, then sew triangles to the remaining 2 sides. Press seams of triangles towards the centre square and press all log cabin strips towards the **outside** of the block, away from the centre.
Sew shorter 12½in (31.8cm) Fabric 5 strips to the block sides, then sew longer 15½in (39.4cm) Fabric 5 strips to the top and bottom.
Sew shorter 15½in (39.4cm) Fabric 10 strips to the block sides, then sew longer 18½in (47cm) Fabric 10 strips to the top and bottom to complete the block. Make 9 blocks in total, 5 using Fabric 1 as the centre square and 4 blocks using Fabric 2 as the centre square.

Shell Blocks
Referring to the Shell Block Assembly Diagram, take a fussy-cut Fabric 4 shell 6½in (16.5cm) square and sew 4 rounds of strips around it in the following order:

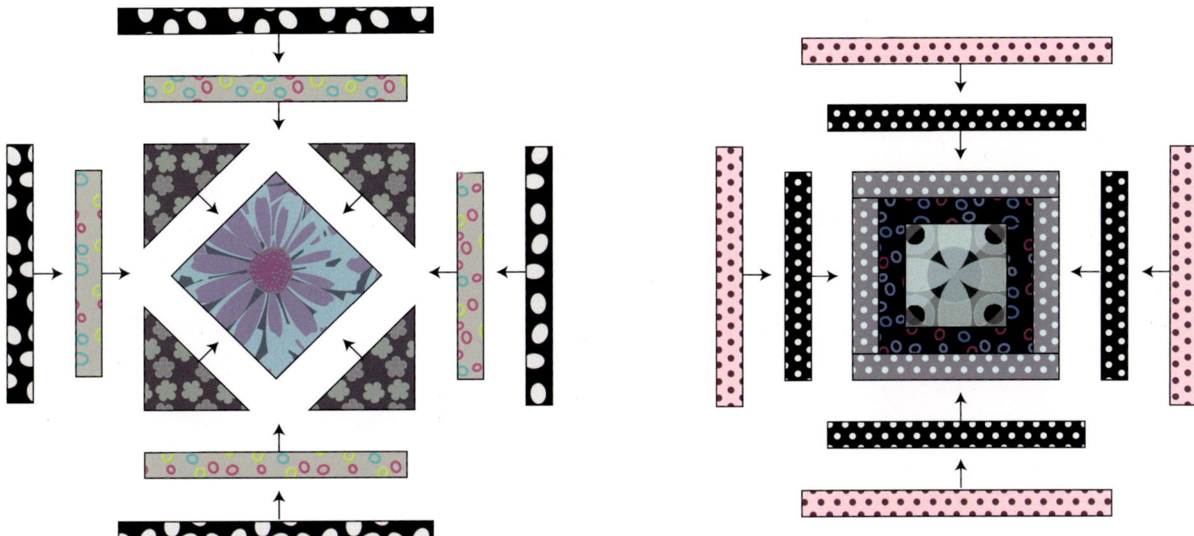

Flower Block

Shell Block

Fabric 6 6½in (16.5cm) strips and 9½in (24.1cm) strips;
Fabric 7 9½in (24.1cm) strips and 12½in (31.8cm) strips;
Fabric 8 12½in (31.8cm) strips and 15½in (39.4cm) strips; and
Fabric 9 15½in (39.4cm) strips and 18½in (47cm) strips.
For each round, first sew the shorter strips to the block sides, then sew the longer strips to the top and bottom. Press all seams towards the outside of the block. Make 4 blocks in total.

Side-setting Half Blocks
Setting blocks are made using the same method as the square shell blocks as shown in the Shell Block Assembly Diagram, but are slightly larger to allow for them to be cut in half and used as setting triangles.
Take a Fabric 4 7⅜in (18.7cm) square and sew 4 rounds of strips around it in the following order:
Fabric 6 7⅜in (18.7cm) strips and 10⅜in (26.4cm) strips;
Fabric 9 10⅜in (26.4cm) strips and 13⅜in (34cm) strips;
Fabric 8 13⅜in (34cm) strips and 16⅜in (41.6cm) strips; and
Fabric 7 16⅜in (41.6cm) strips and 19⅜in (49.2cm) strips.
Make 4 blocks in total and cross cut each diagonally once to make 8 side-setting

half blocks. Stay-stitch each diagonal edge ⅛in (3mm) from the fabric edge to prevent stretching.

Corner-setting Quarter Blocks
The corner-setting quarter blocks are made from one large square block using the same method as the shell blocks as shown in the Shell Block Assembly Diagram. These blocks are larger than the side-setting blocks.
Use the Fabric 4 7¾in (19.7cm) square and sew 4 rounds of strips around it in the following order:
Fabric 6 7¾in (19.7cm) strips and 10¾in (27.3cm) strips;
Fabric 9 10¾in (27.3cm) strips and 13¾in (34.9cm) strips;
Fabric 8 13¾in (34.9cm) strips and 16¾in (42.5cm) strips; and
Fabric 7 16¾in (42.5cm) strips and 19¾in (50.2cm) strips.
Cut the finished square in half diagonally twice to make 4 corner-setting quarter blocks. Stay-stitch the short sides of each triangle ⅛in (3mm) from the fabric edge to prevent stretching.

Quilt Assembly
Lay out the blocks on point referring to the Quilt Assembly Diagram on page 68 and quilt photograph. Use the side-setting and corner-setting blocks to complete the layout.

Sew the blocks together in diagonal rows, pressing seams in opposite directions on alternate rows – odd rows to the left, even rows to the right – to allow the finished seams to lie flat. Sew the diagonal rows together, taking care to align crossing seams.

FINISHING THE QUILT
Remove selvedges from the Fabric 11 sections and sew the 4 smallest pieces together end to end to form a long strip measuring 86in x 9½in (218cm x 24.1cm). Sew this strip and the 2 large sections together down their long sides to make a backing approximately 86in x 89in (218cm x 226cm).

Press the quilt top. Layer the quilt top, batting and backing, and baste together (see page 140).
Quilt as desired.
Trim the quilt edges and attach the binding (see page 141).

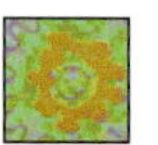 Fabric 1

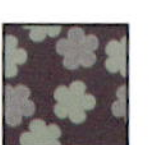 Fabric 3

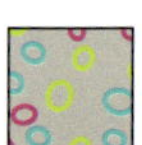 Fabric 5

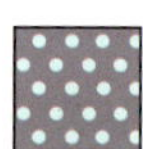 Fabric 7

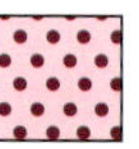 Fabric 9

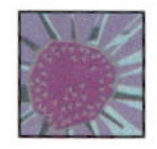 Fabric 2

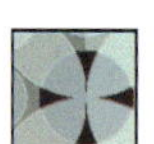 Fabric 4

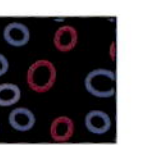 Fabric 6

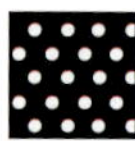 Fabric 8

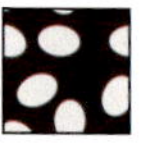 Fabric 10

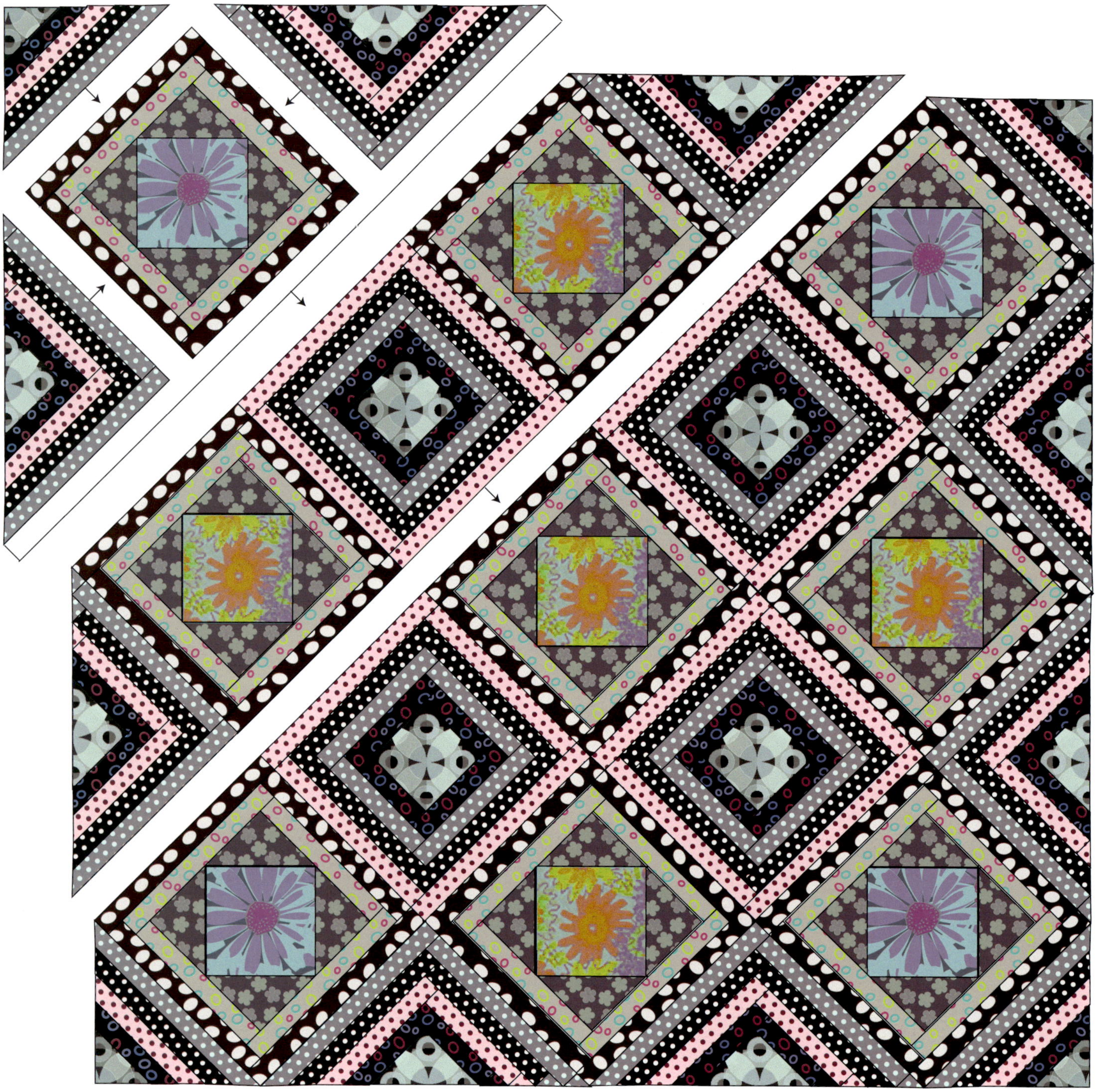

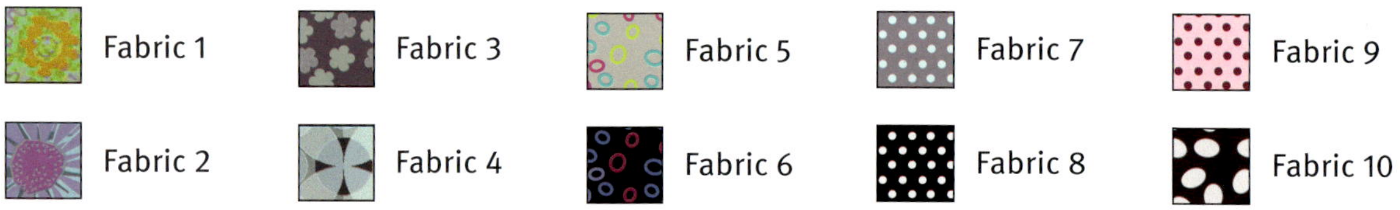

golden stars **

Kaffe Fassett

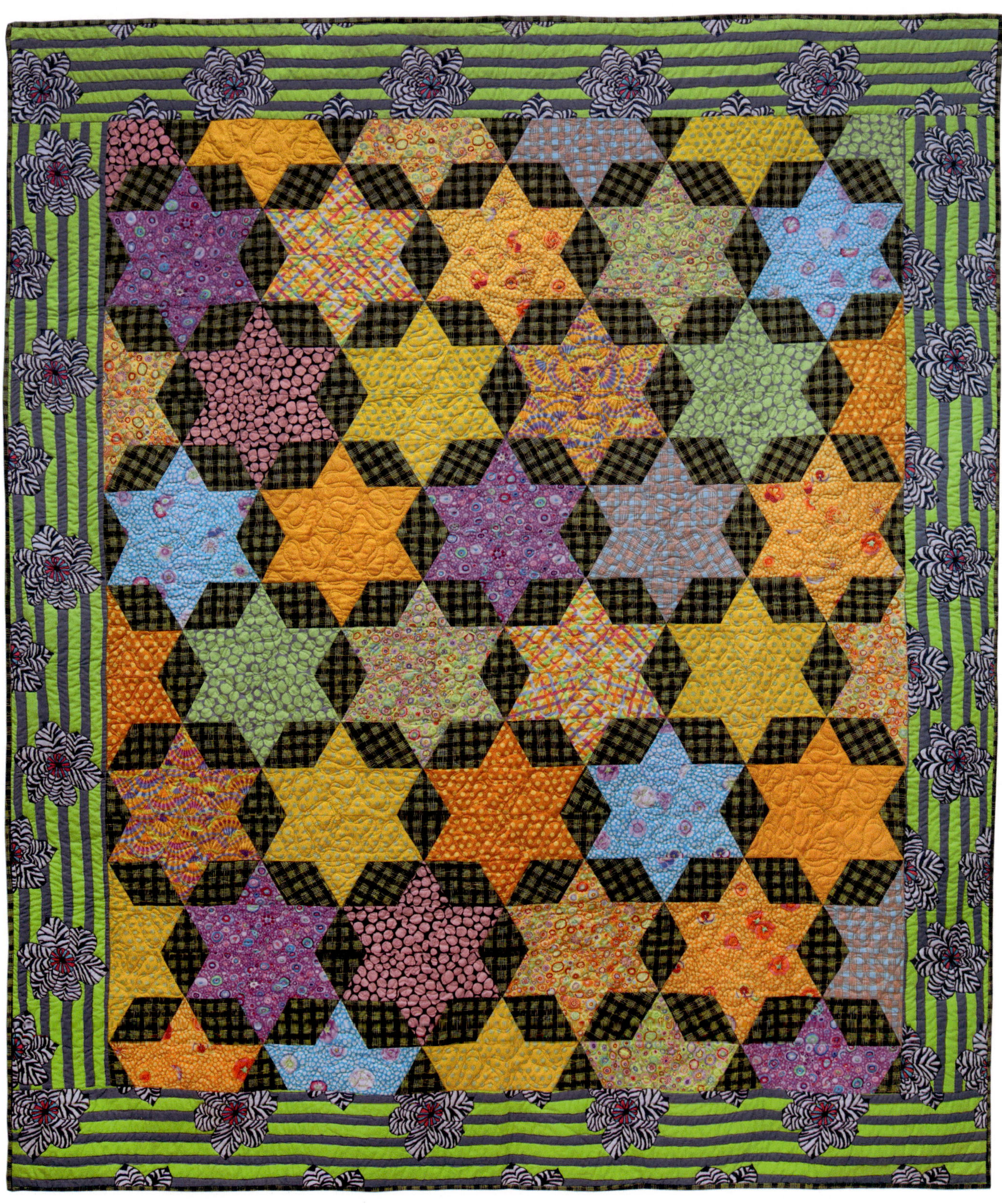

The effect of Brandon's black Gingham
fabric surrounding all these sunny
yellow-pointed stars was the inspiration
for the quilt's name. All the vertical
diamonds have been made from two
triangles, thus allowing the quilt to be
sewn without the inset seams usually
associated with diamond quilts.

SIZE OF FINISHED QUILT
86in x 72in (218cm x 183cm)

FABRICS
Fabrics have been calculated at a
maximum width of 40in (102cm). Fabrics
have been given a number – see the
Fabric Swatch Diagram for details.

Patchwork Fabrics
GINGHAM
Fabric 1   Black   1¾yd (1.7m)
* see also Binding Fabric
Fabric 2   Grey   ¼yd (25cm)
ROMAN GLASS
Fabric 3   Lavender   ⅜yd (40cm)
PAPERWEIGHT
Fabric 4   Lime   ¼yd (25cm)
Fabric 5   Yellow   ¼yd (25cm)
SPOT
Fabric 6   Yellow   ½yd (50cm)
Fabric 7   Ochre   ¼yd (25cm)
GUINEA FLOWER
Fabric 8   Turquoise   ⅜yd (40cm)
Fabric 9   Gold   ⅜yd (40cm)
JUMBLE
Fabric 10   Rose   ¼yd (25cm)
Fabric 11   Moss   ¼yd (25cm)
ABORIGINAL DOT
Fabric 12   Gold   ¼yd (25cm)
PAPER FANS
Fabric 13   Yellow   ¼yd (25cm)
MAD PLAID
Fabric 14   Gold   ¼yd (25cm)
ZEBRA LILY
Fabric 15   Green   2¼yd (2.1m)

Backing and Binding Fabrics
LOTUS LEAF extra-wide backing
Fabric 16   Jade   2⅜yd (2.25m)
GINGHAM
Fabric 1   Black   ¾yd (70cm)
* see also Patchwork Fabrics

Batting
96in x 82in (245cm x 208cm)

FABRIC SWATCH DIAGRAM

Patchwork Fabrics

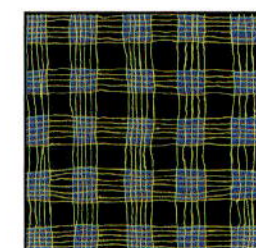

Fabric 1
GINGHAM
Black
BM89BK

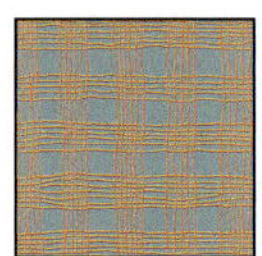

Fabric 2
GINGHAM
Grey
BM89GY

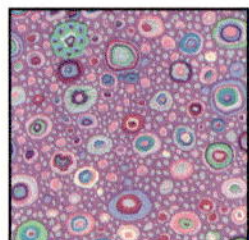

Fabric 3
ROMAN GLASS
Lavender
GP01LV

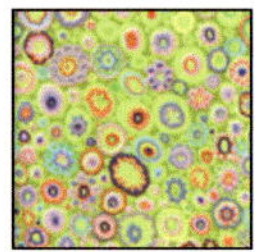

Fabric 4
PAPERWEIGHT
Lime
GP20LM

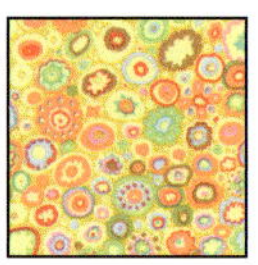

Fabric 5
PAPERWEIGHT
Yellow
GP20YE

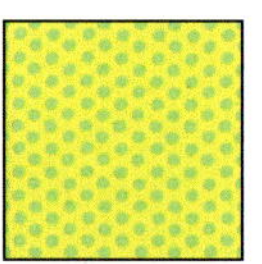

Fabric 6
SPOT
Yellow
GP70YE

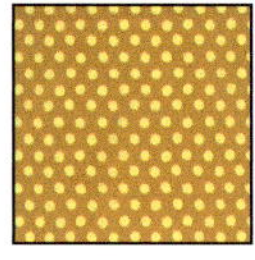

Fabric 7
SPOT
Ochre
GP70OC

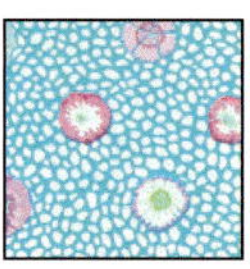

Fabric 8
GUINEA FLOWER
Turquoise
GP59TQ

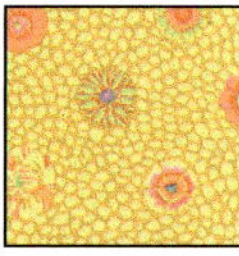

Fabric 9
GUINEA FLOWER
Gold
GP59GD

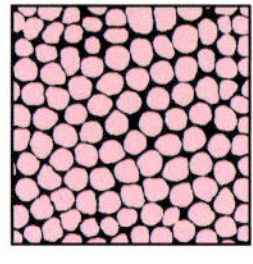

Fabric 10
JUMBLE
Rose
BM53RO

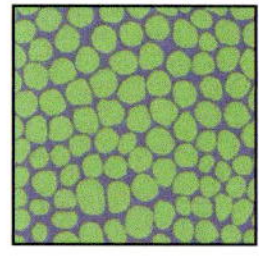

Fabric 11
JUMBLE
Moss
BM53MS

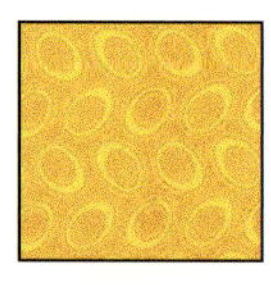

Fabric 12
ABORIGINAL DOT
Gold
GP71GD

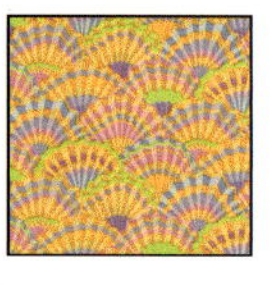

Fabric 13
PAPER FANS
Yellow
GP143YE

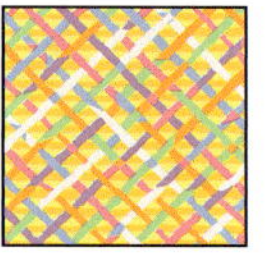

Fabric 14
MAD PLAID
Gold
BM37GD

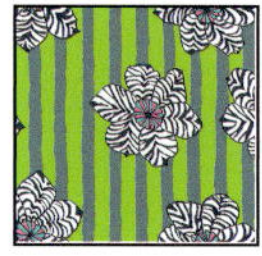

Fabric 15
ZEBRA LILY
Green
BM91GN

Backing and Binding Fabrics

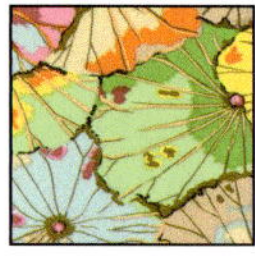

Fabric 16
LOTUS LEAF
Jade
QB07JA

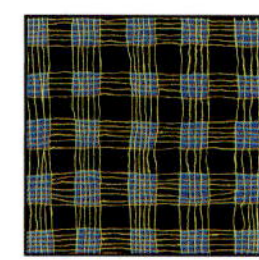

Fabric 1
GINGHAM
Black
BM89BK

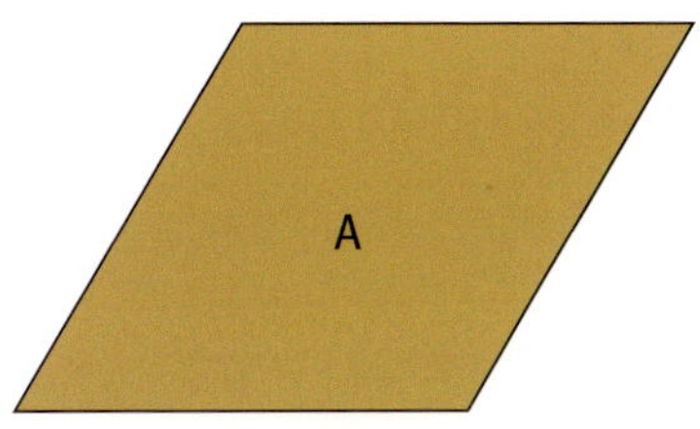

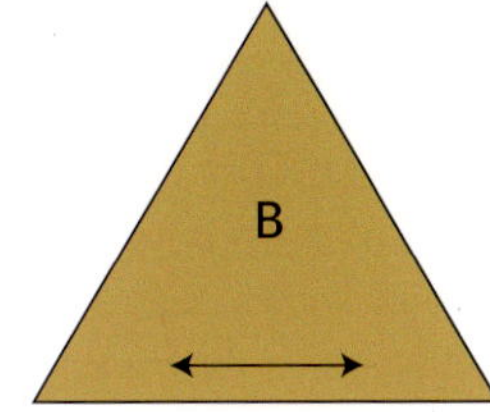

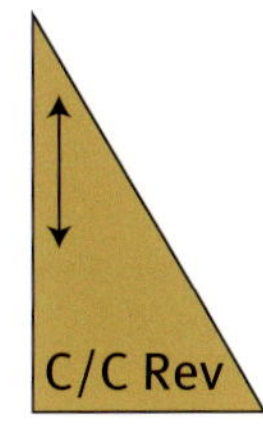

FABRIC	STRIPS	Diamonds A	Half-diamonds B	Quarter-diamonds C	Reverse Quarter-Diamonds C Rev
Fabric 1 Gingham Black	14	70	63	7	7
Fabric 2 Gingham Grey	2	8	6	2	2
Fabric 3 Roman Glass Lavender	3	14	14	-	-
Fabric 4 Paperweight Lime	2	10	10	-	-
Fabric 5 Paperweight Yellow	2	10	6	4	4
Fabric 6 Spot Yellow	4	18	16	2	2
Fabric 7 Spot Ochre	2	8	4	4	4
Fabric 8 Guinea Flower Turquoise	3	14	14	-	-
Fabric 9 Guinea Flower Gold	3	14	14	-	-
Fabric 10 Jumble Rose	2	9	8	1	1
Fabric 11 Jumble Moss	2	9	8	1	1
Fabric 12 Aboriginal Dot Gold	2	10	10	-	-
Fabric 13 Paper Fans Yellow	2	8	8	-	-
Fabric 14 Mad Plaid Gold	2	8	8	-	-

PATCHES

This quilt is made from 60° diamonds (Template A), half-diamonds (Template B) and quarter-diamonds (Template C/C Reverse), all cut from 4in (10.2cm) strips. Each full star consists of 4 diamonds and 4 half-diamonds. Partial stars at the top and bottom of the quilt consist of 2 diamonds and 2 half-diamonds. Quarter-diamonds are used at the quilt sides.

CUTTING OUT

Fabric is cut across the width unless otherwise stated. When cutting different pieces from the same fabric, always cut the larger pieces first.

Diamonds, Half-diamonds and Quarter-diamonds

Cut strips 4in (10.2cm) wide and cross cut 60° diamonds, half-diamonds and quarter-diamonds, using templates A, B and C/C Reverse. Each strip will yield 8 diamonds or 14 half-diamonds. Quarter-diamonds can be cut from either end of strips as well as along the strip so, if required, start or end strips with a quarter-diamond, depending on whether C or C Reverse quarter-diamonds are required. Cut diamonds, half-diamonds and quarter-diamonds/reverse quarter-diamonds from fabrics as shown in the Cutting Table.

Border

From Fabric 15 cut 4 strips **down the length of the fabric** 6½in (16.5cm) wide. Trim 2 lengths to 74in x 6½in (188cm x 16.5cm) for the side borders; Trim 2 lengths to 72½in x 6½in (184.2cm x 16.5cm) for the top and bottom borders.

Backing

Trim Fabric 16 to 96in x 82in (245cm x 208cm).

Binding

From Fabric 1 cut 9 strips 2½in (6.4cm) wide. Remove selvedges and sew end to end with 45° seams (see page 141).

MAKING THE QUILT

Using a design wall will help to place patches in the required layout. Use ¼in (6mm) seams throughout.

Centre

Referring to the Quilt Assembly Diagram on page 73 and quilt photograph, lay out the diamonds, half-diamonds and quarter-diamonds to form the stars, noting that all vertical diamonds are formed of 2 half-diamonds, and that points at the sides of the quilt are formed of C and C Reverse quarter-diamonds.

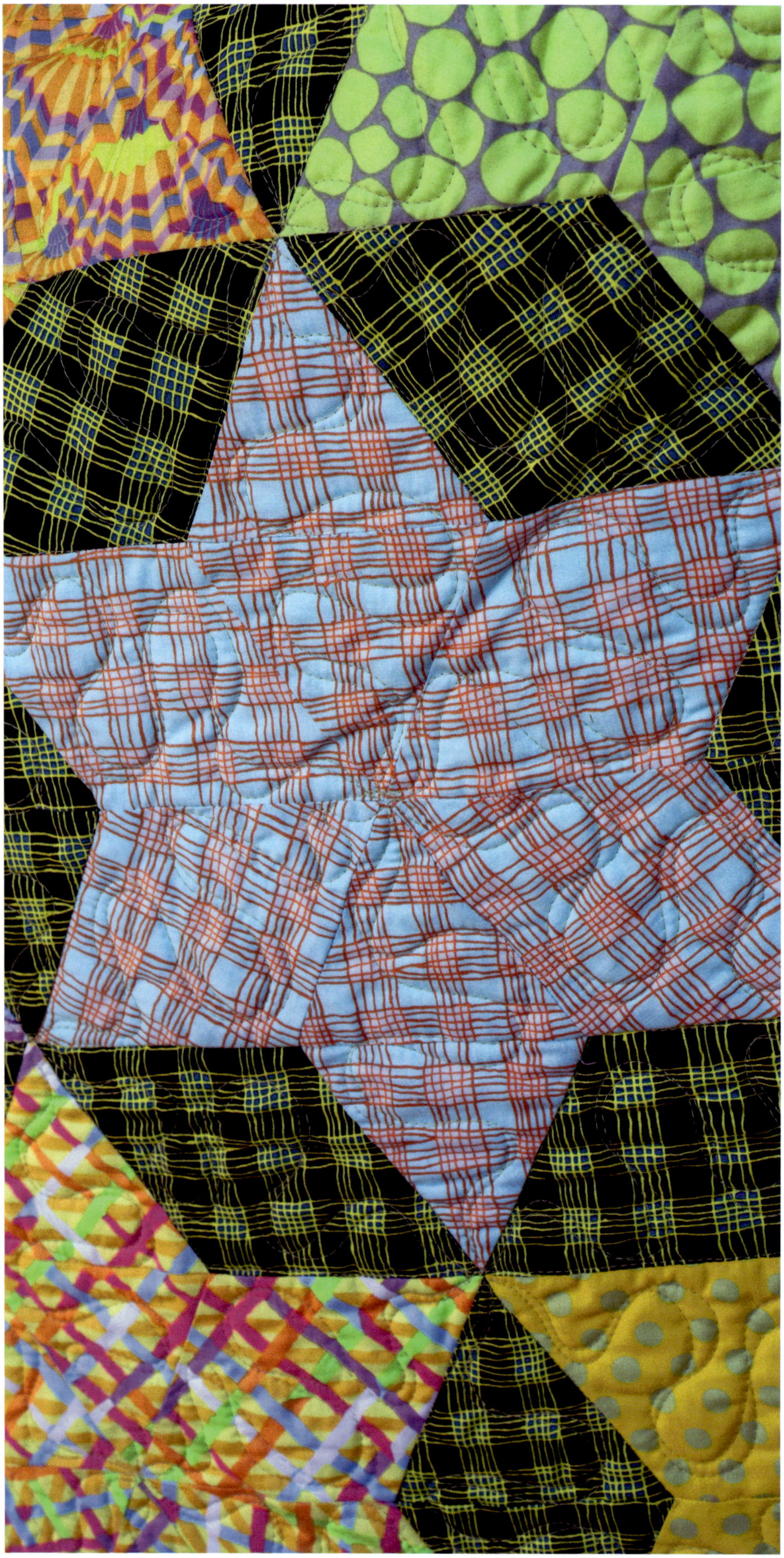

Check your layout is correct, then sew together one row at a time, pressing seams in opposite directions on alternate rows – odd rows to the left, even rows to the right – to allow the finished seams to lie flat. Sew the rows together taking care to align crossing seams.

Borders
Pin (to prevent stretching borders) then sew the longer side borders to the centre and press seams towards the border. Then pin and sew the top and bottom borders to the centre to complete the quilt top.

FINISHING THE QUILT
Press the quilt top. Layer the quilt top, batting and backing, and baste together (see page 140).
Quilt as desired.
Trim the quilt edges and attach the binding (see page 141).

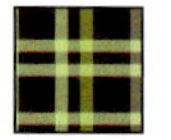 Fabric 1   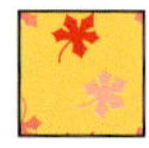 Fabric 9

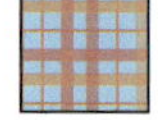 Fabric 2   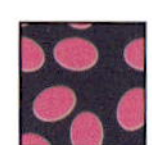 Fabric 10

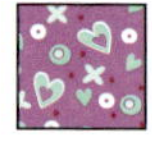 Fabric 3   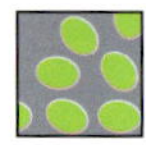 Fabric 11

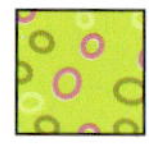 Fabric 4   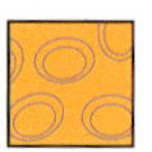 Fabric 12

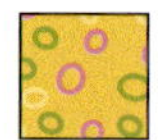 Fabric 5   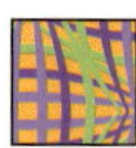 Fabric 13

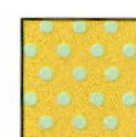 Fabric 6   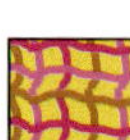 Fabric 14

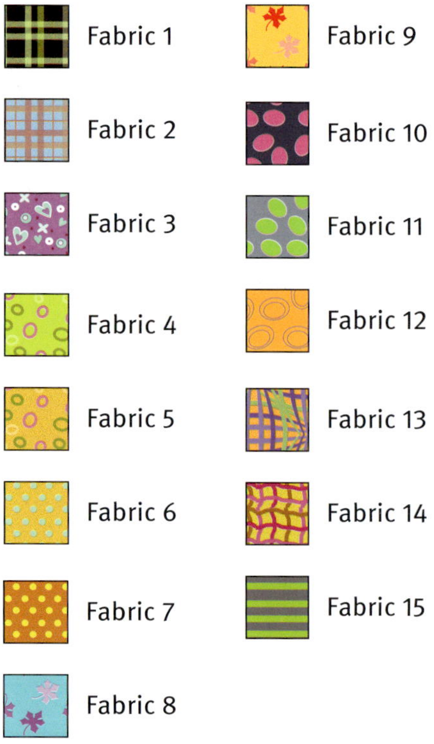

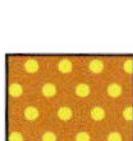 Fabric 7   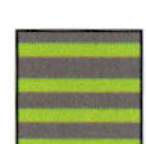 Fabric 15

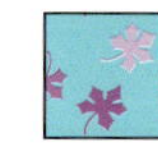 Fabric 8

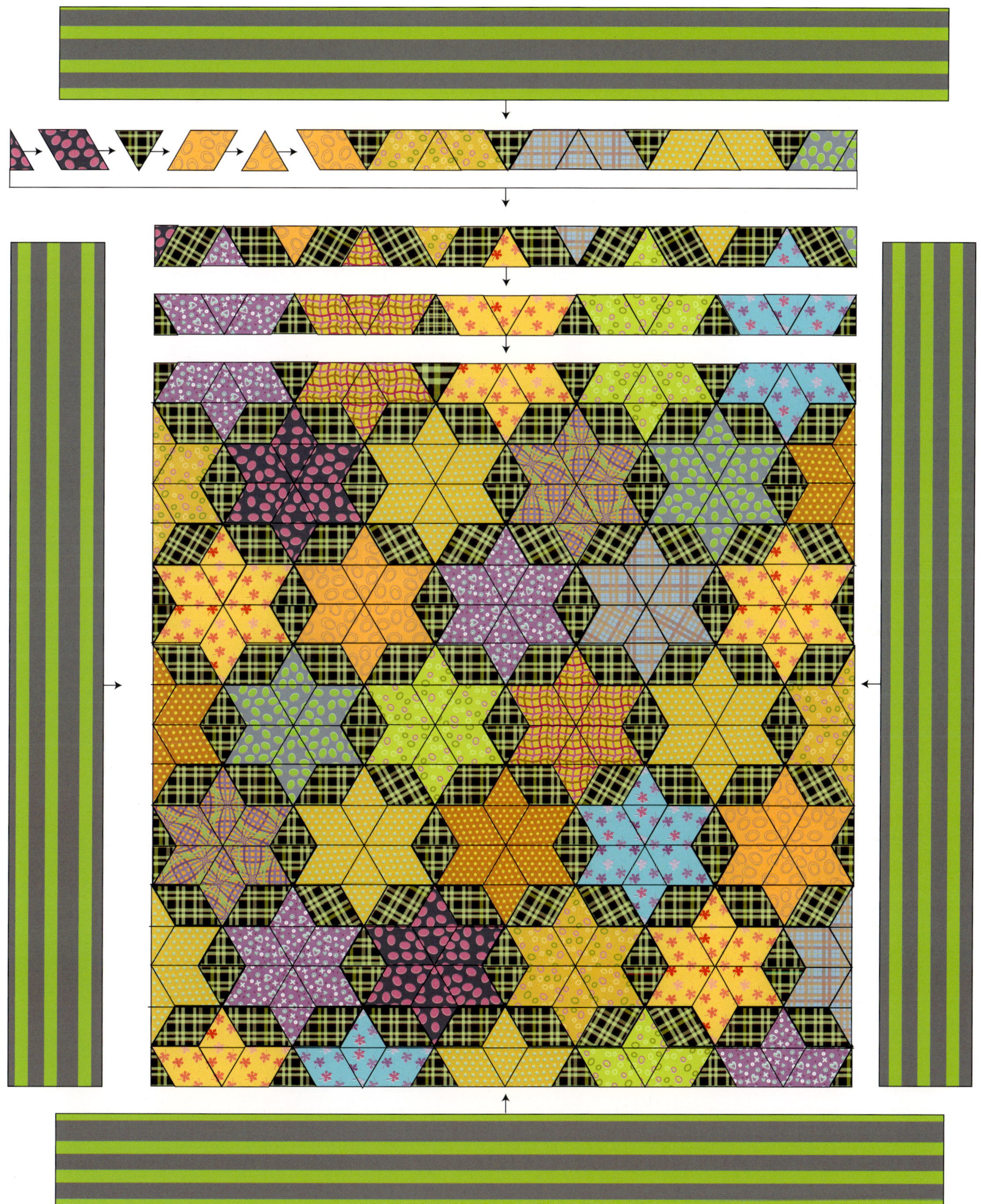

criss cross **

Kaffe Fassett

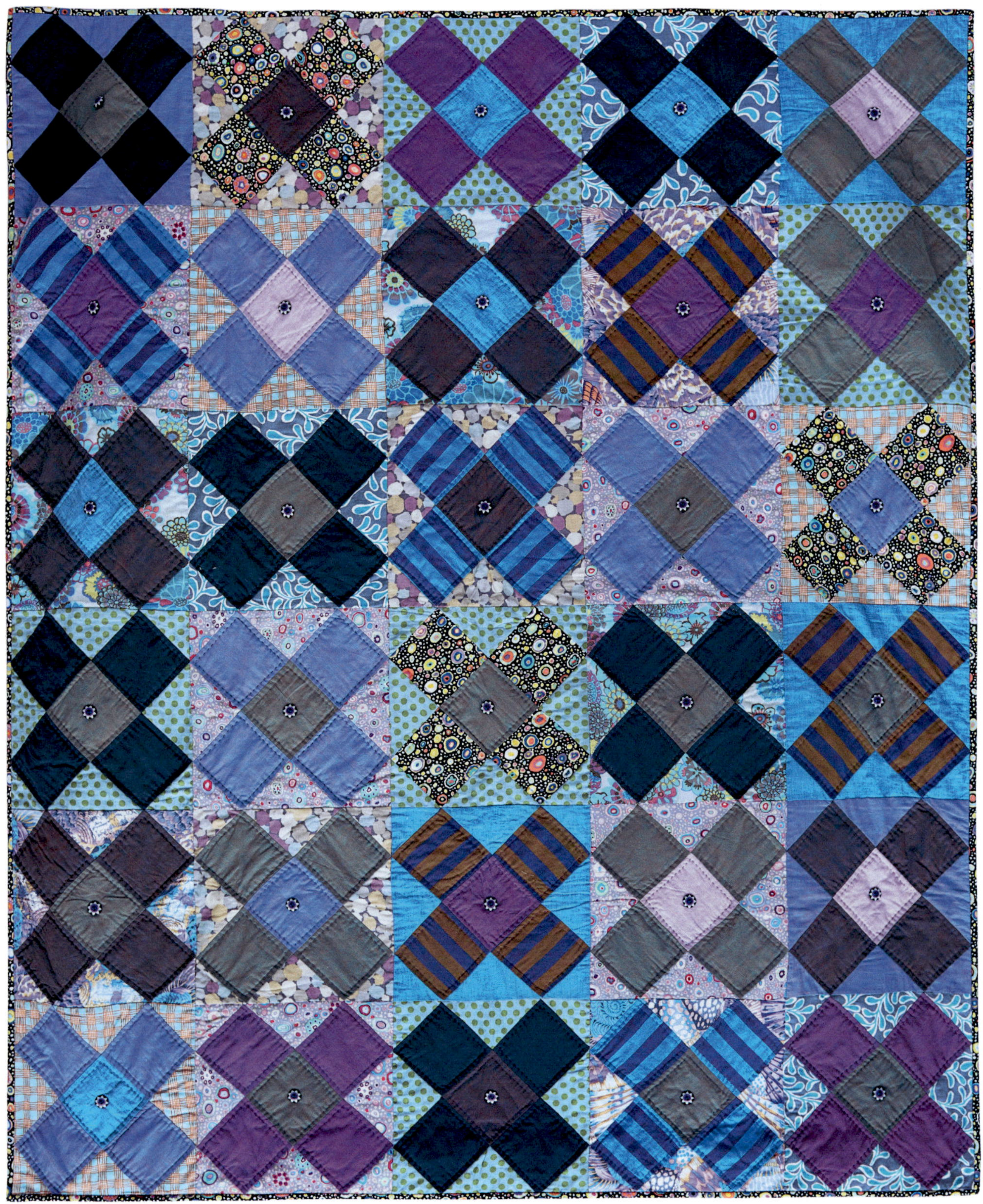

The crosses on this soft tonal quilt remind me of the rusty metal ties often seen supporting bulging brickwork on old farmhouses and barns. I designed a series of buttons for Dill Buttons that have been put to good use in the centre of each cross in this quilt.

SIZE OF FINISHED QUILT
72in x 60in (183cm x 152cm)

FABRICS
Fabrics have been calculated at a maximum width of 40in (102cm). Fabrics have been given a number – see the Fabric Swatch Diagram for details.

Patchwork Fabrics
ROMAN GLASS
| Fabric 1 | Grey | 3/8yd (40cm) |
| Fabric 2 | Contrast | 3/8yd (40cm) |

* see also Binding Fabric

ASIAN CIRCLES
| Fabric 3 | Turquoise | 3/8yd (40cm) |

SHOT COTTON
Fabric 4	Opal	3/4yd (70cm)
Fabric 5	Dawn	1/4yd (25cm)
Fabric 6	Mist	1/2yd (50cm)
Fabric 7	Shadow	1/2yd (50cm)
Fabric 8	Dusk	1/2yd (50cm)
Fabric 9	Lupin	3/8yd (40cm)
Fabric 10	Galvanised	5/8yd (60cm)

GINGHAM
| Fabric 11 | Grey | 3/8yd (40cm) |

REFLECTIONS
| Fabric 12 | Putty | 3/8yd (40cm) |

SAILOR VALENTINE
| Fabric 13 | Grey | 3/8yd (40cm) |

TWIG
| Fabric 14 | Grey | 3/8yd (40cm) |

SPOT
| Fabric 15 | Sage | 3/8yd (40cm) |

WIDE STRIPE
| Fabric 16 | Blueberry | 3/8yd (40cm) |
| Fabric 17 | Butterscotch | 3/8yd (40cm) |

Backing and Binding Fabrics
TONAL FLORAL
| Fabric 18 | Charcoal | 4 1/2yd (4.2m) |

ROMAN GLASS
| Fabric 2 | Contrast | 5/8yd (60cm) |

* see also Patchwork Fabrics

Batting
80in x 70in (203cm x 178cm)

FABRIC SWATCH DIAGRAM

Patchwork Fabrics

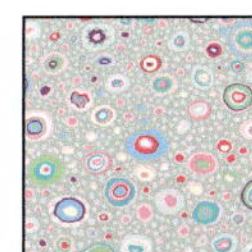
Fabric 1
ROMAN GLASS
Grey
GP01GY

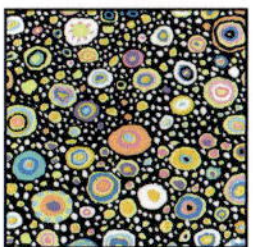
Fabric 2
ROMAN GLASS
Contrast
GP01CN

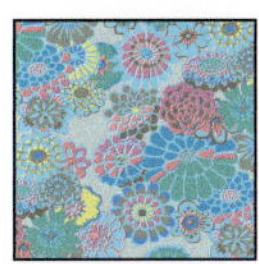
Fabric 3
ASIAN CIRCLES
Turquoise
GP89TQ

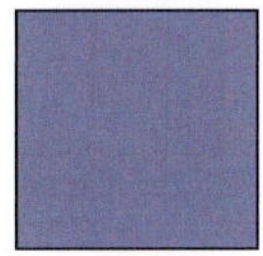
Fabric 4
SHOT COTTON
Opal
SC114OP

Fabric 5
SHOT COTTON
Dawn
SC121DN

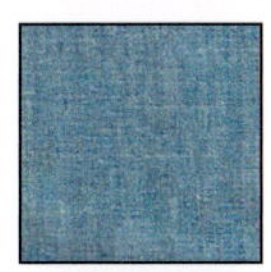
Fabric 6
SHOT COTTON
Mist
SC128MI

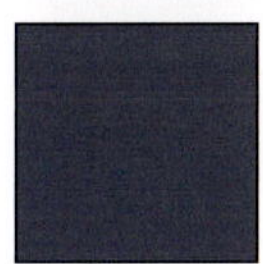
Fabric 7
SHOT COTTON
Shadow
SC108SD

Fabric 8
SHOT COTTON
Dusk
SC129DU

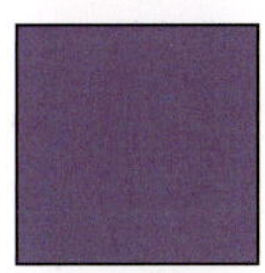
Fabric 9
SHOT COTTON
Lupin
SC113LU

Fabric 10
SHOT COTTON
Galvanised
SC130GA

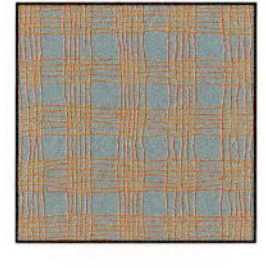
Fabric 11
GINGHAM
Grey
BM89GY

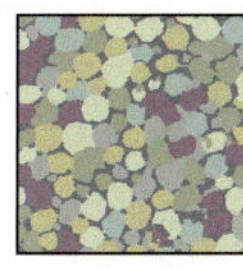
Fabric 12
REFLECTIONS
Putty
BM87PT

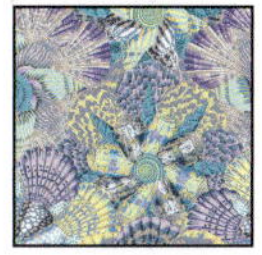
Fabric 13
SAILOR VALENTINE
Grey
PJ121GY

Fabric 14
TWIG
Grey
GP196GY

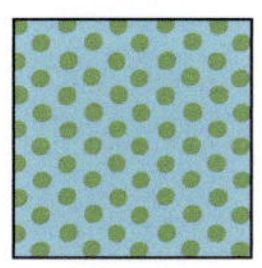
Fabric 15
SPOT
Sage
GP70SJ

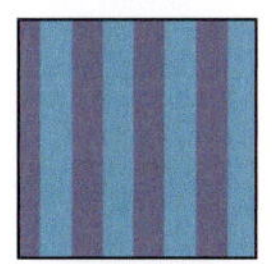
Fabric 16
WIDE STRIPE
Blueberry
SS01BB

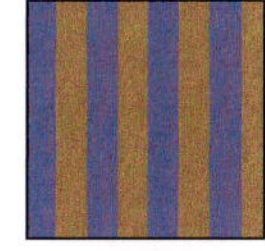
Fabric 17
WIDE STRIPE
Butterscotch
SS01BC

Backing and Binding Fabrics

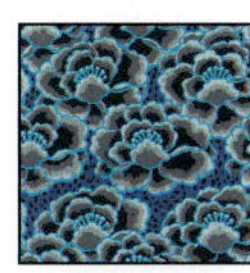
Fabric 18
TONAL FLORAL
Charcoal
GP197CC

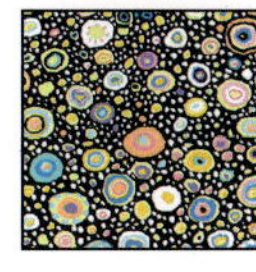
Fabric 2
ROMAN GLASS
Contrast
GP01CN

Extras

For the cross centres: 30 size $\frac{7}{8}$ in
(20mm) Star Flower buttons from Dill.

PATCHES

Patches are squares and half- and
quarter-square triangles. A cross shape,
made from 5 squares cut $4\frac{3}{4}$ in (12.1cm),
is set on point with side-setting triangles
cut as quarter-square triangles from
larger $7\frac{1}{4}$ in (18.4cm) squares and
corner-setting triangles cut as half-
square triangles from smaller $3\frac{5}{8}$ in
(9.2cm) squares. Finished blocks are
12in (30.5cm) square and set in 6 rows
of 5.

CUTTING OUT

Fabric is cut across the width unless
otherwise stated. When cutting different
pieces from the same fabric, always cut
the larger pieces first.

Side-setting Triangles

Cut a strip $7\frac{1}{4}$ in (18.4cm) wide and
cross cut squares at $7\frac{1}{4}$ in (18.4cm).
Each strip will yield 5 squares. Cut
each square diagonally twice to create
4 quarter-square triangles from each.
Cut 30 squares to yield 120 side-setting
triangles from fabrics as follows:
Fabric 1 5 squares – 20 triangles;
Fabric 3 3 squares – 12 triangles;
Fabric 4 2 squares – 8 triangles;
Fabric 6 3 squares – 12 triangles;
Fabric 11 3 squares – 12 triangles;
Fabric 12 3 squares –12 triangles;
Fabric 13 3 squares – 12 triangles;
Fabric 14 3 squares – 12 triangles;
Fabric 15 5 squares – 20 triangles.

Cross Squares

Cut strips $4\frac{3}{4}$ in (12.1cm) wide. Cross cut
squares at $4\frac{3}{4}$ in (12.1cm). Each strip
will yield 8 squares. Cut a total of 150
squares from fabrics as follows:
Fabric 2 (2 strips) 12 squares;
Fabric 4 (3 strips) 18 squares;
Fabric 5 (1 strip) 4 squares;
Fabric 6 (1 strip) 5 squares;
Fabric 7 (3 strips) 24 squares;
Fabric 8 (3 strips) 19 squares;
Fabric 9 (2 strips) 16 squares;
Fabric 10 (4 strips) 28 squares;
Fabric 16 (2 strips) 12 squares;
Fabric 17 (2 strips) 12 squares.

Corner-setting Triangles

Cut a strip $3\frac{5}{8}$ in (9.2cm) wide and cross
cut squares at $3\frac{5}{8}$ in (9.2cm). Each strip
will yield 10 squares. Cut each square
once diagonally to yield 2 half-square
triangles from each. Cut 60 squares to
yield 120 corner-setting triangles from
fabrics as follows:
Fabric 1 10 squares – 20 triangles;
Fabric 3 6 squares – 12 triangles;
Fabric 4 4 squares – 8 triangles;
Fabric 6 6 squares – 12 triangles;
Fabric 11 6 squares – 12 triangles;
Fabric 12 6 squares – 12 triangles;
Fabric 13 6 squares – 12 triangles;
Fabric 14 6 squares – 12 triangles;
Fabric 15 10 squares – 20 triangles.

Backing

From Fabric 18 cut 2 pieces 80in x 40in
(203cm x 102cm).

Binding

From Fabric 2 cut 7 strips $2\frac{1}{2}$ in (6.4cm)
wide. Remove selvedges and sew end to
end with 45° seams (see page 141).

MAKING THE QUILT

Using a design wall will help to place
patches in the required layout.
Use $\frac{1}{4}$ in (6mm) seams throughout.

Making the Blocks

Referring to the Block Assembly
Diagram, the Quilt Assembly Diagram
and the quilt photograph for fabric
placements, select 4 matching squares
and a corresponding centre square, then
select side-setting triangles and corner-
setting triangles. Sew the squares and
setting triangles in diagonal rows as
shown in the Block Assembly Diagram.
Make 30 blocks in total.

Quilt Assembly

Lay out the blocks in 6 rows of 5 blocks,
referring to the Quilt Assembly Diagram
and the quilt photograph. Sew together
one row at a time, pressing seams in
opposite directions on alternate rows
– odd rows to the left, even rows to the
right – to allow the finished seams to lie
flat. Sew the rows together, taking care
to align crossing seams.

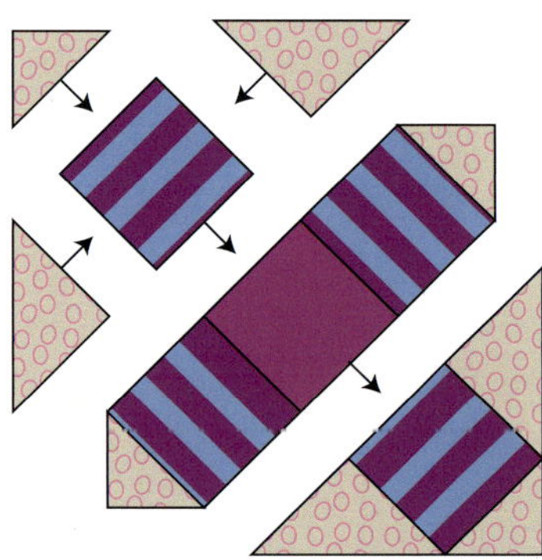

BLOCK ASSEMBLY DIAGRAM

FINISHING THE QUILT

Remove selvedges and sew the Fabric 18
backing pieces together down their long
edges and trim to form a piece 80in x
70in (203cm x 178cm).

Press the quilt top. Layer the quilt top,
batting and backing, and baste together
(see page 140).
Quilt as desired and sew a button to the
centre of each cross.
Note: This quilt was hand-quilted with
Aurifil size 12 cotton thread: 1 spool of
each of shades 4241, 2566, 1128, 2581,
1248 and 2540.
Trim the quilt edges and attach the
binding (see page 141).

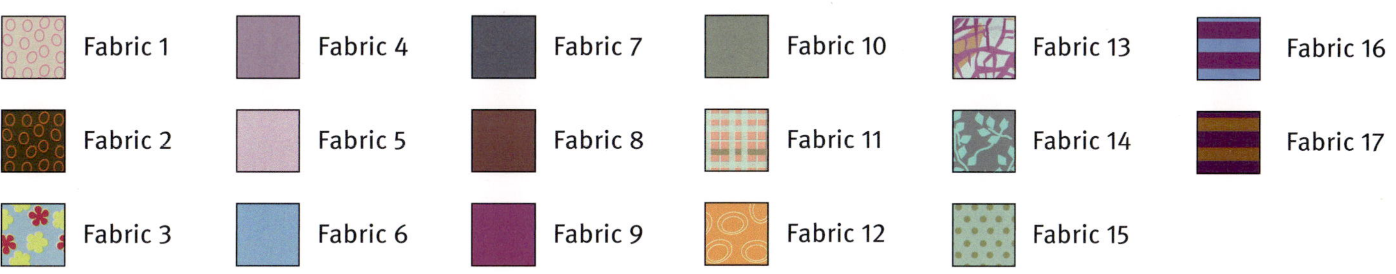

Fabric 1
Fabric 2
Fabric 3
Fabric 4
Fabric 5
Fabric 6
Fabric 7
Fabric 8
Fabric 9
Fabric 10
Fabric 11
Fabric 12
Fabric 13
Fabric 14
Fabric 15
Fabric 16
Fabric 17

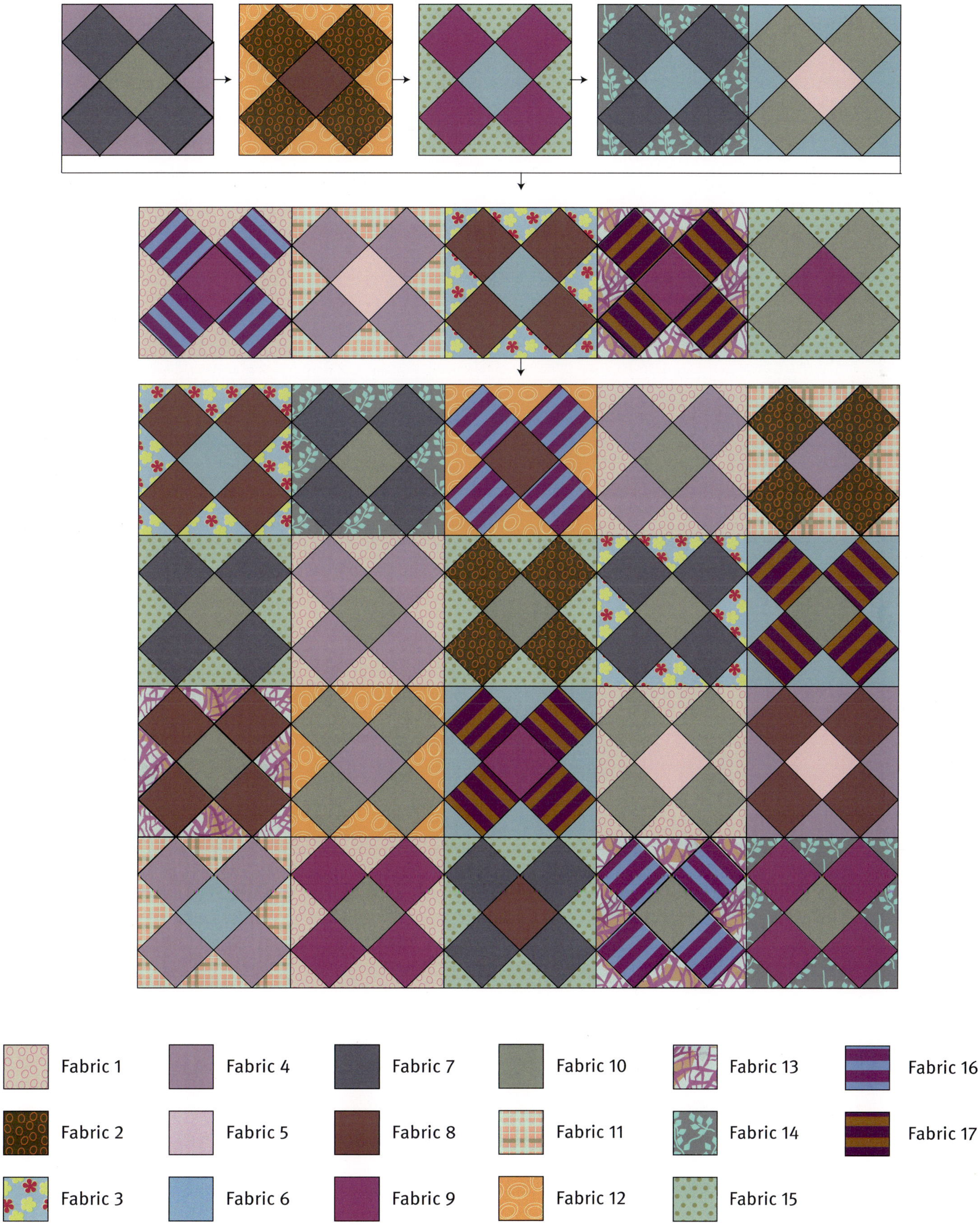

garden bricks *

Kaffe Fassett

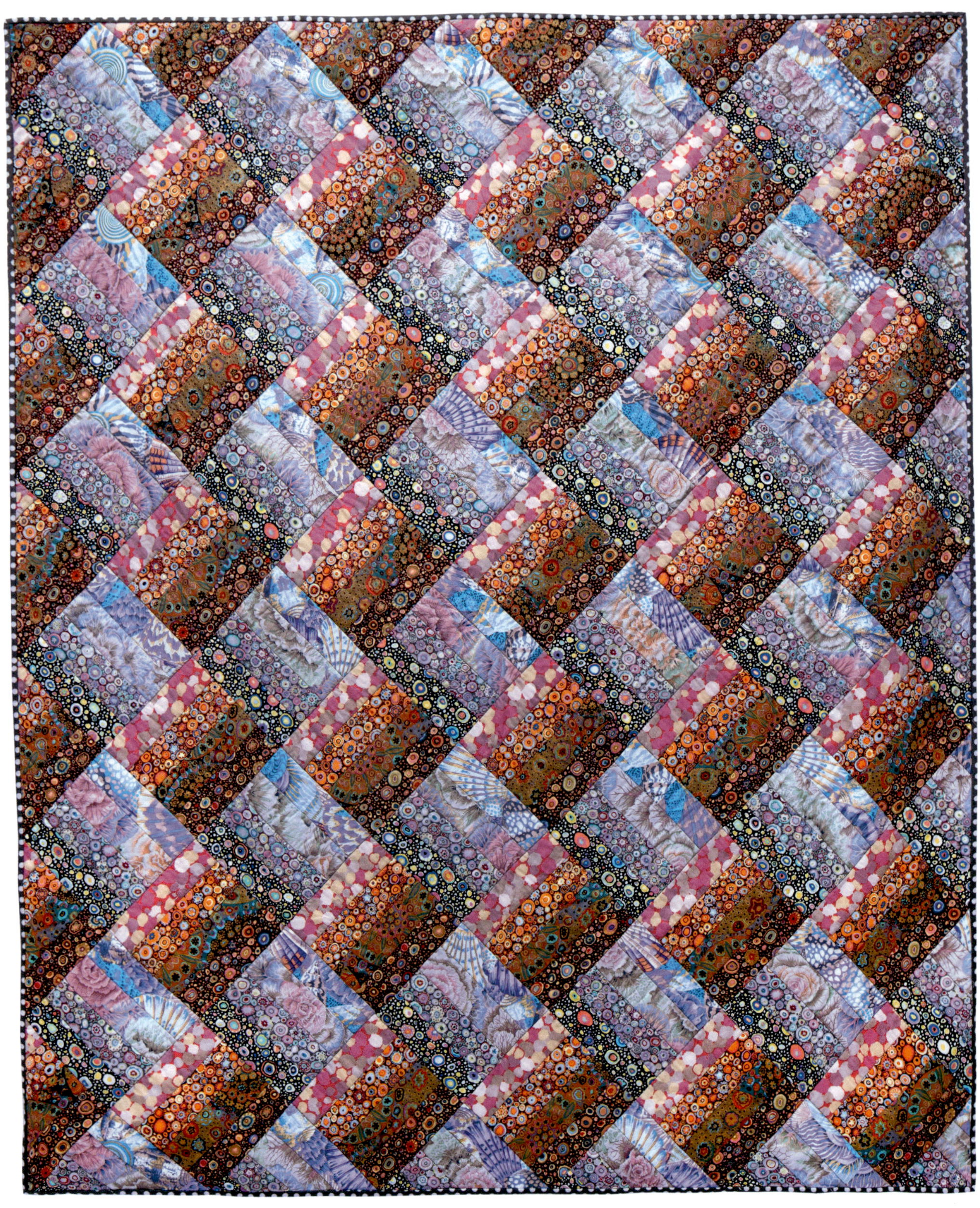

This simple quilt, made from two variations of the same block, creates a shaded geometric pattern from some of our classic fabrics in pastels and contrasts.

SIZE OF FINISHED QUILT
74in x 62in (188cm x 157.5cm)

FABRICS
Fabrics have been calculated at a maximum width of 40in (102cm). Fabrics have been given a number – see the Fabric Swatch Diagram for details.

Patchwork Fabrics
ROMAN GLASS
Fabric 1   Byzantine   1yd (95cm)
MILLEFIORE
Fabric 2   Antique   1yd (95cm)
PAPERWEIGHT
Fabric 3   Pumpkin   1yd (95cm)
REFLECTIONS
Fabric 4   Neutral   1yd (95cm)
ROMAN GLASS
Fabric 5   Contrast   1yd (95cm)
PAPERWEIGHT
Fabric 6   Grey   1yd (95cm)
BRASSICA
Fabric 7   Grey   1yd (95cm)
SAILOR VALENTINE
Fabric 8   Grey   1yd (95cm)

Backing and Binding Fabrics
ONION RINGS extra-wide backing
Fabric 9   Black   2yd (1.9m)
SPOT
Fabric 10   Charcoal   ⅝yd (60cm)

Batting
84in x 72in (213cm x 183cm)

PATCHES
The blocks (in two different sets of fabrics) are formed of 4 rectangular 'bricks' finished at 2in x 8in (5.1cm x 20.3cm), set in a dark to light order, to form squares finished at 8in (20.3cm). As seen in the quilt photograph, the blocks are set on point in rows in alternating directions so the fabrics form zigzag lines down the quilt. Pieced blocks are cut to form setting triangles around the quilt edges and two smaller corner triangles for the top left and bottom right corners of the quilt.

CUTTING OUT
Fabric is cut across the width unless otherwise stated.

Blocks
Cut strips 2½in (6.4cm) wide and cross cut rectangles 8½in x 2½in (21.6cm x 6.4cm). Each strip will yield 4 rectangles. Cut 13 strips from each of Fabrics 1, 2, 3, 4, 5, 6, 7 and 8 and crosscut 42 rectangles from each fabric. Cut a total of 336 rectangles.

Backing
Trim Fabric 9 to 84in x 72in (213cm x 183cm).

Binding
From Fabric 10, cut 8 strips 2½in (6.4cm) wide. Remove selvedges and sew end to end with 45° seams (see page 141).

MAKING THE QUILT
Using a design wall will help to place patches in the required layout.
Use ¼in (6mm) seams throughout.

Making the Blocks
Block 1 is made using rectangles in Fabrics 1, 2, 3 and 4.
Block 2 is made using rectangles in Fabrics 5, 6, 7 and 8.

Referring to the Block Assembly Diagram, sew 4 rectangles together for each block, ordering them from dark to light, following fabric numbers, and press all seams towards the darker fabrics. Make a total of 42 blocks in each colour combination.

Patchwork Fabrics

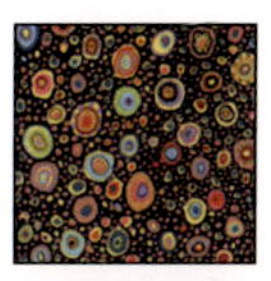

Fabric 1
ROMAN GLASS
Byzantine
GP01BY

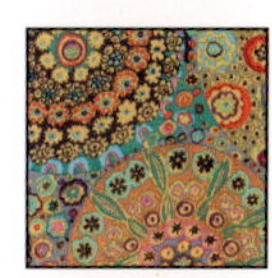

Fabric 2
MILLEFIORE
Antique
GP92AN

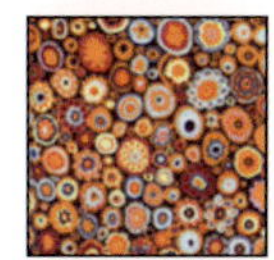

Fabric 3
PAPERWEIGHT
Pumpkin
GP20PN

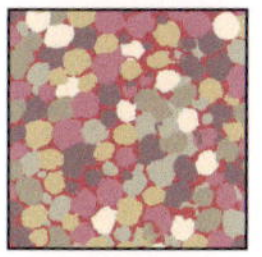

Fabric 4
REFLECTIONS
Neutral
BM87NE

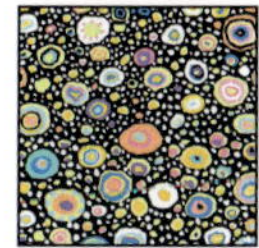

Fabric 5
ROMAN GLASS
Contrast
GP01CN

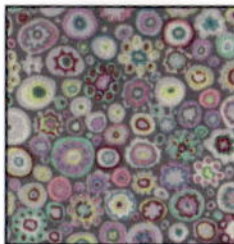

Fabric 6
PAPERWEIGHT
Grey
GP20GY

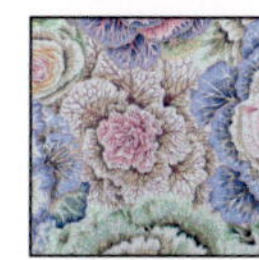

Fabric 7
BRASSICA
Grey
PJ51GY

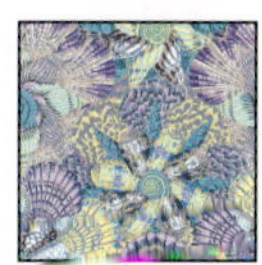

Fabric 8
SAILOR VALENTINE
Grey
PJ12IGY

Backing and Binding Fabrics

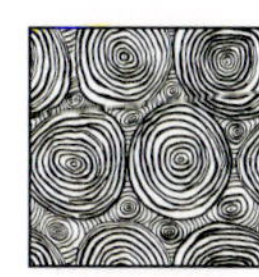

Fabric 9
ONION RINGS
Black
QM01BK

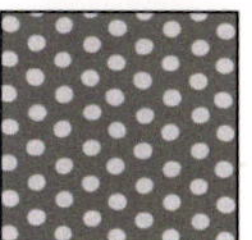

Fabric 10
SPOT
Charcoal
GP70CC

BLOCK ASSEMBLY DIAGRAM

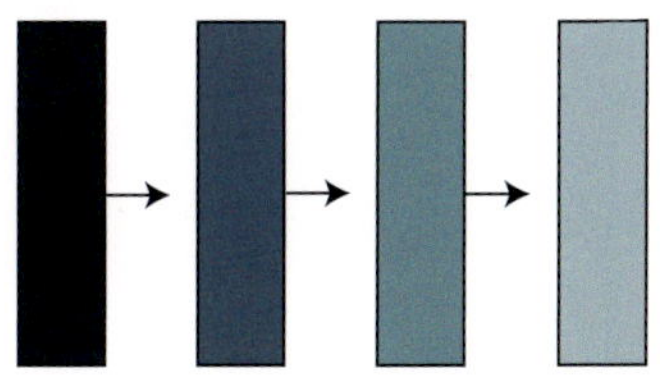

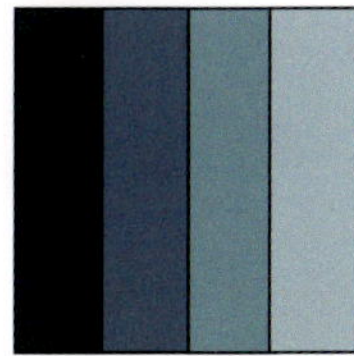

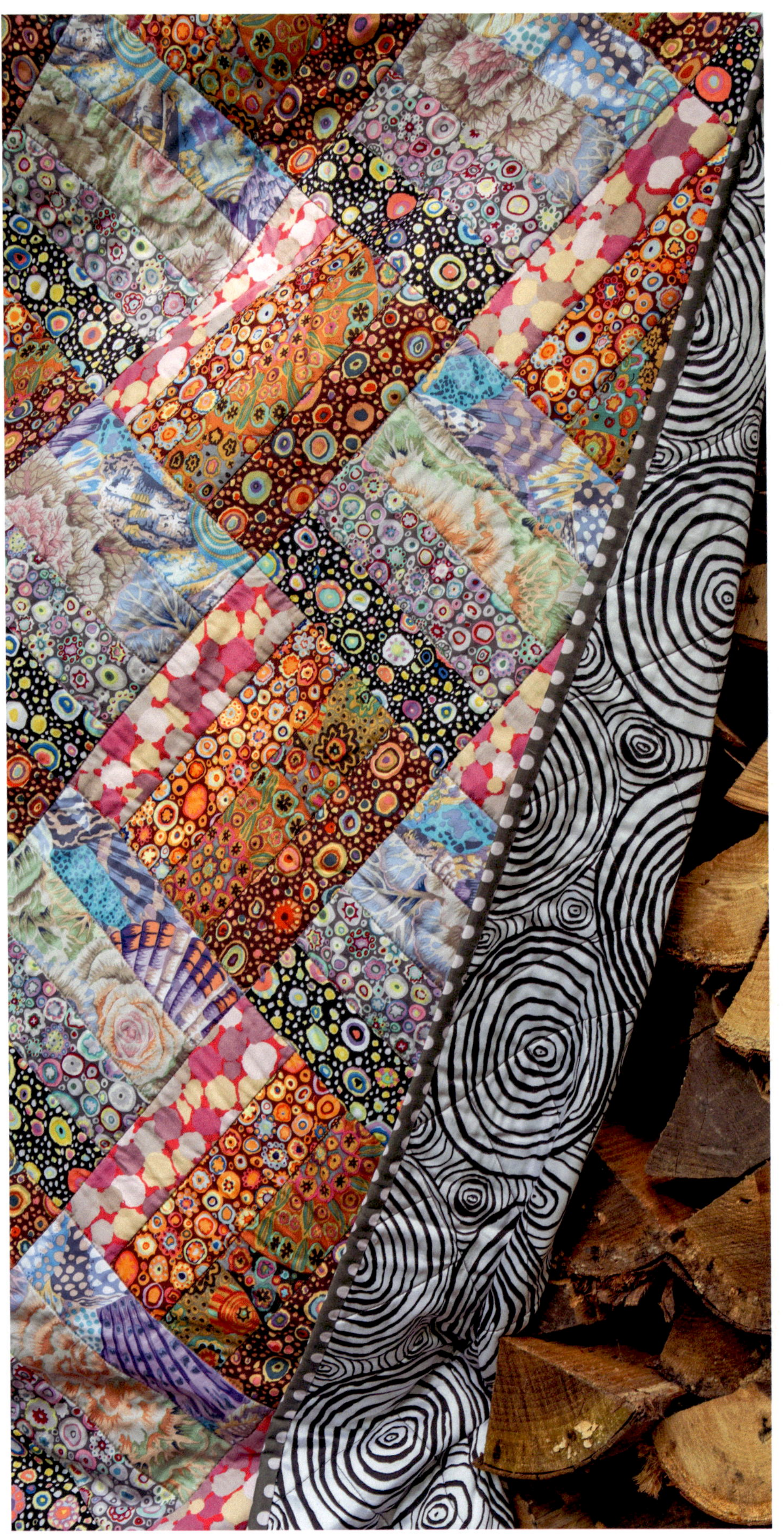

Centre
Referring to the Quilt Assembly Diagram and quilt photograph, lay out the blocks on point in 14 rows of 6, ensuring the blocks are orientated correctly to form the zigzag lines down the quilt – Block 1 angled to the left, Block 2 angled to the right.

Setting and Corner Triangles
Once correctly positioned, the blocks forming the outer edges of the quilt need to be cut down to form setting triangles. Press the blocks using spray starch and stay-stitch the long side of the triangles as you make them to avoid distorting the quilt edges when sewing together.

Use a safety pin to mark the required diagonal half of each side-setting block and with a soft pencil or chalk pencil and ruler, draw a diagonal seam line from corner to corner. Mark a cutting line ¼in (6mm) outside the seam line on the unwanted (un-pinned) side and cut away the excess. Repeat for all the side, top and bottom-setting triangles.

Using the same method for the top left and bottom right corner triangles, mark the quarter block required for the corner triangle with a safety pin. Mark both diagonal seam lines from corner to corner, then mark cutting lines ¼in (6mm) outside both seam lines. Cut along both diagonal cutting lines to leave the required corner triangles with seam allowances.

Sew the setting triangles and blocks together in diagonal rows as shown in the Quilt Assembly Diagram, pressing seams in opposite directions on alternate rows – odd rows to the left, even rows to the right – to allow the finished seams to lie flat. Sew the diagonal rows together, taking care to align crossing seams.

FINISHING THE QUILT
Press the quilt top. Layer the quilt top, batting and backing, and baste together (see page 140).
Quilt as desired.
Trim the quilt edges and attach the binding (see page 141).

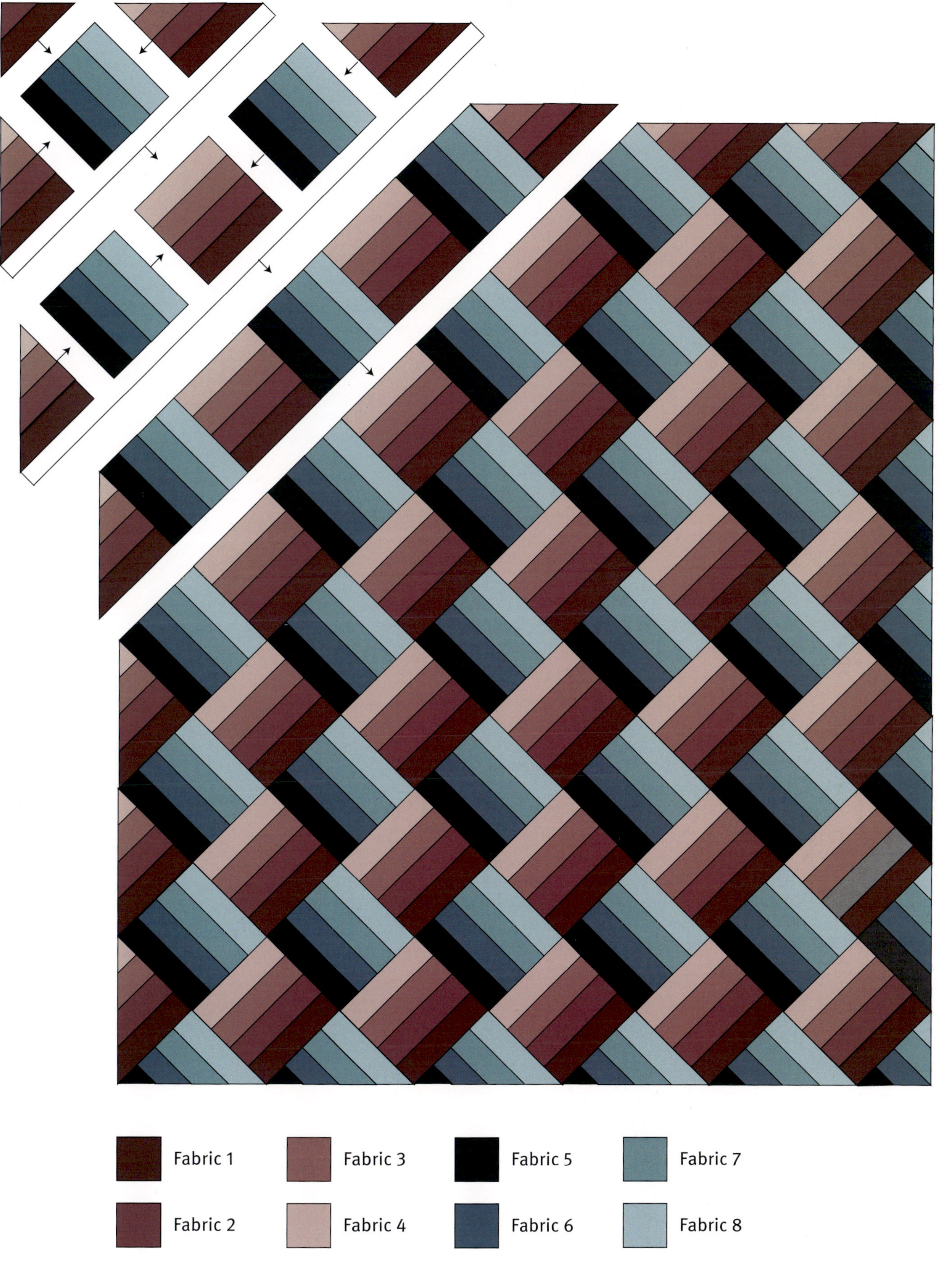

Fabric 1
Fabric 2
Fabric 3
Fabric 4
Fabric 5
Fabric 6
Fabric 7
Fabric 8

lightning strike *

Kaffe Fassett

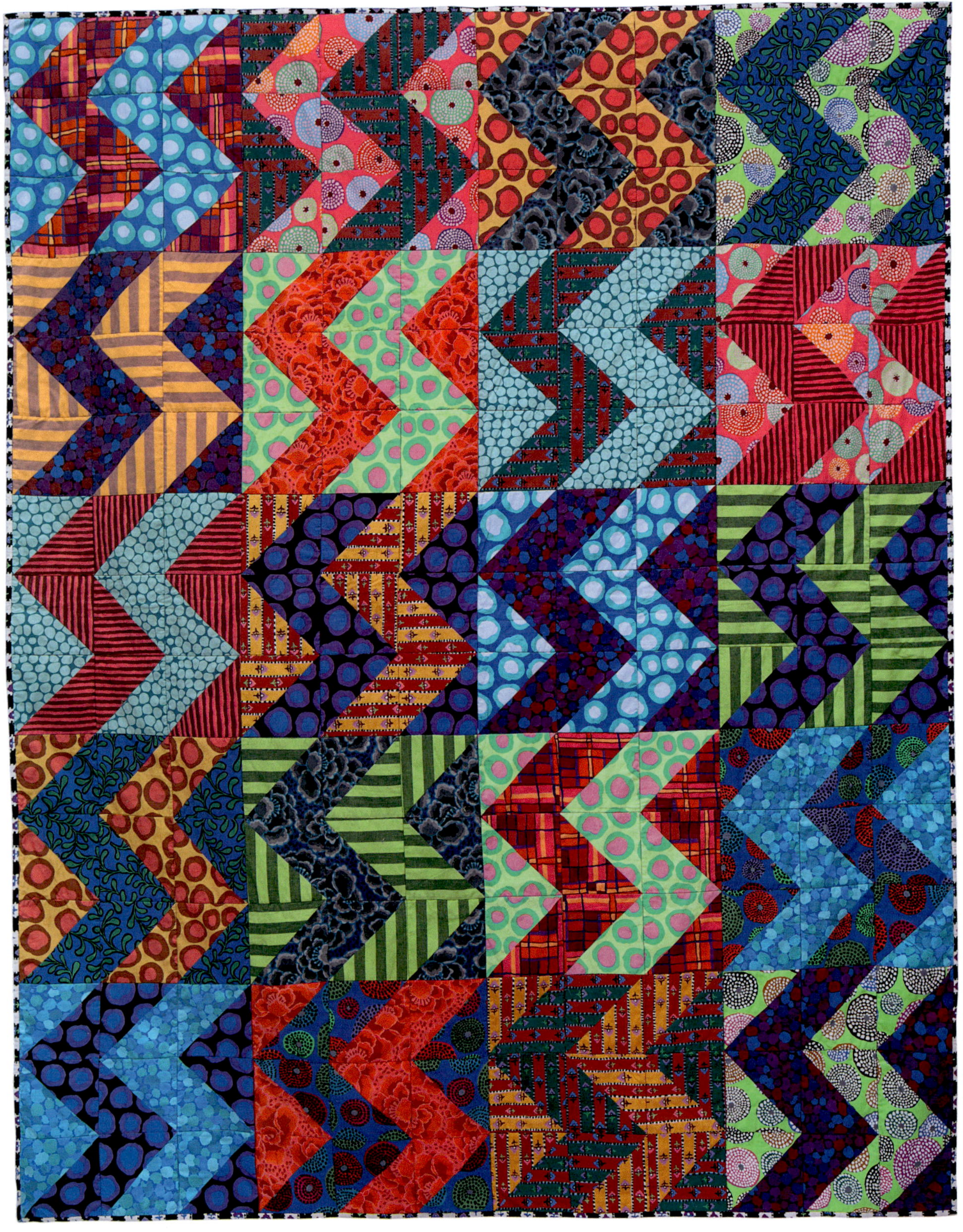

This dynamic quilt is simple to make and shows off a good selection of our recent fabrics. It is a great quilt for anybody who likes strong colours and bold graphics.

SIZE OF FINISHED QUILT
90in x 72in (229cm x 183cm)

FABRICS
Fabrics have been calculated at a maximum width of 40in (102cm). Fabrics have been given a number – see the Fabric Swatch Diagram for details.

Patchwork Fabrics
FISH LIPS
Fabric 1	Banana	½yd (50cm)
Fabric 2	Black	⅝yd (60cm)
Fabric 3	Blue	½yd (50cm)
Fabric 4	Green	½yd (50cm)

WIDE STRIPE
| Fabric 5 | Cantaloupe | ¼yd (25cm) |
| Fabric 6 | Watermelon | ½yd (50cm) |

CHECKMATE
| Fabric 7 | Pink | ½yd (50cm) |

JUMBLE
| Fabric 8 | Turquoise | ½yd (50cm) |

COMB STRIPE
| Fabric 9 | Pink | ½yd (50cm) |

REFLECTIONS
| Fabric 10 | Purple | ⅝yd (60cm) |
| Fabric 11 | Teal | ½yd (50cm) |

DISKS
Fabric 12	Blue	½yd (50cm)
Fabric 13	Lime	½yd (50cm)
Fabric 14	Pink	½yd (50cm)

SHIRAZ
| Fabric 15 | Dark | ⅝yd (60cm) |
| Fabric 16 | Red | ½yd (50cm) |

TWIG
| Fabric 17 | Blue | ½yd (50cm) |

TONAL FLORAL
| Fabric 18 | Charcoal | ½yd (50cm) |
| Fabric 19 | Red | ½yd (50cm) |

Backing and Binding Fabrics
PEBBLE MOSAIC extra-wide backing
| Fabric 20 | Prune | 2⅜yd (2.25m) |

SHIRAZ
| Fabric 21 | Contrast | ¾yd (70cm) |

Batting
100in x 82in (254cm x 208cm)

Patchwork Fabrics

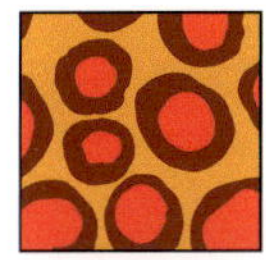
Fabric 1
FISH LIPS
Banana
BM07BA

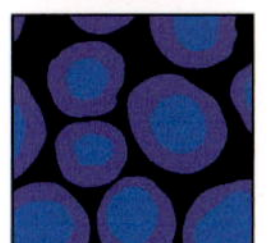
Fabric 2
FISH LIPS
Black
BM07BK

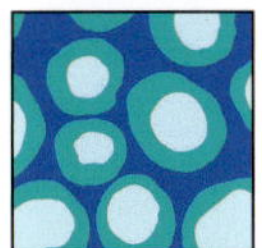
Fabric 3
FISH LIPS
Blue
BM07BL

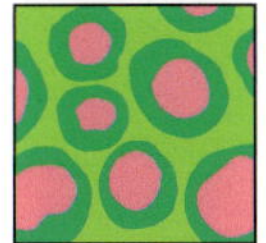
Fabric 4
FISH LIPS
Green
BM07GN

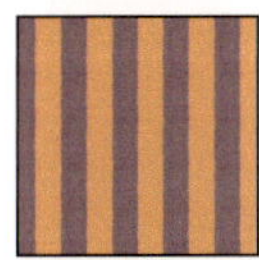
Fabric 5
WIDE STRIPE
Cantaloupe
SS01CA

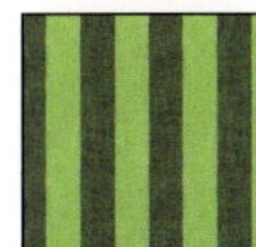
Fabric 6
WIDE STRIPE
Watermelon
SS01WL

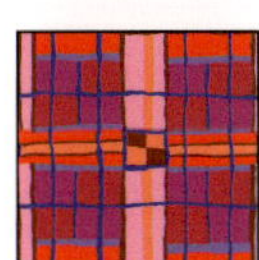
Fabric 7
CHECKMATE
Pink
BM86PK

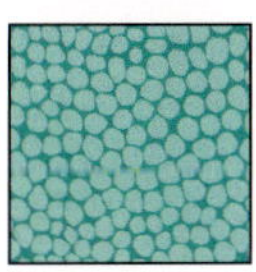
Fabric 8
JUMBLE
Turquoise
BM53TQ

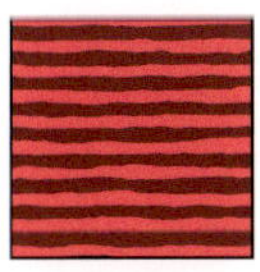
Fabric 9
COMB STRIPE
Pink
BM84PK

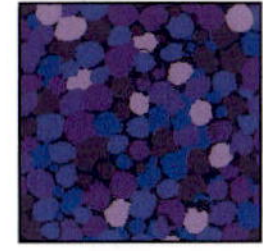
Fabric 10
REFLECTIONS
Purple
BM87PU

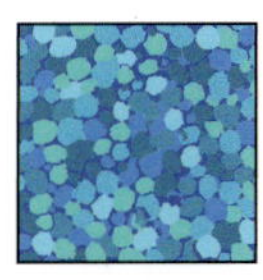
Fabric 11
REFLECTIONS
Teal
BM87TE

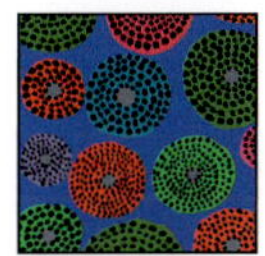
Fabric 12
DISKS
Blue
GP193BL

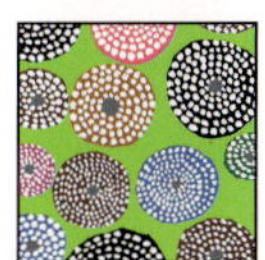
Fabric 13
DISKS
Lime
GP193LM

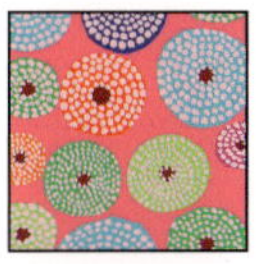
Fabric 14
DISKS
Pink
GP193PK

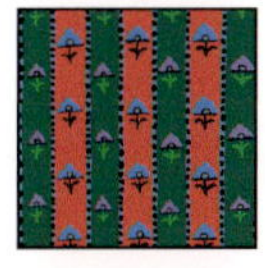
Fabric 15
SHIRAZ
Dark
GP194DK

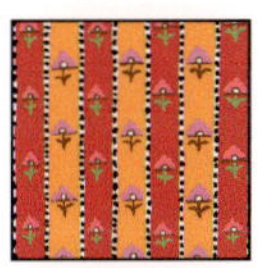
Fabric 16
SHIRAZ
Red
GP194RD

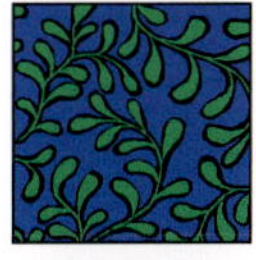
Fabric 17
TWIG
Blue
GP196BL

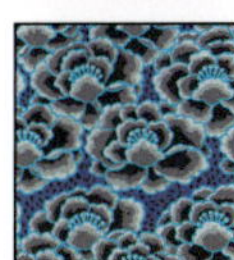
Fabric 18
TONAL FLORAL
Charcoal
GP197RD

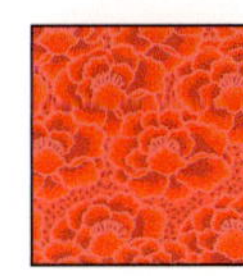
Fabric 19
TONAL FLORAL
Red
GP193PK

Backing and Binding Fabrics

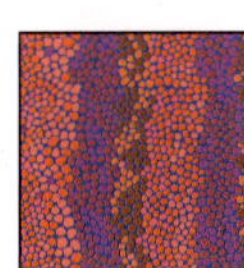
Fabric 20
PEBBLE MOSAIC
Prune
QM04PV

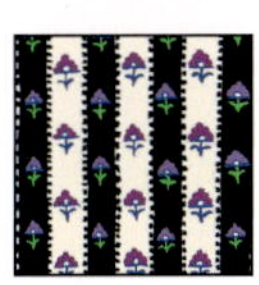
Fabric 21
SHIRAZ
Contrast
GP194CN

PATCHES

Patches are finished 6in (15.2cm) squares, each made from 2 half-square triangles (HSTs). The squares are arranged in 9-square blocks, each finished at 18in (45.7cm). These create zigzag lines that continue through the blocks down the length of the quilt. The lightning effect alternates between dark and light fabrics throughout the blocks. Blocks are set in 5 rows of 4.

CUTTING OUT

Fabric is cut across the width unless otherwise stated.

Triangles

Cut strips 6⅞in (17.5cm) wide and cross cut squares at 6⅞in (17.5cm). Each strip will yield 5 squares. Cross cut each square once diagonally to make 2 HSTs. Cut a total of 180 squares to make 360 triangles from fabrics as follows:
Fabric 1 (2 strips) 9 squares – 18 triangles;
Fabric 2 (3 strips) 14 squares – 27 triangles;
Fabric 3 (2 strips) 9 squares – 18 triangles;
Fabric 4 (2 strips) 9 squares – 18 triangles;
Fabric 5 (1 strip) 5 squares – 9 triangles;
Fabric 6 (2 strips) 9 squares – 18 triangles;
Fabric 7 (2 strips) 9 squares – 18 triangles;
Fabric 8 (2 strips) 9 squares – 18 triangles;
Fabric 9 (2 strips) 9 squares – 18 triangles;
Fabric 10 (3 strips) 14 squares – 27 triangles;
Fabric 11 (2 strips) 9 squares – 18 triangles;
Fabric 12 (2 strips) 9 squares – 18 triangles;
Fabric 13 (2 strips) 9 squares – 18 triangles;
Fabric 14 (2 strips) 9 squares – 18 triangles;
Fabric 15 (3 strips) 14 squares – 27 triangles;
Fabric 16 (2 strips) 9 squares – 18 triangles;
Fabric 17 (2 strips) 9 squares – 18 triangles;

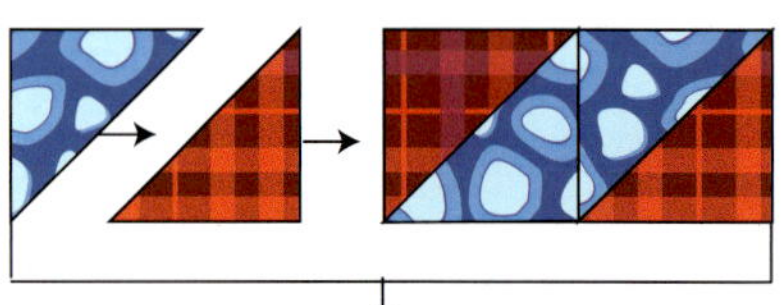
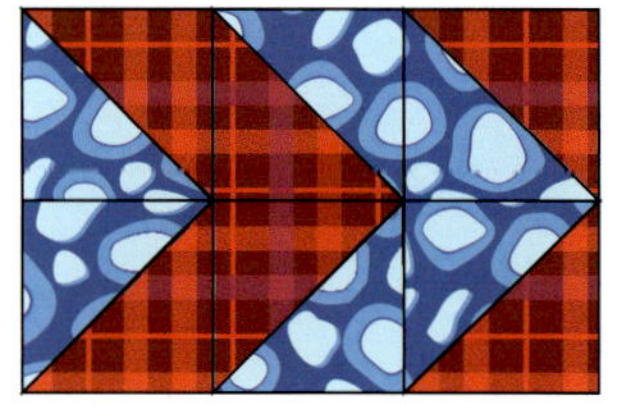

Fabric 18 (2 strips) 9 squares – 18 triangles;
Fabric 19 (2 strips) 9 squares – 18 triangles.

Backing

Trim Fabric 20 to 100in x 82in (254cm x 208cm).

Binding

From Fabric 21 cut 9 strips 2½in (6.4cm) wide. Remove selvedges and sew end to end with 45° seams (see page 141).

MAKING THE QUILT

Using a design wall will help to place patches in the required layout.
Use ¼in (6mm) seams throughout.

Making the Blocks

Referring to the Block Assembly Diagram, as well as the Quilt Assembly Diagram and the quilt photograph for fabric pairings, sew pairs of light and dark triangles together along their long diagonal edges to make each half-square patch. As these are bias seams, take care not to pull the seam as you sew. Make 9 half-square patches for each block and press seams gently, without stretching, towards the darker fabric.
Referring to the Block Assembly Diagram for positioning, sew the patches together in 3 rows of 3, then sew the 3 rows together to form each block. Make 20 blocks in total.

Quilt Assembly

Lay out the blocks referring to the Quilt Assembly Diagram and quilt photograph.

Sew the blocks together one row at a time, pressing seams in opposite directions on alternate rows – odd rows to the left, even rows to the right – to allow the finished seams to lie flat. Sew the 5 rows together, taking care to align crossing seams.

FINISHING THE QUILT

Press the quilt top. Layer the quilt top, batting and backing, and baste together (see page 140).
Quilt as desired.
Trim the quilt edges and attach the binding (see page 141).

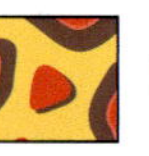 Fabric 1
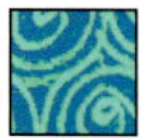 Fabric 11
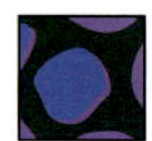 Fabric 2
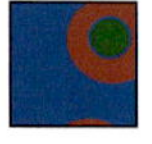 Fabric 12
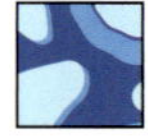 Fabric 3
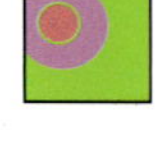 Fabric 13
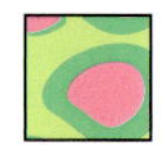 Fabric 4
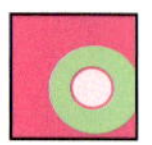 Fabric 14
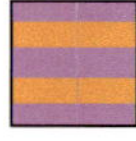 Fabric 5
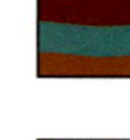 Fabric 15
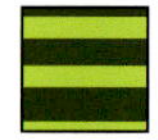 Fabric 6
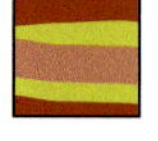 Fabric 16
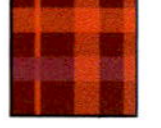 Fabric 7
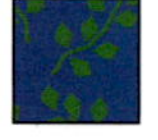 Fabric 17
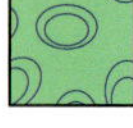 Fabric 8
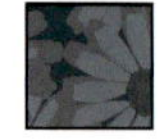 Fabric 18
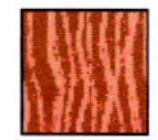 Fabric 9
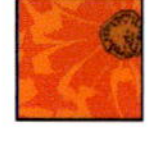 Fabric 19
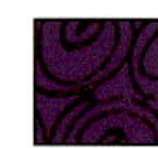 Fabric 10

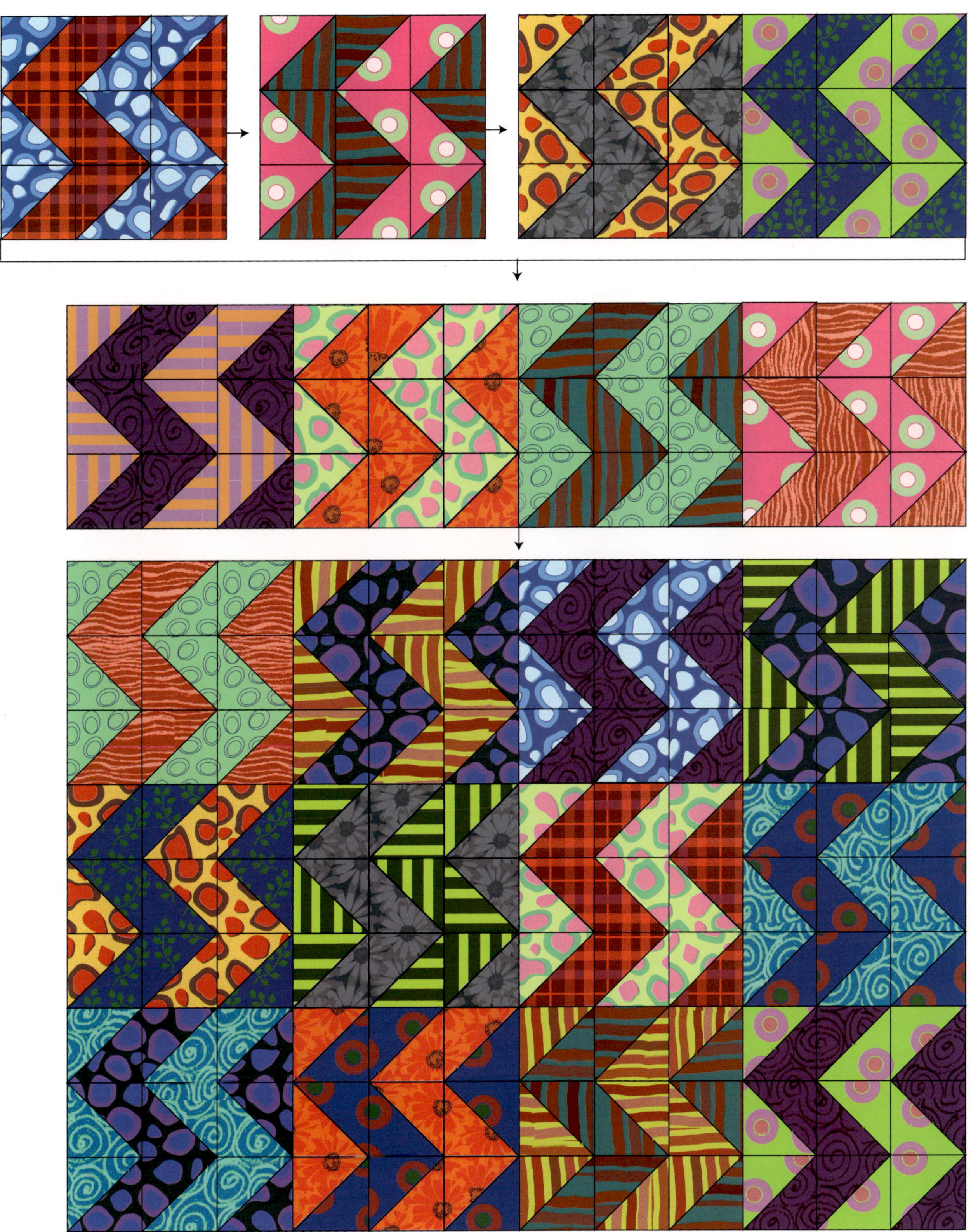

gingham lattice *

Kaffe Fassett

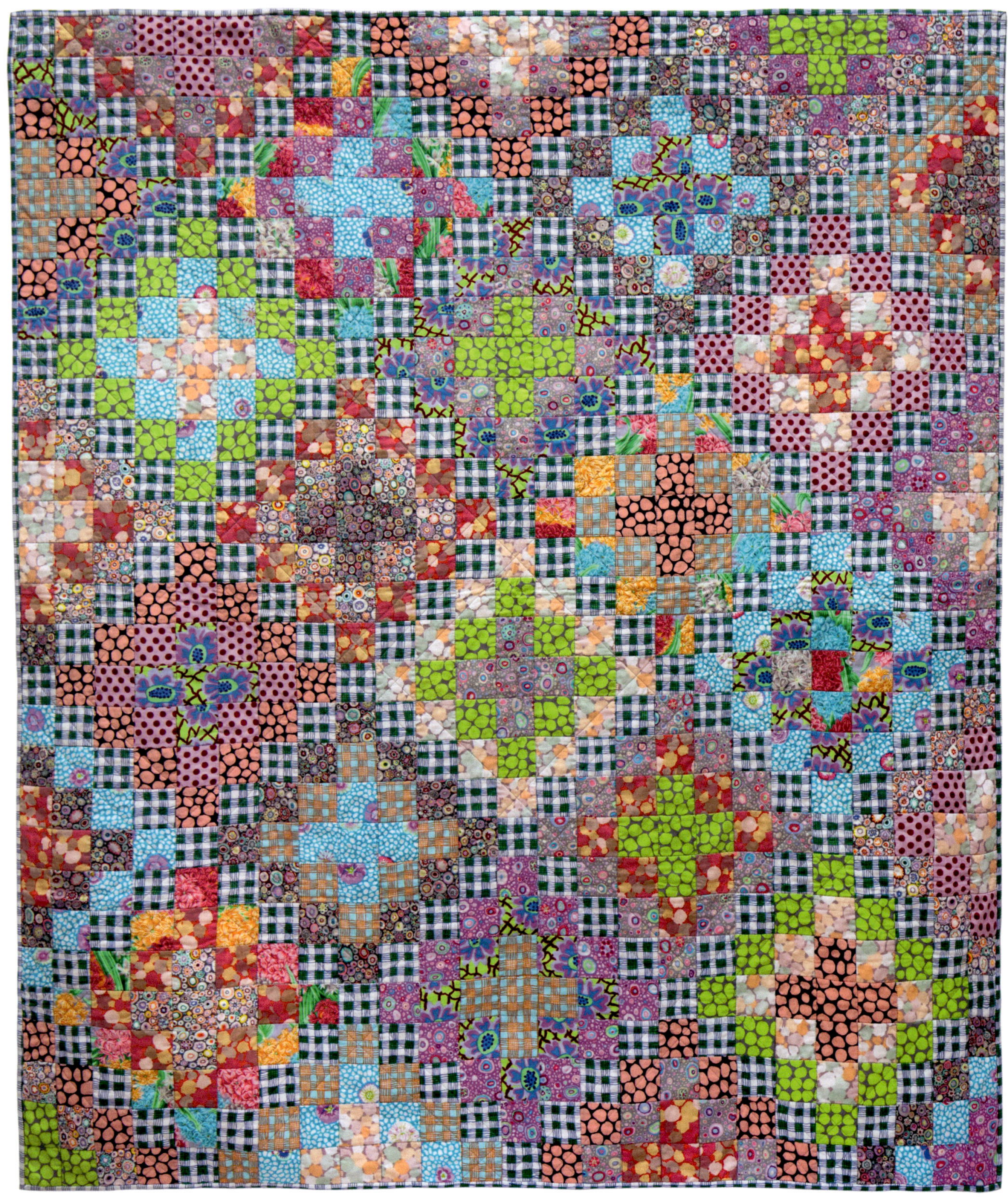

This quilt of simple squares looks
more complex than it is, as it is sewn
together in rows, making it easy to
construct. The squares are laid out in
diagonal 16-square blocks that have a
central cross formation. Each block is
surrounded with sashing squares of
Brandon's Gingham fabric in green.

SIZE OF FINISHED QUILT
73in x 63in (185cm x 160cm)

FABRICS
Fabrics have been calculated at a
maximum width of 40in (102cm). Fabrics
have been given a number – see the
Fabric Swatch Diagram for details.

Patchwork Fabrics
GINGHAM

Fabric 1	Green	1⅛yd (1.1m)

* see also Binding Fabric

Fabric 2	Grey	⅜yd (40cm)

JUMBLE

Fabric 3	Lime	⅜yd (40cm)
Fabric 4	Rose	⅜yd (40cm)

REFLECTIONS

Fabric 5	Neutral	½yd (50cm)
Fabric 6	Pastel	½yd (50cm)

FLOWER NET

Fabric 7	Lime	⅜yd (40cm)

GUINEA FLOWER

Fabric 8	Turquoise	½yd (50cm)

ROMAN GLASS

Fabric 9	Grey	⅜yd (40cm)
Fabric 10	Lavender	⅜yd (40cm)

PAPERWEIGHT

Fabric 11	Pastel	⅜yd (40cm)
Fabric 12	Grey	⅜yd (40cm)

SPOT

Fabric 13	Mauve	⅜yd (40cm)

HYACINTHS

Fabric 14	Grey	⅜yd (40cm)

Backing and Binding Fabrics
MILLEFIORE extra-wide backing

Fabric 15	Pastel	2⅛yd (2m)

GINGHAM

Fabric 1	Green	⅝yd (60cm)

* see also Patchwork Fabrics

Batting
83in x 73in (207cm x 185cm)

Patchwork Fabrics

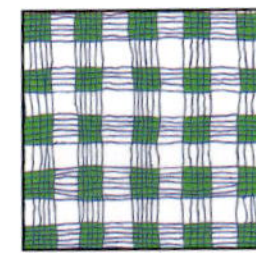

Fabric 1
GINGHAM
Green
BM89GN

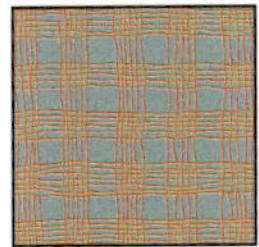

Fabric 2
GINGHAM
Grey
BM89GY

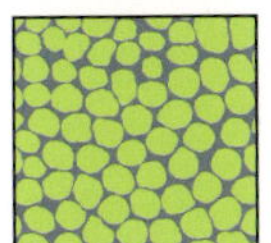

Fabric 3
JUMBLE
Lime
BM53LM

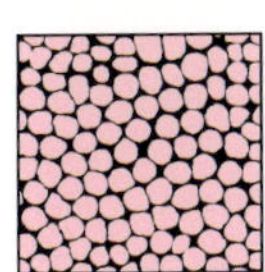

Fabric 4
JUMBLE
Rose
BM53RO

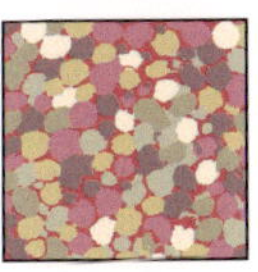

Fabric 5
REFLECTIONS
Neutral
BM87NE

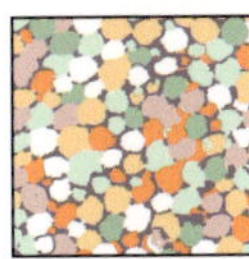

Fabric 6
REFLECTIONS
Pastel
BM87PT

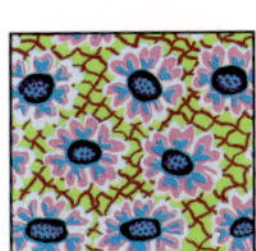

Fabric 7
FLOWER NET
Lime
BM81LM

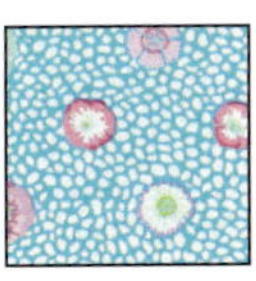

Fabric 8
GUINEA FLOWER
Turquoise
GP59TQ

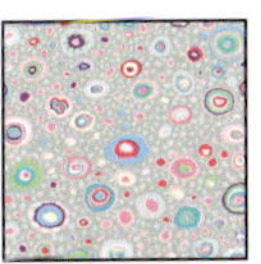

Fabric 9
ROMAN GLASS
Grey
GP01GY

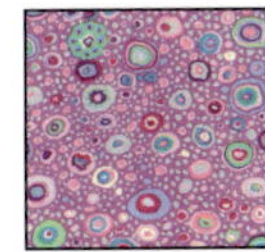

Fabric 10
ROMAN GLASS
Lavender
GP01LV

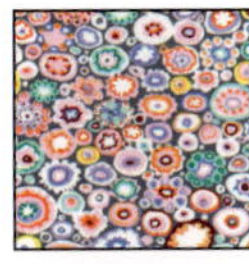

Fabric 11
PAPERWEIGHT
Pastel
GP20PT

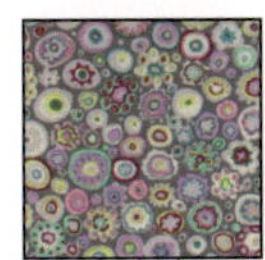

Fabric 12
PAPERWEIGHT
Grey
GP20GY

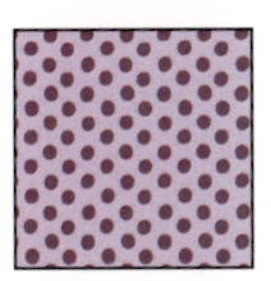

Fabric 13
SPOT
Mauve
GP70MV

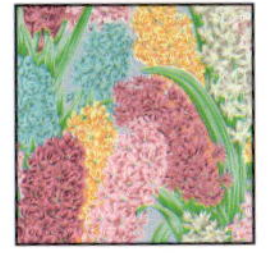

Fabric 14
HYACINTHS
Grey
PJ123GY

Backing and Binding Fabrics

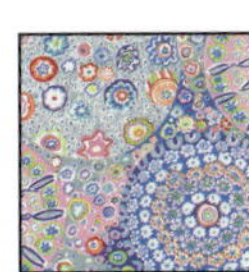

Fabric 15
MILLEFIORE
Pastel
QB06PT

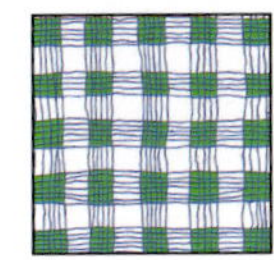

Fabric 1
GINGHAM
Green
BM89GN

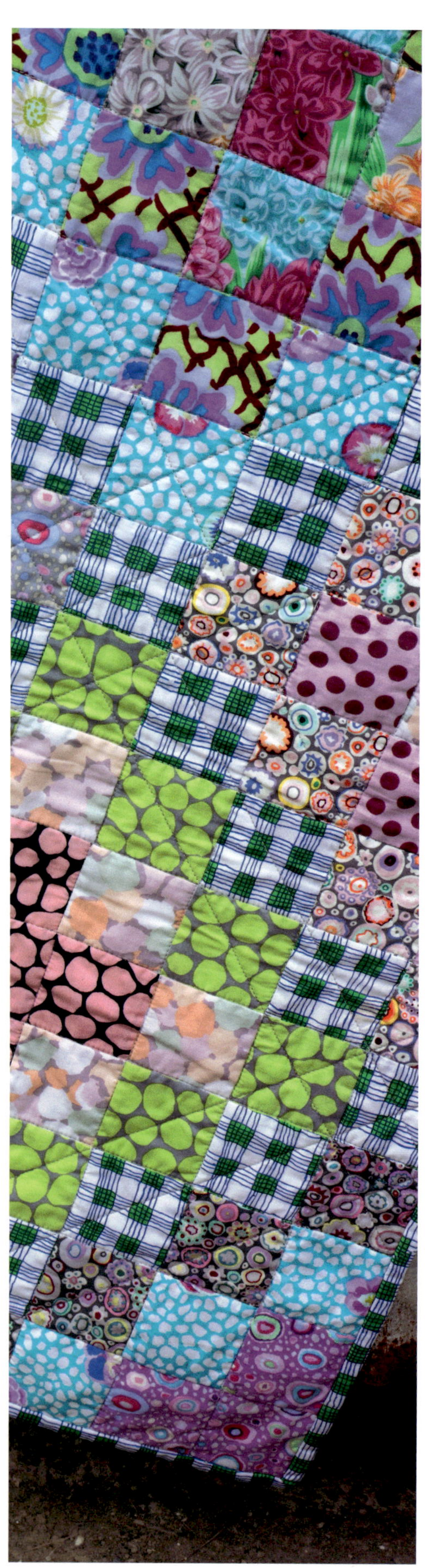

PATCHES

Patches are squares finished at 2½in (6.4cm), laid out in diagonal 16-square blocks with a central cross formation. Each block is surrounded by diagonal rows of sashing squares in Fabric 1. Patches are set in 29 rows of 25 squares.

CUTTING OUT

Fabric is cut across the width unless otherwise stated.

Patches

Cut strips 3in (7.6cm) wide and cross cut squares at 3in (7.6cm). Each strip will yield 13 squares. Cut a total of 725 squares from fabrics as follows:
Fabric 1 (12 strips) 154 squares;
Fabric 2 (3 strips) 39 squares;
Fabric 3 (4 strips) 49 squares;
Fabric 4 (4 strips) 45 squares;
Fabric 5 (5 strips) 58 squares;
Fabric 6 (5 strips) 53 squares;
Fabric 7 4 strips) 45 squares;
Fabric 8 (5 strips) 53 squares;
Fabric 9 (4 strips) 45 squares;
Fabric 10 (3 strips) 35 squares;
Fabric 11 (3 strips) 37 squares;
Fabric 12 (4 strips) 42 squares;
Fabric 13 (3 strips) 29 squares;
Fabric 14 (4 strips) 41 squares.

Backing

Trim Fabric 15 to 83in x 73in (207cm x 185cm).

Binding

From Fabric 1 cut 8 strips 2½in (6.4cm) wide. Remove selvedges and sew end to end with 45° seams (see page 141).

MAKING THE QUILT

Using a design wall will help to place patches in the required layout.
Use ¼in (6mm) seams throughout.

Quilt Assembly

Lay out the patches in rows, forming diagonal 16-square blocks, each with a central cross formation and with Fabric 1 diagonal sashing squares between them, referring to the Quilt Assembly Diagram and quilt photograph for placement.

Sew the patches together one row at a time, pressing seams in opposite directions on alternate rows – odd rows to the left, even rows to the right – to allow the finished seams to lie flat. Sew the rows together, taking care to align crossing seams.

FINISHING THE QUILT

Press the quilt top. Layer the quilt top, batting and backing, and baste together (see page 140).
Quilt as desired.
Trim the quilt edges and attach the binding (see page 141).

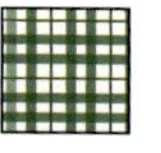 Fabric 1
 Fabric 8
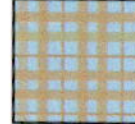 Fabric 2
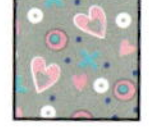 Fabric 9
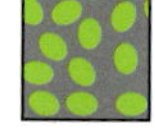 Fabric 3
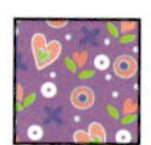 Fabric 10
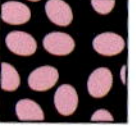 Fabric 4
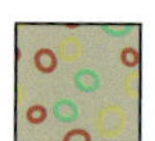 Fabric 11
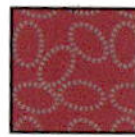 Fabric 5
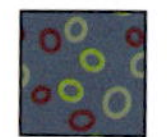 Fabric 12
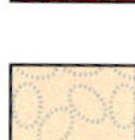 Fabric 6
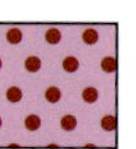 Fabric 13
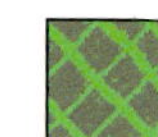 Fabric 7
 Fabric 14

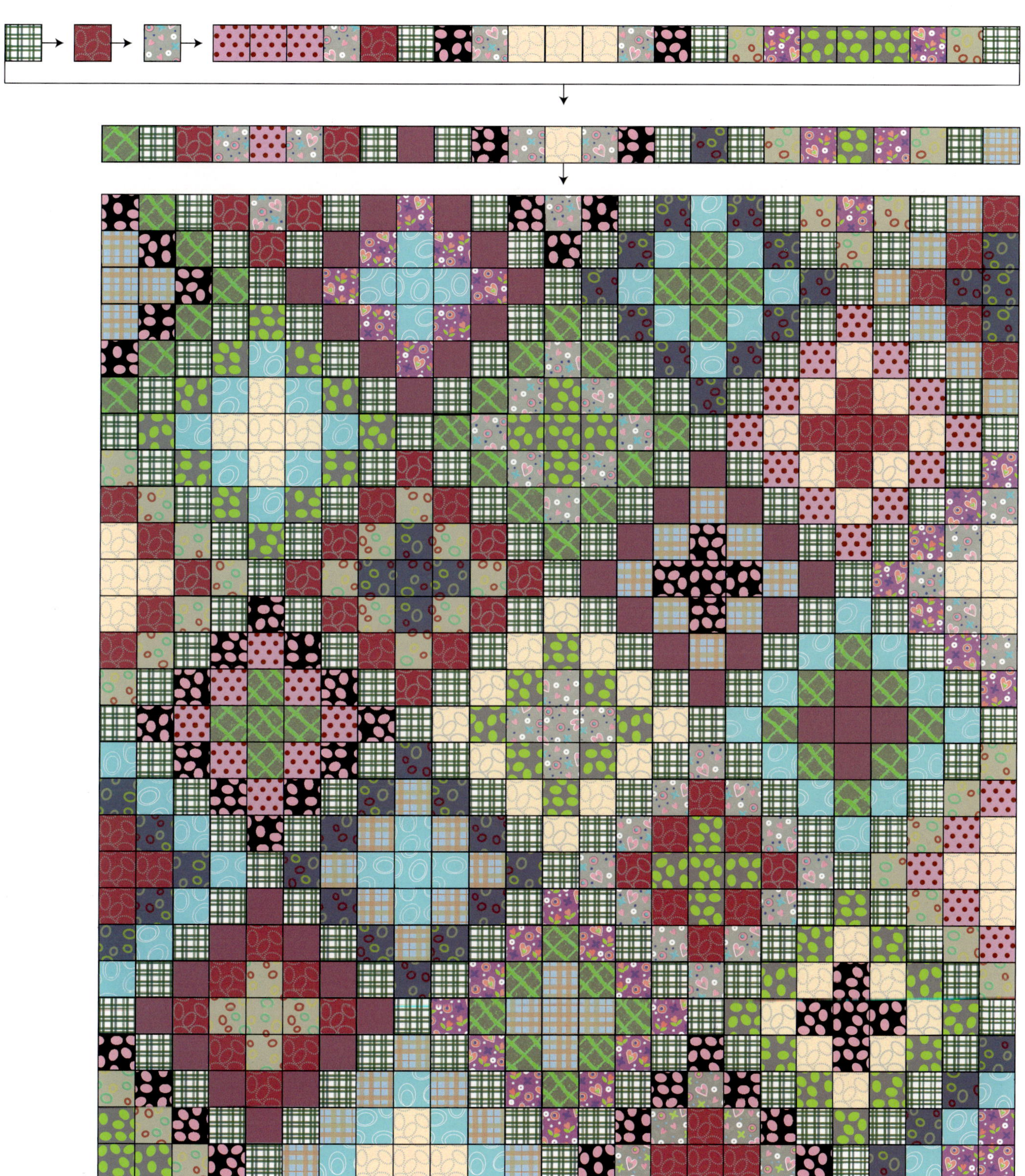

flowers and fences **

Kaffe Fassett

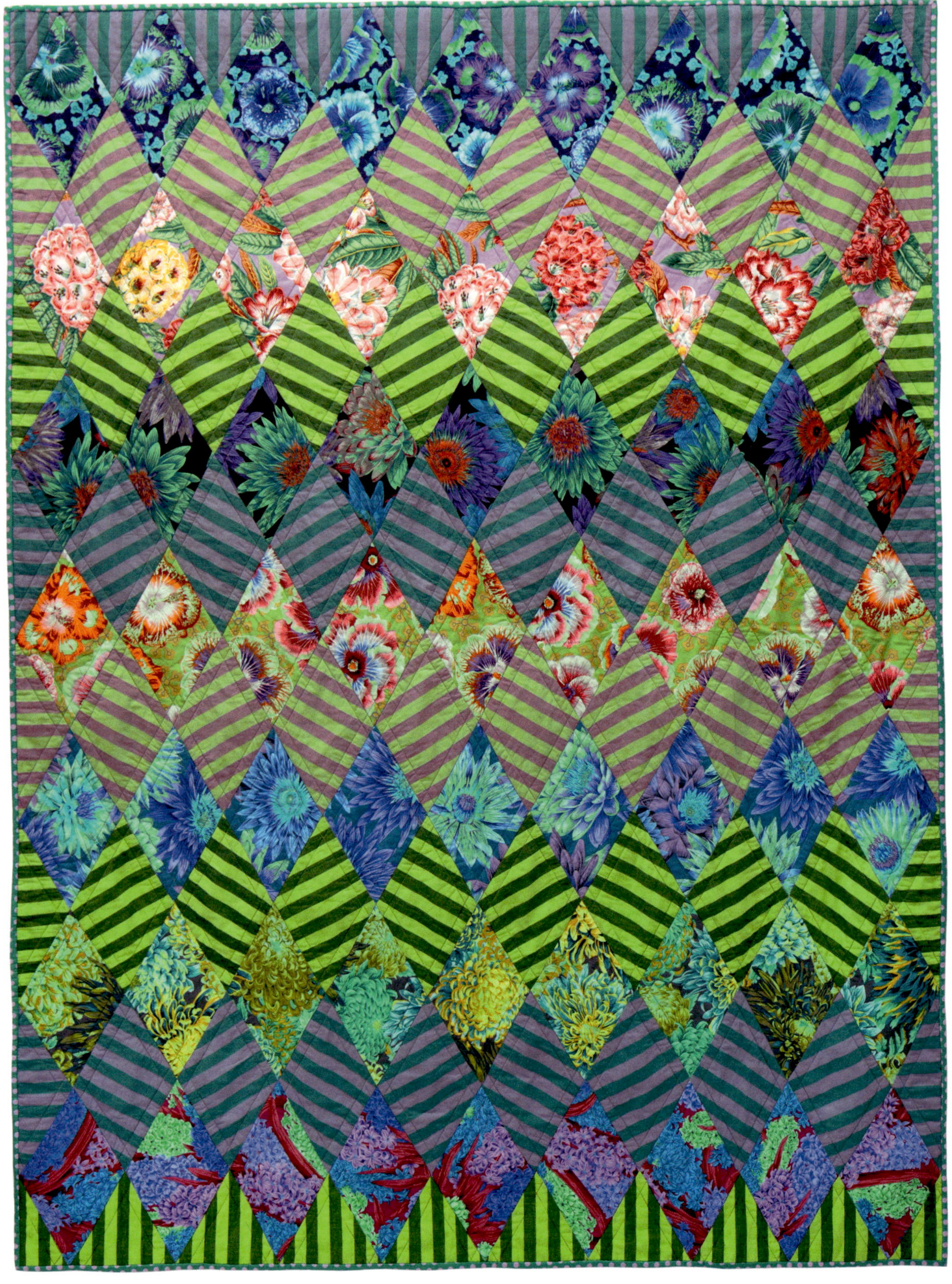

This quilt features charmingly fresh rows of striped fabrics alternating with rows of large flowered ones, inspired by flower heads seen above a picket fence.

SIZE OF FINISHED QUILT
84in x 62½in (213.3cm x 158.8cm)

FABRICS
Fabrics have been calculated at a maximum width of 40in (102cm). Fabrics have been given a number – see the Fabric Swatch Diagram for details.

Patchwork Fabrics
WIDE STRIPE
Fabric 1	Heather	1⅛yd (1.1m)
Fabric 2	Apple	⅞yd (85cm)
Fabric 3	Watermelon	1⅛yd (1.1m)

FLOATING HIBISCUS
Fabric 4	Blue	⅝yd (60cm)
Fabric 5	Green	⅝yd (60cm)

HYACINTHS
Fabric 6	Blue	⅝yd (60cm)

JAPANESE CHRYSANTHEMUM
Fabric 7	Forest	⅝yd (60cm)

TROPICAL WATER LILIES
Fabric 8	Blue	⅝yd (60cm)
Fabric 9	Dark	⅝yd (60cm)

RHODODENDRONS
Fabric 10	Lavender	⅝yd (60cm)

Backing and Binding Fabrics
MILLEFIORE extra-wide backing
Fabric 11	Jade	2yd (1.9m)

SPOT
Fabric 12	Guava	⅝yd (60cm)

Batting
94in x 72in (239cm x 183cm)

TEMPLATES

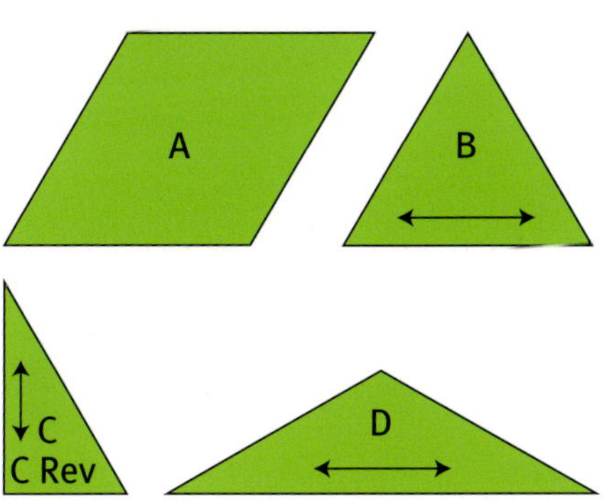

PATCHES
The quilt is made of 60° diamond, half-diamond and quarter-diamond patches, cut using Templates A, B and C/C Rev. Long half-diamond patches are cut using Template D to complete rows at the sides of the quilt.

Patches are set in horizontal rows alternating between striped Fabrics 1, 2 and 3 and flowery Fabrics 4, 5, 6, 7, 8, 9 and 10.

FABRIC SWATCH DIAGRAM

Patchwork Fabrics

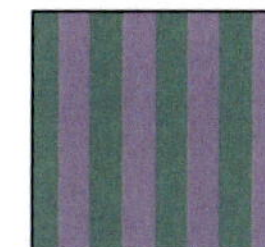
Fabric 1
WIDE STRIPE
Heather
SS01HE

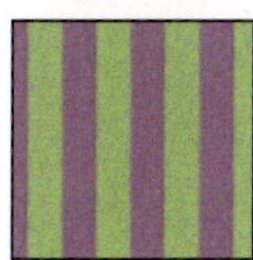
Fabric 2
WIDE STRIPE
Apple
SS01AL

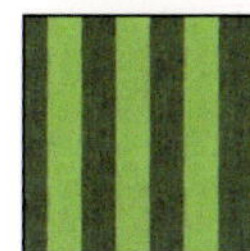
Fabric 3
WIDE STRIPE
Watermelon
SS01WL

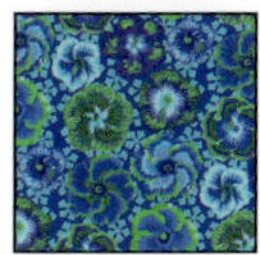
Fabric 4
FLOATING HIBISCUS
Blue
PJ122BL

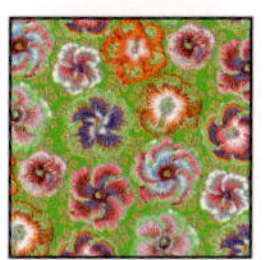
Fabric 5
FLOATING HIBISCUS
Green
PJ122GN

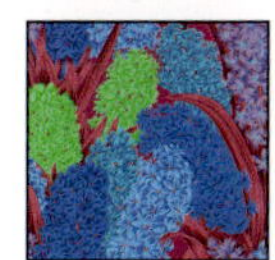
Fabric 6
HYACINTHS
Blue
PJ123BL

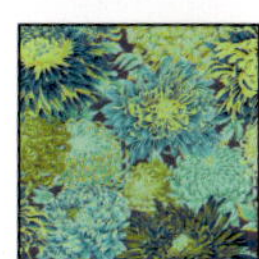
Fabric 7
JAPANESE CHRYSANTHEMUM
Forest
PJ41FO

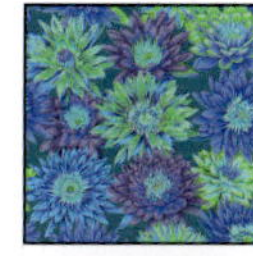
Fabric 8
TROPICAL WATER LILIES
Blue
PJ119BL

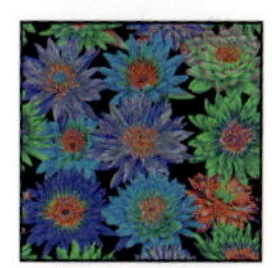
Fabric 9
TROPICAL WATER LILIES
Dark
PJ119DK

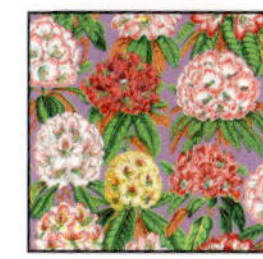
Fabric 10
RHODODENDRONS
Lavender
PJ124LV

Backing and Binding Fabrics

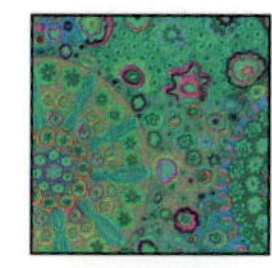
Fabric 11
MILLEFIORE
Jade
QB06JA

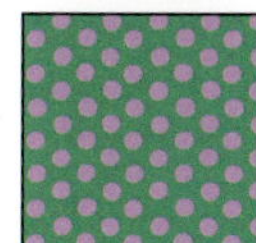
Fabric 12
SPOT
Guava
GP70GU

CUTTING OUT

Fabric is cut across the width unless otherwise stated. When cutting different pieces from the same fabric, always cut the larger pieces first.

Diamonds

Referring to the Diamond Cutting Diagram, cut approximately half of the diamond patches using Template A Method 1 to cut 60° diamond patches across the strips and the remainder of 60° diamond patches using Method 2. Alternating the two methods allows the bias-cut edges to be sewn to a grain-line edge (strengthening the quilt and preventing stretch) Each strip will yield at least 4 full diamond A patches using either method.

Half and Quarter Diamonds

Cut half diamonds by rotating the template 180° after each cut, and cut quarter diamonds and reverse quarter diamonds, if required, from the remaining pieces.

Diamonds, Half Diamonds and Quarter Diamonds

Cut strips 6½in (16.5cm) wide across the width of the fabric. Cut diamond, half-diamond and quarter-diamond patches from fabrics as follows:
Fabric 1 (5 strips) 16 diamond A, 8 half-diamond B, 1 quarter-diamond C, 1 quarter-diamond C reverse;
Fabric 2 (4 strips) 16 diamond A;
Fabric 3 (5 strips) 16 diamond A, 8 half-diamond B, 1 quarter-diamond C, 1 quarter-diamond C reverse;
Fabric 4 (3 strips) 9 diamond A;
Fabric 5 (3 strips) 9 diamond A;
Fabric 6 (3 strips) 9 diamond A;
Fabric 7 (3 strips) 9 diamond A;
Fabric 8 (3 strips) 9 diamond A;
Fabric 9 (3 strips) 9 diamond A;
Fabric 10 (3 strips) 9 diamond A.

Long Half Diamonds

From each of Fabrics 1, 2 and 3 cut a strip 4¼in (10.8cm) wide. Using Template D, cut long half-diamond patches, rotating the template 180° after each one. Cut 4 long half-diamond patches from each fabric.

Backing

Trim Fabric 11 to 94in x 72in (239cm x 183cm).

Binding

From Fabric 12 cut 8 strips 2½in (6.4cm) wide. Remove selvedges and sew end to end with 45° seams (see page 141).

MAKING THE QUILT

Using a design wall will help to place patches in the required layout.
Use ¼in (6mm) seams throughout.

Quilt Assembly

Referring to the Quilt Assembly Diagram and quilt photograph, lay out the flower Template A diamonds in 7 rows of 9, alternating between cutting Method 1 and Method 2 diamonds. Fill in the rows of striped Template A diamonds, alternating between Method 1 and Method 2 diamonds to ensure the stripes are not all parallel and to strengthen the bias edges.
Add Template B half diamonds to form the top and bottom rows, finishing each corner with a Template C or C reverse quarter diamond. Use corresponding Template D long half diamonds to complete the rows at each side.
Referring to the Quilt Assembly Diagram, sew the patches together in diagonal rows, pressing seams in opposite directions on alternate rows – odd rows to the left, even rows to the right – to allow the finished seams to lie flat.

Take care not to stretch the bias seams as you sew. Sew the diagonal rows together, aligning crossing seams.

FINISHING THE QUILT

Press the quilt top. Layer the quilt top, batting and backing, and baste together (see page 140).
Quilt as desired.
Trim the quilt edges and attach the binding (see page 141).

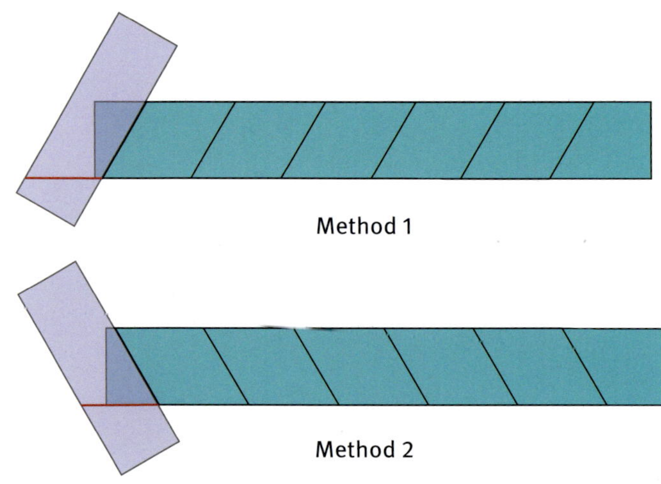

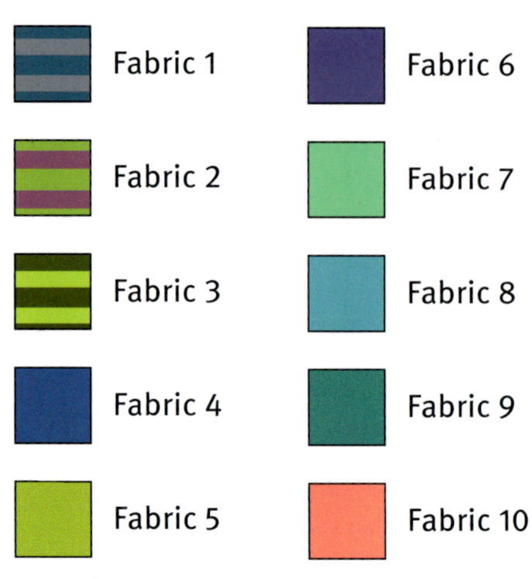

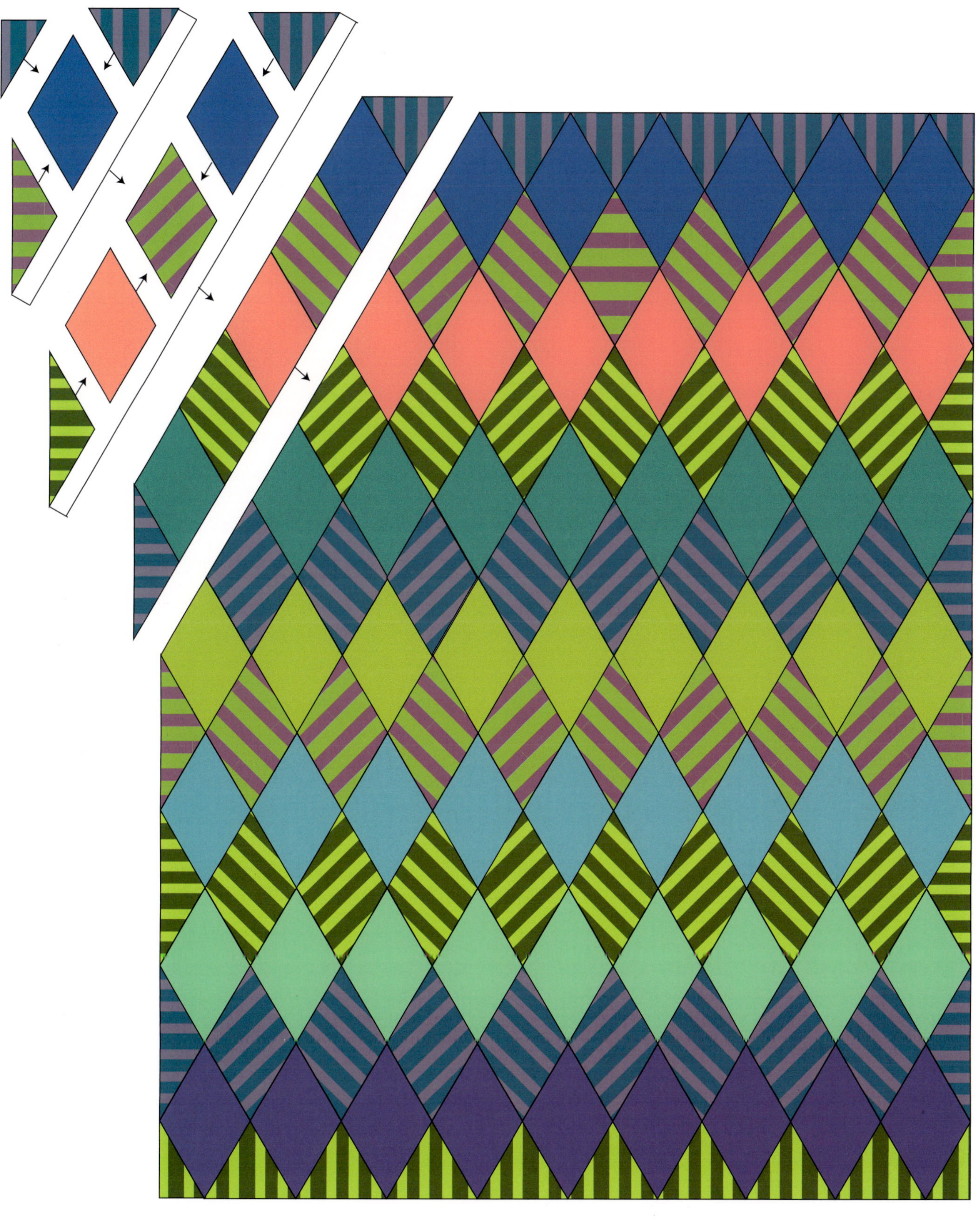

blooming octagons dark ***

Kaffe Fassett

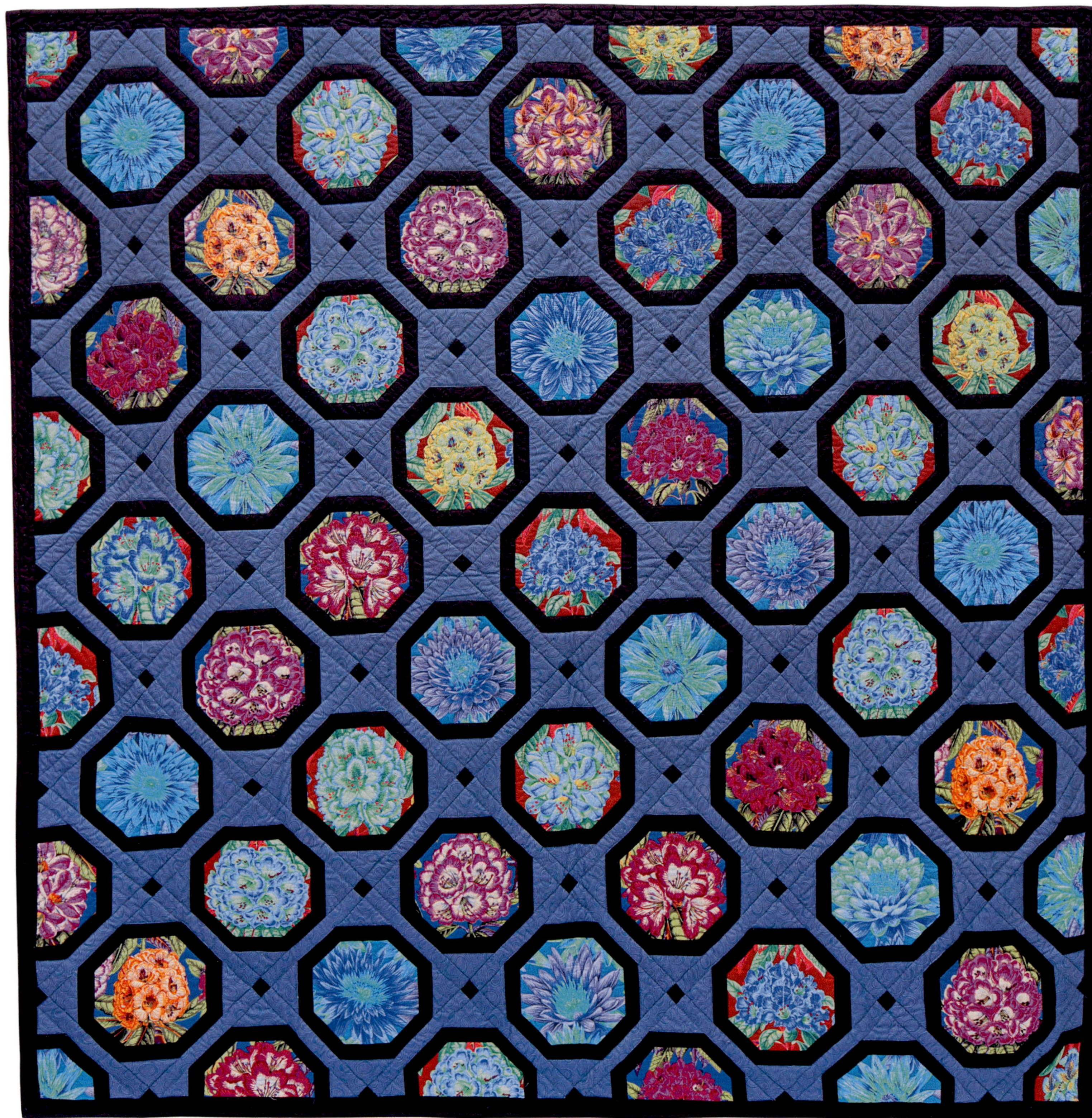

The grey-blue background to the fussy-cut octagons in Philip Jacobs' latest floral fabrics allows them to shine out beautifully, although you will have to discard (or repurpose) the fabric left over from fussy cutting the flowers. The finished effect is really worth it.

SIZE OF FINISHED QUILT
77in x 77in (196cm x 196cm)

FABRICS
Fabrics have been calculated at a maximum width of 40in (102cm). Fabrics have been given a number – see the Fabric Swatch Diagram for details.

Patchwork Fabrics
RHODODENDRONS
Fabric 1   Magenta   3yd (2.8m)
Fabric 2   Green   3yd (2.8m)
TROPICAL WATER LILIES
Fabric 3   Blue   3yd (2.8m)
ABORIGINAL DOT
Fabric 4   Denim   3¼yd (3m)
Fabric 5   Orchid   4¾yd (4.4m)
* see also Binding Fabric

Backing and Binding Fabrics
PEBBLE MOSAIC extra-wide backing
Fabric 6   Prune   2½yd (2.3m)
ABORIGINAL DOT
Fabric 5   Orchid   ¾yd (70cm)
* see also Patchwork Fabrics

Batting
87in x 87in (221cm x 221cm)

PATCHES
The feature octagons are fussy cut from 8in (20.3cm) squares and made with a dark 1in (2.5cm) border. Partial octagons around the edges of the quilt are made as whole octagons and trimmed to the required size, so there are 61 octagon blocks to make in total. The 20 edge blocks can be made from parts of the feature fabrics that don't centre blooms as well as from other parts of the fabric. Blocks are set on point in diagonal rows on a blue/grey background with narrow sashing strips punctuated with small, dark sashing squares.

CUTTING OUT
Fabric is cut across the width unless otherwise stated. When cutting different pieces from the same fabric, always cut the larger pieces first.

Feature Fabric Blooms
From Fabrics 1, 2 and 3 fussy cut 61 squares at 8in (20.3cm), 20–21 from each fabric, with a bloom centred in each square.
Note: Choose the blooms you like best in each fabric – it is not necessary to copy exactly the blooms and their positions in our quilt. Note that the squares will be set on point, so if you want to position the blooms directionally on the quilt, fussy cut the squares on point. Remember that 20 of the squares will be trimmed down to half- or quarter-squares around the edges of the quilt, so use the fabric accordingly. Extra fabric has been allowed for fussy cutting.

Octagon Borders and Sashing Squares
From Fabric 5 cut as follows:
5 strips 10in (25.4cm) wide and cross cut 122 rectangles 10in x 1½in (25.4cm x 3.8cm). Each strip will yield 26 rectangles;
5 strips 8in (20.3cm) wide and cross cut 122 rectangles 8in x 1½in (20.3cm x 3.8cm). Each strip will yield 26 rectangles;
18 strips 2¾in (7cm) wide and cross cut 244 squares at 2¾in (7cm) for the octagon corners. Each strip will yield 14 squares;
3 strips 1½in (3.8cm) wide and cross cut 60 squares at 1½in (3.8cm) for sashing squares. Each strip will yield 26 squares.

Background Sashing and Triangles
From Fabric 4 cut as follows:
4 strips 10in (25.4cm) wide and cross cut 100 rectangles 10in x 1½in (25.4cm x 3.8cm). Each strip will yield 26 rectangles;
21 strips 3¼in (8.3cm) wide and cross cut 244 squares at 3¼in (8.3cm). Each strip will yield 12 squares.

Patchwork Fabrics

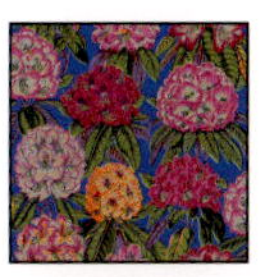
Fabric 1
RHODODENDRONS
Magenta
PJ124MG

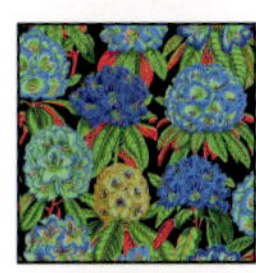
Fabric 2
RHODODENDRONS
Green
PJ124GN

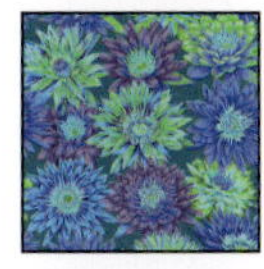
Fabric 3
TROPICAL WATER LILIES
Blue
PJ119BL

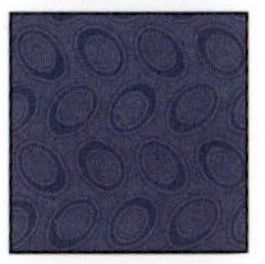
Fabric 4
ABORIGINAL DOT
Denim
GP71DM

Fabric 5
ABORIGINAL DOT
Orchid
GP71OD

Backing and Binding Fabrics

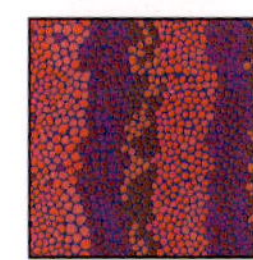
Fabric 6
PEBBLE MOSAIC
Prune
QM04PV

Fabric 5
ABORIGINAL DOT
Orchid
GP71OD

Border

From the remaining Fabric 5 cut 8 strips 1¾in (4.4cm) wide, remove selvedges and sew end to end. From the length, cut as follows:
2 lengths 77¼in (196.2cm) long for the side borders;
2 lengths 74¼in (188.6cm) long for the top and bottom borders.

Backing

Trim Fabric 6 to 87in x 87in (221cm x 221cm).

Binding

From Fabric 5 cut 9 strips 2½in (6.4cm) wide. Remove selvedges and sew end to end with 45° seams (see page 141).

MAKING THE QUILT

Using a design wall will help to place patches in the required layout.
Use ¼in (6mm) seams throughout.

Making the Blocks

Referring to the Block Assembly Diagram and the quilt photograph, position a Fabric 5 octagon border square, right sides together, on each corner of a large feature square and sew diagonally from corner to corner (a). Trim off the excess fabric, leaving a ¼in (6mm) seam allowance and press seams towards the corners (b).
Sew shorter Fabric 5 rectangles to opposite sides of the block (c), then sew longer Fabric 5 rectangles to the remaining 2 sides, pressing seams towards the borders (d).
Position a Fabric 4 background square, right sides together, on each corner of the block and sew diagonally corner to corner (e). Trim off the excess fabric, leaving a ¼in (6mm) seam allowance and press seams towards the corners to complete the block (f).
Make 61 blocks.

Centre

Referring to the Quilt Assembly Diagram and the quilt photograph, lay out the blocks in diagonal rows and add sashing strips and squares between the blocks. Position the more central blooms in the quilt centre and trim the edge octagons as follows:

Side Octagons: Mark the centre line, choosing the best half to show on the quilt, then trim the block a ¼in (6mm) outside the centre line. Return the half-blocks to the layout.

Corner Octagons: Mark the centre lines in both directions and choose the preferred quarter-block to show on the quilt. Trim a ¼in (6mm) outside both centre lines and return each corner quarter-block to the layout.

Check the layout has a good balance of coloured blooms, without any noticeable 'clumping' of the same colours.
Sew together one diagonal row at a time, alternating between octagon rows and sashing rows. Press block seams towards the octagons and press sashing seams towards the sashing (away from the sashing squares). Sew the rows together, taking care to align crossing seams.

Border

Pin (to prevent stretching borders) and sew the shorter Fabric 5 top and bottom borders to the centre, press seams towards the border, then pin and sew the longer side borders to the centre to complete the quilt top.

FINISHING THE QUILT

Press the quilt top. Layer the quilt top, batting and backing, and baste together (see page 140).
Quilt as desired.
Trim the quilt edges and attach the binding (see page 141).

BLOCK ASSEMBLY DIAGRAM

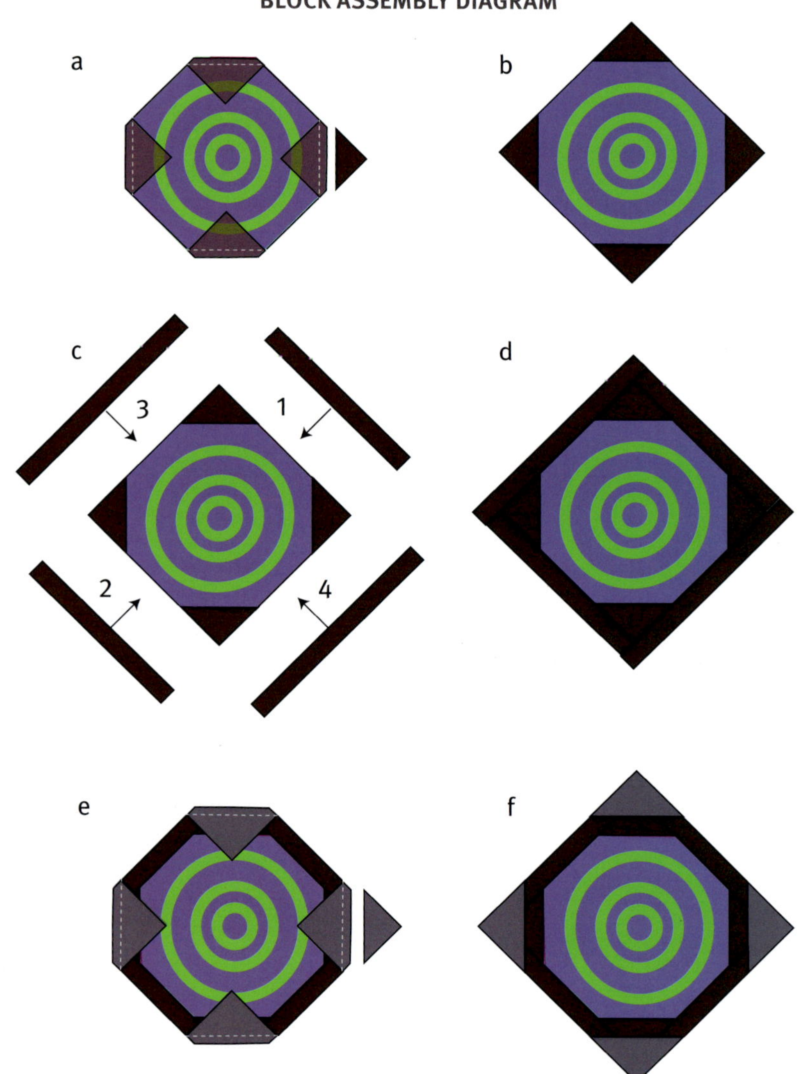

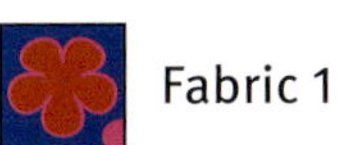 Fabric 1

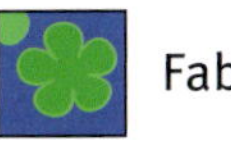 Fabric 2

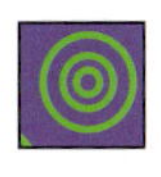 Fabric 3

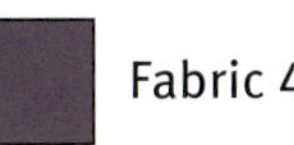 Fabric 4

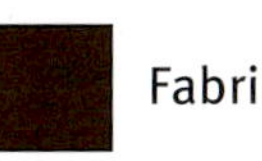 Fabric 5

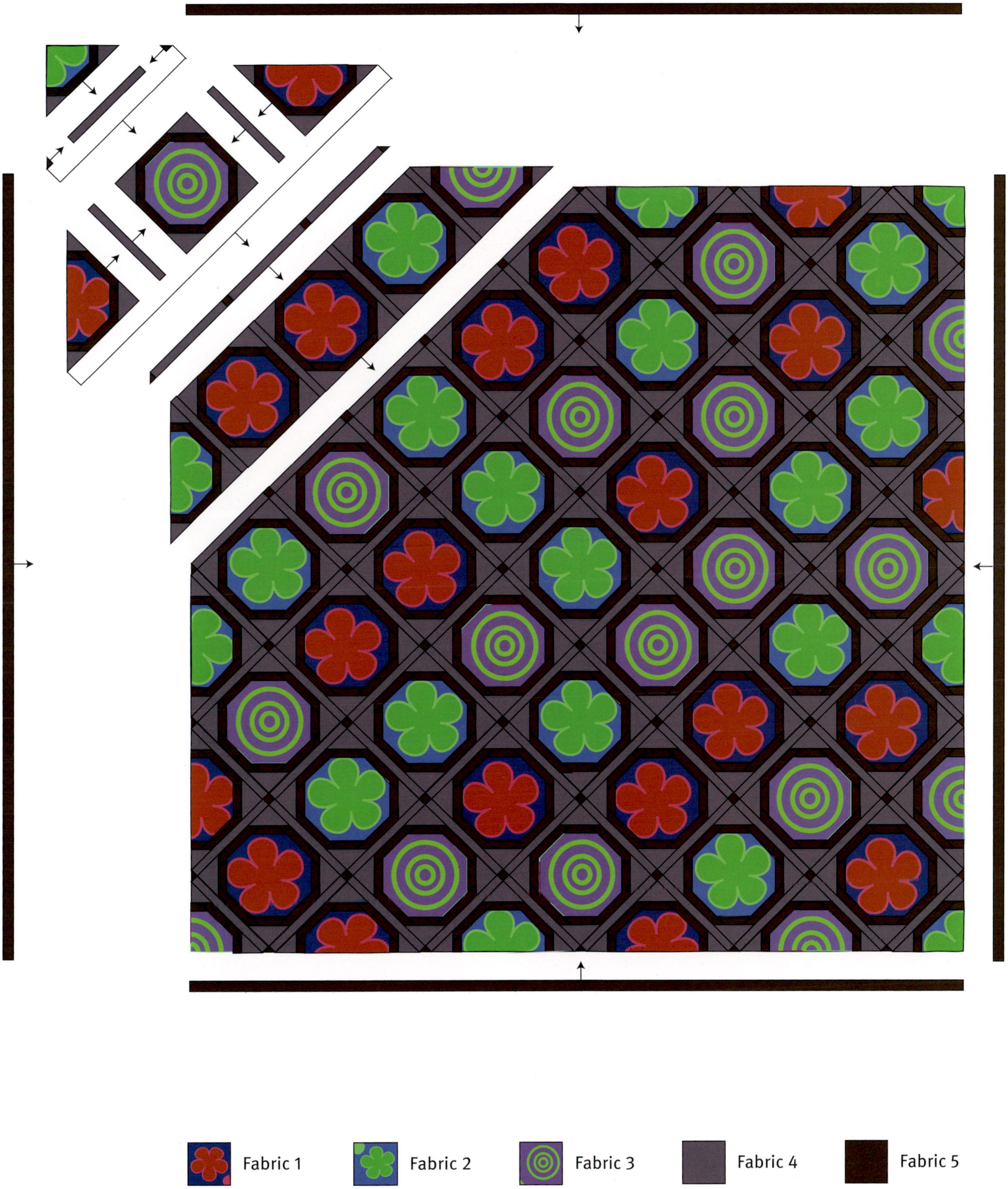

blooming octagons pastel ***

Kaffe Fassett

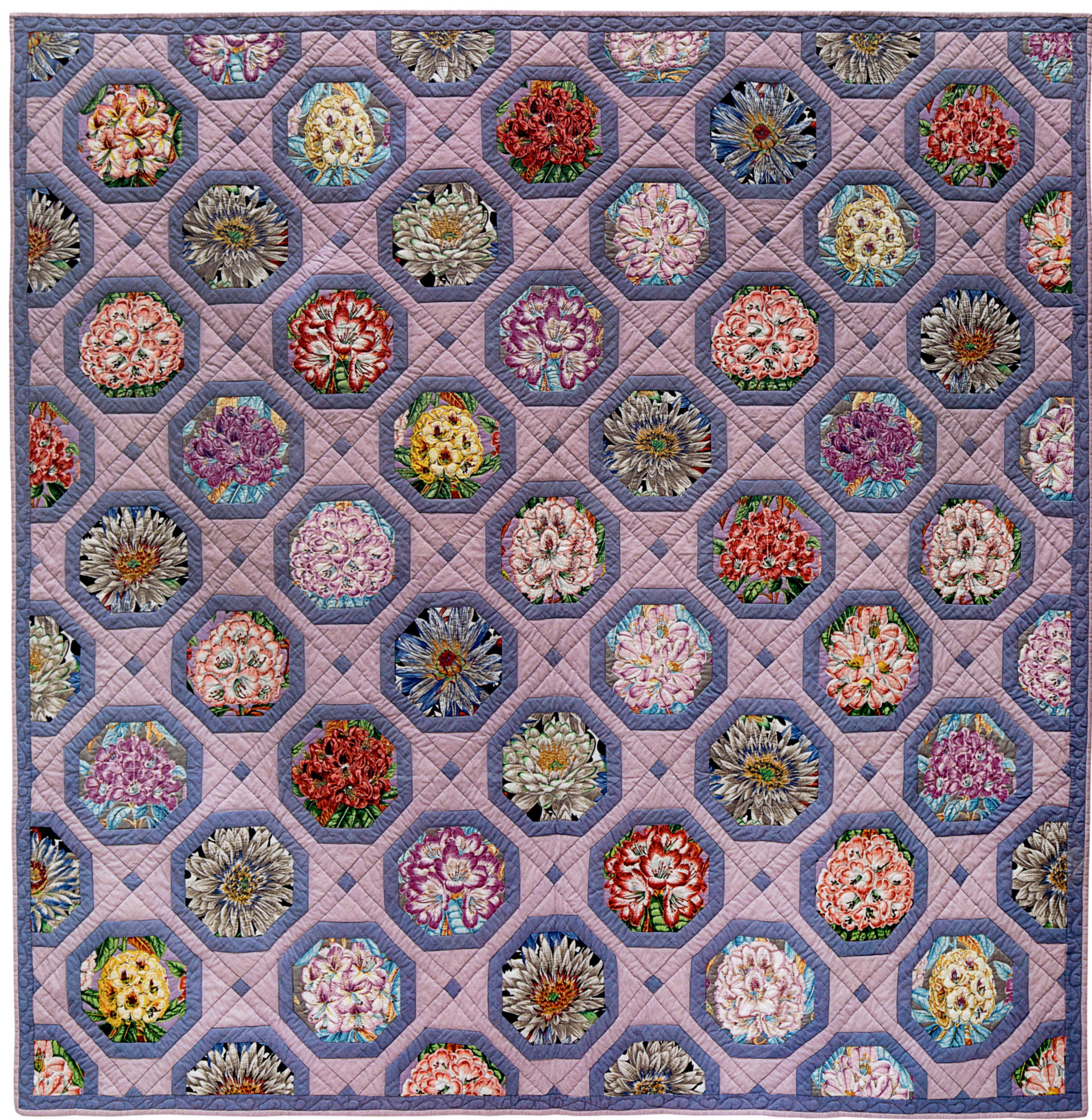

This pastel version of *Blooming Octagons Dark* uses softer colourways of Philip Jacobs' Rhododendrons and Tropical Water Lily prints along with some of my more pastel toned shot cottons.

Follow the instructions for *Blooming Octagons Dark* on page 94.

Note: The only notable difference to the instructions is that the binding is cut from Fabric 4 instead of Fabric 5.

SIZE OF FINISHED QUILT
77in x 77in (196cm x 196cm)

FABRICS
Fabrics have been calculated at a maximum width of 40in (102cm). Fabrics have been given a number – see the Fabric Swatch Diagram for details.

Patchwork Fabrics
RHODODENDRONS

Fabric 1	Grey	3yd (2.8m)
Fabric 2	Lavender	3yd (2.8m)

TROPICAL WATER LILIES

| Fabric 3 | Contrast | 3yd (2.8m) |

SHOT COTTON

| Fabric 4 | Dawn | 3¼yd (3m) |

* see also Binding Fabric

| Fabric 5 | Opal | 4¾yd (4.4m) |

Backing and Binding Fabrics
JAPANESE CHRYSANTHEMUM extra-wide backing

| Fabric 6 | Magenta | 2½yd (2.3m) |

SHOT COTTON

| Fabric 4 | Dawn | ¾yd (70cm) |

* see also Patchwork Fabrics

Batting
87in x 87in (221cm x 221cm)

Patchwork Fabrics

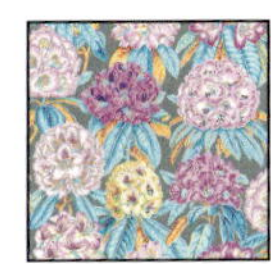

Fabric 1
RHODODENDRONS
Grey
PJ124GY

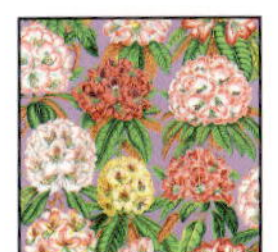

Fabric 2
RHODODENDRONS
Lavender
PJ124LV

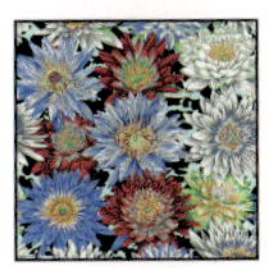

Fabric 3
TROPICAL WATER LILIES
Contrast
PJ119CN

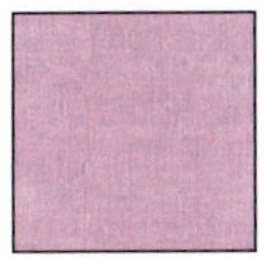

Fabric 4
SHOT COTTON
Dawn
SC121DN

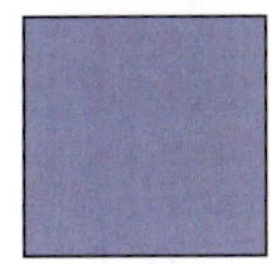

Fabric 5
SHOT COTTON
Opal
SC114OP

Backing and Binding Fabrics

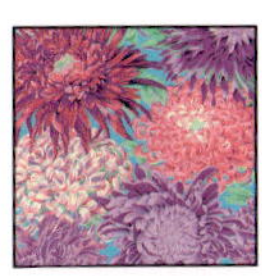

Fabric 6
JAPANESE CHRYSANTHEMUM
Magenta
QJ03MG

Fabric 4
SHOT COTTON
Dawn
SC121DN

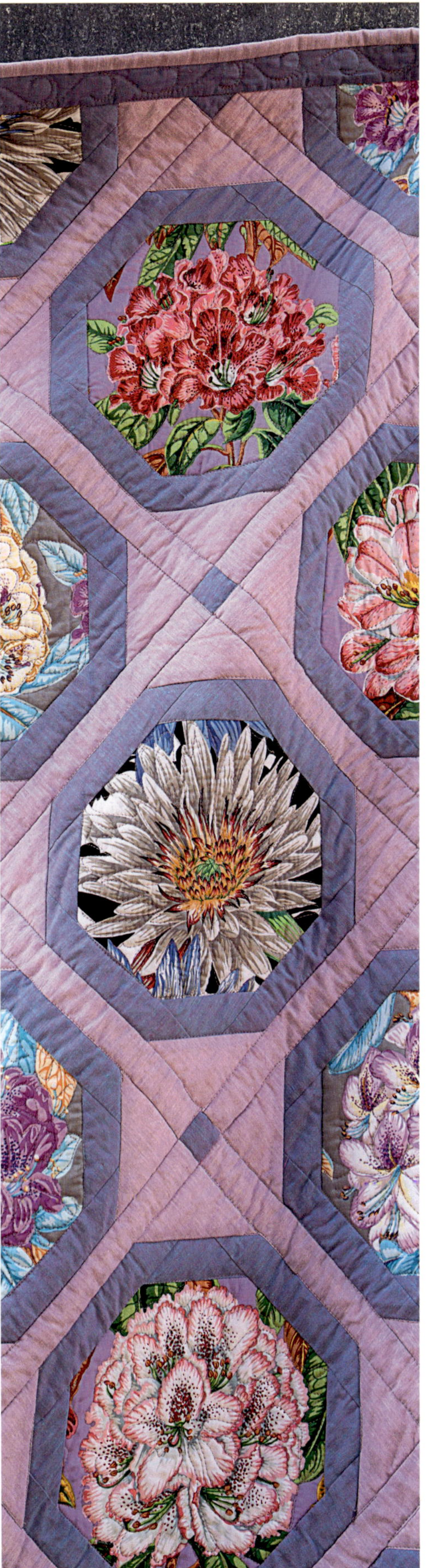

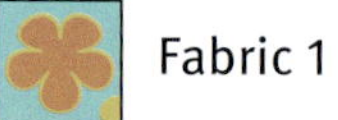 Fabric 1
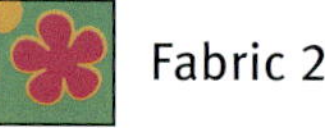 Fabric 2
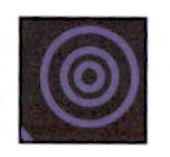 Fabric 3
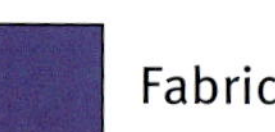 Fabric 4
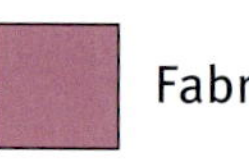 Fabric 5

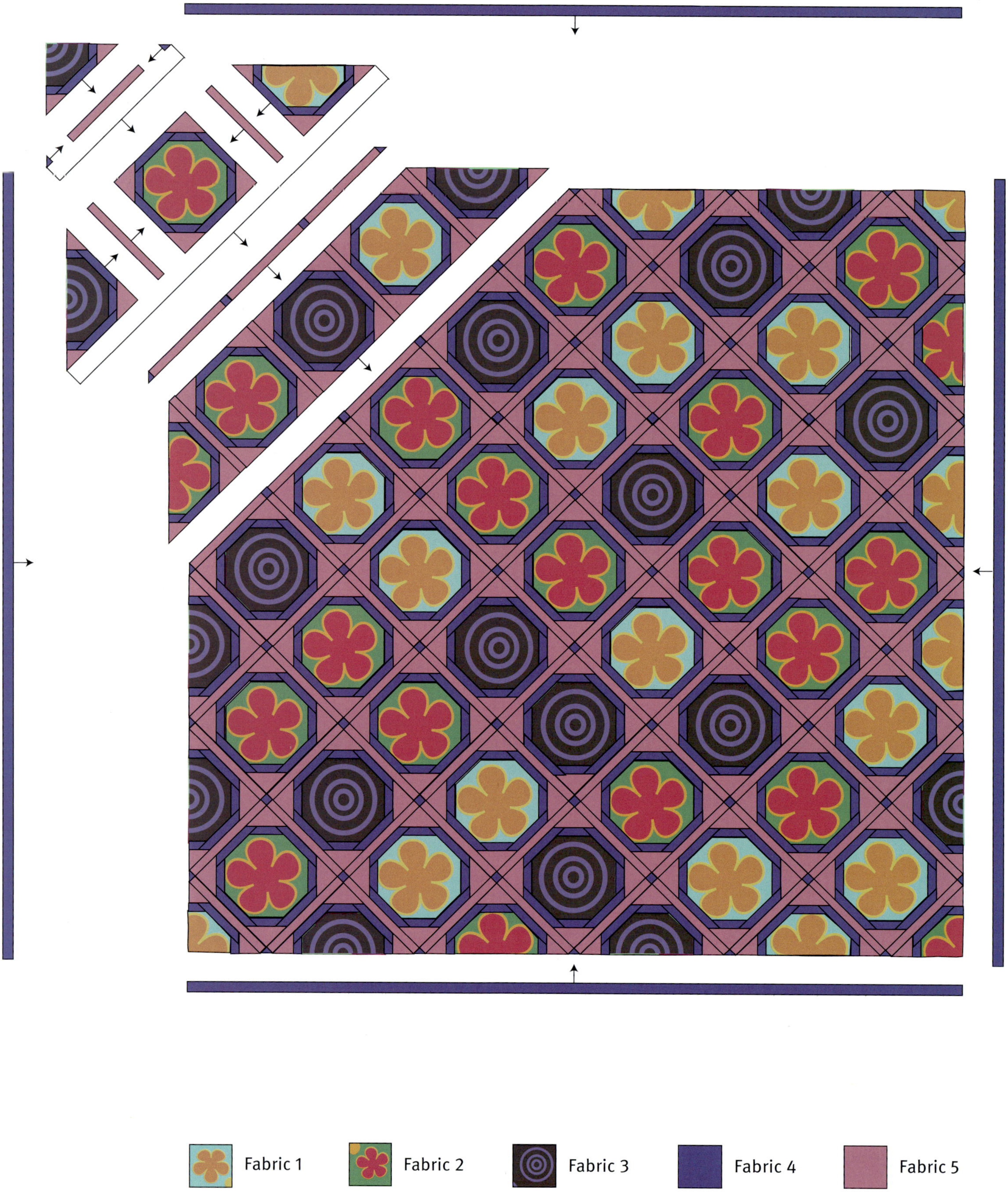

faded shuttles **

Kaffe Fassett

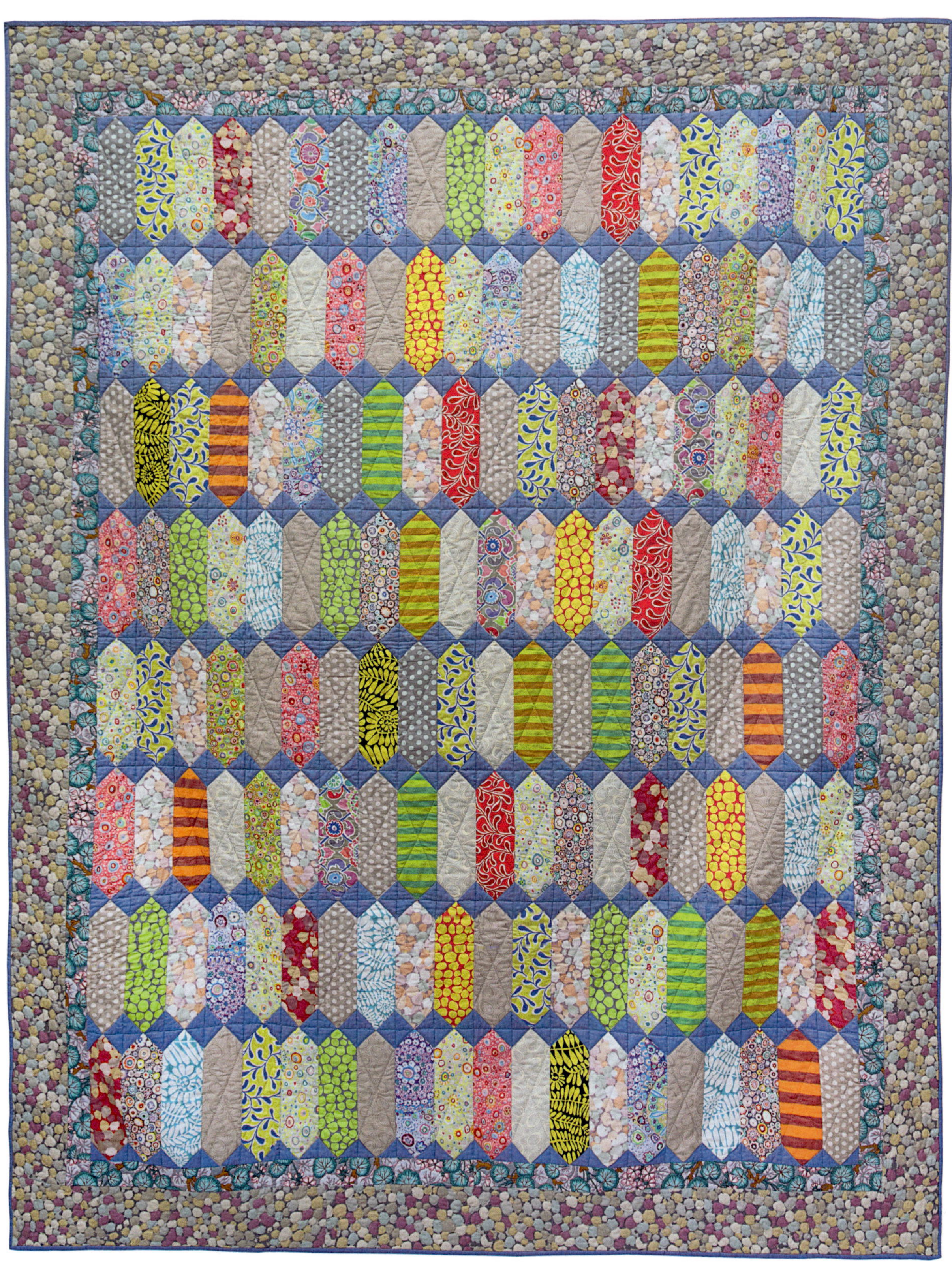

The shuttle blocks in this quilt are simply elongated snowball blocks. With just two shapes to cut, it is relatively easy to make and a great showcase for some of our recent smaller prints, along with some firm favourites.

SIZE OF FINISHED QUILT
94in x 74in (239cm x 188cm)

FABRICS
Fabrics have been calculated at a maximum width of 40in (102cm). Fabrics have been given a number – see the Fabric Swatch Diagram for details.

Patchwork Fabrics
SHOT COTTON
Fabric 1   Opal   2yd (1.9m)
* see also Binding Fabric
CLIMBING GERANIUMS
Fabric 2   Grey   ⅝yd (60cm)
REFLECTIONS
Fabric 3   Putty   1⅜yd (1.3m)
Fabric 4   Neutral   ¼yd (25cm)
Fabric 5   Pastel   ½yd (50cm)
PAPERWEIGHT
Fabric 6   Lime   ¼yd (25cm)
Fabric 7   Pastel   ⅜yd (40cm)
ROMAN GLASS
Fabric 8   Pastel   ½yd (50cm)
Fabric 9   Pink   ⅜yd (40cm)
MILLEFIORE
Fabric 10   Lilac   ⅜yd (40cm)
SPOT
Fabric 11   Silver   ½yd (50cm)
Fabric 12   Steel   ⅜yd (40cm)
JUMBLE
Fabric 13   Lemon   ¼yd (25cm)
Fabric 14   Lime   ¼yd (25cm)
ABORIGINAL DOT
Fabric 15   Cream   ⅜yd (40cm)
Fabric 16   Silver   ½yd (50cm)
FRONDS
Fabric 17   White   ⅜yd (40cm)
Fabric 18   Yellow   ¼yd (25cm)
NARROW STRIPE
Fabric 19   Gooseberry   ¼yd (25cm)
Fabric 20   Sulfur   ¼yd (25cm)
WIDE STRIPE
Fabric 21   Cantaloupe   ¼yd (25cm)
TUDOR
Fabric 22   Pastel   ¼yd (25cm)
TWIG
Fabric 23   Pink   ¼yd (25cm)
Fabric 24   Yellow   ½yd (50cm)

Backing and Binding Fabrics
FLOWER NET extra-wide backing
Fabric 25   White   2½yd (2.3m)
SHOT COTTON
Fabric 1   Opal   ¾yd (70cm)
* see also Patchwork Fabrics

Batting
104in x 84in (264cm x 213cm)

PATCHES
Blocks are elongated snowball blocks finished at 10in x 3in (25.4cm x 7.6cm). Small squares, all in the same fabric, are used to create the block corners. Blocks are set in 8 rows of 20 and bordered with a narrow inner border and a wider outer border.

This is a scrappy quilt and blocks do not need to be positioned identically to the original to have the same overall effect. We have given instructions to provide identical blocks, but you could use more or less of some fabrics, as you wish.

CUTTING OUT
Fabric is cut across the width unless otherwise stated.

Blocks
For the block corners, from Fabric 1 cut 32 strips 2in (5.1cm) wide and cross cut a total of 640 squares at 2in (5.1cm). Each strip will yield 20 squares.

For the feature block rectangles, if more than 6 rectangles are required from a fabric, cut from **wide** 10½in (26.7cm) strips (that will yield up to 11 patches per strip). For up to 6 rectangles, cut from **narrow** 3½in (8.9cm) strips (that will yield 3 patches per strip). Cut a total of 160 rectangles 10½in x 3½in (26.7cm x 8.9cm) from fabrics as follows:
Fabric 4 (2 narrow strips) 6 rectangles;
Fabric 5 (1 wide strip and 2 narrow strips) 16 rectangles;
Fabric 6 (2 narrow strips) 4 rectangles;
Fabric 7 (1 wide strip) 8 rectangles;
Fabric 8 (1 wide strip and 2 narrow strips) 16 rectangles;
Fabric 9 (1 wide strip) 8 rectangles;
Fabric 10 (1 wide strip) 8 rectangles;
Fabric 11 (1 wide strip and 1 narrow strip) 13 rectangles;
Fabric 12 (1 wide strip) 7 rectangles;
Fabric 13 (2 narrow strips) 4 rectangles;
Fabric 14 (2 narrow strips) 6 rectangles;
Fabric 15 (1 wide strip) 8 rectangles;
Fabric 16 (1 wide strip and 1 narrow strip) 13 rectangles;
Fabric 17 (1 wide strip) 8 rectangles;
Fabric 18 (1 narrow strip) 3 rectangles;
Fabric 19 (2 narrow strips) 4 rectangles;
Fabric 20 (2 narrow strips) 4 rectangles;
Fabric 21 (2 narrow strips) 4 rectangles;
Fabric 22 (2 narrow strips) 4 rectangles;
Fabric 23 (2 narrow strips) 4 rectangles;
Fabric 24 (1 wide strip and 1 narrow strip) 12 rectangles.

Inner Border
From Fabric 2 cut 8 strips 2½in (6.4cm) wide, remove selvedges and sew together end to end. From the length, cut pieces as follows:
2 pieces 80½in (204.5cm) for the side borders;
2 pieces 64½in (163.8cm) for the top and bottom borders.

Outer Border
From Fabric 3 cut 8 strips 5½in (14cm) wide, remove selvedges and sew together end to end. From the length, cut pieces as follows:
2 pieces 84½in (214.6cm) for the side borders;
2 pieces 74½in (189.2cm) for the top and bottom borders.

Backing
Trim Fabric 25 to 104in x 84in (264cm x 213cm).

Binding
From Fabric 1 cut 9 strips 2½in (6.4cm) wide. Remove selvedges and sew end to end with 45° seams (see page 141).

FABRIC SWATCH DIAGRAM

Patchwork Fabrics

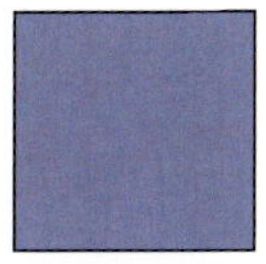
Fabric 1
SHOT COTTON
Opal
SC114OP

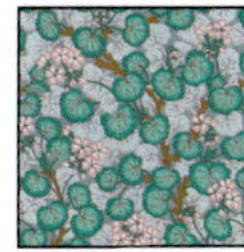
Fabric 2
CLIMBING GERANIUMS
Grey
PJ110GY

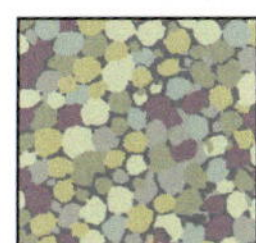
Fabric 3
REFLECTIONS
Putty
BM87PY

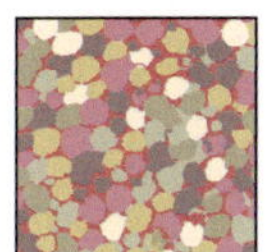
Fabric 4
REFLECTIONS
Neutral
BM87NE

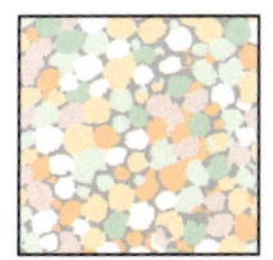
Fabric 5
REFLECTIONS
Pastel
BM87PT

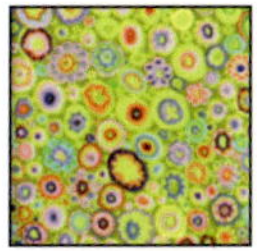
Fabric 6
PAPERWEIGHT
Lime
GP20LM

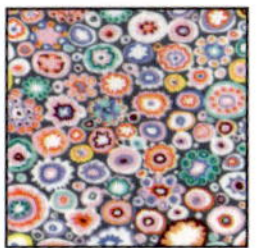
Fabric 7
PAPERWEIGHT
Pastel
GP20PT

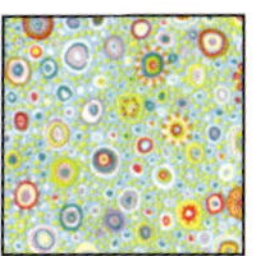
Fabric 8
ROMAN GLASS
Pastel
GP01PT

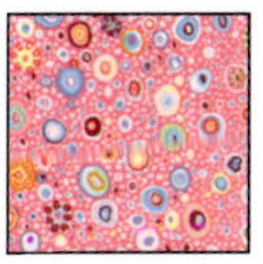
Fabric 9
ROMAN GLASS
Pink
GP01PK

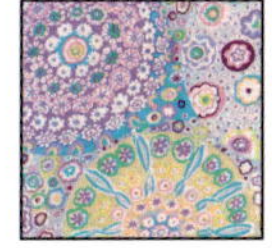
Fabric 10
MILLEFIORE
Lilac
GP92LI

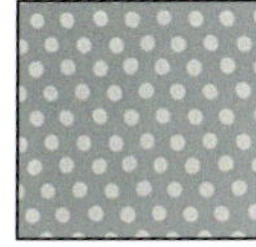
Fabric 11
SPOT
Silver
GP70SV

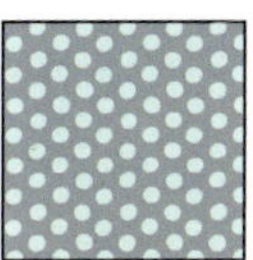
Fabric 12
SPOT
Steel
GP70ST

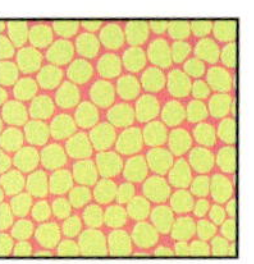
Fabric 13
JUMBLE
Lemon
BM53LE

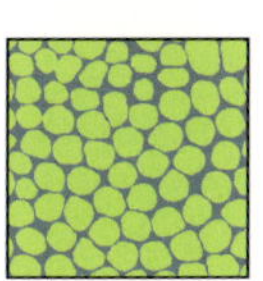
Fabric 14
JUMBLE
Lime
BM53LM

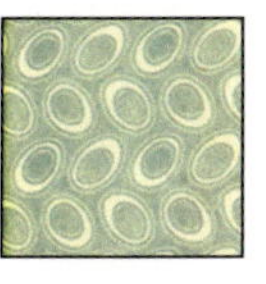
Fabric 15
ABORIGINAL DOT
Cream
GP71CM

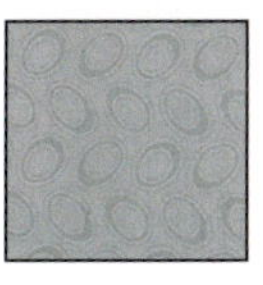
Fabric 16
ABORIGINAL DOT
Silver
GP71SV

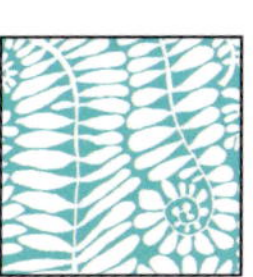
Fabric 17
FRONDS
White
BM85WH

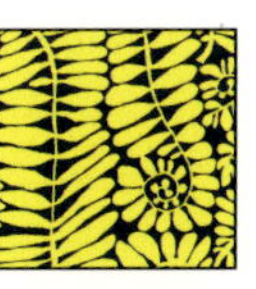
Fabric 18
FRONDS
Yellow
BM85YE

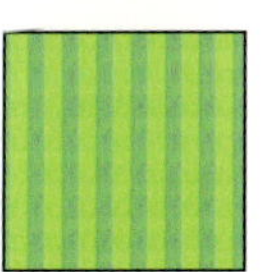
Fabric 19
NARROW STRIPE
Gooseberry
SS02GY

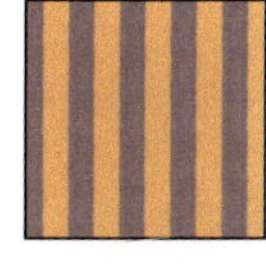
Fabric 20
NARROW STRIPE
Sulfur
SS02SU

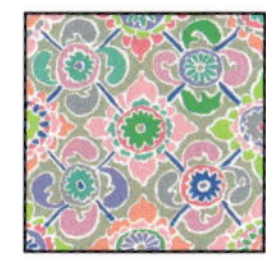
Fabric 21
WIDE STRIPE
Cantaloupe
SS01CA

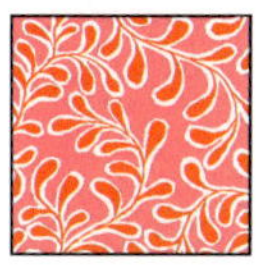
Fabric 22
TUDOR
Pastel
GP195PT

Fabric 23
TWIG
Pink
GP196PK

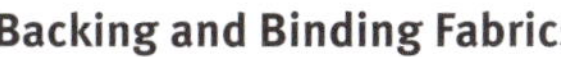
Fabric 24
TWIG
Yellow
GP196YE

Backing and Binding Fabrics

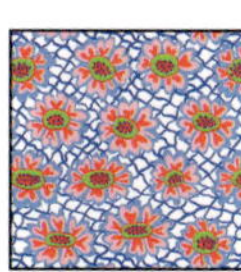
Fabric 25
FLOWER NET
White
QM03WH

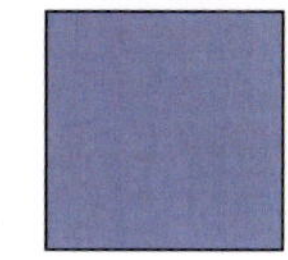
Fabric 1
SHOT COTTON
Opal
SC114OP

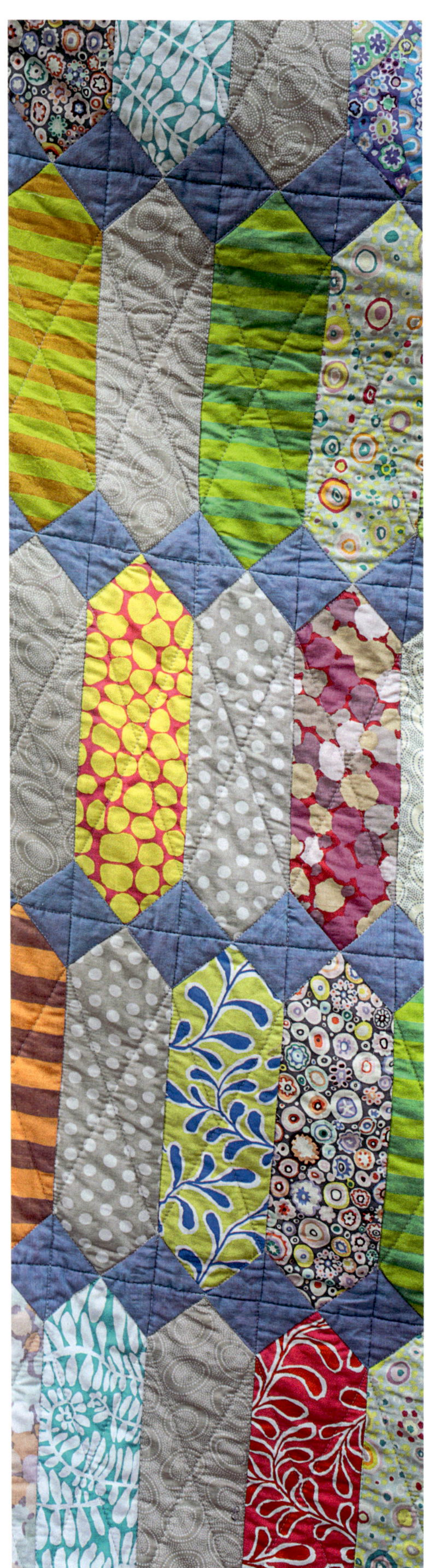

MAKING THE QUILT

Using a design wall will help to place patches in the required layout.
Use ¼in (6mm) seams throughout.

Making the Blocks

Referring to the Block Assembly Diagram, take a rectangle and 4 small squares. Position a small square right sides together on each corner of the rectangle and sew diagonally (a). Trim off the excess fabric, leaving a ¼in (6mm) seam allowance (b). Press seams towards the corners to finish the block (c). Make 160 blocks.

Centre

Referring to the Quilt Assembly Diagram and the quilt photograph, or, if deciding on your own mix of blocks, lay out the blocks in 8 rows of 20. Stand back and check there are no areas with too much of the same colour or tone. Once happy with the overall layout, sew together one row at a time, pressing seams in opposite directions on alternate rows – odd rows to the left, even rows to the right – to allow the finished seams to lie flat. Sew the rows together, taking care to align crossing seams.

Borders

Pin (to prevent stretching borders) and sew the longer side inner border pieces to the centre, press seams towards the border, then pin and sew the top and bottom inner border pieces to the centre. Repeat with the outer border pieces, first sides, then top and bottom, to complete the quilt top.

FINISHING THE QUILT

Press the quilt top. Layer the quilt top, batting and backing, and baste together (see page 140).
Quilt as desired.
Trim the quilt edges and attach the binding (see page 141).

BLOCK ASSEMBLY DIAGRAM

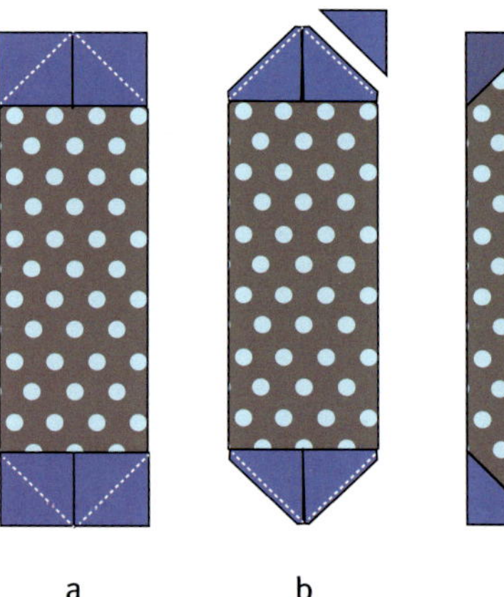

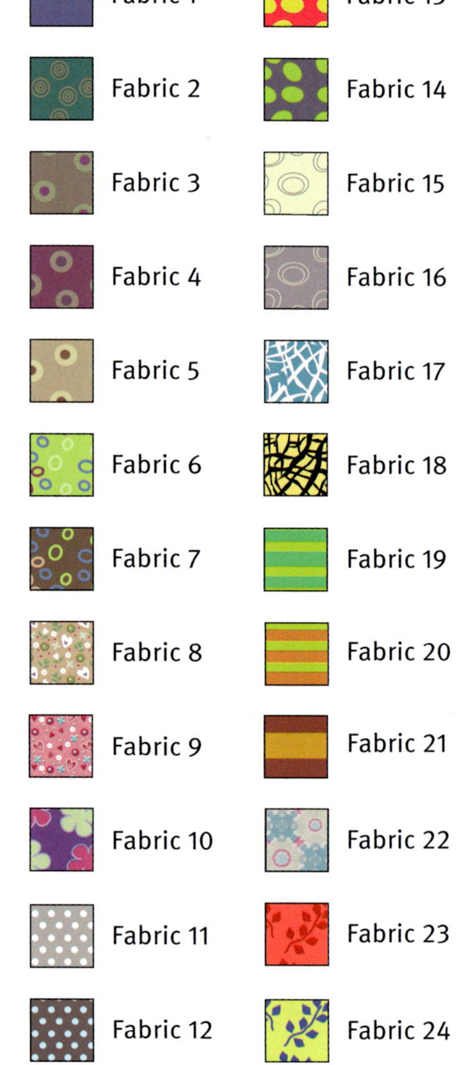

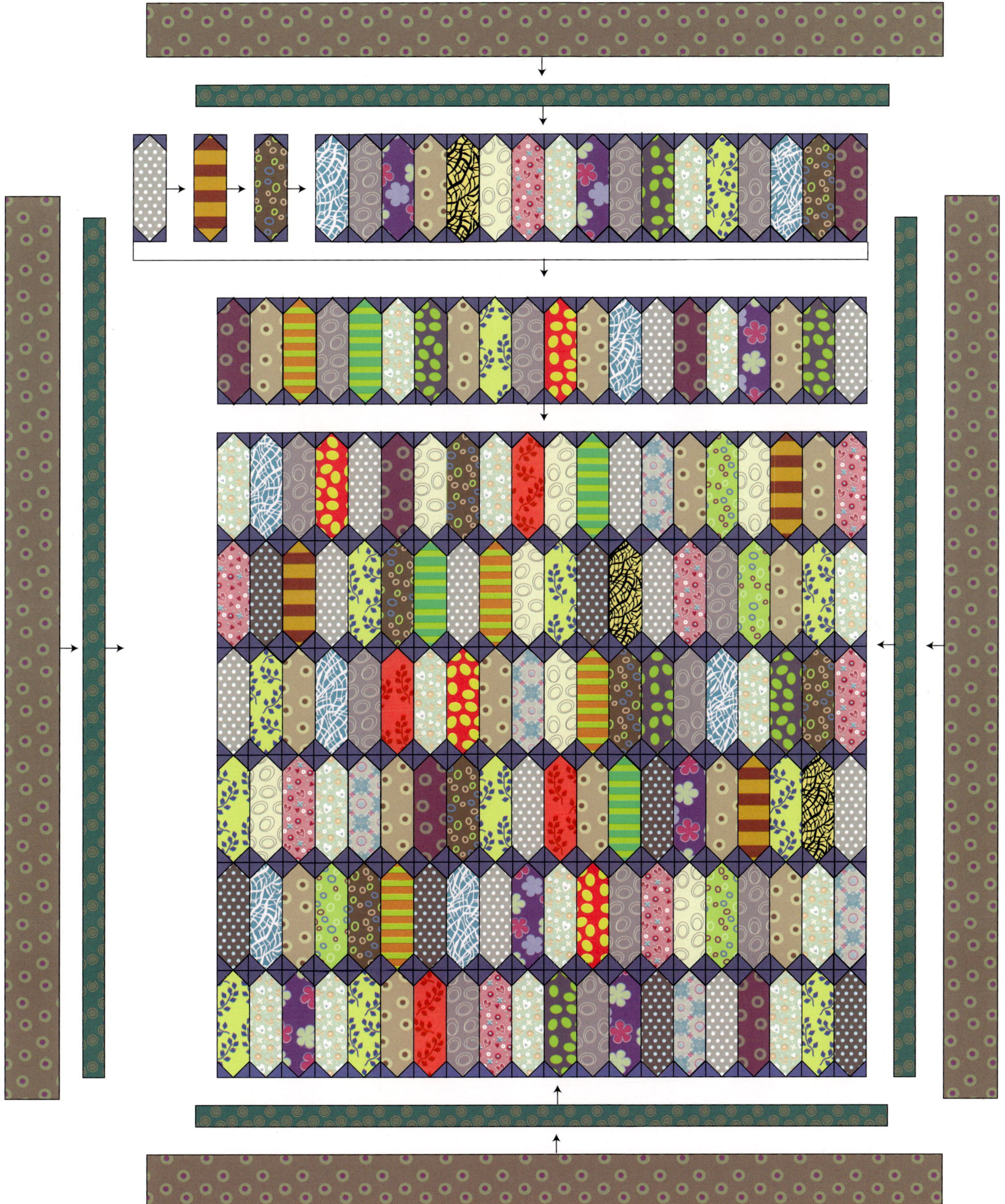

bean stalks **

Kaffe Fassett

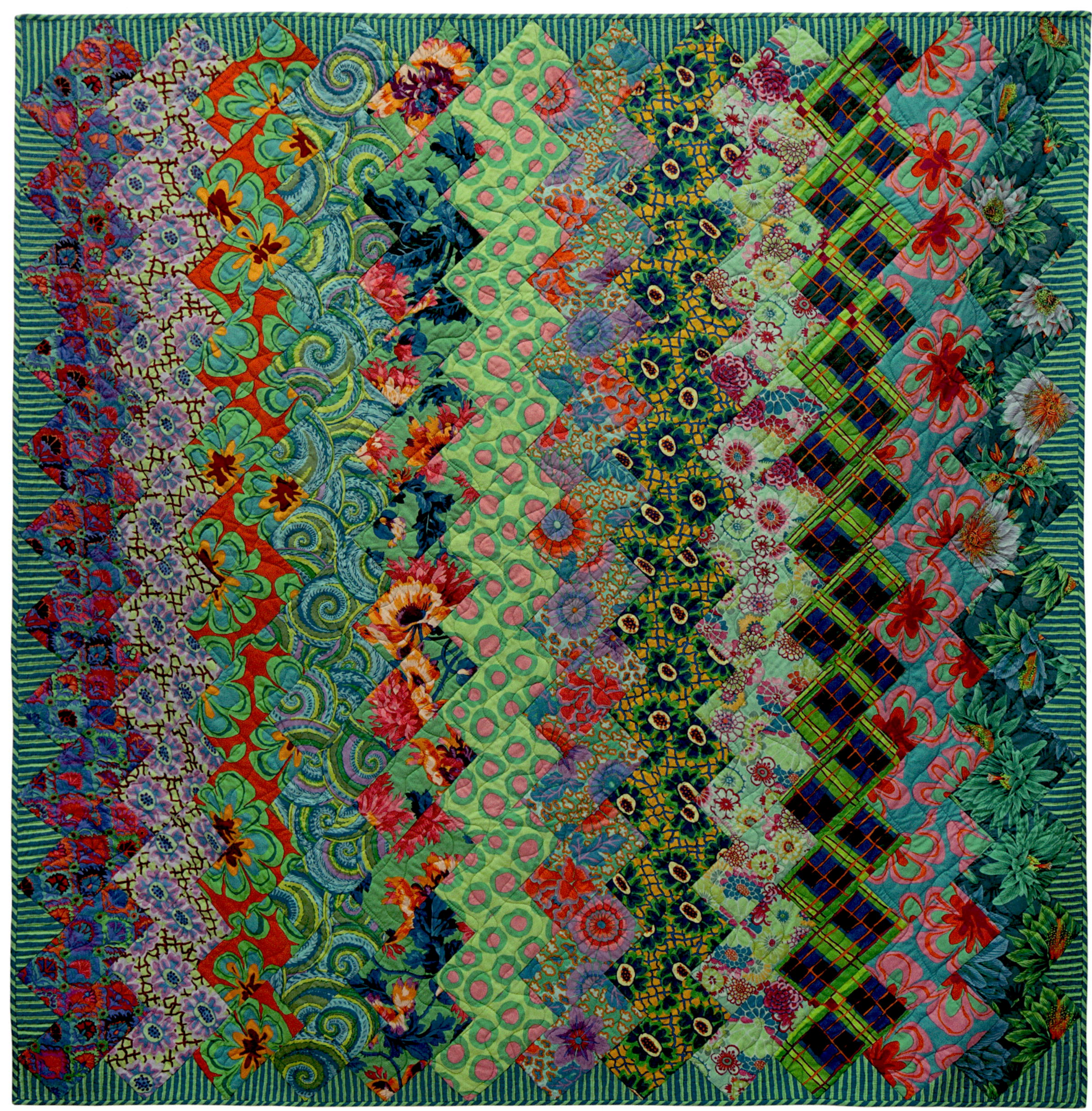

This fresh, country-style take on Judy Baldwin's *Diagonal Bricks* quilt from *Quilt Grandeur*, showcases a selection of our recent floral and graphic fabrics in shades of cool green.

SIZE OF FINISHED QUILT
71in x 71in (180cm x 180cm)

FABRICS
Fabrics have been calculated at a maximum width of 40in (102cm). Fabrics have been given a number – see the Fabric Swatch Diagram for details.

Patchwork Fabrics

COMB STRIPE		
Fabric 1	Teal	¾yd (70cm)
* see also Binding Fabric		
STEP FLOWER		
Fabric 2	Multi	½yd (50cm)
FLOWER NET		
Fabric 3	Lime	½yd (50cm)
FUNKY FLORA		
Fabric 4	Watermelon	½yd (50cm)
CURLY BASKETS		
Fabric 5	Green	½yd (50cm)
GARDEN PARTY		
Fabric 6	Pink	½yd (50cm)
FISH LIPS		
Fabric 7	Green	½yd (50cm)
DREAM		
Fabric 8	Aqua	½yd (50cm)
FLOWER NET		
Fabric 9	Citrus	½yd (50cm)
ASIAN CIRCLES		
Fabric 10	Green	½yd (50cm)
CHECKMATE		
Fabric 11	Green	½yd (50cm)
FUNKY FLORA		
Fabric 12	Aqua	½yd (50cm)
CACTUS FLOWER		
Fabric 13	Green	½yd (50cm)

Backing and Binding Fabrics

ENCHANTED extra-wide backing

Fabric 14	Red	2¼yd (2.1m)
COMB STRIPE		
Fabric 1	Teal	¾yd (70cm)

* see also Patchwork Fabrics

Batting
81in x 81in (206cm x 206cm)

FABRIC SWATCH DIAGRAM

Patchwork Fabrics

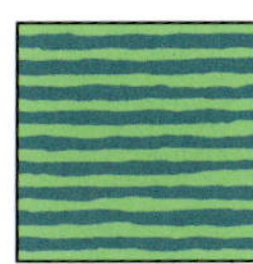

Fabric 1
COMB STRIPE
Teal
BM84TE

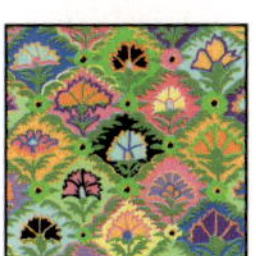

Fabric 2
STEP FLOWER
Multi
GP202MU

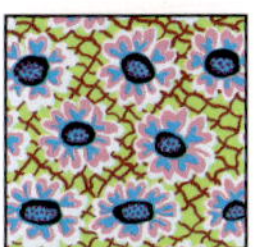

Fabric 3
FLOWER NET
Lime
BM81LM

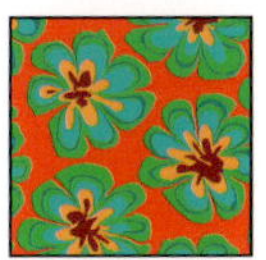

Fabric 4
FUNKY FLORA
Watermelon
BM11WL

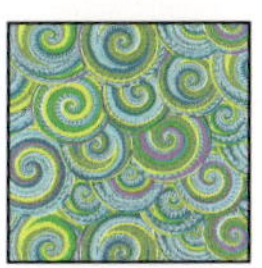

Fabric 5
CURLY BASKETS
Green
PJ66GN

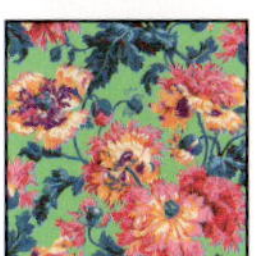

Fabric 6
GARDEN PARTY
Pink
PJ20PK

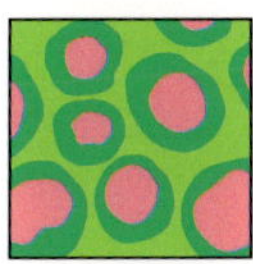

Fabric 7
FISH LIPS
Green
BM07GN

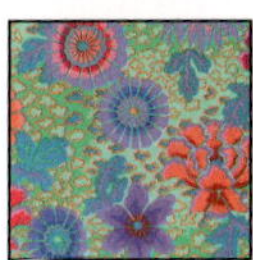

Fabric 8
DREAM
Aqua
GP148AQ

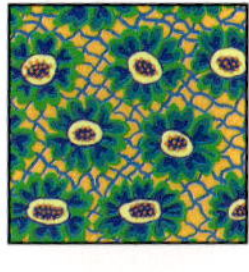

Fabric 9
FLOWER NET
Citrus
BM81CT

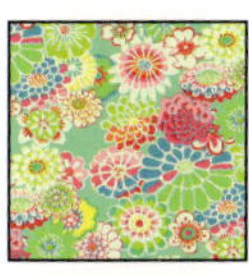

Fabric 10
ASIAN CIRCLES
Green
GP89GN

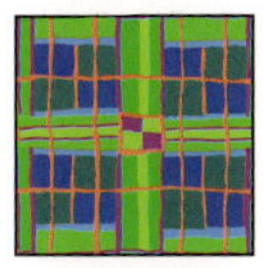

Fabric 11
CHECKMATE
Green
BM86GN

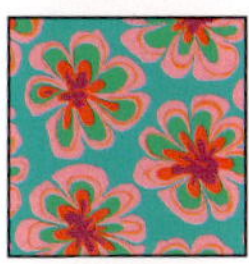

Fabric 12
FUNKY FLORA
Aqua
BM11AQ

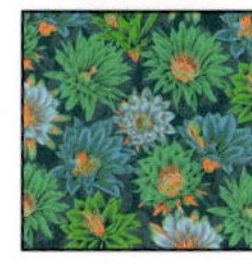

Fabric 13
CACTUS FLOWER
Green
PJ96GN

Backing and Binding Fabrics

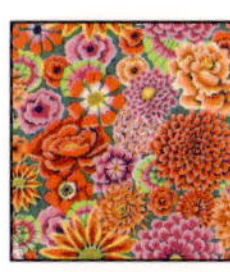

Fabric 14
ENCHANTED
Red
QP08RD

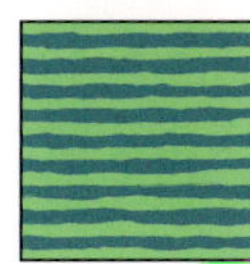

Fabric 1
COMB STRIPE
Teal
BM84TE

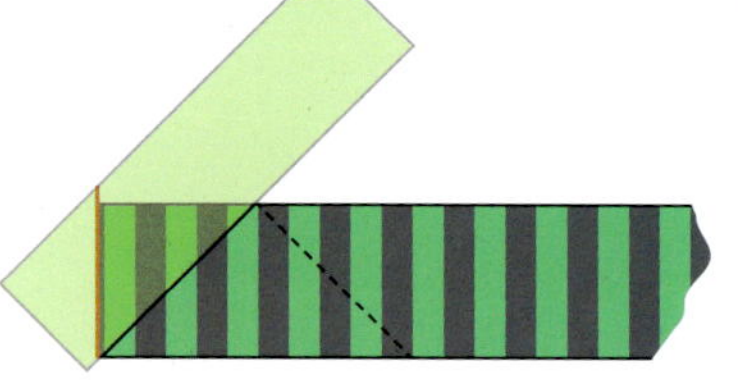

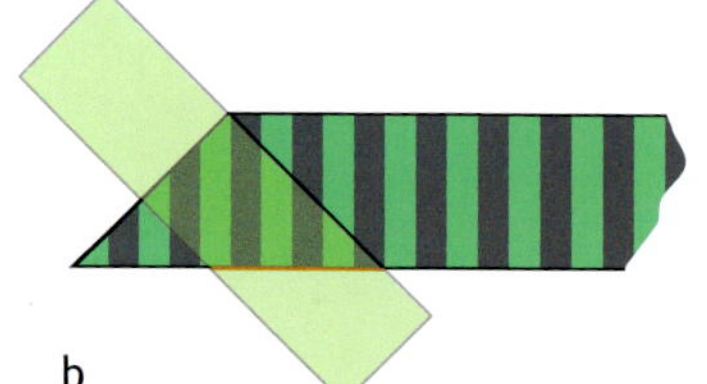

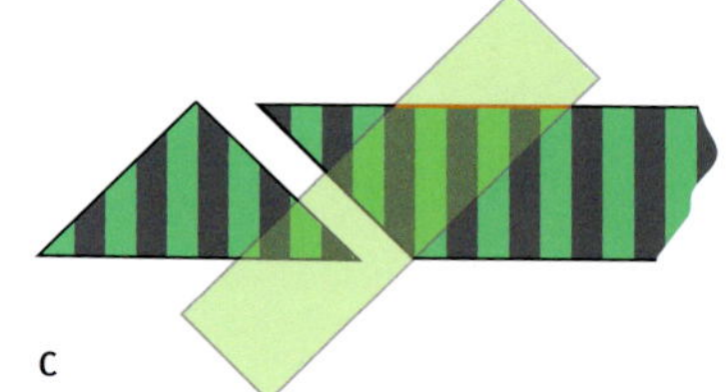

a

b

c

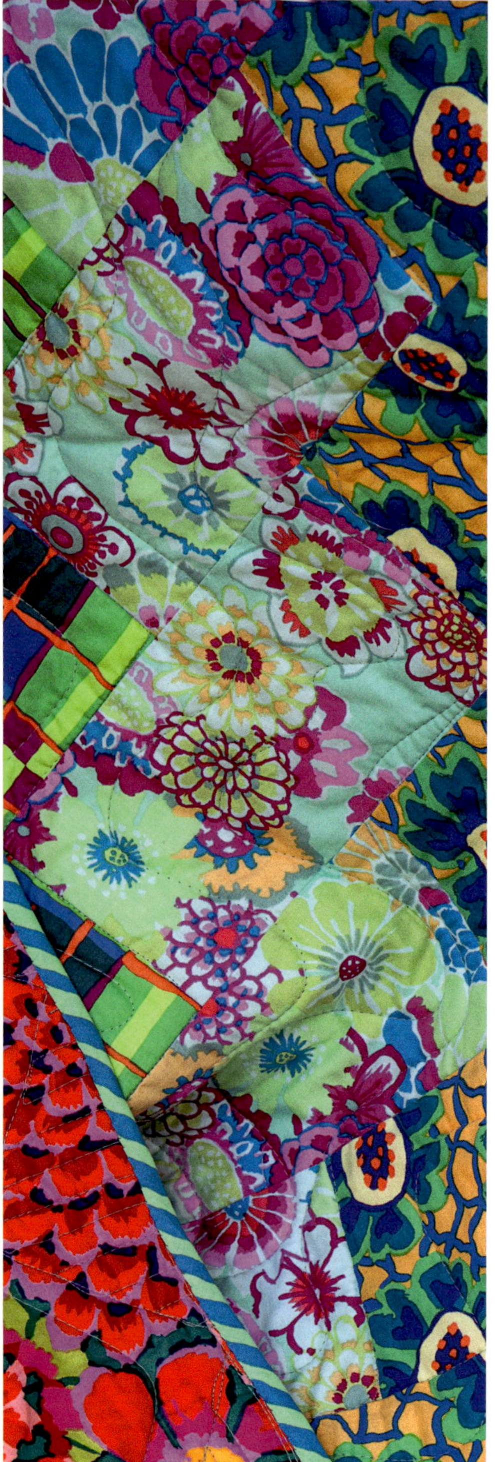

PATCHES

The patches are rectangles, finished at 8in x 4in (20.3cm x 10.2cm), laid out in columns at a 45° angle. There are 12 columns of different fabric 'bricks', each column composed of 12 bricks.

The four edges of the quilt are finished with striped setting triangles, all cut with the stripes running from the quilt centre to the quilt edges.

Note: There is enough fabric to make each column with 16 bricks, if preferred.

CUTTING OUT

Fabric is cut across the width unless otherwise stated.

'Brick' Rectangles

From each of Fabrics 2, 3, 4, 5, 6, 7, 8, 9, 10, 11, 12 and 13 cut 2 strips 8½in (21.6cm) wide and cross cut 12 rectangles 8½in x 4½in (21.6cm x 11¼cm).

Setting Triangles

Edge-setting Triangles: From Fabric 1 remove selvedges and, **down the length of the fabric (across the stripes)**, cut 8 strips 3½in (9cm) wide. Referring to the cutting diagram, cut a total of 44 right-angled triangles. Align the 45° line on your ruler with the straight side edge of the strip and cut a diagonal line (a). Rotate the ruler and align the 45° line with the lower edge, intersecting the first cut and cut diagonally (b). Flip the ruler over and continue cutting triangles across the strip (c). Each strip will yield 6 triangles with short edges measuring 6½in (16.5cm) and the long edge measuring 9¼in (23.5cm).

Large Corner Triangles: From the remaining Fabric 1 cut a square 6½in x 6½in (16.5cm x 16.5cm). With the stripes vertical, cut the square diagonally from the top right to the bottom left to form 2 large corner triangles for the top left and bottom right corners of the quilt.

Small Corner Triangles: Also from Fabric 1 cut a square 3¾in x 3¾in (9.5cm x 9.5cm). With the stripes vertical, cut the square diagonally from the top left to the bottom right to form 2 small corner triangles for the top right and bottom left corners of the quilt.

Backing

Trim Fabric 14 to 81in x 81in (206cm x 206cm).

Binding

From Fabric 1 cut 8 strips 2½in (6.4cm) wide **on the bias** (diagonally at 45°). Remove selvedges and sew end to end with 45° seams (see page 141). You will need at least 8¼yd (7.6m) of binding.

MAKING THE QUILT

Using a design wall will help to place patches in the required layout.

Use ¼in (6mm) seams throughout.

Centre

Referring to the Quilt Assembly Diagram and quilt photograph, lay out the blocks in 12 columns, each angled to 45° with 12 matching 'brick' rectangles. Add 11 edge-setting triangles around all 4 sides and add the large and small corner triangles as shown in the diagram.

Sew the blocks together in diagonal rows, starting at the top left corner as shown in the Quilt Assembly Diagram. Sew one row at a time, pressing seams, then sew the rows together, pinning together to avoid stretching the rows.

FINISHING THE QUILT

Press the quilt top. Layer the quilt top, batting and backing, and baste together (see page 140).

Quilt as desired.

Trim the quilt edges and attach the binding (see page 141).

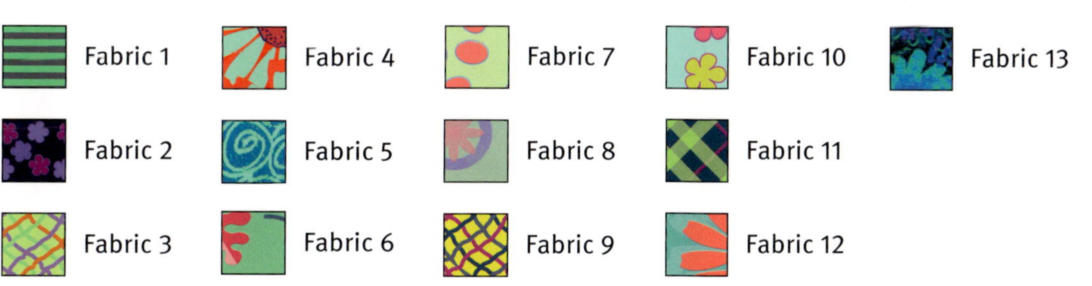

Fabric 1
Fabric 2
Fabric 3
Fabric 4
Fabric 5
Fabric 6
Fabric 7
Fabric 8
Fabric 9
Fabric 10
Fabric 11
Fabric 12
Fabric 13

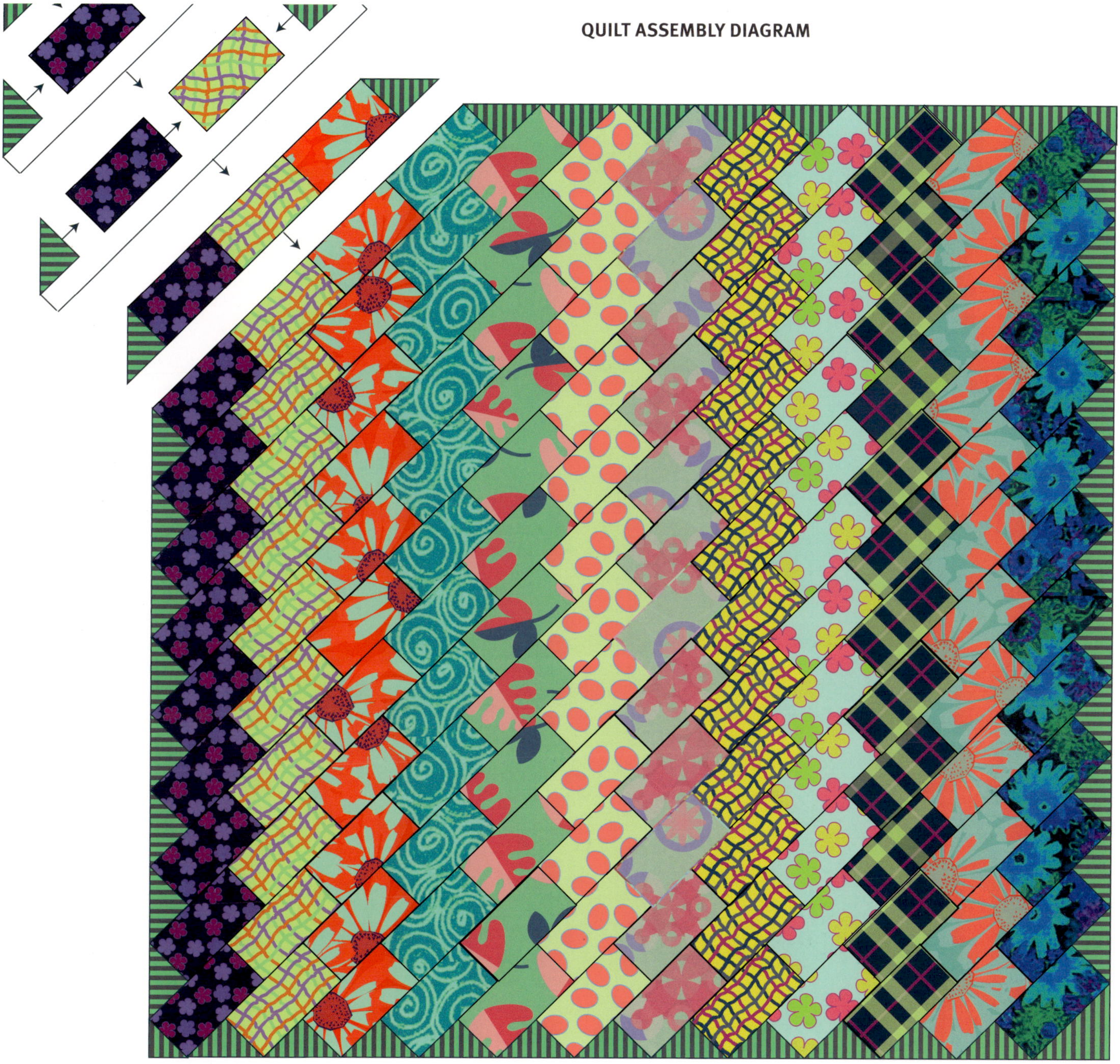

windmills **

Kaffe Fassett

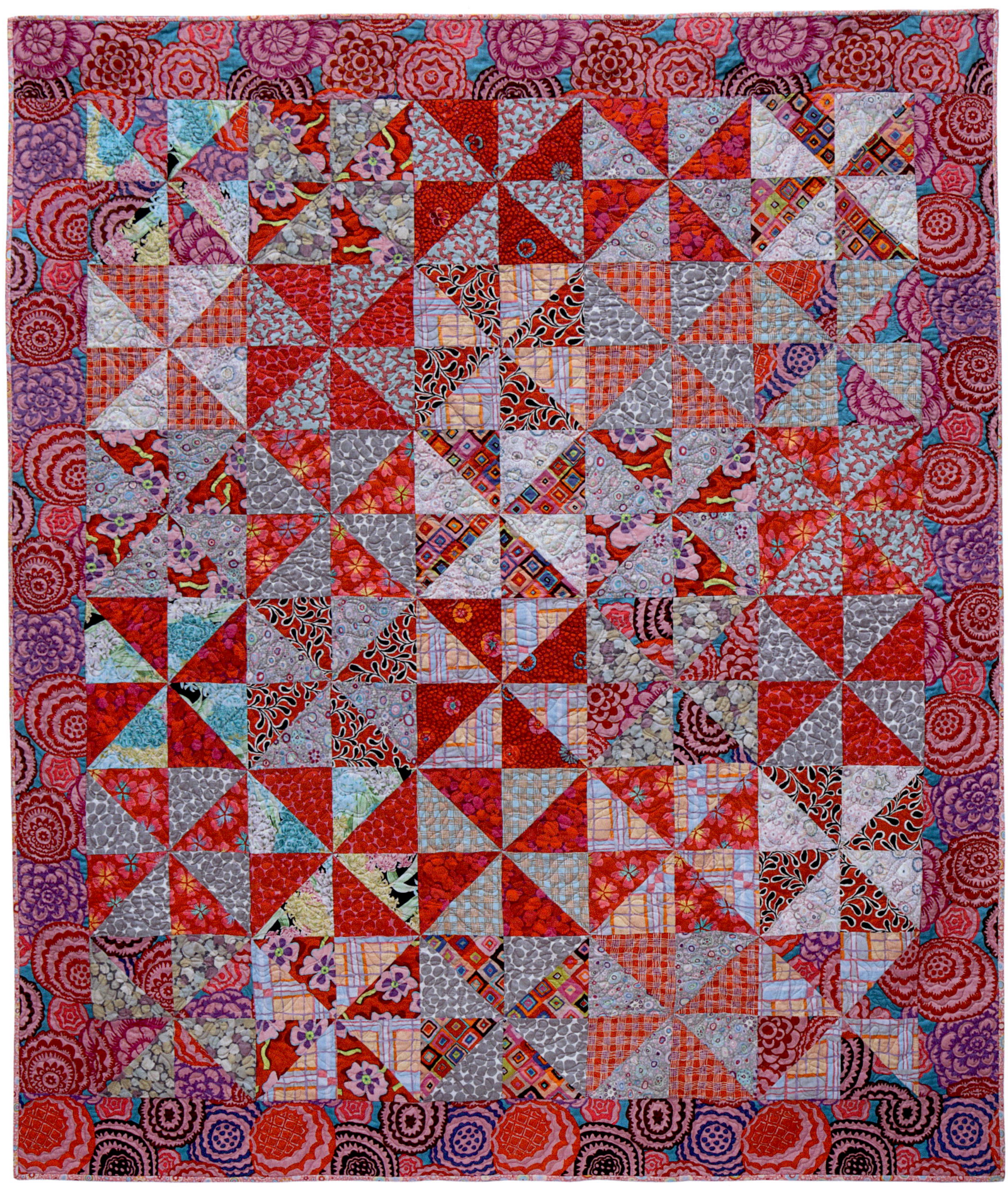

Made from a traditional pinwheel block, this is a scrappy quilt that shows off how well the contrasting red and grey fabrics from our recent collections pair up together. The circular motion of the windmills is reflected in my Deco flower motifs around the border.

SIZE OF FINISHED QUILT
84in x 72in (213cm x 183cm)

FABRICS
Fabrics have been calculated at a maximum width of 40in (102cm). Fabrics have been given a number – see the Fabric Swatch Diagram for details.

Patchwork Fabrics
Reds
DECO
Fabric 1   Hot   2⅛yd (2m)
GUINEA FLOWER
Fabric 2   Red   ¼yd (25cm)
JUMBLE
Fabric 3   Ruby   ½yd (50cm)
REFLECTIONS
Fabric 4   Fuchsia   ½yd (50cm)
CAMO FLOWER
Fabric 5   Red   ½yd (50cm)
GINGHAM
Fabric 6   Red   ½yd (50cm)
TWIG
Fabric 7   Red   ½yd (50cm)
PETALS
Fabric 8   Red   ½yd (50cm)
SQUARE DANCE
Fabric 9   Red   ½yd (50cm)
Greys
GINGHAM
Fabric 10   Grey   ¼yd (25cm)
JUMBLE
Fabric 11   Grey   ½yd (50cm)
CHECKMATE
Fabric 12   Pastel   ½yd (50cm)
REFLECTIONS
Fabric 13   Putty   ½yd (50cm)
ROMAN GLASS
Fabric 14   Grey   ½yd (50cm)
MILLEFIORE
Fabric 15   Grey   ½yd (50cm)
CORAL
Fabric 16   Duck Egg   ½yd (50cm)
HYACINTHS
Fabric 17   Contrast   ½yd (50cm)

Patchwork Fabrics

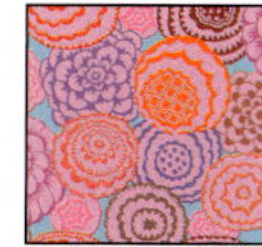
Fabric 1
DECO
Hot
GP199HT

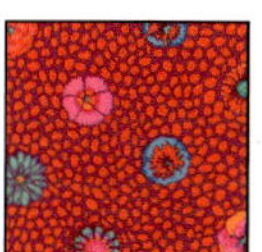
Fabric 2
GUINEA FLOWER
Red
GP59RD

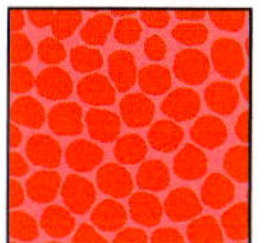
Fabric 3
JUMBLE
Ruby
BM53RB

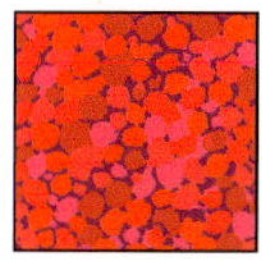
Fabric 4
REFLECTIONS
Fuchsia
BM87FU

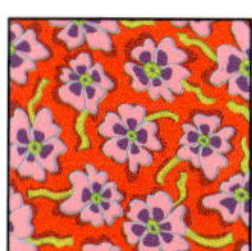
Fabric 5
CAMO FLOWER
Red
BM88RD

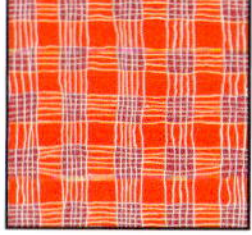
Fabric 6
GINGHAM
Red
BM89RD

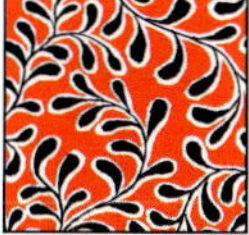
Fabric 7
TWIG
Red
GP196RD

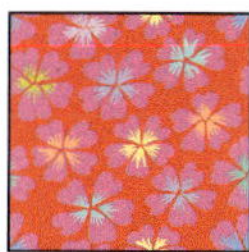
Fabric 8
PETALS
Red
GP201RD

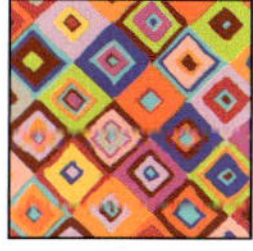
Fabric 9
SQUARE DANCE
Red
GP203RD

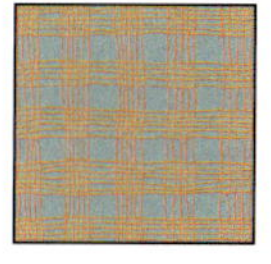
Fabric 10
GINGHAM
Grey
BM89GY

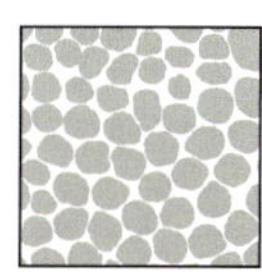
Fabric 11
JUMBLE
Grey
BM53GY

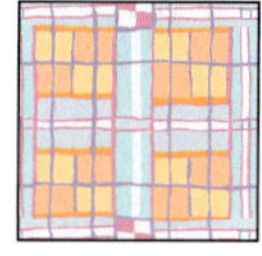
Fabric 12
CHECKMATE
Pastel
BM86PT

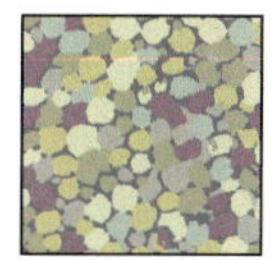
Fabric 13
REFLECTIONS
Putty
BM87PY

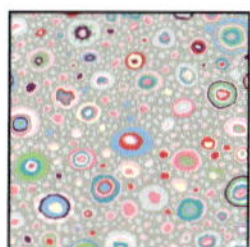
Fabric 14
ROMAN GLASS
Grey
GP01GY

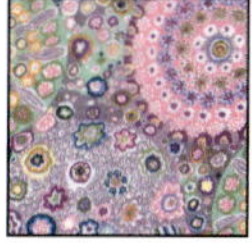
Fabric 15
MILLEFIORE
Grey
GP92GY

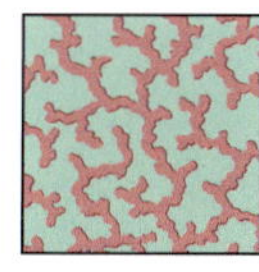
Fabric 16
CORAL
Duck Egg
PJ04DE

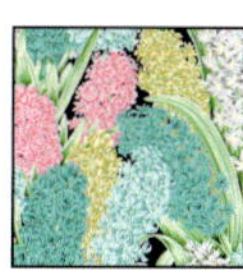
Fabric 17
HYACINTHS
Contrast
PJ123CN

Backing and Binding Fabrics

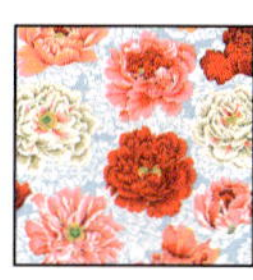
Fabric 18
BROCADE PEONY
Natural
QJ03NL

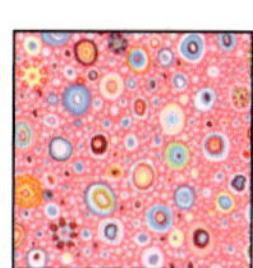
Fabric 19
ROMAN GLASS
Pink
GP01PK

Backing and Binding Fabrics
BROCADE PEONY extra-wide backing
Fabric 18   Natural   2¾yd (2.6m)
ROMAN GLASS
Fabric 19   Pink   ¾yd (70cm)

Batting
94in x 82in (239cm x 208cm)

PATCHES
Patches are half-square triangles
(HSTs) cut from 6⅞in (17.5cm) squares,
which are sewn together in pairs of red
and grey fabrics to make finished 6in
(15.2cm) squares. Pinwheels are created
using 4 HST squares to make 12in
(30.5cm) finished blocks that are set in
6 rows of 5 and bordered with a finished
6in (15.2cm) border.

CUTTING OUT
Fabric is cut across the width unless
otherwise stated.

Border
From Fabric 1 cut **down the length of the
fabric** 4 strips 6½in x 72½in (16.5cm x
184.2cm).

Pinwheels
From the remaining Fabric 1 cut 5
strips 6⅞in (17.5cm) wide **across** the
remaining piece (leaving a usefully
shaped surplus piece) and cross cut
10 squares at 6⅞in (17.5cm), with 2
squares from each strip. Cut each square
once diagonally to yield 2 HSTs from
each square: 20 HSTs in total.

To make the rest of the pinwheels, cut
strips 6⅞in (17.5cm) wide and cross cut
squares at 6⅞in (17.5cm). Each strip will
yield 5 squares. Cut each square once
diagonally to yield 2 HSTs from each
square. Cut strips, squares and triangles
from fabrics as follows:
Fabric 2 (1 strip) 4 squares –
8 triangles;
Fabric 3 (2 strips) 6 squares –
12 triangles;
Fabric 4 (2 strips) 6 squares –
12 triangles;
Fabric 5 (2 strips) 8 squares –
16 triangles;
Fabric 6 (2 strips) 6 squares –
12 triangles;

Fabric 7 (2 strips) 6 squares –
12 triangles;
Fabric 8 (2 strips) 8 squares –
16 triangles;
Fabric 9 (2 strips) 6 squares –
12 triangles;
Fabric 10 (1 strip) 4 squares –
8 triangles;
Fabric 11 (2 strips) 10 squares –
20 triangles;
Fabric 12 (2 strips) 10 squares –
20 triangles;
Fabric 13 (2 strips) 6 squares –
12 triangles;
Fabric 14 (2 strips) 10 squares –
20 triangles;
Fabric 15 (2 strips) 8 squares –
16 triangles;
Fabric 16 (2 strips) 6 squares –
12 triangles;
Fabric 17 (2 strips) 6 squares –
12 triangles.

Backing
Trim Fabric 18 to 94in x 82in (239cm x
208cm).

Binding
From Fabric 19 cut 9 strips 2½in (6.4cm)
wide. Remove selvedges and sew end to
end with 45° seams (see page 141).

MAKING THE QUILT
Using a design wall will help to place
patches in the required layout.
Use ¼in (6mm) seams throughout.

Making the Blocks
Referring to the Block Assembly
Diagram, sew pairs of red and grey
triangles together along the long edge
(a) to form a square and press seams
towards the red fabric. Sew pairs of
squares together (b), then sew the
pairs together to form each pinwheel
block. Referring to the Quilt Assembly
Diagram and quilt photograph for fabric
placement, make 30 blocks.

Centre
Lay out the blocks in 6 rows of 5,
referring to the Quilt Assembly Diagram
and the quilt photograph.
Sew together one row at a time,
pressing seams in opposite directions
on alternate rows – odd rows to the left,
even rows to the right – to allow the

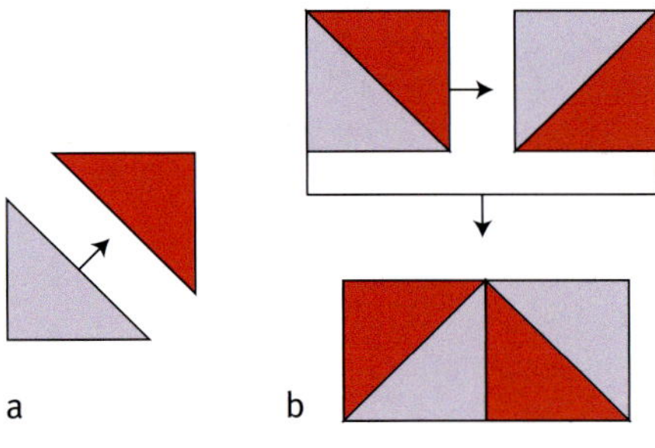

BLOCK ASSEMBLY DIAGRAM

finished seams to lie flat. Sew the rows
together taking care to align crossing
seams.

Borders
Pin (to prevent stretching borders) and
sew the side borders to the centre, press
seams towards the border, then pin and
sew the top and bottom borders to the
centre to complete the quilt top.

FINISHING THE QUILT
Press the quilt top. Layer the quilt top,
batting and backing, and baste together
(see page 140).
Quilt as desired.
Trim the quilt edges and attach the
binding (see page 141).

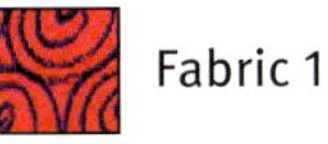
Fabric 1

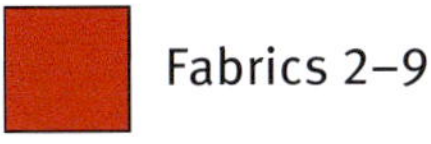
Fabrics 2–9

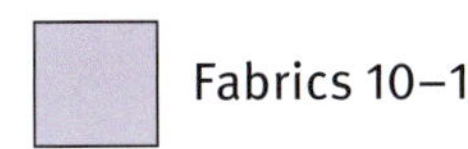
Fabrics 10–17

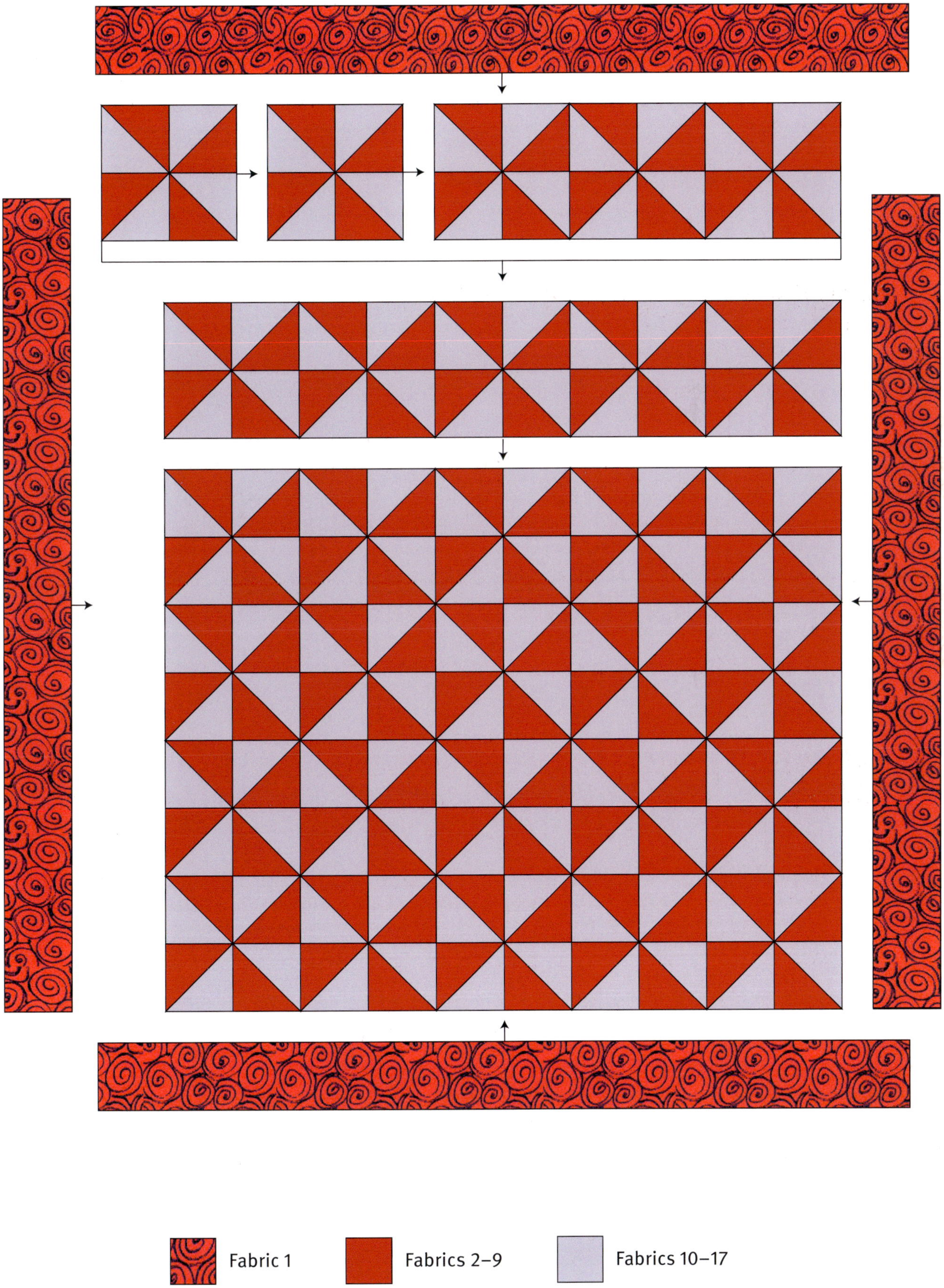

blushing nine-patch *

Kaffe Fassett

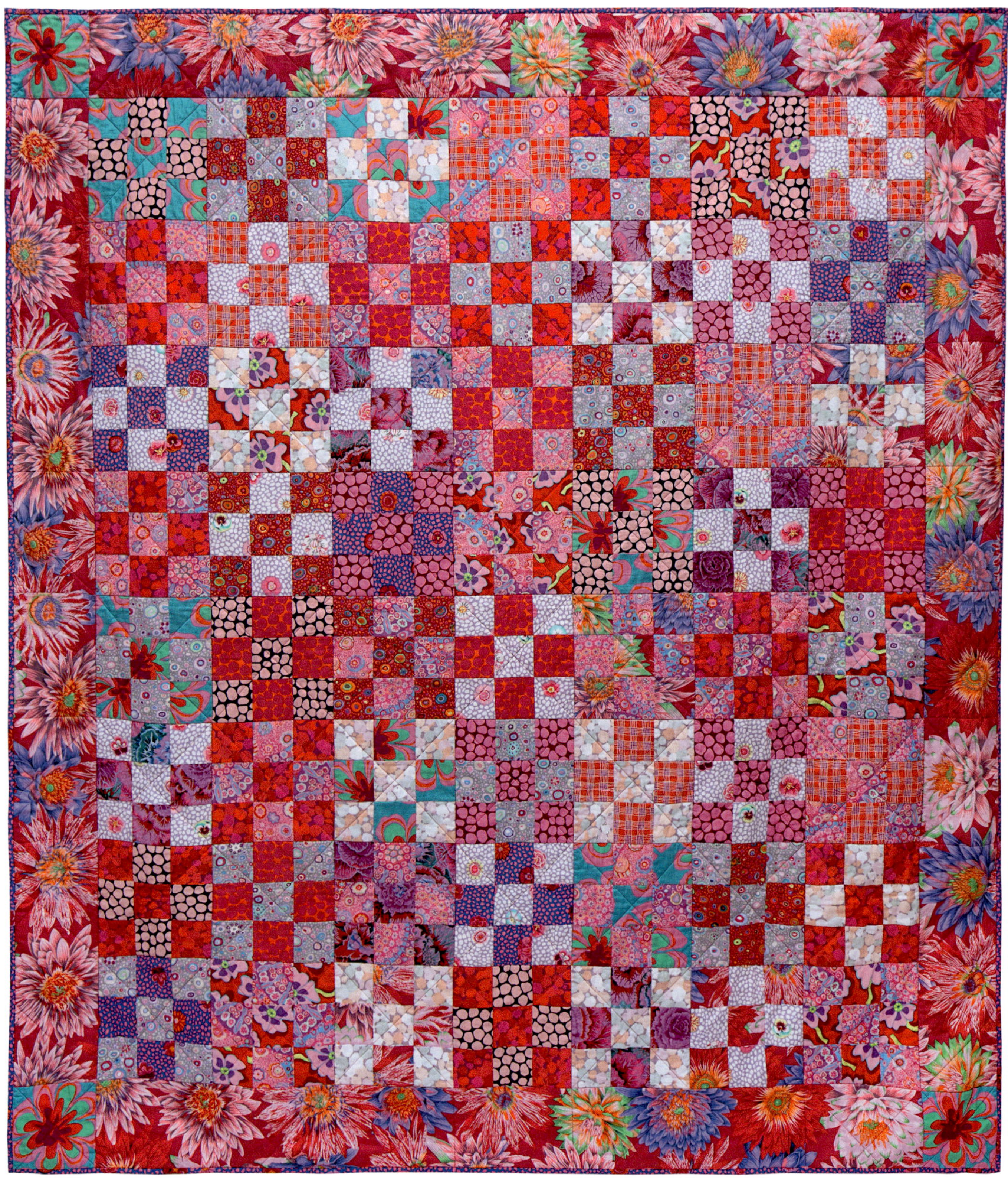

This pretty design showcases a checkerboard pattern of mostly small-scale pink/red and pale grey fabrics set in 9-patch blocks, with alternating darker and paler squares. The wide border in Philip Jacobs' Tropical Water Lilies fabric, along with the Funky Flora corner squares, finish it off beautifully.

SIZE OF FINISHED QUILT
84in x 75in (214cm x 191cm)

FABRICS
Fabrics have been calculated at a maximum width of 40in (102cm). Fabrics have been given a number – see the Fabric Swatch Diagram for details.

Patchwork Fabrics
TROPICAL WATER LILIES
| Fabric 1 | Red | 1⅝yd (1.5m) |
FUNKY FLORA
| Fabric 2 | Aqua | ⅝yd (60cm) |
JUMBLE
Fabric 3	Rose	⅜yd (40cm)
Fabric 4	Bubblegum	⅜yd (40cm)
Fabric 5	Magenta	⅜yd (40cm)
ROMAN GLASS
Fabric 6	Grey	⅝yd (60cm)
Fabric 7	Red	⅜yd (40cm)
REFLECTIONS
Fabric 8	Red	½yd (50cm)
Fabric 9	Pastel	½yd (50cm)
MILLEFIORE
Fabric 10	Pink	¾yd (70cm)
GINGHAM
Fabric 11	Red	⅜yd (40cm)
CAMO FLOWER
Fabric 12	Red	⅜yd (40cm)
GUINEA FLOWER
Fabric 13	Lavender	⅝yd (60cm)
Fabric 14	Pink	¼yd (25cm)
* see also Binding Fabric
BRASSICA
| Fabric 15 | Magenta | ⅜yd (40cm) |

Backing and Binding Fabrics
CHECKMATE
| Fabric 16 | Blush | 5½yd (5.1m) |
GUINEA FLOWER
| Fabric 14 | Pink | ¾yd (70cm) |
* see also Patchwork Fabrics

Batting
92in x 83in (234cm x 211cm)

FABRIC SWATCH DIAGRAM

Patchwork Fabrics

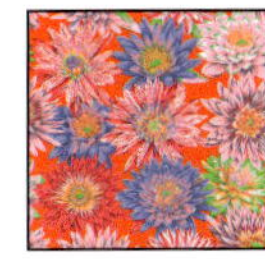
Fabric 1
TROPICAL WATER LILIES
Red
PJ119RD

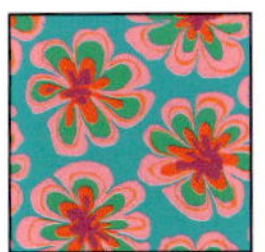
Fabric 2
FUNKY FLORA
Aqua
BM11AQ

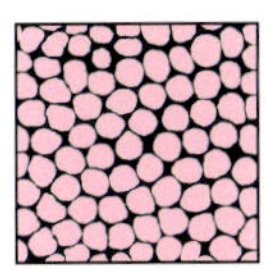
Fabric 3
JUMBLE
Rose
BM53RO

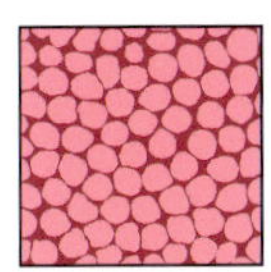
Fabric 4
JUMBLE
Bubblegum
BM53BB

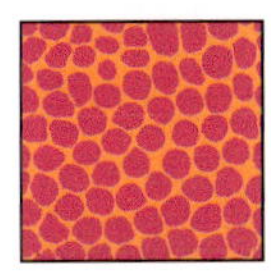
Fabric 5
JUMBLE
Magenta
BM53MG

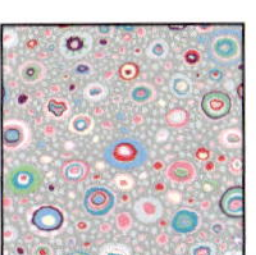
Fabric 6
ROMAN GLASS
Grey
GP01GY

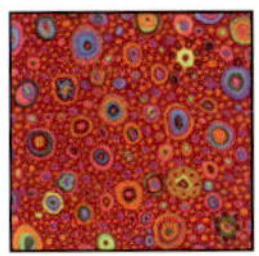
Fabric 7
ROMAN GLASS
Red
GP01RD

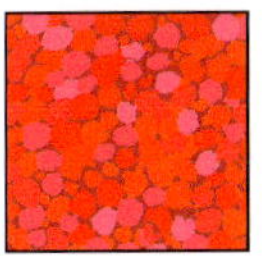
Fabric 8
REFLECTIONS
Red
BM87RD

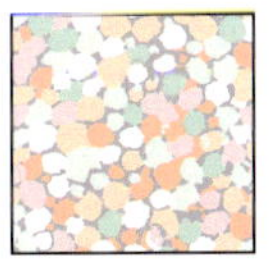
Fabric 9
REFLECTIONS
Pastel
BM87PT

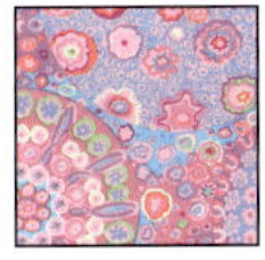
Fabric 10
MILLEFIORE
Pink
GP92PK

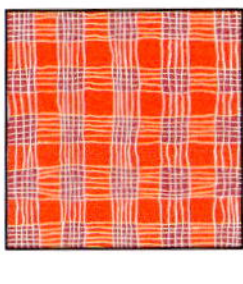
Fabric 11
GINGHAM
Red
BM89RD

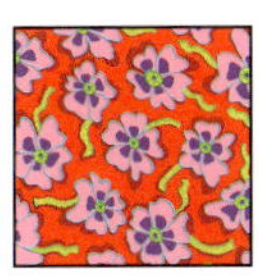
Fabric 12
CAMO FLOWER
Red
BM88RD

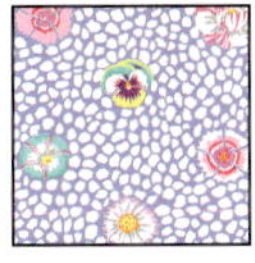
Fabric 13
GUINEA FLOWER
Lavender
GP59LV

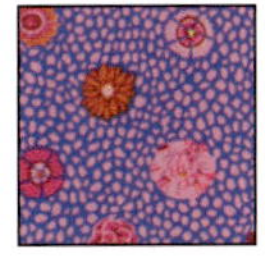
Fabric 14
GUINEA FLOWER
Pink
GP59PK

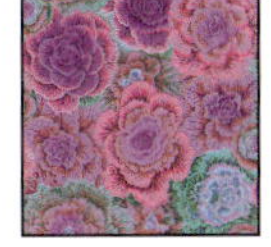
Fabric 15
BRASSICA
Magenta
PJ51MG

Backing and Binding Fabrics

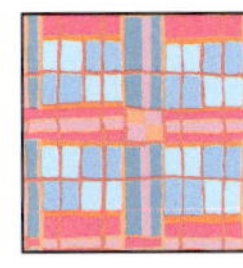
Fabric 16
CHECKMATE
Blush
BM86BS

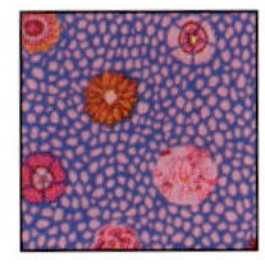
Fabric 14
GUINEA FLOWER
Pink
GP59PK

PATCHES

Square patches finished at 3in (7.6cm) are used to make 9-patch blocks in alternating paler and darker fabrics forming finished blocks at 9in (22.9cm) square. Blocks are set in 8 rows of 7 and surrounded with a 6in (15.2cm) border completed with 6in (15.2cm) fussy-cut corner squares.

CUTTING OUT

Fabric is cut across the width unless otherwise stated. When cutting different pieces from the same fabric, always cut the larger pieces first.

Border and Corner Squares

From Fabric 1 cut 7 strips 6½in (16.5cm) wide, remove selvedges and join strips end to end using ¼in (6mm) seams, and press seams open.
From the length cut:
2 pieces 72½in x 6½in (184.2cm x 16.5cm) for the longer side borders;
2 pieces 63½in x 6½in (161.3cm x 16.5cm) for the shorter top and bottom borders.
Retain the remaining fabric for the 9-patch squares.

From Fabric 2 fussy cut 4 squares at 6½in (16.5cm) square, centring a flower in each for the border corner squares. Retain the remaining fabric for the 9-patch squares.

Nine-patch Blocks

Cut strips 3½in (8.9cm) wide and cross cut squares at 3½in (8.9cm). Each strip will yield 11 squares. Cut a total of 504 squares from fabrics as follows:
Fabric 1 (2 strips) 19 squares;
Fabric 2 (3 strips) 28 squares;
Fabric 3 (3 strips) 27 squares;
Fabric 4 (3 strips) 25 squares;
Fabric 5 (3 strips) 24 squares;
Fabric 6 (5 strips) 49 squares;
Fabric 7 (3 strips) 23 squares;
Fabric 8 (4 strips) 42 squares;
Fabric 9 (4 strips) 42 squares;
Fabric 10 7 strips) 73 squares;
Fabric 11 (3 strips) 26 squares;
Fabric 12 (3 strips) 27 squares;
Fabric 13 (5 strips) 51 squares;
Fabric 14 (2 strips) 21 squares;
Fabric 15 (3 strips) 27 squares.

Backing

From Fabric 16 cut 2 pieces 83in x 40in (211cm x 101cm) and 1 piece 28in x 40in (71.1cm x 101cm).

Binding

From Fabric 14 cut 9 strips 2½in (6.4cm) wide. Remove selvedges and sew end to end with 45° seams (see page 141).

MAKING THE QUILT

Using a design wall will help to place patches in the required layout.
Use ¼in (6mm) seams throughout.

Making the Blocks

Referring to the Block Assembly Diagram, select squares in 1 darker and 1 paler fabric and arrange 9 squares alternating dark and pale into 3 rows of 3.
Note: it is not necessary to follow the original fabric pairings, but there are enough squares in each fabric for you to follow the layout exactly if preferred. Sew each row of squares together, pressing seams in opposite directions on alternate rows – odd rows to the left, even rows to the right – to allow the finished seams to lie flat. Sew the 3 rows together, taking care to align crossing seams. Make 56 blocks, 28 with dark squares in the corners and 28 with pale squares in the corners.

Centre

Lay out the blocks in 8 rows of 7, referring to the Quilt Assembly Diagram and the quilt photograph for block and fabric placement. Sew the blocks together one row at a time, pressing seams in opposite directions on alternate rows – odd rows to the left, even rows to the right – to allow the finished seams to lie flat. Sew the rows together, taking care to align crossing seams.

Borders and Corner squares

Pin (to prevent stretching borders) and sew the longer Fabric 1 side borders to the centre. Press seams towards the border. Sew a Fabric 2 fussy-cut square to each end of the top and bottom borders, then pin and sew the top and bottom borders to the centre to complete the quilt top.

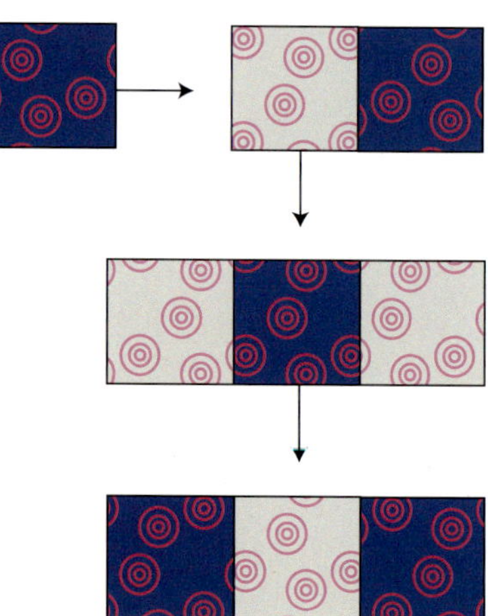

FINISHING THE QUILT

Remove selvedges from the Fabric 16 backing pieces. Cross cut the short section into 3 equal pieces measuring approximately 28in x 13½in (71.1cm x 34.3cm) and sew them together end to end to make a piece approximately 83in x 13½in (211cm x 34.3cm). Pin and sew the 3 sections together down their long edges and trim to form a piece 92in x 83in (234cm x 211cm).

Press the quilt top. Layer the quilt top, batting and backing, and baste together (see page 140).
Quilt as desired.
Trim the quilt edges and attach the binding (see page 141).

QUILT ASSEMBLY DIAGRAM

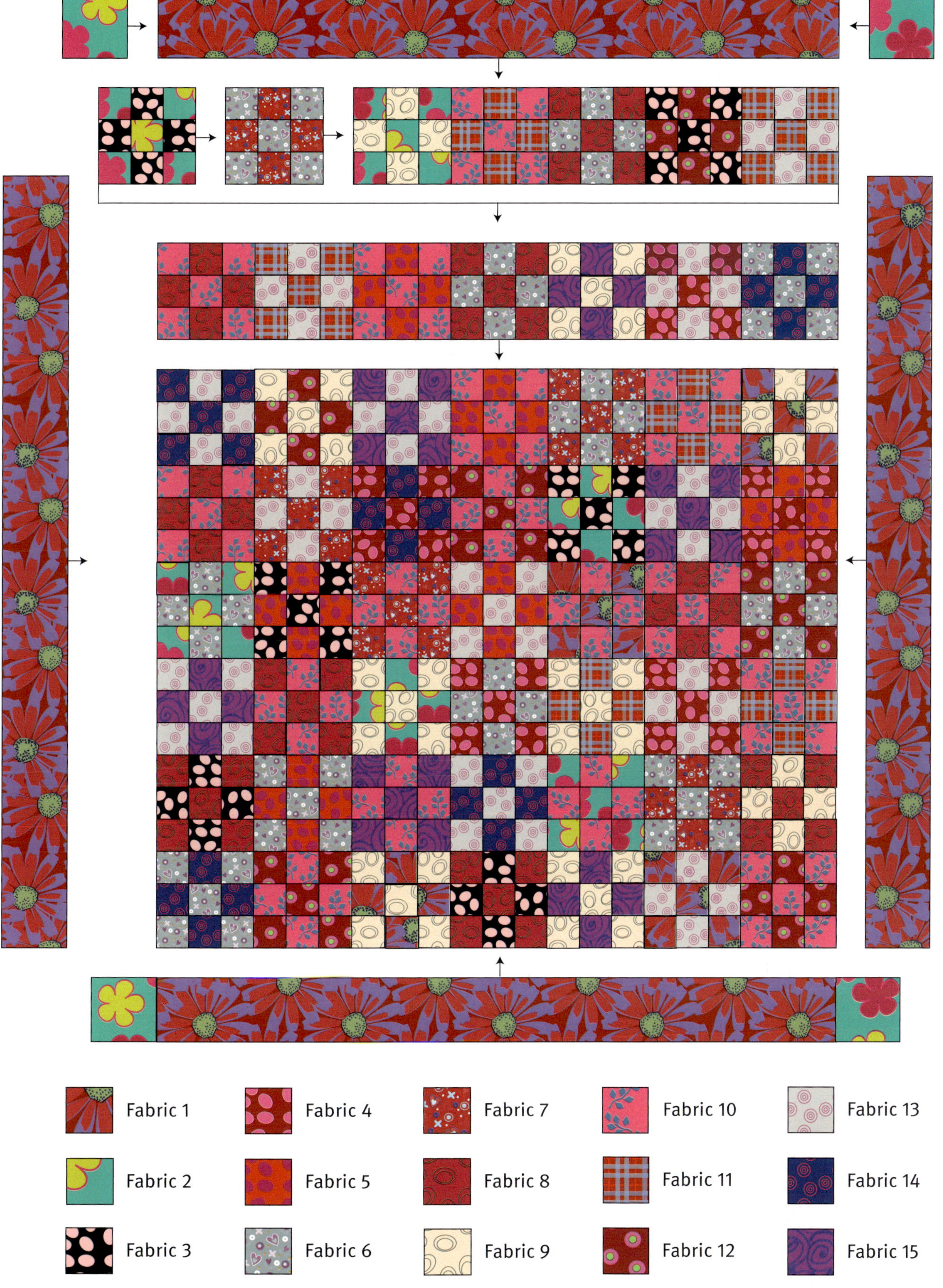

gentleman's relish *

Kaffe Fassett

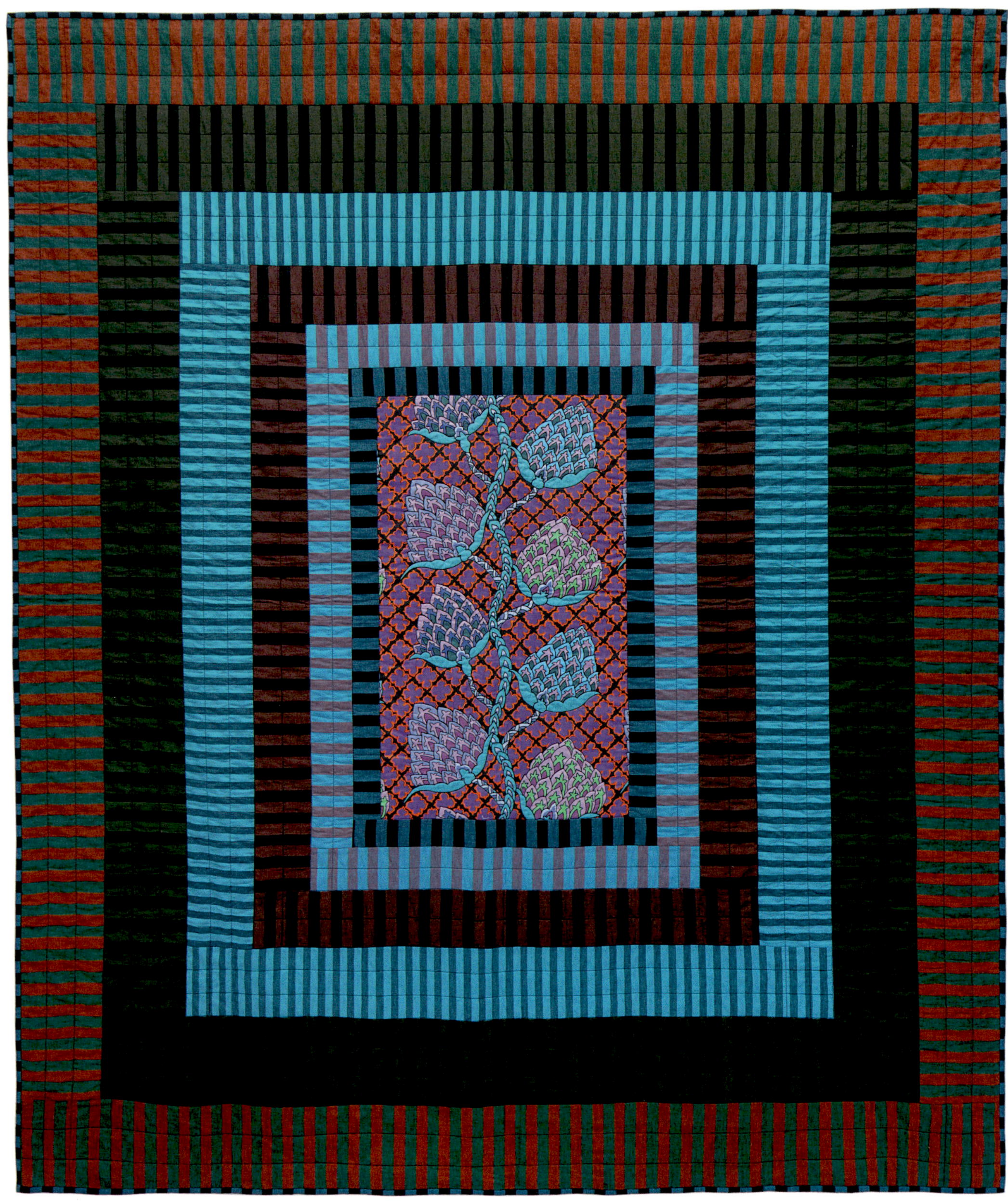

Patchwork Fabrics

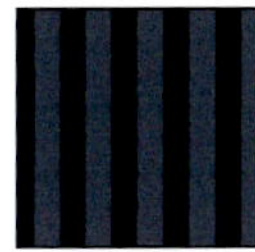

Fabric 1
WIDE STRIPE
Fjord
SS01FJ

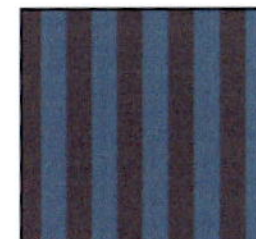

Fabric 2
WIDE STRIPE
Embers
SS01EB

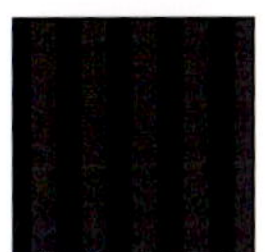

Fabric 3
WIDE STRIPE
Peat
SS01PZ

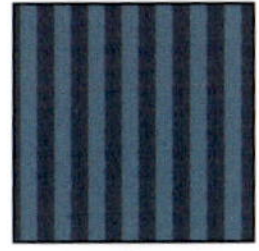

Fabric 4
NARROW STRIPE
Mallard
SS02ML

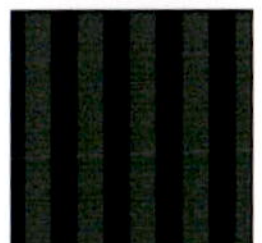

Fabric 5
WIDE STRIPE
Kiwi
SS01KI

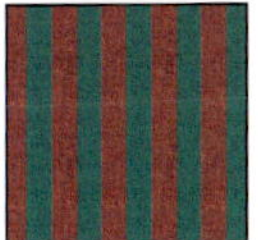

Fabric 6
WIDE STRIPE
Russet
SS01RT

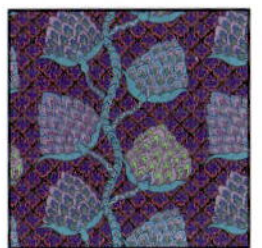

Fabric 7
PAISLEY FLOWER
Blue
GP200BL

Backing and Binding Fabrics

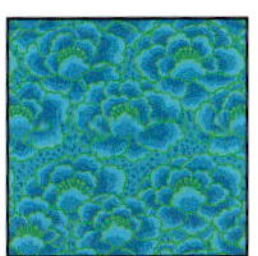

Fabric 8
TONAL FLORAL
Turquoise
QB09TQ

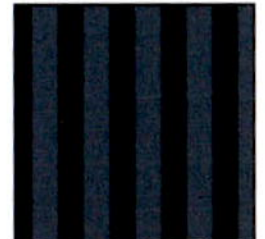

Fabric 1
WIDE STRIPE
Fjord
SS01FJ

Using my Shot Cotton Stripes fabrics in increasingly wide borders makes a delightful contrasting frame for my Paisley Flower fabric in the central medallion.

SIZE OF FINISHED QUILT
82in x 70in (208cm x 178cm)

FABRICS
Fabrics have been calculated at a maximum width of 40in (102cm). Fabrics have been given a number – see the Fabric Swatch Diagram for details.

Patchwork Fabrics
WIDE STRIPE
Fabric 1	Fjord	¼yd (25cm)
* see also Binding Fabric		
Fabric 2	Embers	½yd (50cm)
Fabric 3	Peat	⅝yd (60cm)

NARROW STRIPE
Fabric 4	Mallard	⅞yd (85cm)

WIDE STRIPE
Fabric 5	Kiwi	1¼yd (1.2m)
Fabric 6	Russet	1⅝yd (1.5m)

PAISLEY FLOWER
Fabric 7	Blue	1yd (95cm)

Backing and Binding Fabrics
TONAL FLORAL extra-wide backing
Fabric 8	Turquoise	2⅝yd (2.45m)

WIDE STRIPE
Fabric 1	Fjord	¾yd (70cm)
* see also Patchwork Fabrics		

Batting
92in x 80in (234cm x 203cm)

PATCHES
The central medallion is fussy cut and finished at 30in x 18in (76.2cm x 45.7cm). Six concentric borders finished at 2in, 3in, 4in, 5in, 6in and 6in (5.1cm, 7.6cm, 10.2cm, 12.7cm, 15.2cm and 15.2cm) wide respectively, complete the quilt. The side borders are attached before the top and bottom ones for each border in turn.

CUTTING OUT
Fabric is cut across the width unless otherwise stated.

Centre Medallion
From Fabric 7 fussy cut a rectangle 30½in long x 18½in wide (77.5cm x 47cm), centring a vine with Paisley flowers in a pleasing arrangement.
Extra fabric has been allowed for this.

Borders
The 6 borders are various widths and all require a number of strips cut across the width of the fabric and then joined. For all borders, remove selvedges, join strips end to end using ¼in (6mm) seams and press seams open.
Border 1: From Fabric 1 cut 3 strips 2½in (6.4cm) wide. From the length cut:
2 pieces 30½in x 2½in (77.5cm x 6.4cm) for the side borders;
2 pieces 22½in x 2½in (57.2cm x 6.4cm) for the top and bottom borders.
Border 2: From Fabric 2 cut 4 strips 3½in (8.9cm) wide. From the length cut:
2 pieces 34½in x 3½in (87.6cm x 8.9cm) for the side borders;
2 pieces 28½in x 3½in (72.4cm x 8.9cm) for the top and bottom borders.
Border 3: From Fabric 3 cut 4 strips 4½in (11.4cm) wide. From the length cut:
2 pieces 40½in x 4½in (102.9cm x 11.4cm) for the side borders;
2 pieces 36½in x 4½in (92.7cm x 11.4cm) for the top and bottom borders.
Border 4: From Fabric 4 cut 5 strips 5½in (14cm) wide. From the length cut:
2 pieces 48½in x 5½in (123.2cm x 14cm) for the side borders;
2 pieces 46½in x 5½in (118.1cm x 14cm) for the top and bottom borders.
Border 5: From Fabric 5 cut 6 strips 6½in (16.5cm) wide. From the length cut 4 pieces 58½in x 6½in (148.6cm x 16.5cm).
Border 6: From Fabric 6 cut 8 strips 6½in (16.5cm) wide. From the length cut 4 pieces 70½in x 6½in (179.1cm x 16.5cm).

Backing
Trim Fabric 8 to 92in long x 80in wide (234cm x 203cm).

Binding
From Fabric 1 cut 9 strips 2½in (6.4cm) wide. Remove selvedges and sew end to end with 45° seams (see page 141).

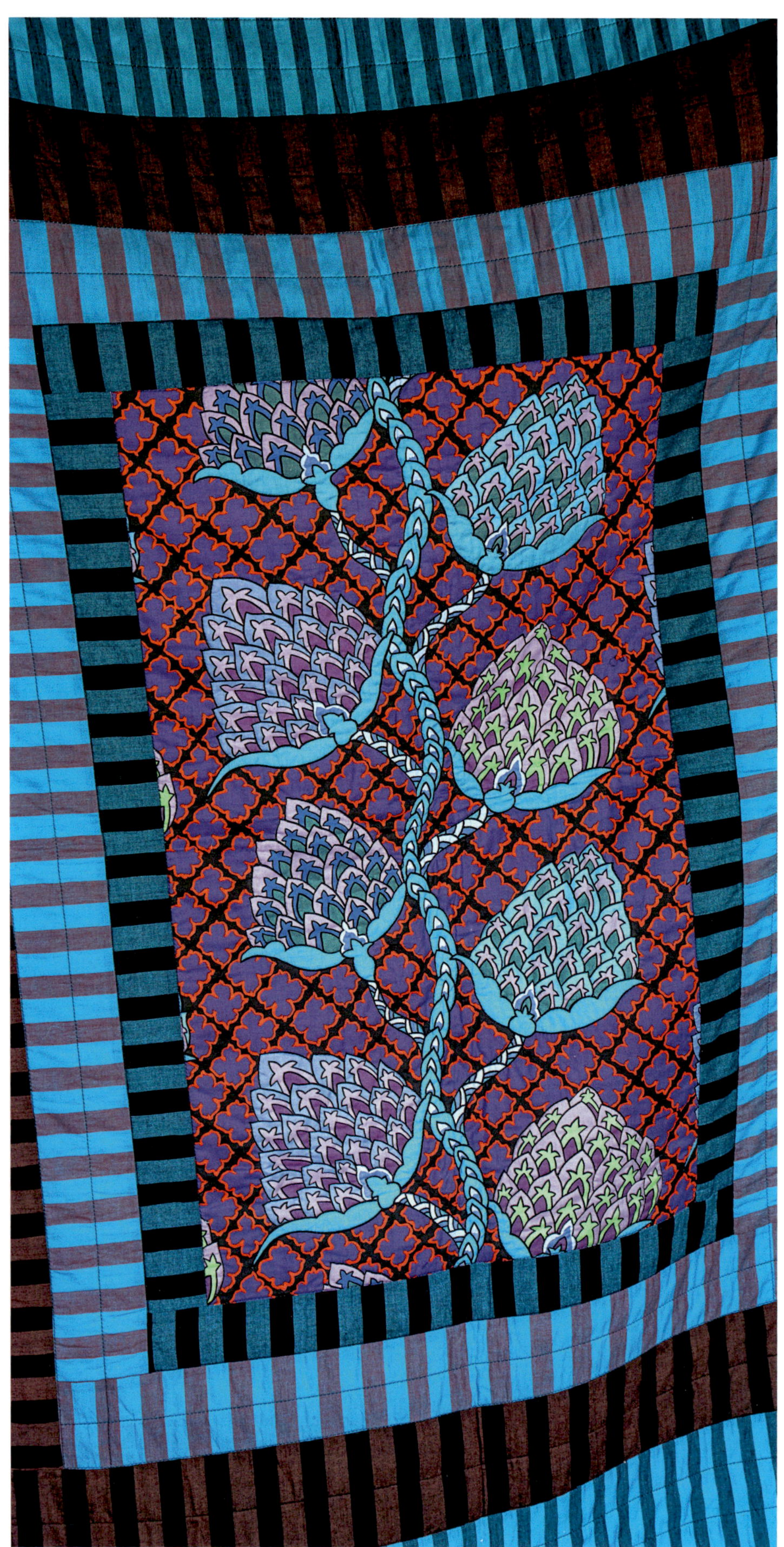

MAKING THE QUILT

Using a design wall will help to place borders in the required layout.
Use ¼in (6mm) seams throughout.

Assembly

Mark the centre on each border strip and on the quilt top, so you can match centre marks when adding each border. Working from the centre out, add each border in turn, from 1 to 6, referring to the Quilt Assembly Diagram and the quilt photograph, and attaching first the side borders, then top and bottom borders. Pin (to prevent stretching borders) and sew the side borders to the centre, press seams towards the outside edge of the quilt, then pin and sew the top and bottom borders to the centre.
Repeat these steps for the remaining 5 borders to complete the quilt top.

FINISHING THE QUILT

Press the quilt top. Layer the quilt top, batting and backing, and baste together (see page 140).
Quilt as desired.
Trim the quilt edges and attach the binding (see page 141).

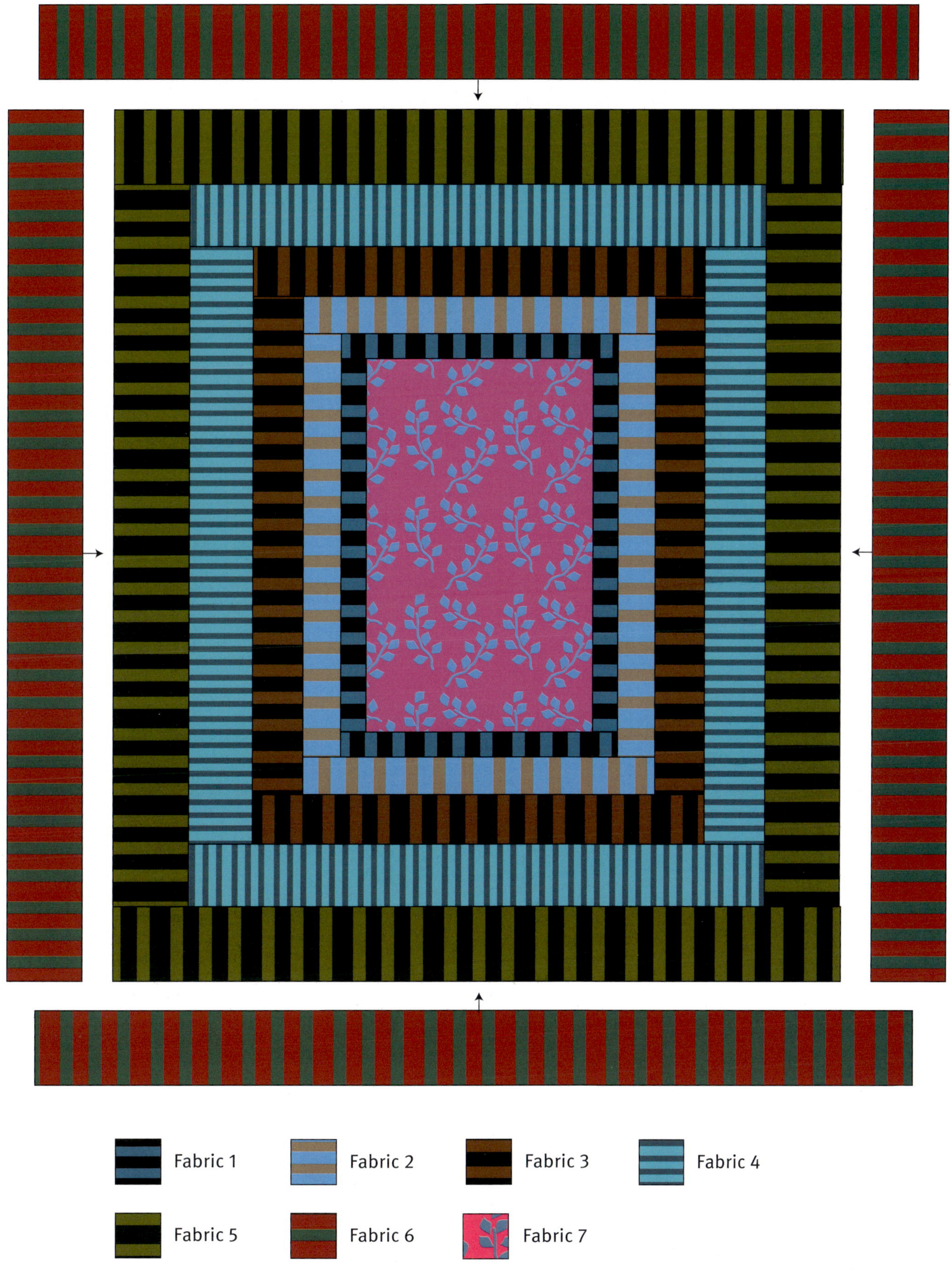

Fabric 1
Fabric 2
Fabric 3
Fabric 4
Fabric 5
Fabric 6
Fabric 7

country snowballs **

Kaffe Fassett

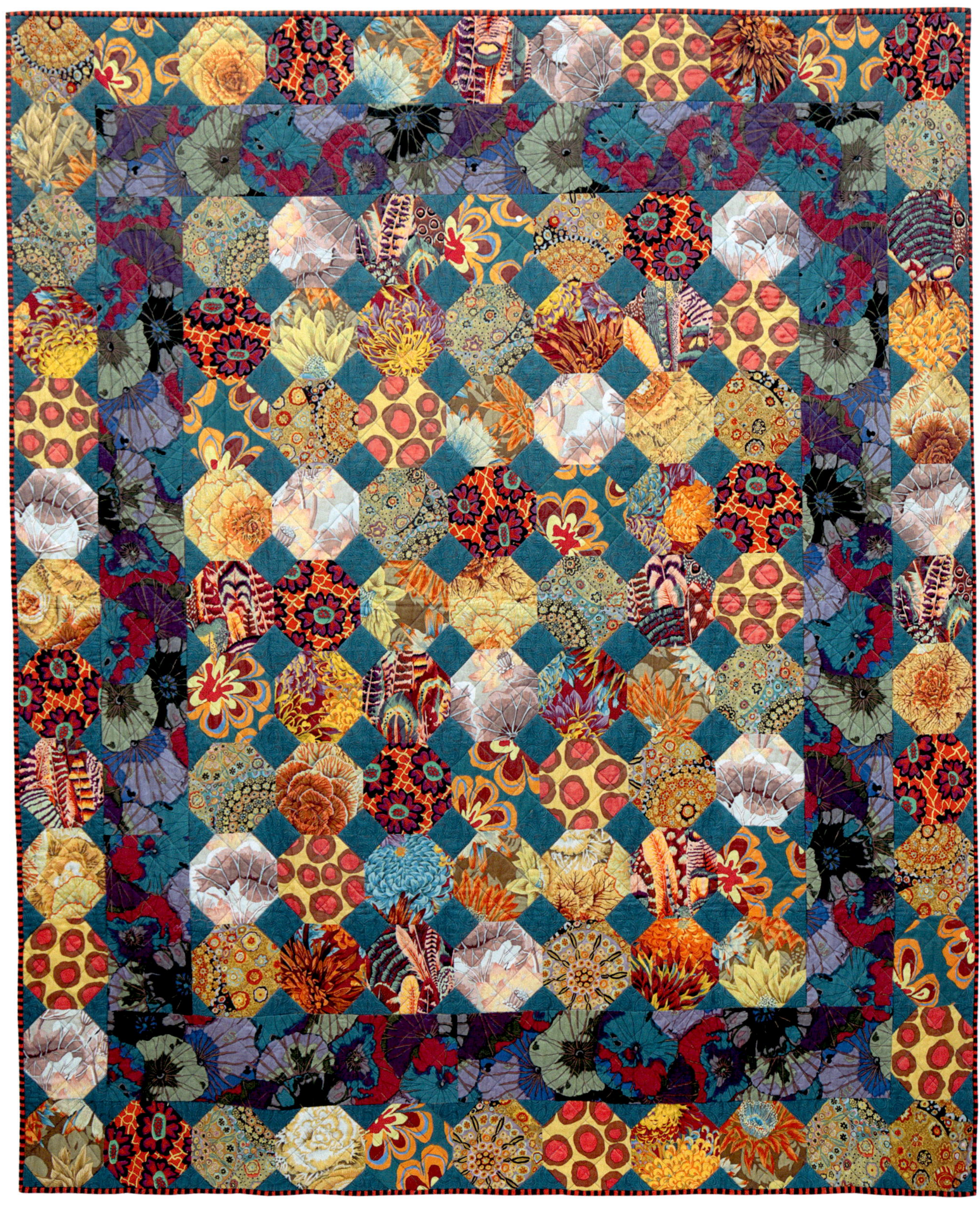

This quilt uses the ever-popular snowball block to highlight some of our recent fabric collections in golden harvest colours, set off with rich dark green corners and my shady, dark Lotus Leaf print as an inset border.

SIZE OF FINISHED QUILT
78in x 66in (198cm x 168cm)

FABRICS
Fabrics have been calculated at a maximum width of 40in (102cm). Fabrics have been given a number – see the Fabric Swatch Diagram for details.

Patchwork Fabrics
LAKE BLOSSOMS
Fabric 1   Antique   ½yd (50cm)
MILLEFIORE
Fabric 2   Brown   ½yd (50cm)
Fabric 3   Antique   ½yd (50cm)
JAPANESE CHRYSANTHEMUM
Fabric 4   Autumn   ½yd (50cm)
BRASSICA
Fabric 5   Brown   ½yd (50cm)
FEATHERS
Fabric 6   Summer   ½yd (50cm)
CACTUS FLOWER
Fabric 7   Brown   ½yd (50cm)
FLOWER NET
Fabric 8   Crimson   ½yd (50cm)
FUNKY FLORA
Fabric 9   Forest   ½yd (50cm)
FISH LIPS
Fabric 10   Banana   ½yd (50cm)
ABORIGINAL DOT
Fabric 11   Charcoal   1⅞yd (1.8m)
LOTUS LEAF
Fabric 12   Dark   1¼yd (1.2m)
* See also Backing Fabric

Backing and Binding Fabrics
LOTUS LEAF
Fabric 12   Dark   5yd (4.65m)
* see also Patchwork Fabrics
COMB STRIPE
Fabric 13   Rust   ¾yd (70cm)

Batting
88in x 76in (224cm x 193cm)

FABRIC SWATCH DIAGRAM

Patchwork Fabrics

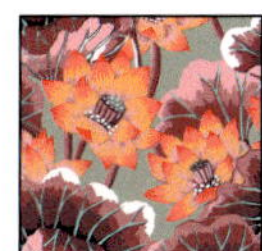

Fabric 1
LAKE BLOSSOMS
Antique
GP93AN

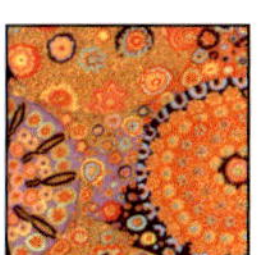

Fabric 2
MILLEFIORE
Brown
GP92BR

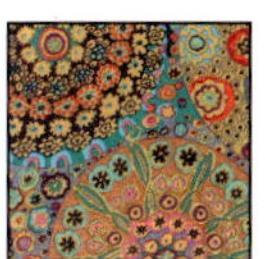

Fabric 3
MILLEFIORE
Antique
GP92AN

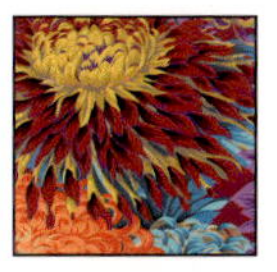

Fabric 4
JAPANESE CHRYSANTHEMUM
Autumn
PJ41AU

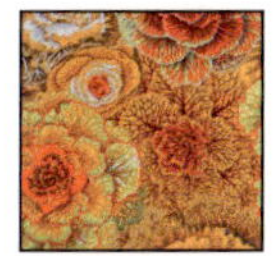

Fabric 5
BRASSICA
Brown
PJ51BR

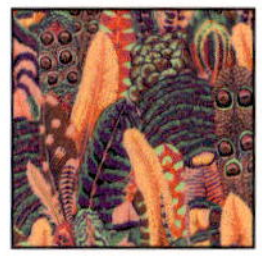

Fabric 6
FEATHERS
Summer
PJ55SU

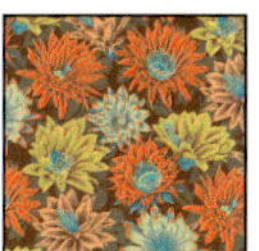

Fabric 7
CACTUS FLOWER
Brown
PJ96BR

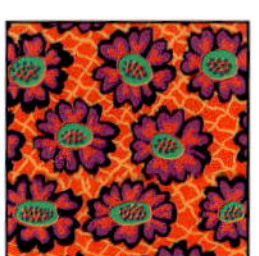

Fabric 8
FLOWER NET
Crimson
BM81CR

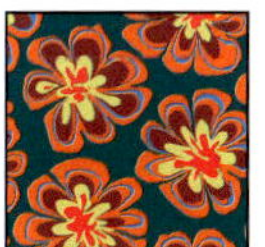

Fabric 9
FUNKY FLORA
Forest
BM11FO

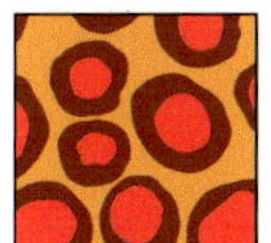

Fabric 10
FISH LIPS
Banana
BM07BA

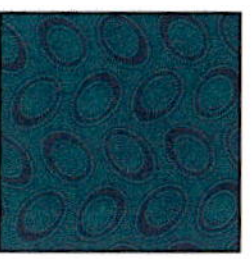

Fabric 11
ABORIGINAL DOT
Charcoal
GP71CC

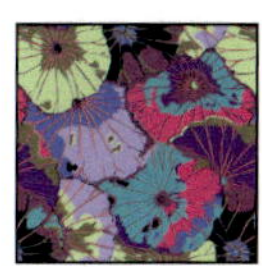

Fabric 12
LOTUS LEAF
Dark
GP29DK

Backing and Binding Fabrics

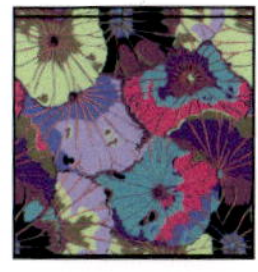

Fabric 12
LOTUS LEAF
Dark
GP29DK

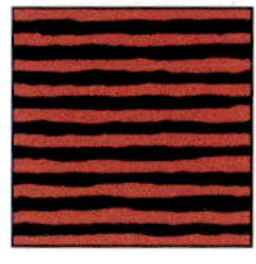

Fabric 13
COMB STRIPE
Rust
BM84RU

PATCHES

The quilt is constructed using traditional octagonal snowball blocks, made the easy way using a large feature square and 4 small corner squares. The small corner squares are stitched diagonally to the corners of the large square to produce snowball blocks finished at 6in (15.2cm) square.

Blocks are set in 9 rows of 7 with an inset 6in (15.2cm) border before the final round of snowball blocks.

CUTTING OUT

Fabric is cut across the width unless otherwise stated.

Feature Squares

From each of the following fabrics cut 2 strips 6½in (16.5cm) wide and cross cut squares at 6½in (16.5cm). Each strip will yield 6 squares. Cut a total of 107 squares from fabrics as follows:
Fabric 1 12 squares;
Fabric 2 10 squares;
Fabric 3 10 squares;
Fabric 4 12 squares;
Fabric 5 11 squares;
Fabric 6 11 squares;
Fabric 7 10 squares;
Fabric 8 11 squares;
Fabric 9 10 squares;
Fabric 10 10 squares.

Corner Squares

From Fabric 11 cut 26 strips 2¼in (5.7cm) wide and cross cut squares at 2¼in (5.7cm). Each strip will yield 17 squares. Cut a total of 428 squares.

Inset Border

From Fabric 12 cut 6 strips 6½in (16.5cm) wide, remove selvedges and join strips end to end using ¼in (6mm) seams and press seams open. From this length cut 4 pieces 54½in (138.4cm) long.

Backing

From Fabric 12 cut 2 pieces 88in x 40in (224cm x 101.6cm).

Binding

From Fabric 13 remove selvedges and cut 12 strips **down the length of the fabric (ie across the stripes)** 2½in (6.4cm) wide. Sew end to end with 45° seams (see page 141).

MAKING THE QUILT

Using a design wall will help to place patches in the required layout.
Use ¼in (6mm) seams throughout.

Making the Blocks

Referring to the Block Assembly Diagram, take a large feature square and 4 small Fabric 11 corner squares. Position a small square right sides together on each corner of the large square and sew diagonally (a). Trim off the excess, leaving a ¼in (6mm) seam allowance (b). Press seams towards the corners to finish the block (c). Make 107 blocks.

Centre

Referring to the Quilt Assembly Diagram and the quilt photograph, layout the snowball blocks in 9 rows of 7. Sew together one row at a time, pressing seams in opposite directions on alternate rows – odd rows to the left, even rows to the right – to allow the finished seams to lie flat. Sew the rows together taking care to align crossing seams.

Add the inset border. Mark the centre of each strip and the centre of each side of the quilt. Match the centre marks and pin, then sew the side borders to the centre. Press seams towards the border, then repeat with the top and bottom borders.

For the outer round of snowball blocks, sew 11 snowball blocks together for each of the 4 sides. As before, match the centres, pin, then sew a strip of 11 snowball blocks to each side of the quilt. Press seams towards the inset border. Repeat with the top and bottom outer round of snowball blocks to complete the quilt top.

FINISHING THE QUILT

Remove selvedges and sew the Fabric 12 backing pieces together down their long edges and trim them to form a piece 88in x 76in (224cm x 193cm).

Press the quilt top. Layer the quilt top, batting and backing, and baste together (see page 140).
Quilt as desired.
Trim the quilt edges and attach the binding (see page 141).

BLOCK ASSEMBLY DIAGRAM

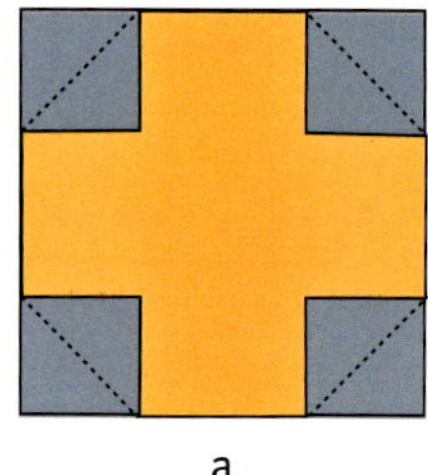 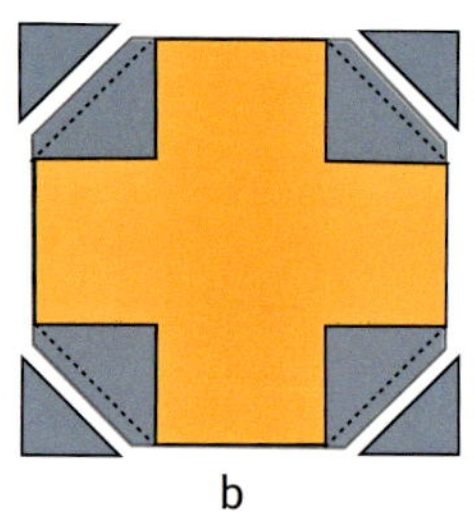 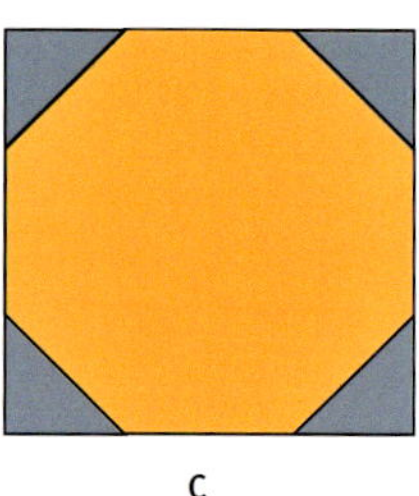

a   b   c

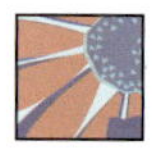 Fabric 1   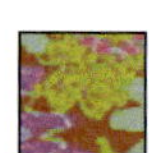 Fabric 7

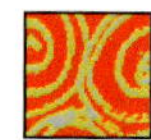 Fabric 2   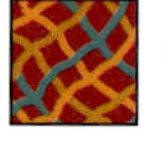 Fabric 8

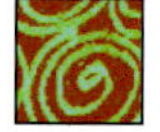 Fabric 3   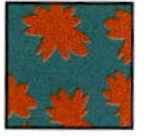 Fabric 9

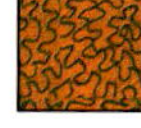 Fabric 4   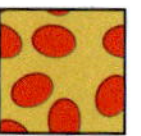 Fabric 10

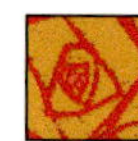 Fabric 5   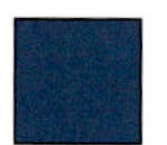 Fabric 11

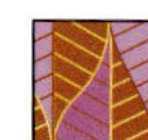 Fabric 6   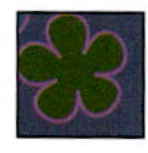 Fabric 12

QUILT ASSEMBLY DIAGRAM

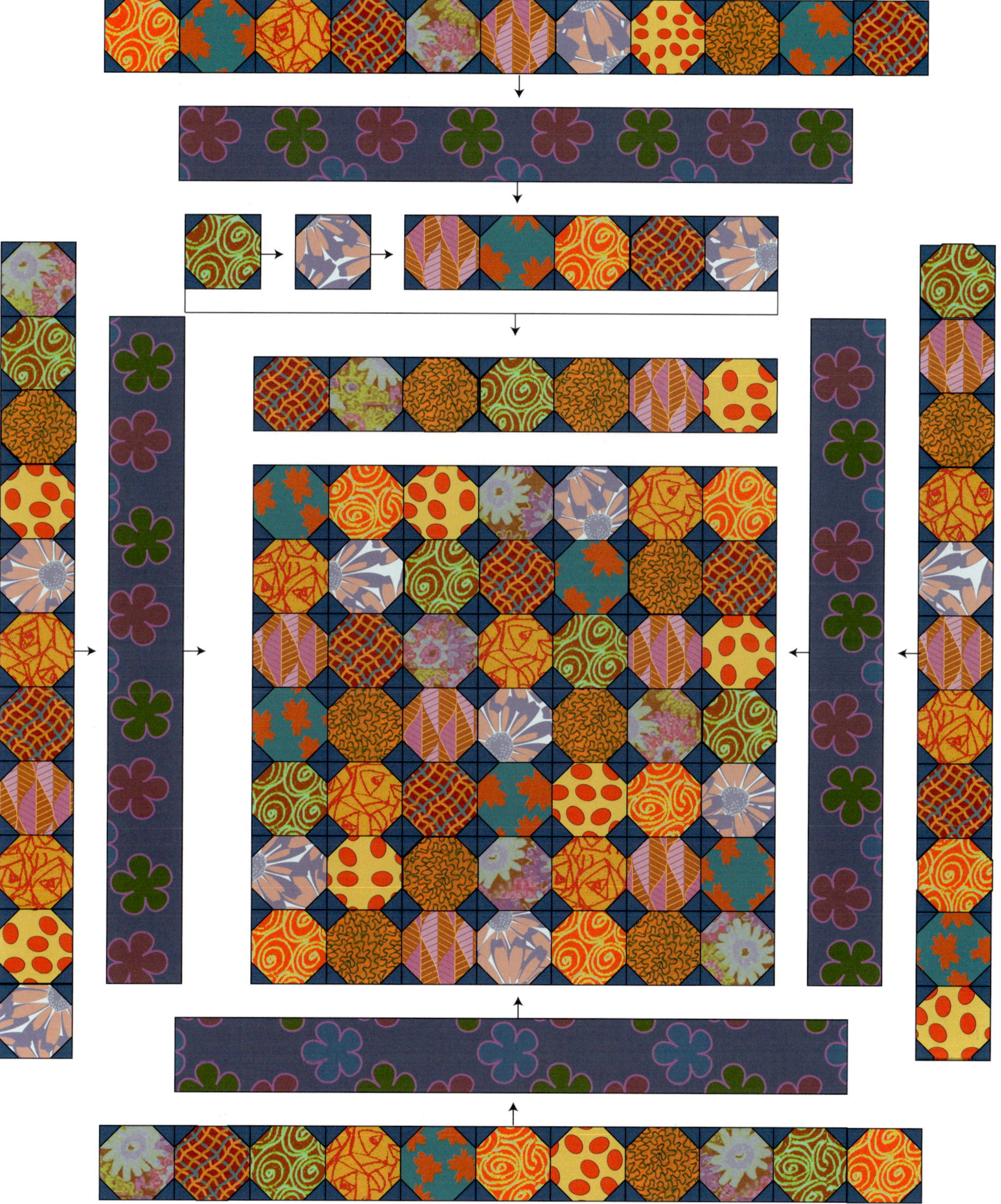

leafy circles *

Kaffe Fassett

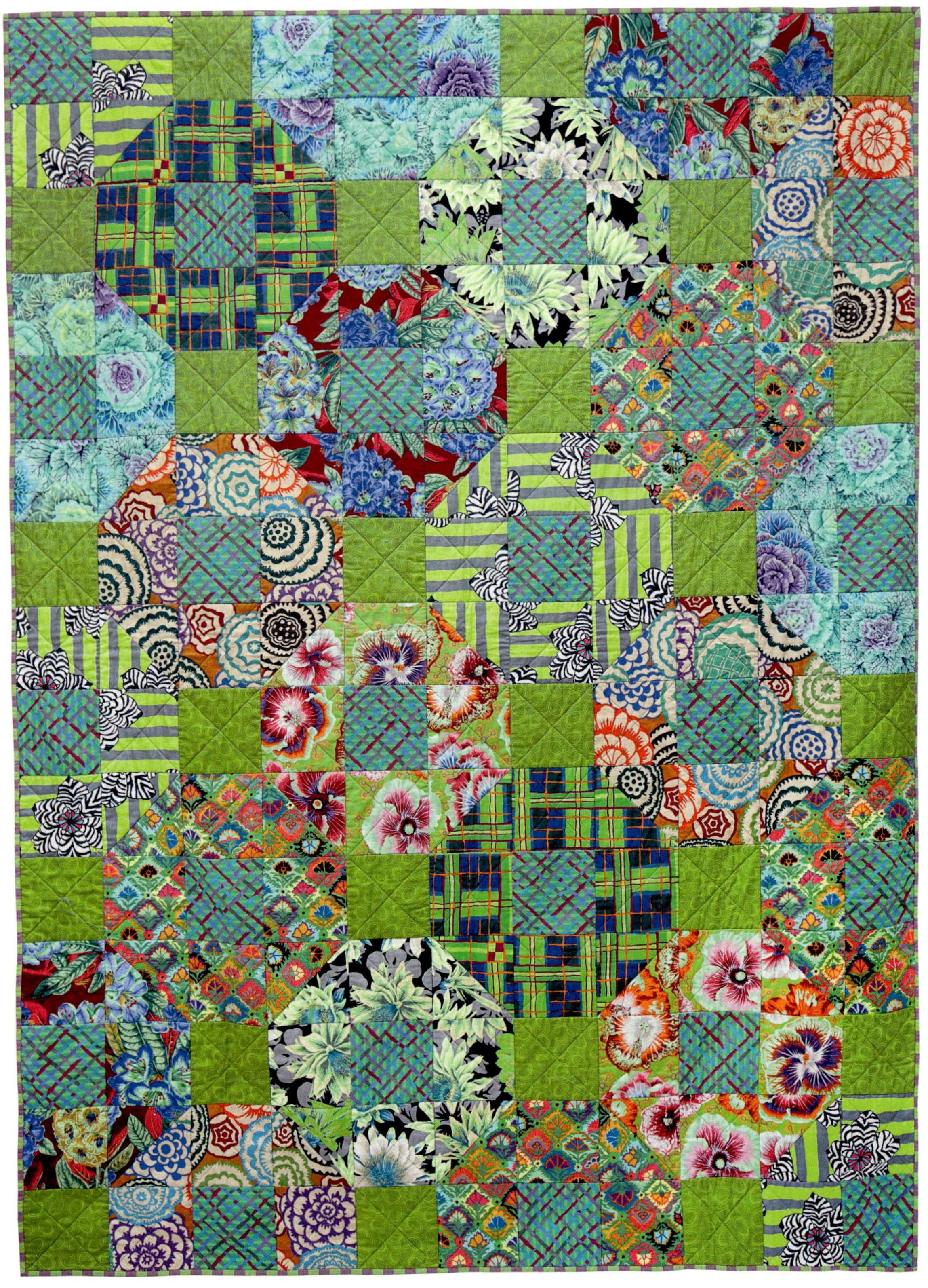

This rich green quilt is simple to make and is anchored by the use of Brandon's Mad Plaid fabric in the centre of each 9-patch square, with half-square triangles (HSTs) in each corner, creating leafy circles, and my Aboriginal Dot fabric in between them.

SIZE OF FINISHED QUILT
90in x 66in (228cm x 167cm)

FABRICS
Fabrics have been calculated at a maximum width of 40in (102cm). Fabrics have been given a number – see the Fabric Swatch Diagram for details.

Patchwork Fabrics
ABORIGINAL DOT
Fabric 1   Leaf   1yd (95cm)
MAD PLAID
Fabric 2   Green   1yd (95cm)
CHECKMATE
Fabric 3   Green   ⅝yd (60cm)
ZEBRA LILY
Fabric 4   Green   ⅝yd (60cm)
DECO
Fabric 5   Antique   ⅞yd (85cm)
STEP FLOWER
Fabric 6   Multi   ⅞yd (85cm)
BRASSICA
Fabric 7   Green   ⅝yd (60cm)
CACTUS FLOWER
Fabric 8   Contrast   ⅝yd (60cm)
FLOATING HIBISCUS
Fabric 9   Green   ⅝yd (60cm)
RHODODENDRONS
Fabric 10   Green   ⅝yd (60cm)

Backing and Binding Fabrics
ENCHANTED extra-wide backing
Fabric 11   Green   2⅛yd (2m)
WIDE STRIPE
Fabric 12   Apple   ¾yd (70cm)

Batting
100in x 76in (254cm x 193cm)

FABRIC SWATCH DIAGRAM

Patchwork Fabrics

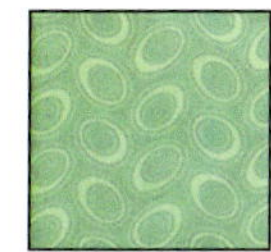

Fabric 1
ABORIGINAL DOT
Leaf
GP71LF

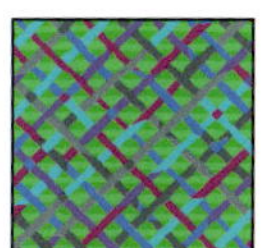

Fabric 2
MAD PLAID
Green
BM37GN

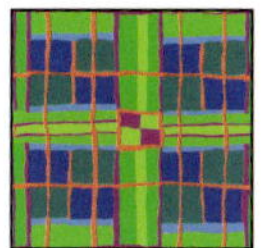

Fabric 3
CHECKMATE
Green
BM86GN

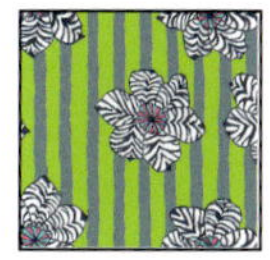

Fabric 4
ZEBRA LILY
Green
BM91GN

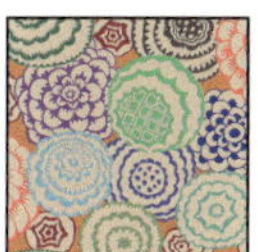

Fabric 5
DECO
Antique
GP199AN

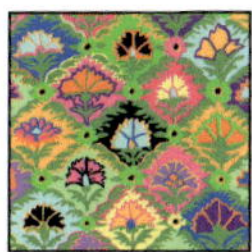

Fabric 6
STEP FLOWER
Multi
GP202MU

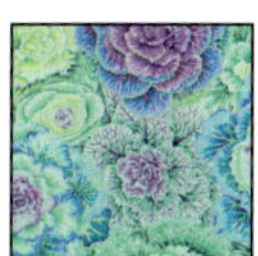

Fabric 7
BRASSICA
Green
PJ51GN

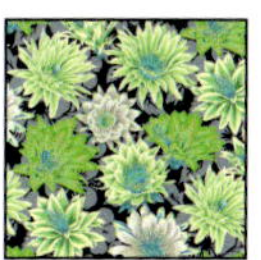

Fabric 8
CACTUS FLOWER
Contrast
PJ96CN

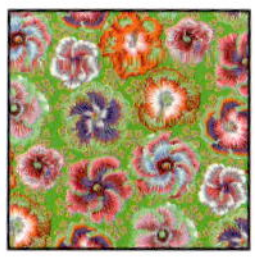

Fabric 9
FLOATING HIBISCUS
Green
PJ122GN

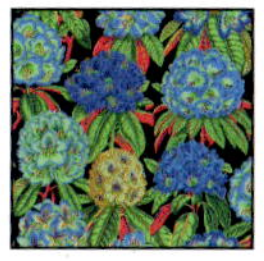

Fabric 10
RHODODENDRONS
Green
PJ124GN

Backing and Binding Fabrics

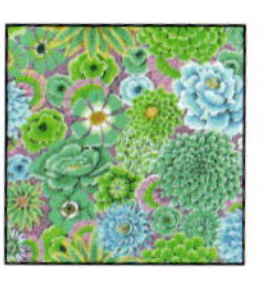

Fabric 11
ENCHANTED
Green
QB08GN

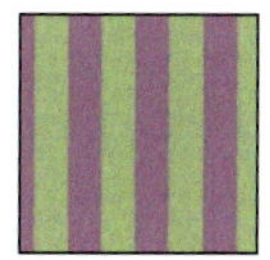

Fabric 12
WIDE STRIPE
Apple
SS01AL

PATCHES
Patches are squares and HSTs finished at 6in (15.2cm). They are arranged as 9-patch squares with HST blocks at each corner, forming circles. Each circle has the same centre square fabric and each space between the circles has the same fabric creating the background. Patches are set in 15 rows of 11, sewn together in rows.

CUTTING OUT
Fabric is cut across the width unless otherwise stated. When cutting different pieces from the same fabric, always cut the larger pieces first.

Half-square Triangles (HSTs)
Cut strips 6⅞in (17.5cm) wide and cross cut squares at 6⅞in (17.5cm). Cut each square in half diagonally once to create 2 HSTs from each square. Each strip will yield 5 squares. Cut a total of 35 squares, making 70 HSTs, from fabrics as follows:
Fabric 3 (1 strip) 4 squares – 8 triangles;
Fabric 4 (1 strip) 4 squares – 8 triangles;
Fabric 5 (2 strips) 6 squares – 12 triangles;
Fabric 6 (2 strips) 6 squares – 12 triangles;
Fabric 7 (1 strip) 3 squares – 6 triangles;
Fabric 8 (1 strip) 4 squares – 8 triangles;
Fabric 9 (1 strip) 4 squares – 8 triangles;
Fabric 10 1 strip) 4 squares – 8 triangles.

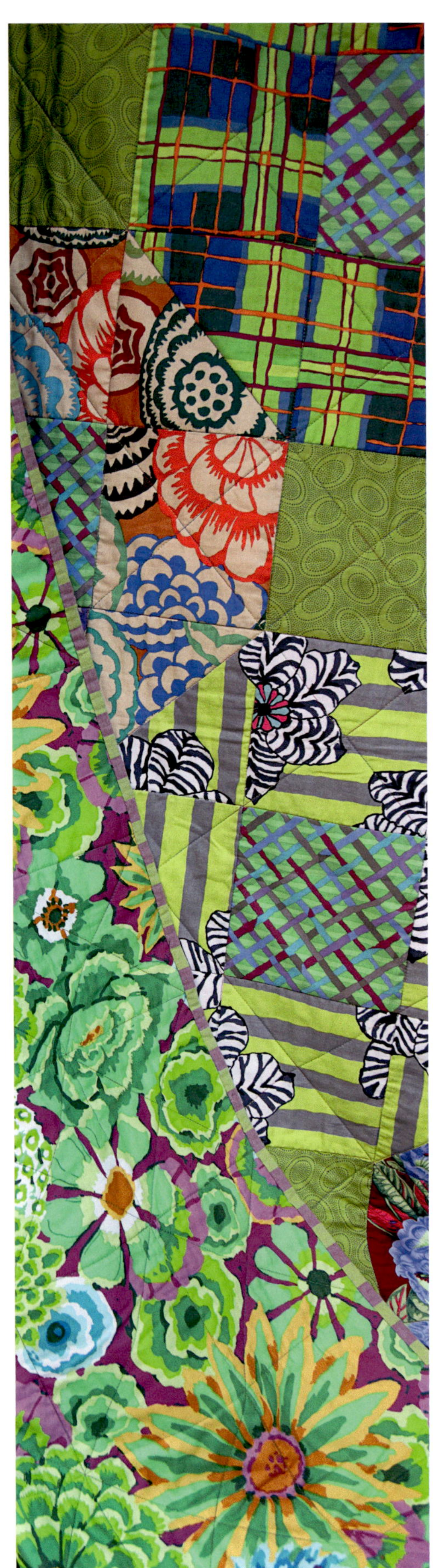

Squares

Trim down the remaining strips from the HSTs plus additional strips needed at 6½in (16.5cm) wide, and cross cut squares at 6½in (16.5cm). Each full strip will yield 6 squares. Cut a total of 130 squares from fabrics as follows:
Fabric 1 (5 strips) 24 squares;
Fabric 2 (5 strips) 24 squares;
Fabric 3 (2 strips) 8 squares;
Fabric 4 (2 strips) 11 squares;
Fabric 5 (remaining piece + 2 strips) 14 squares;
Fabric 6 (remaining piece +2 strips) 14 squares;
Fabric 7 9 squares;
Fabric 8 (2 strips) 8 squares;
Fabric 9 (2 strips) 8 squares;
Fabric 10 (2 strip) 10 squares.

Backing

Trim Fabric 11 backing fabric to 100in x 76in (254cm x 193cm).

Binding

From Fabric 12 cut 9 strips 2½in (6.4cm) wide. Remove selvedges and sew end to end with 45° seams (see page 141).

MAKING THE QUILT

Using a design wall will help to place patches in the required layout.
Use ¼in (6mm) seams throughout.

Making the Patches

Referring to the Quilt Assembly Diagram and the quilt photograph, lay out the squares and HSTs in 15 rows of 11 squares, ensuring the 'leafy circles' have correctly positioned HST squares at the corners.

Take each set of HSTs from the layout and sew the triangles together along their long edges. Press gently to avoid stretching the bias seams and return them to the layout. Double check the layout is correct, especially that the HST squares are correctly orientated for each circle.

Assembly

Sew together one row at a time, pressing seams in opposite directions on alternate rows – odd rows to the left, even rows to the right – to allow the finished seams to lie flat. Sew the rows together taking care to align crossing seams.

FINISHING THE QUILT

Press the quilt top. Layer the quilt top, batting and backing, and baste together (see page 140).
Quilt as desired.
Trim the quilt edges and attach the binding (see page 141).

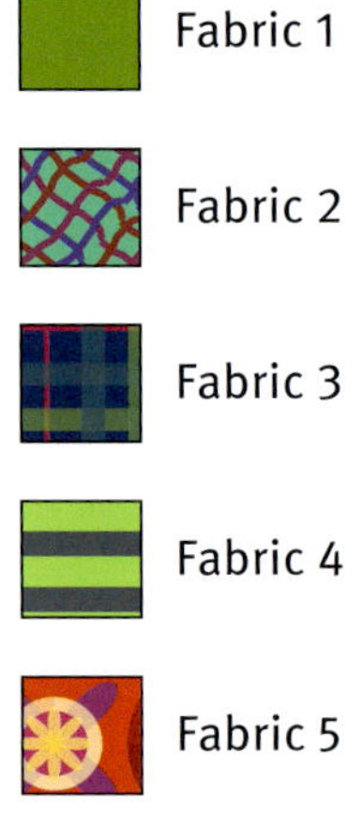

Fabric 1

Fabric 2

Fabric 3

Fabric 4

Fabric 5

Fabric 6

Fabric 7

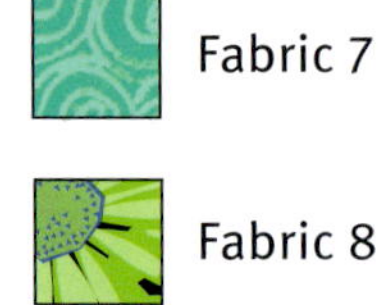

Fabric 8

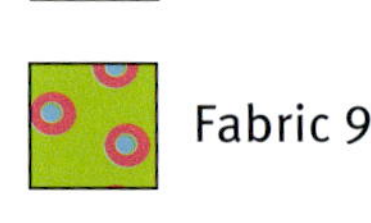

Fabric 9

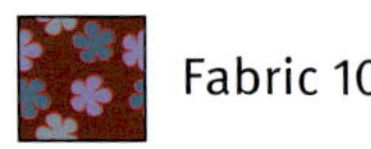

Fabric 10

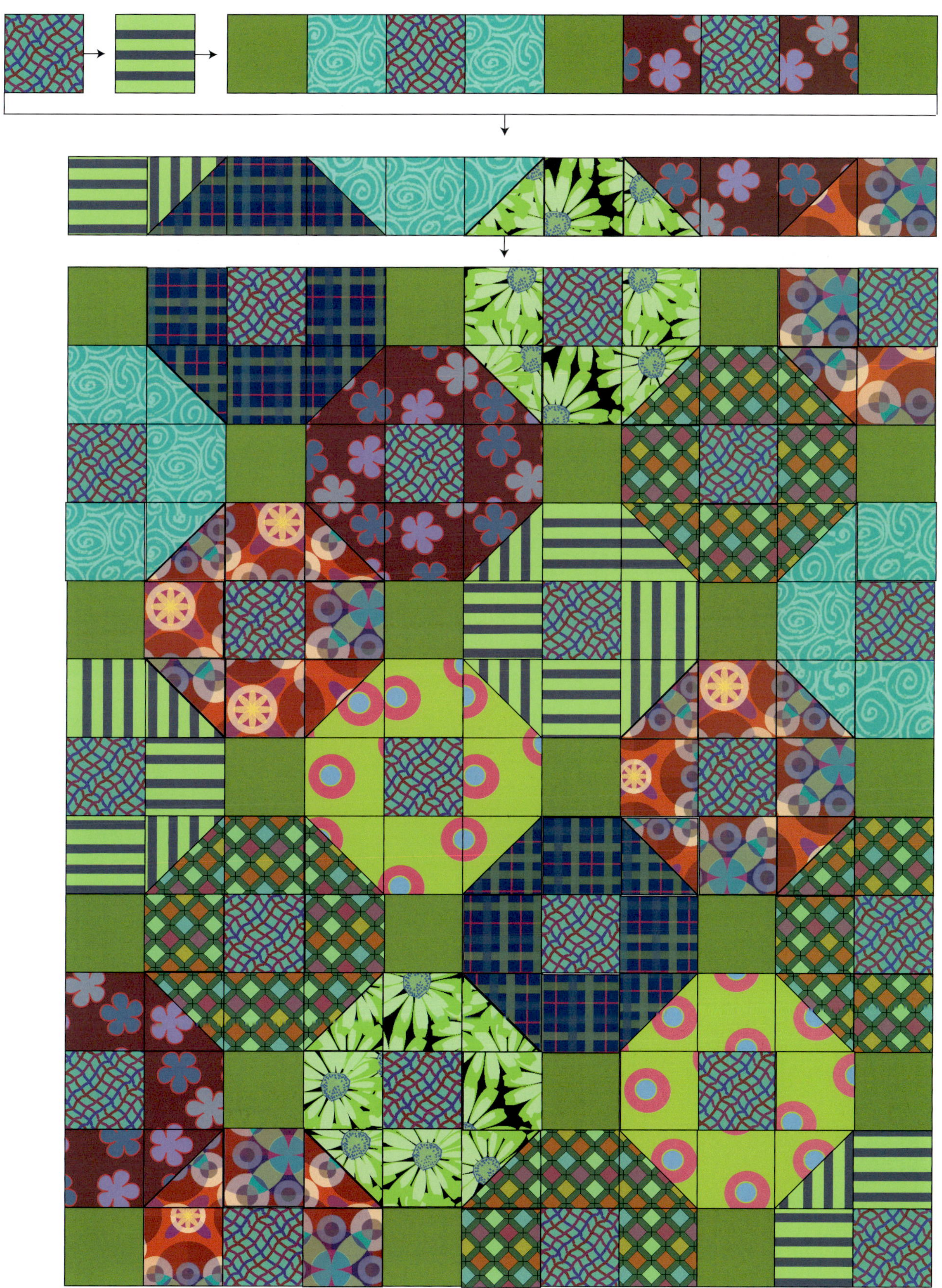

deco floral *

Kaffe Fassett

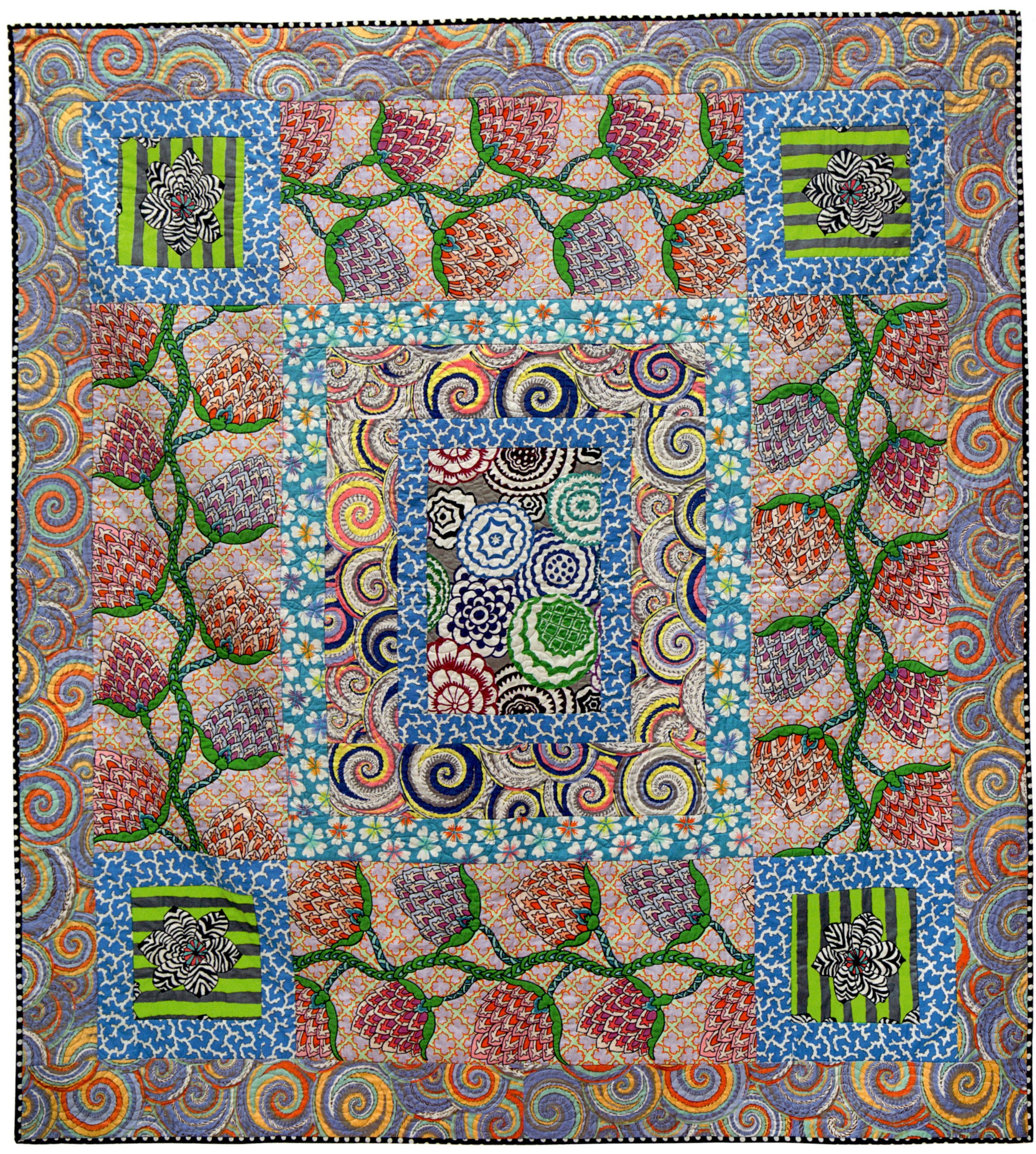

This medallion quilt has borders in various sizes. The widest border, which is fussy cut using my Paisley Flower vine print, surrounds the centre and two narrower inner borders. It has contrasting framed corner squares, giving the quilt a more architectural appearance, and a further narrow border provides the outer frame.

SIZE OF FINISHED QUILT
76in x 70in (193cm x 177cm)

FABRICS
Fabrics have been calculated at a maximum width of 40in (102cm). Fabrics have been given a number – see the Fabric Swatch Diagram for details.

Patchwork Fabrics
DECO
Fabric 1   Cool   ³⁄₈yd (40cm)
CORAL
Fabric 2   Blue   ⁵⁄₈yd (60cm)
CURLY BASKETS
Fabric 3   Contrast   ½yd (50cm)
CURLY BASKETS
Fabric 4   Multi   1⅛yd (1.1m)
PETALS
Fabric 5   Sky   ½yd (50cm)
PAISLEY FLOWER
Fabric 6   Pastel   2yd (1.9m)
ZEBRA LILY
Fabric 7   Green   ½yd (50cm)

Backing and Binding Fabrics
JAPANESE CHRYSANTHEMUM
extra-wide backing
Fabric 8   Magenta   2½yd (2.3m)
SPOT
Fabric 9   Noir   ⁵⁄₈yd (60cm)

Batting
86in x 80in (218cm x 203cm)

PATCHES
The quilt is constructed around a rectangular centre panel with a succession of 5 borders. Borders 1, 2, 3 and 5 are cut across the width of the fabric. Border 4 is fussy cut lengthwise to centre the vine and flowers pattern. This border wraps clockwise around the quilt and is separated by framed fussy-cut corner squares.

CUTTING OUT
Fabric is cut across the width unless otherwise stated. When required strips are longer than 40in (102cm) – the usable width of the fabric – remove selvedges and join strips end to end to obtain the required length. Use ¼in (6mm) seams and press seams open.

Centre Panel
From Fabric 1 cut a rectangle 12½in x 18½in (31.8cm x 47cm).

Border 1
From Fabric 2 cut 2 strips 2½in (6.4cm) wide and cross cut:
2 pieces 18½in x 2½in (47cm x 6.4cm) for the side borders;
2 pieces 16½in x 2½in (41.9cm x 6.4cm) for the top and bottom borders.

Border 2
From Fabric 3 cut 3 strips 5½in (14cm) wide, remove selvedges and join end to end. From the length cut:
2 pieces 22½in x 5½in (57.2cm x 14cm) for the side borders;
2 pieces 26½in x 5½in (67.3cm x 14cm) for the top and bottom borders.

Border 3
From Fabric 5 cut 4 strips 3½in (8.9cm) wide, remove selvedges and join end to end. From the length cut 4 pieces 32½in x 3½in (82.6cm x 8.9cm).

Border 4
From Fabric 6 cut a strip 38½in (97.8cm) wide. **Cutting down the length of the fabric**, fussy cut 2 panels of vines 14½in (36.8cm) wide and 38½in (97.8cm) long for the side borders.
Also from Fabric 6 cut a strip 32½in (82.6cm) wide. **Cutting down the length of the fabric**, fussy cut 2 panels of vines 14½in (36.8cm) wide and 32½in (82.6cm) long for the top and bottom borders.

Patchwork Fabrics

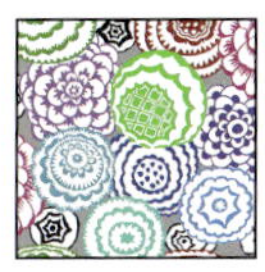

Fabric 1
DECO
Cool
GP199CL

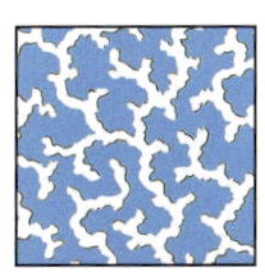

Fabric 2
CORAL
Blue
PJ04BL

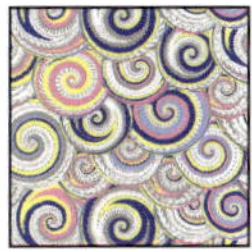

Fabric 3
CURLY BASKETS
Contrast
PJ66CN

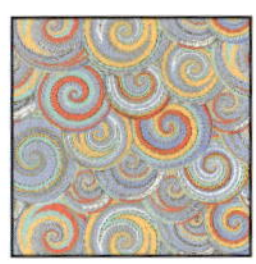

Fabric 4
CURLY BASKETS
Multi
PJ66MU

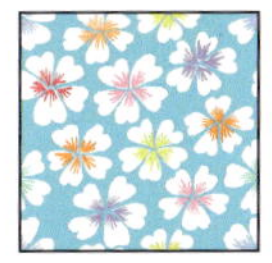

Fabric 5
PETALS
Sky
GP201SK

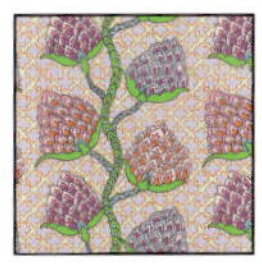

Fabric 6
PAISLEY FLOWER
Pastel
GP200PT

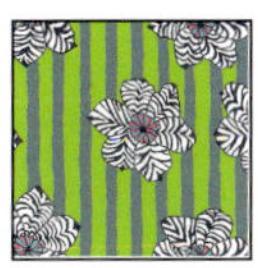

Fabric 7
ZEBRA LILY
Green
BM91GN

Backing and Binding Fabrics

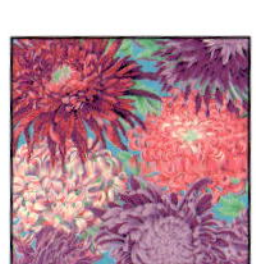

Fabric 8
JAPANESE CHRYSANTHEMUM
Magenta
QJ03MG

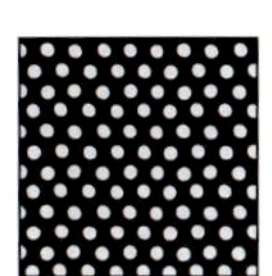

Fabric 9
SPOT
Noir
GP70NO

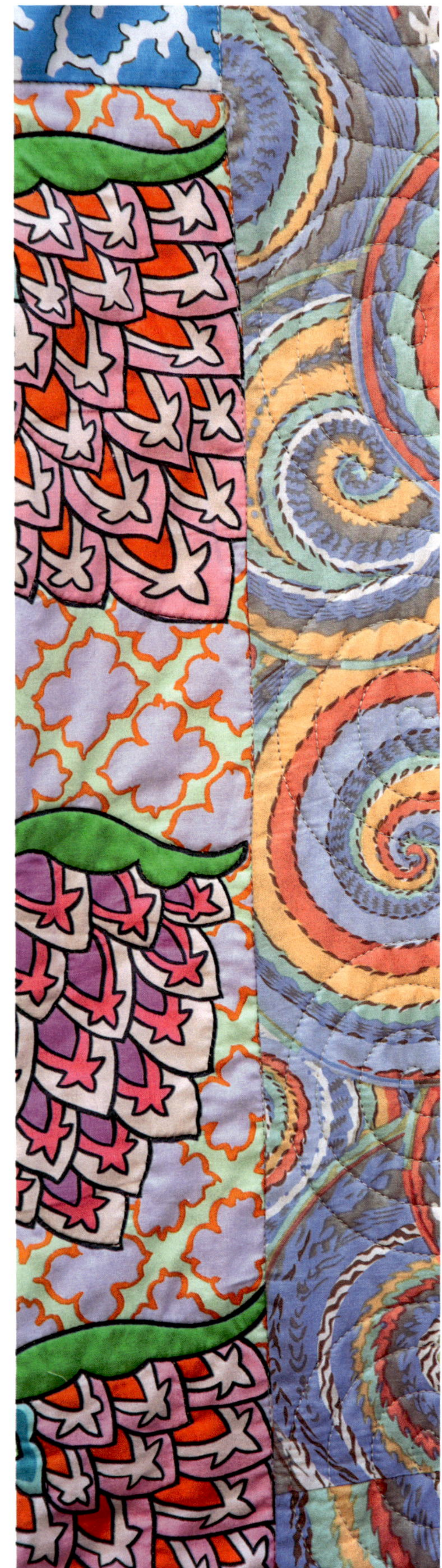

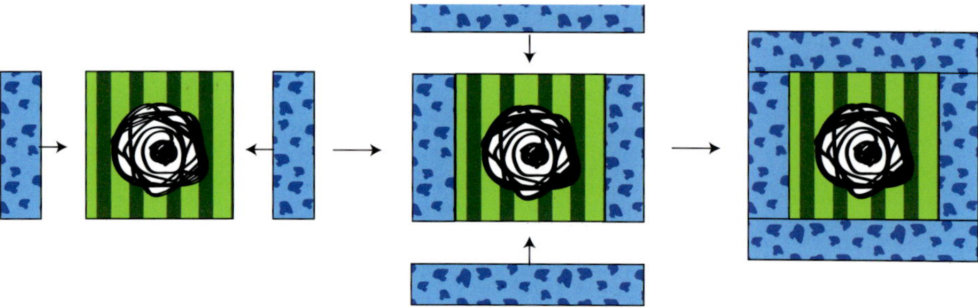

Border 4 Corner Squares
From Fabric 2 cut 5 strips 3in (7.6cm) wide, remove selvedges and join end to end. From the length cut:
8 long pieces 14½in x 3in (36.8cm x 7.6cm);
8 short pieces 9½ x 3in (24.1cm x 7.6cm).
From Fabric 7 fussy cut 4 flower motifs centred in 9½in (24.1cm) squares. Extra fabric has been allowed for this.

Border 5
From Fabric 4 cut 7 strips 5½in (14cm) wide, remove selvedges and join end to end. From the length cut:
2 pieces 66½in x 5½in (168.9cm x 14cm) for the side borders;
2 pieces 70½in x 5½in (179.1cm x 14cm) for the top and bottom borders.

Backing
Trim Fabric 8 to 86in x 80in (218cm x 203cm).

Binding
From Fabric 9 cut 8 strips 2½in (6.4cm) wide. Remove selvedges and sew end to end with 45° seams (see page 141).

MAKING THE QUILT
Using a design wall will help to place patches in the required layout.
Use ¼in (6mm) seams throughout.

Assembly of Borders 1, 2 and 3
Referring to the Quilt Assembly Diagram and the quilt photograph, lay out the centre panel and borders. Pin (to prevent stretching borders) and sew the side borders to the centre, press seams away from the centre, then pin and sew the top and bottom borders. Repeat for Borders 2 and 3.

Assembly of Borders 4 and 5
For Border 4, referring to the Corner Assembly Diagram, sew a Fabric 2 short strip to each side of a Fabric 7 fussy-cut square and press seams towards the borders. Sew a Fabric 2 long strip to the top and bottom then press seams towards the borders. Make all 4 framed corner squares and return them to the layout, arranging them with stripes positioned as in the quilt photograph, or as you prefer.

Pin and sew a longer Fabric 6 panel to each side of the quilt centre, checking the vine is facing the correct direction. Sew a framed corner square to each end of the shorter Fabric 6 panels, press seams towards the corner squares, then pin and sew the top and bottom borders to the centre, checking that crossing seams line up. Press seams away from the centre.
For Border 5, add the 2 side borders, then the top and bottom borders to complete the quilt top.

FINISHING THE QUILT
Press the quilt top. Layer the quilt top, batting and backing, and baste together (see page 140).
Quilt as desired.
Trim the quilt edges and attach the binding (see page 141).

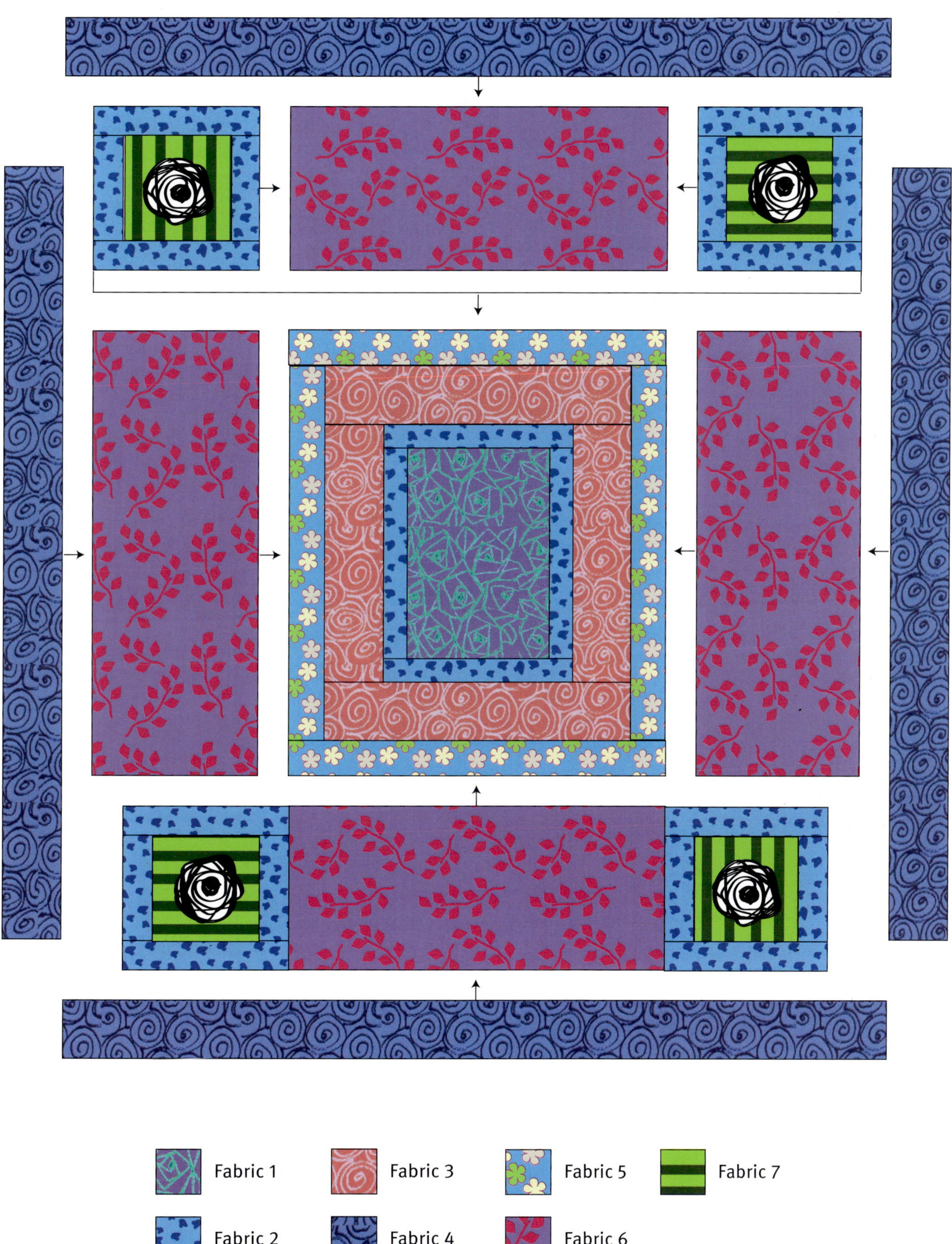

Fabric 1
Fabric 3
Fabric 5
Fabric 7
Fabric 2
Fabric 4
Fabric 6

templates

Refer to the individual quilt instructions for the templates needed. Look for the quilt name on the templates to make sure you are using the correct shapes for the project. Arrows on templates should be lined up with the straight grain of the fabric, which runs either along the selvedge or at 90 degrees to the selvedge. Following marked grain lines is important to avoid bias edges, which can cause distortion.

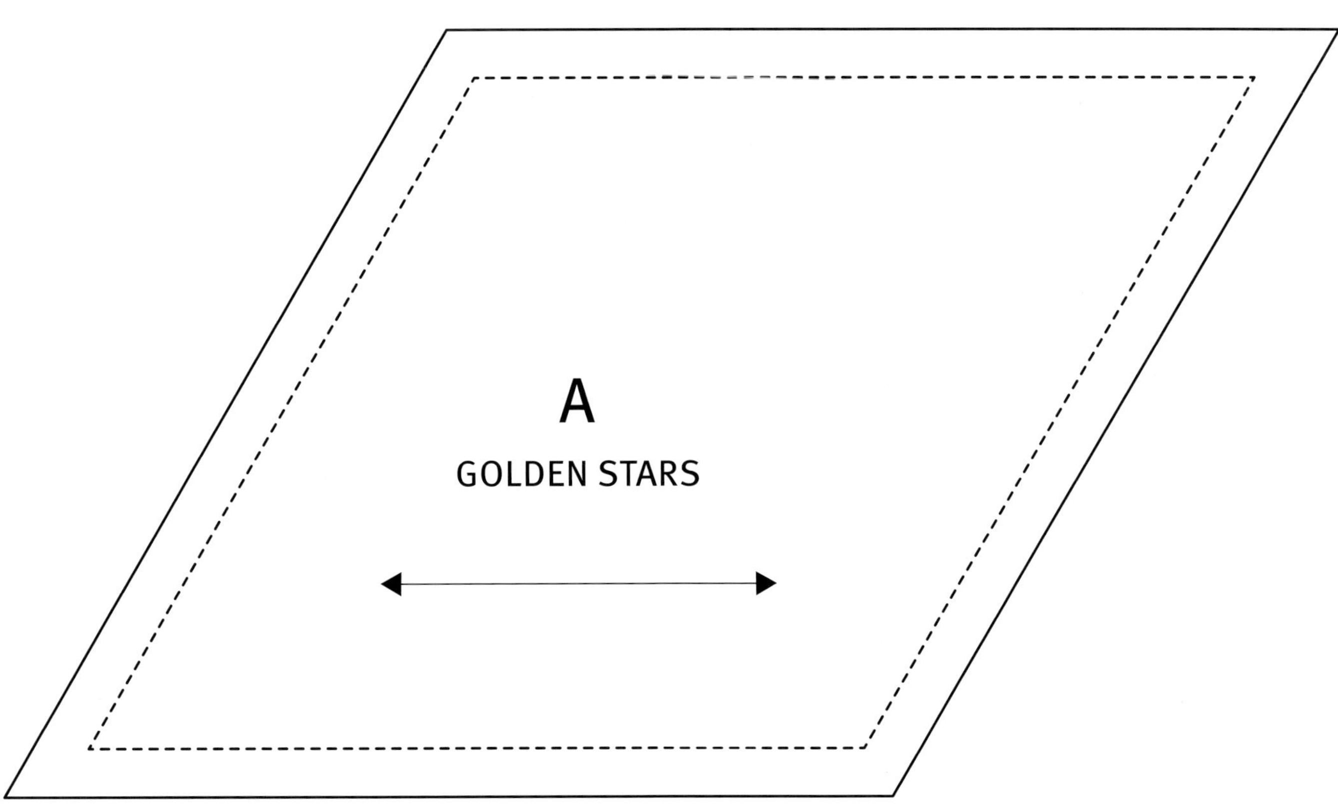

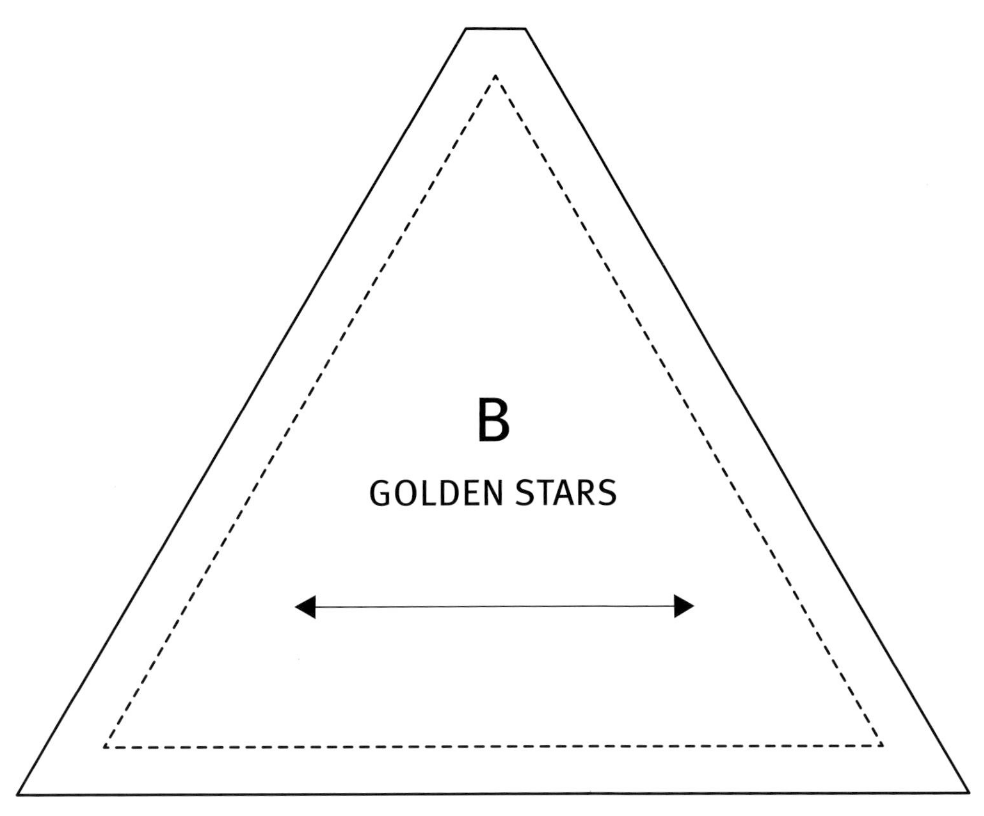

B
GOLDEN STARS

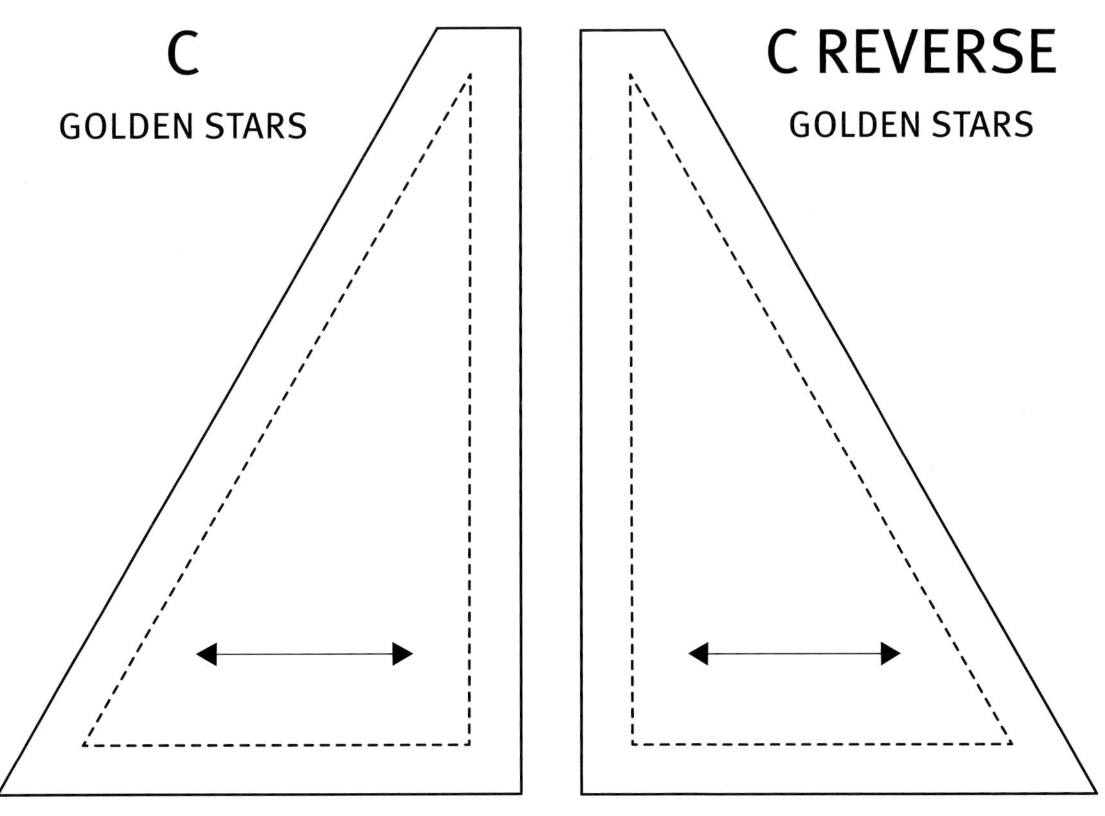

C
GOLDEN STARS
C REVERSE
GOLDEN STARS

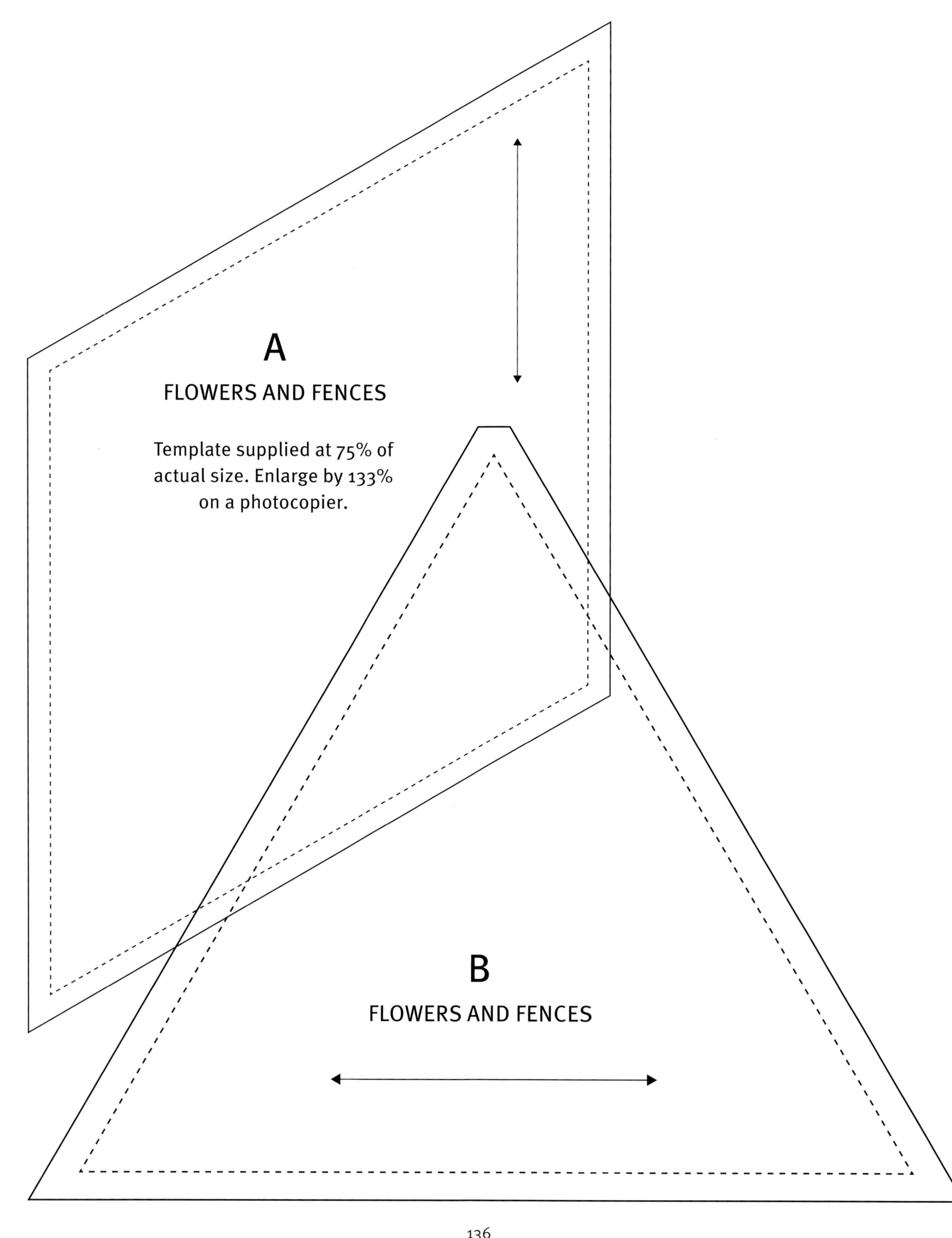

A
FLOWERS AND FENCES
Template supplied at 75% of actual size. Enlarge by 133% on a photocopier.
B
FLOWERS AND FENCES

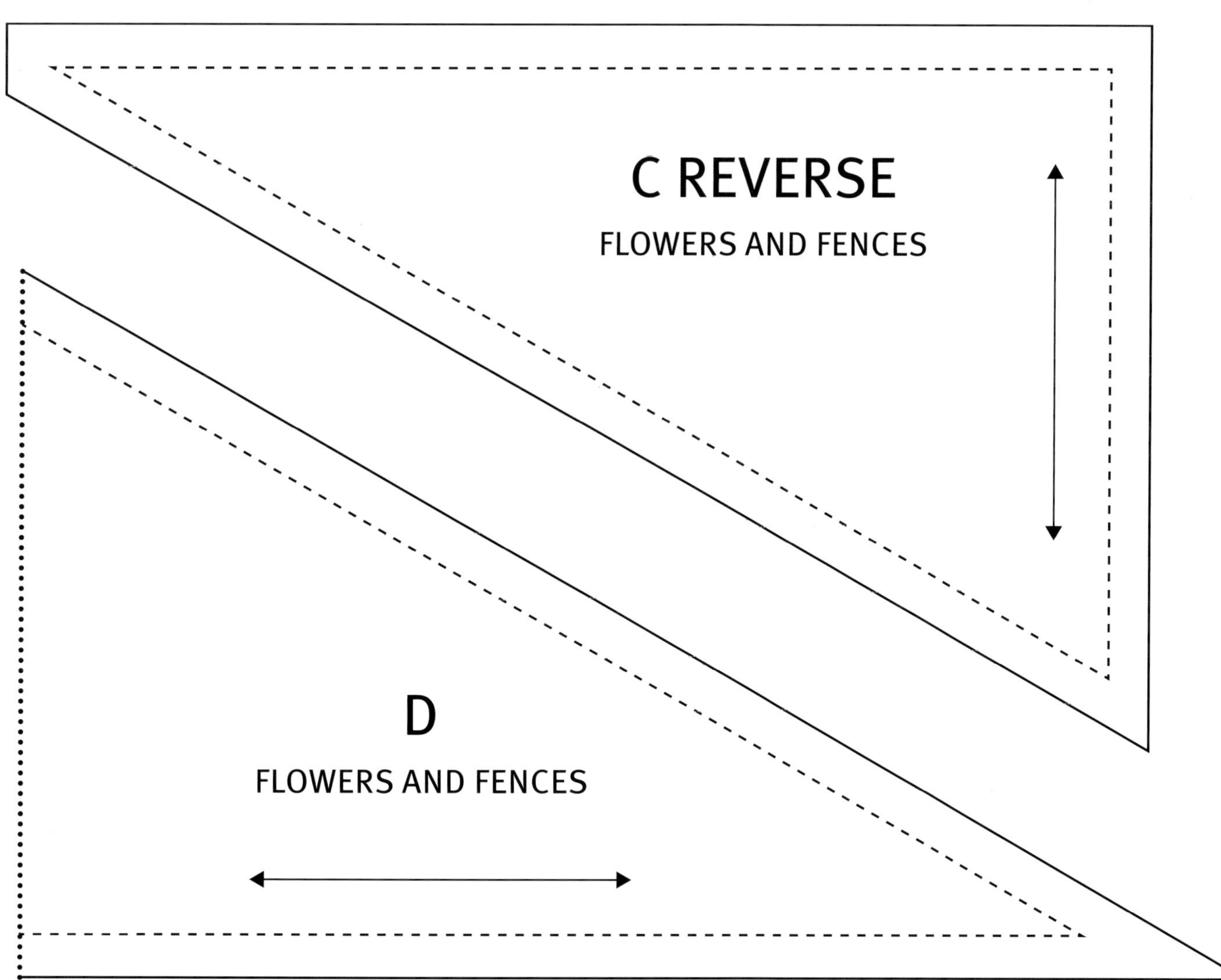

C
FLOWERS AND FENCES
C REVERSE
FLOWERS AND FENCES
D
FLOWERS AND FENCES
Place on fold of paper to complete the template

patchwork and quilting know-how

These instructions are intended for the novice quilt maker, providing the basic information needed to make the projects in this book, along with some useful tips.

EXPERIENCE RATINGS
* Easy, straightforward, suitable for a beginner.
** Suitable for the average patchworker and quilter.
*** For the more experienced patchworker and quilter.

ABOUT THE FABRICS
The fabrics used for the quilts in this book are mainly from Kaffe Fassett Collective:
GP is the code for Kaffe Fassett's designs, PJ for Philip Jacobs' and BM for Brandon Mably's.
The other fabrics used are Shot Cottons and Stripes with SC or SS prefixes as well as wide backing fabrics with QB prefixes.

PREPARING THE FABRIC
Prewash all new fabrics before you begin, to ensure that there will be no uneven shrinkage and no bleeding of colours when the finished quilt is laundered. Press the fabric whilst it is still damp to return crispness to it. All fabric requirements in this book are calculated on a 40in (102cm) usable fabric width, to allow for shrinkage and selvedge removal.

MAKING TEMPLATES
Transparent template plastic is the best material to use: it is durable and allows you to see the fabric and select certain motifs. You can also use tracing paper and thin stiff cardboard.

Templates for machine piecing
1 Trace off the actual-sized template provided either directly on to template plastic, or on to tracing paper and then on to thin cardboard. Use a ruler to help you trace off the straight cutting line, dotted seam line and grain lines.
   Sometimes templates are too large to print complete. Transfer the template on to the fold of a large sheet of paper, cut out and open out for the full template. Some templates are printed at a reduced size and need to be scaled up on a photocopier.
2 Cut out the traced off template using a craft knife, a ruler and a self-healing cutting mat.
3 Punch holes in the corners of the template, at each point on the seam line, using a hole punch.

Templates for hand piecing
• Make a template as for machine piecing, but do not trace off the cutting line. Use the dotted seam line as the outer edge of the template.

• This template allows you to draw the seam lines directly on to the fabric. The seam allowances can then be cut by eye around the patch.

CUTTING THE FABRIC
On the individual instructions for each project, you will find a summary of all the patch shapes used.
   Always mark and cut out any border and binding strips first, followed by the largest patch shapes and finally the smallest ones, to make the most efficient use of your fabric. The border and binding strips are best cut using a rotary cutter.

Rotary cutting
Rotary cut strips are usually cut across the fabric from selvedge to selvedge, but some projects may vary, so please read through all the instructions before you start cutting the fabrics.

1 Before beginning to cut, press out any folds or creases in the fabric. If you are cutting a large piece of fabric, you will need to fold it several times to fit the cutting mat. When there is only a single fold, place the fold facing you. If the fabric is too wide to be folded only once, fold it concertina-style until it fits your mat. A small rotary cutter with a sharp blade will cut up to six layers of fabric; a large cutter up to eight layers.

2 To ensure that your cut strips are straight and even, the folds must be placed exactly parallel to the straight edges of the fabric and along a line on the cutting mat.

3 Place a rotary ruler over the raw edge of the fabric, overlapping it about ½in (1.25cm). Make sure that the ruler is at right angles to both the straight edges and the fold to ensure that you cut along the straight grain. Press down on the ruler and wheel the cutter away from you along the edge of the ruler.

4 Open out the fabric to check the edge. Don't worry if it's not perfectly straight – a little wiggle will not show when the quilt is stitched together. Re-fold the fabric, then place the ruler over the trimmed edge, aligning the edge with the markings on the ruler that match the correct strip width. Cut strip along the edge of the ruler.

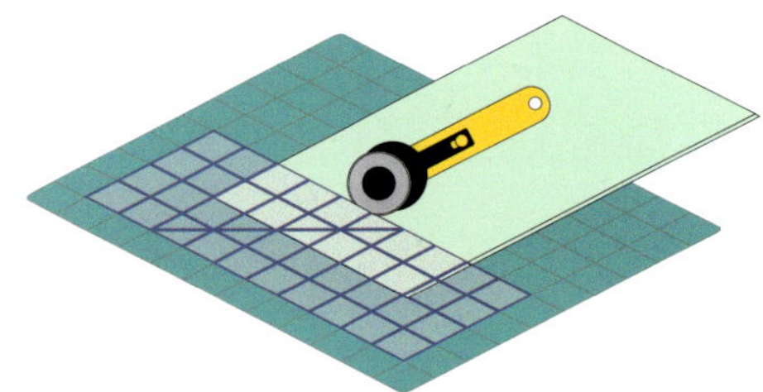

USING TEMPLATES
The most efficient way to cut out templates is by first rotary cutting a strip of fabric to the width stated for your template, and then marking off your templates along the strip, edge to edge at the required angle. This method leaves hardly any waste and gives a random effect to your patches.
   A less efficient method is to fussy cut them, where the templates are cut individually by placing them on particular motifs or stripes, to create special effects. Although this method is more wasteful, it yields very interesting results.

1 Place the template face down, on the wrong side of the fabric, with the grain-line arrow following the straight grain of the fabric, if indicated. Be careful though – check with your individual instructions, as some instructions may ask you to cut patches on varying grains.

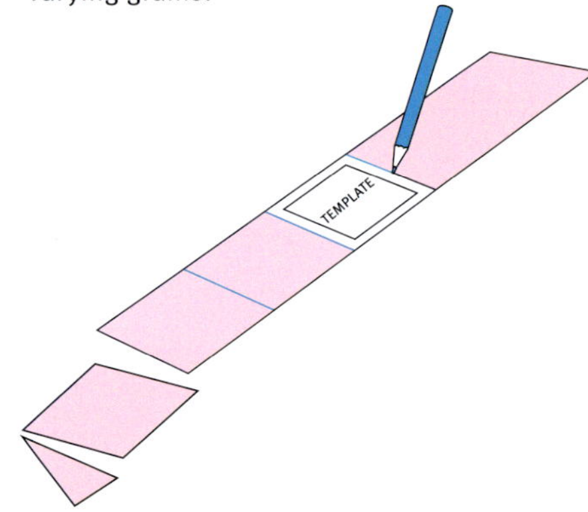

2 Hold the template firmly in place and draw around it with a sharp pencil or crayon, marking in the corner dots or seam lines. To save fabric, position patches close together or even touching. Don't worry if outlines positioned on the straight grain when drawn on striped fabrics do not always match the stripes when cut – this will add a degree of visual excitement to the patchwork!

3 Once you've drawn all the pieces needed, you are ready to cut the fabric, with either a rotary cutter and ruler or a pair of sharp sewing scissors.

Basic hand and machine piecing
Patches can be stitched together by hand or machine. Machine stitching is quicker, but hand assembly allows you to carry your patches around with you and work on them in every spare moment. The choice is yours. For techniques that are new to you, practise on scrap pieces of fabric until you feel confident.

Hand piecing

1 Pin two patches with right sides together, so that the marked seam lines are facing outwards.

2 Using a single strand of strong thread, secure the corner of a seam line with a couple of back stitches.

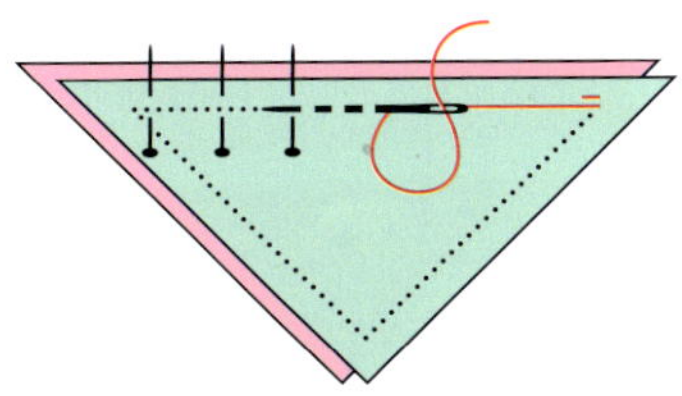

3 Sew running stitches along the marked line, working 8–10 stitches per inch (2.5cm) and ending at the opposite seam line corner with a few back stitches. When hand piecing never stitch over the seam allowances.

4 Press the seams to one side, as shown in machine piecing (Step 2).

Machine piecing

Follow the quilt instructions for the order in which to piece the individual patchwork blocks and then assemble the blocks together in rows.

1 Seam lines are not marked on the fabric for simple shapes, so stitch ¼in (6mm) seams using the machine needle plate, a ¼in (6mm) wide machine foot, or tape stuck to the machine as a guide. Pin two patches with right sides together, matching edges.

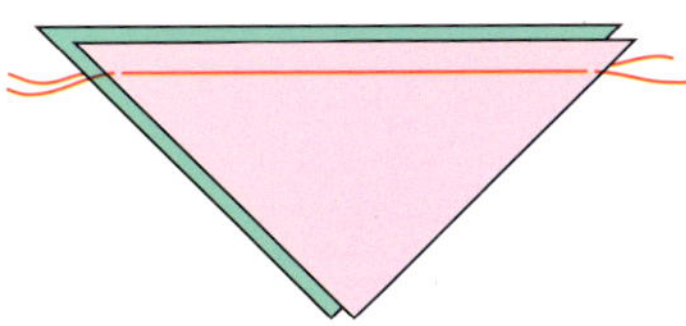

For some shapes, particularly diamonds, you need to match the sewing lines, not the fabric edges. Place 2 diamonds right sides together but offset so that the sewing lines intersect at the correct position. Use pins to secure for sewing.

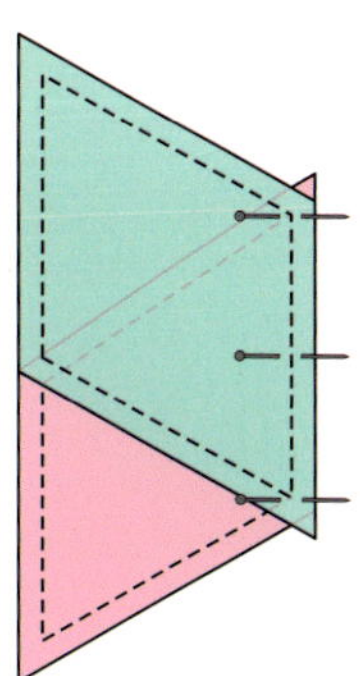

Set your machine at 10–12 stitches per inch (2.5cm) and stitch seams from edge to edge, removing pins as you feed the fabric through the machine.

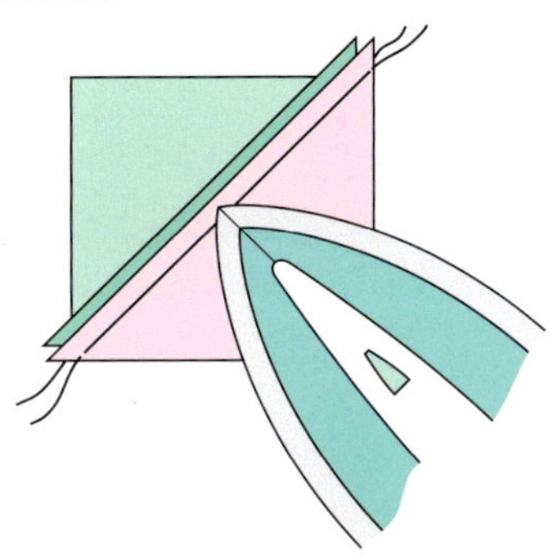

2 Press the seams of each patchwork block to one side before attempting to join it to another block. When joining diamond shaped blocks you will need to offset the blocks in the same way as diamond shaped patches, matching the sewing lines, not the fabric edges.

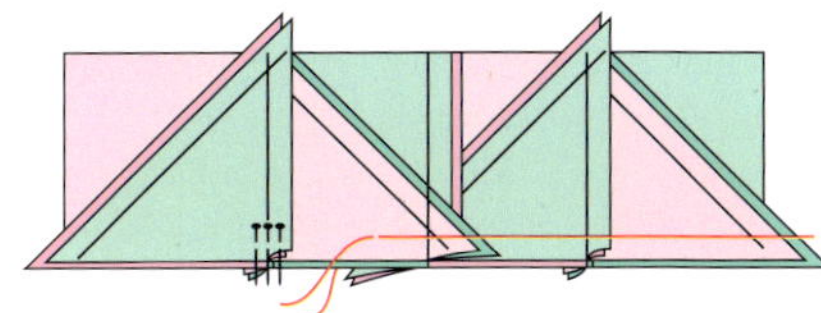

3 When joining rows of blocks, make sure that adjacent seam allowances are pressed in opposite directions to reduce bulk and make matching easier. Pin pieces together directly through the stitch line and to the right and left of the seam. Remove pins as you sew. Continue pressing seams to one side as you work.

Inset (Y) seams

When 3 or more patches have seams that come together without making a rectangle (i.e. in a Y-shape), an inset seam is needed. As shown in the diagram, with RS together, first sew the A–B seam. Then, starting from an inner point to an outer point, sew the A–C seam, and finally the A–D seam. Make sure you start and finish each ¼in (6mm) seam exactly at the beginning and end (as marked by dots on the diagram) and do not stitch into the seam allowance.

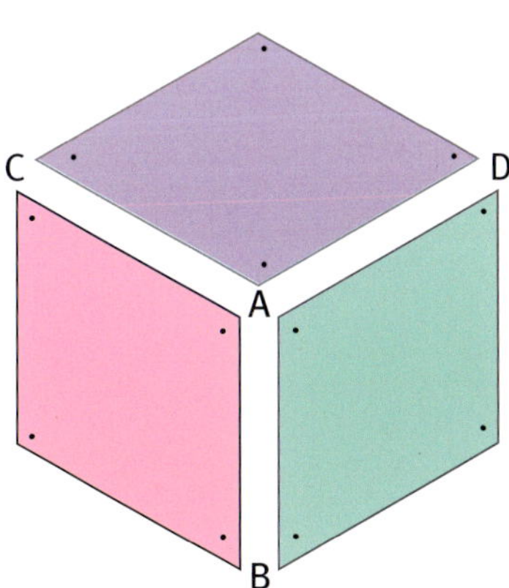

MACHINE APPLIQUÉ WITH ADHESIVE WEB

To make appliqué very easy you can use adhesive web (which comes attached to a paper backing sheet) to bond the motifs to the background fabric. There are two types of web available: the first keeps the pieces in place while they are stitched, the second permanently attaches the pieces so that no sewing is required. Follow steps 1 and 2 for the non-sew type and steps 1–3 for the type that requires sewing.

1 Trace the reversed appliqué design onto the paper side of the adhesive web, leaving a ¼in (6mm) gap between all the shapes. Roughly cut out the motifs ⅛in (3mm) outside your drawn line.

2 Bond the motifs to the reverse of your chosen fabrics. Cut out on the drawn line with very sharp scissors. Remove the backing paper by scoring the centre of the motif carefully with a scissor point and peeling the paper away from the centre out (to prevent damage to the edges). Place the motifs onto the background, noting any which may be layered. Cover with a clean cloth and bond with a hot iron (check instructions for temperature setting as adhesive web can vary depending on the manufacturer).

3 Using a contrasting or toning coloured thread in your machine, work small close zig zag stitches (or a blanket stitch if your machine has one) around the edge of the motifs; the majority of the stitching should sit on the appliqué shape. When stitching up to points, stop with the machine needle in the down position, lift the foot of your machine, pivot the work, lower the foot and continue to stitch. Make sure all the raw edges are stitched.

HAND APPLIQUÉ

Good preparation is essential for speedy and accurate hand appliqué. The finger-pressing method is suitable for needle-turning application, used for simple shapes like leaves and flowers. Using a card template is the best method for bold simple motifs such as circles.

Finger–pressing method

1 To make your template, transfer the appliqué design using carbon paper on to stiff card, and cut out the template. Trace around the outline of your appliquéd shape on to the right side of your fabric using a well sharpened pencil. Cut out shapes, adding by eye a ¼in (6mm) seam allowance all around.

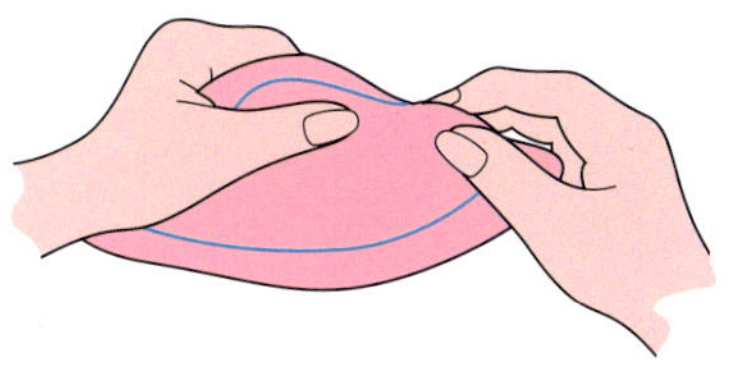

2 Hold the shape right side up and fold under the seam, turning along your drawn line, pinch to form a crease. Dampening the fabric makes this very easy. When using shapes with points such as leaves, turn in the seam allowance at the point first, as shown in the diagram. Then continue all round the shape. If your shapes have sharp curves, you can snip the seam allowance to ease the curve. Take care not to stretch the appliqué shapes as you work.

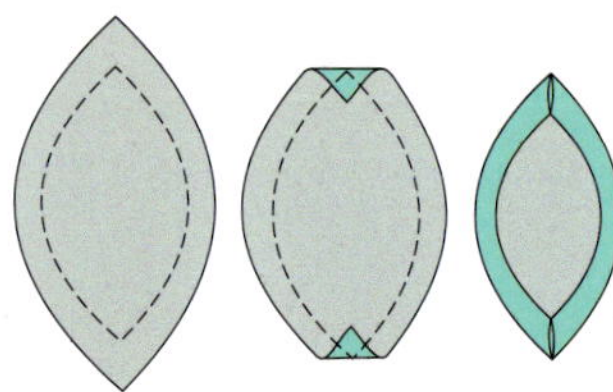

Straight stems
Place fabric face down and simply press over the ¼in (6mm) seam allowance along each edge. You don't need to finish the ends of stems that are layered under other appliqué shapes. Where the end of the stem is visible, simply tuck under the end and finish neatly.

Needle-turning application
Take the appliqué shape and pin in position. Stroke the seam allowance under with the tip of the needle as far as the creased pencil line, and hold securely in place with your thumb. Using a matching thread, bring the needle up from the back of the block into the edge of the shape and proceed to blind-hem in place. (This stitch allows the motifs to appear to be held on invisibly.) To do this, bring the thread out from below through the folded edge of the motif, never on the top. The stitches must be small, even and close together to prevent the seam allowance from unfolding and from frayed edges appearing. Try to avoid pulling the stitches too tight, as this will cause the motifs to pucker up. Work around the whole shape, stroking under each small section before sewing.

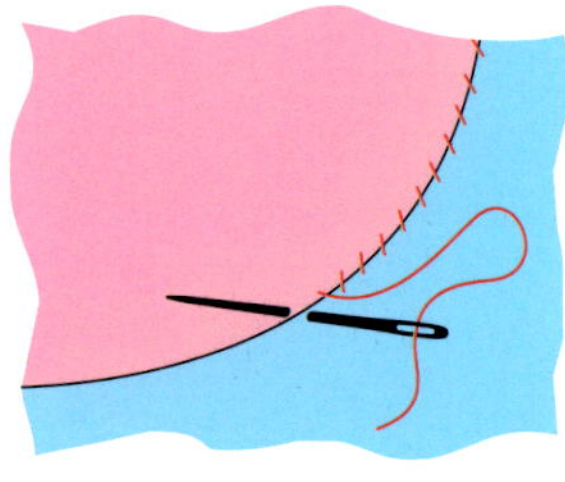

QUILTING
When you have finished piecing your patchwork and added any borders, press it carefully. It is now ready for quilting.

Marking quilting designs and motifs
Many tools are available for marking quilting patterns, check the manufacturer's instructions for use and test on scraps of fabric from your project. Use an acrylic ruler for marking straight lines.

Stencils
Some designs require stencils; these can be made at home, by transferring the designs on to template plastic, or stiff cardboard. The design is then cut away in the form of long dashes, to act as guides for both internal and external lines. These stencils are a quick method for producing an identical set of repeated designs.

BACKING FABRIC
The quilts in this book use two different widths of backing fabric – the standard width of 44in (112cm) and a wider one of 108in (274cm). If you can't find (or don't want to use) the wider fabric then select a standard-width fabric instead and adjust the amount accordingly. For most of the quilts in the book, using a standard-width fabric will probably mean joins in the fabric. The material list for each quilt assumes that an extra 4in of backing fabric is needed all round (8in in total) when making up the quilt sandwich, to allow for long-arm quilting if needed. We have assumed a usable width of 40in (102cm), to allow for selvedge removal and possible shrinkage after washing.

Preparing the backing and batting
• Remove the selvedges and piece together the backing fabric to form a backing at least 4in (10cm) larger all around than the patchwork top.

• Choose a fairly thin batting, preferably pure cotton, to give your quilt a flat appearance. If your batting has been rolled up, unroll it and let it rest before cutting it to the same size as the backing.

• For a large quilt it may be necessary to join two pieces of batting to fit. Lay the pieces of batting on a flat surface so that they overlap by around 8in (20cm). Cut a curved line through both layers.

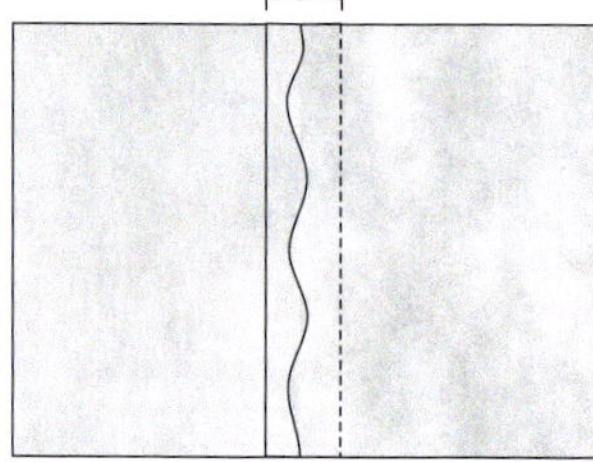

• Carefully peel away the two narrow pieces and discard. Butt the curved cut edges back together. Stitch the two pieces together using a large herringbone stitch.

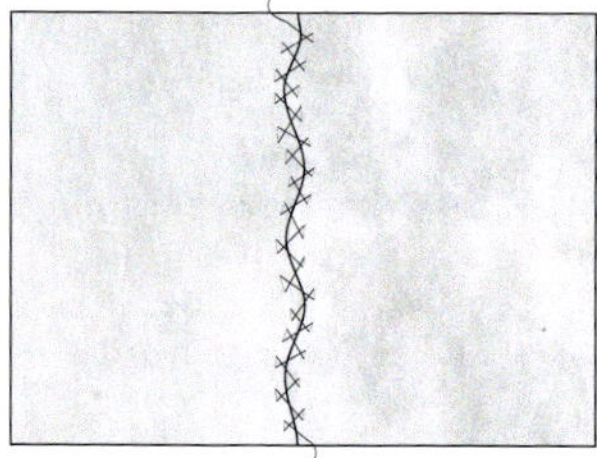

BASTING THE LAYERS TOGETHER
1 On the floor or on a large work surface, lay out the backing with wrong side uppermost. Use weights along the edges to keep it taut.

2 Lay the batting on the backing and smooth it out gently. Next lay the patchwork top, right side up, on top of the batting and smooth gently until there are no wrinkles. Pin at the corners and at the midpoints of each side, close to the edges.

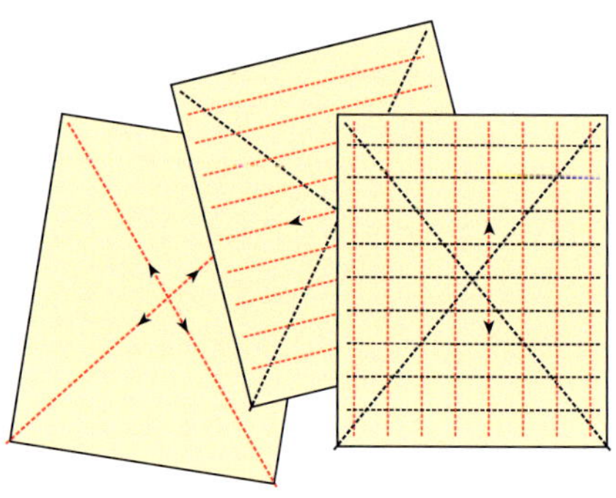

3 Beginning at the centre, baste diagonal lines outwards to the corners, making your stitches about 3in (7.5cm) long. Then, again starting at the centre, baste horizontal and vertical lines out to the edges. Continue basting until you have basted a grid of lines about 4in (10cm) apart over the entire quilt.

4 For speed, when machine quilting, some quilters prefer to baste their quilt sandwich layers together using rust-proof safety pins, spaced at 4in (10cm) intervals over the entire quilt.

HAND QUILTING
This is best done with the quilt mounted on a quilting frame or hoop, but as long as you have basted the quilt well, a frame is not essential. With the quilt top facing upwards, begin at the centre of the quilt and make even running stitches following the design. It is more important to make even stitches on both sides of the quilt than to make small ones. Start and finish your stitching with back stitches and bury the ends of your threads in the batting.

TIED QUILTING
If you prefer you could use tied quilting rather than machine quilting. For tied quilting, use a strong thread that will withstand being pulled through the quilt layers and tied in a knot. You can tie with the knot on the front of the quilt or the back, as preferred. Leaving tufts of thread gives an attractive, rustic look.

Thread a needle with a suitable thread, using the number of strands noted in the project. Put the needle and thread through from the front of the work, leaving a long tail. Go through to the back of the quilt, make a small stitch and then come back through to the front. Tie the threads together using a reef knot and trim the thread ends to the desired length. For extra security, you could tie a double knot or add a spot of fabric glue on the knot.

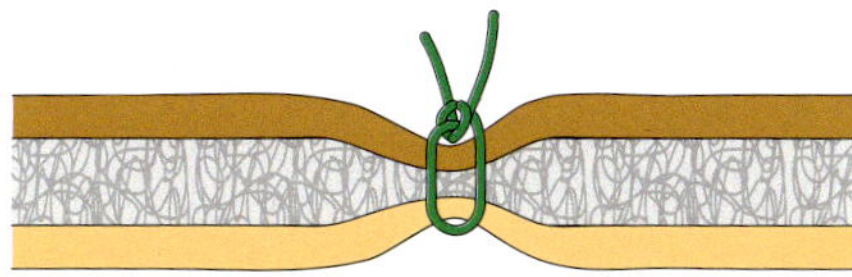

MACHINE QUILTING

• For a flat looking quilt, always use a walking foot on your machine for stitching straight lines, and a darning foot for free-motion quilting.

• It is best to start your quilting at the centre of the quilt and work out towards the borders, doing the straight quilting lines first (stitch-in-the-ditch) followed by the free-motion quilting.

• When free-motion quilting, stitch in a loose meandering style as shown in the diagrams. Do not stitch too closely as this will make the quilt feel stiff when finished. If you wish you can include floral themes or follow shapes on the printed fabrics for added interest.

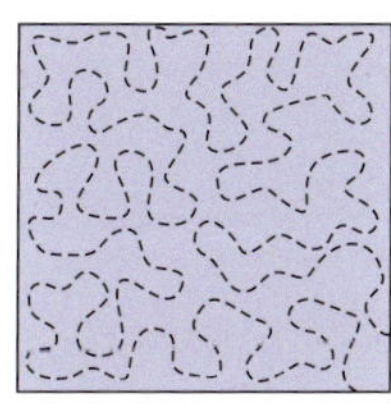

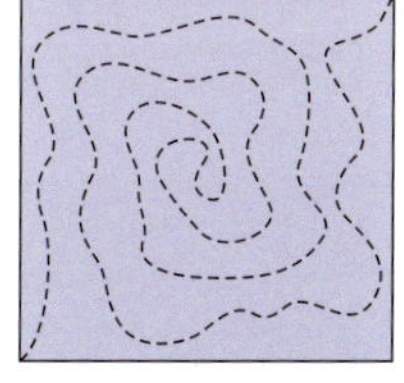

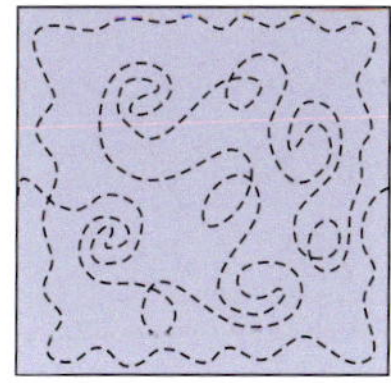

• Make it easier for yourself by handling the quilt properly. Roll up the excess quilt neatly to fit under your sewing machine arm, and use a table or chair to help support the weight of the quilt that hangs down the other side.

FINISHING
Preparing to bind the edges
Once you have quilted or tied your quilt sandwich together, remove all the basting stitches. Then, baste around the outer edge of the quilt ¼in (6mm) from the edge of the top patchwork layer. Trim the back and batting to the edge of the patchwork and straighten the edge of the patchwork if necessary.

Binding and 45-degree seams
1 Cut bias or straight grain strips the width required for your binding, making sure the grain-line is running the correct way on your straight grain strips. Cut enough strips until you have the required length to go around the edge of your quilt.

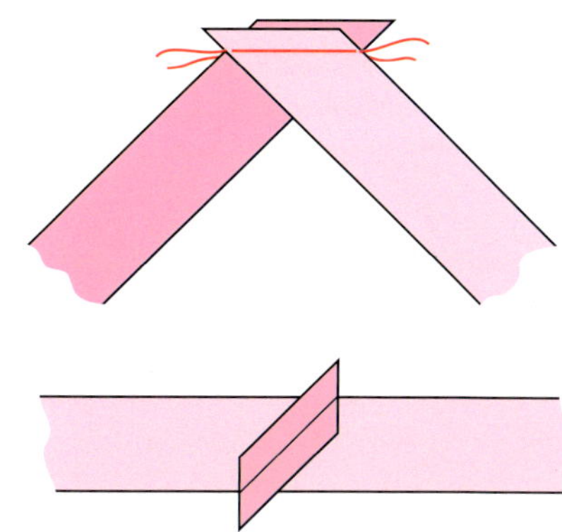

2 To join strips together, the two ends that are to be joined must be cut at a 45-degree angle, as above. Stitch right sides together, trim turnings and press seam open.

Binding the edges

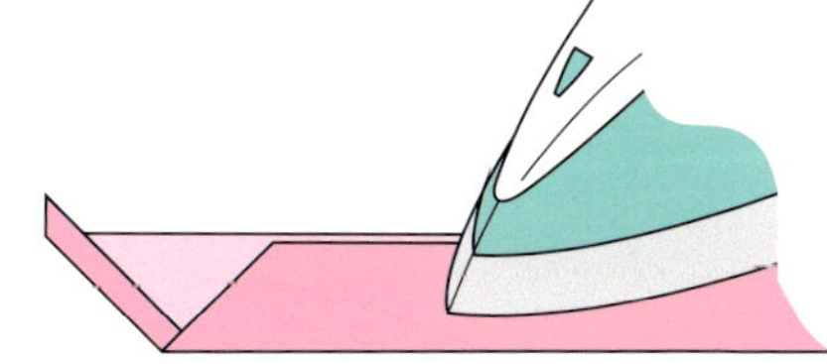

1 Cut the starting end of binding strip at a 45-degree angle, fold a ¼in (6mm) turning to wrong side along cut edge and press in place. With wrong sides together, fold strip in half lengthways, keeping raw edges level, and press.

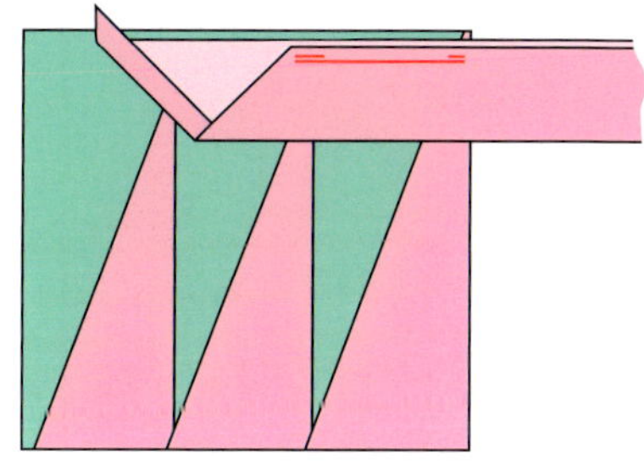

2 Starting at the centre of one of the long edges, place the doubled binding on to the right side of the quilt keeping raw edges level. Stitch the binding in place. starting ¼in (6mm) in from the diagonal folded edge. Reverse stitch to secure, and work ¼in (6mm) in from edge of the quilt towards first corner of quilt. Stop ¼in (6mm) in from corner and work a few reverse stitches.

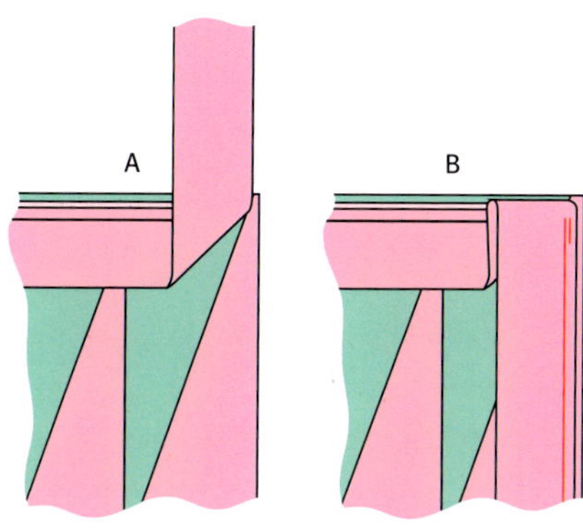

3 Fold the loose end of the binding up, making a 45-degree angle (see A). Keeping the diagonal fold in place, fold the binding back down, aligning the raw edges with the next side of the quilt. Starting at the point where the last stitch ended, stitch down the next side (see B).

4 Continue to stitch the binding in place around all the quilt edges in this way, tucking the finishing end of the binding inside the diagonal starting section.

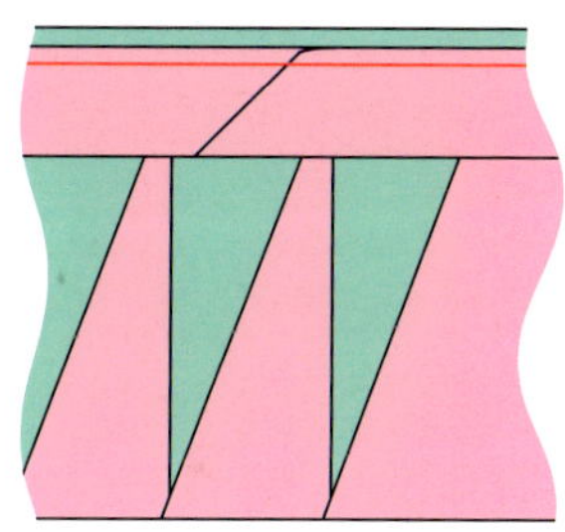

5 Turn the folded edge of the binding on to the back of the quilt. Hand stitch the folded edge in place just covering binding machine stitches, and folding a mitre at each corner.

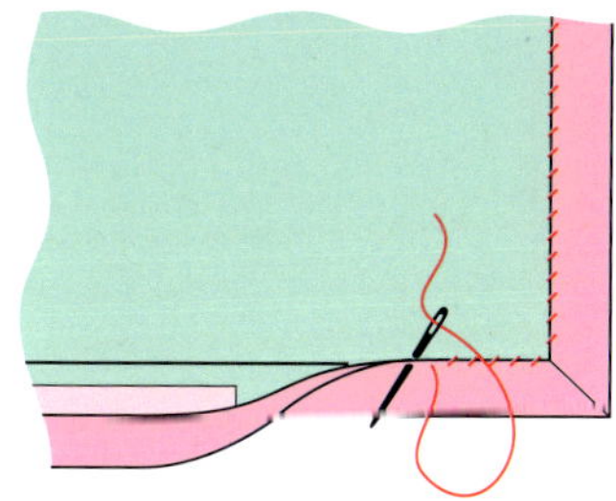

glossary of terms

Adhesive or fusible web This comes attached to a paper-backed sheet and is used to bond appliqué motifs to a background fabric. There are 2 types of web available, the first keeps the pieces in place whilst they are stitched, the second permanently attaches the pieces so that no sewing is required.

Appliqué The technique of stitching fabric shapes on to a background to create a design. It can be applied either by hand or machine with a decorative embroidery stitch, such as buttonhole, or satin stitch.

Backing The bottom layer of a quilt sandwich. It is made of fabric pieced to the size of the quilt top with the addition of about 4in (10cm) all around to allow for quilting take-up.

Basting or tacking This is a means of holding two fabric layers or the layers of a quilt sandwich together temporarily with large hand stitches or pins.

Batting or wadding This is the middle layer, or padding in a quilt. It can be made of cotton, wool, silk or synthetic fibres.

Bias The diagonal grain of a fabric. This is the direction which has the most give or stretch, making it ideal for bindings, especially on curved edges.

Binding A narrow strip of fabric used to finish off the edges of quilts or projects; it can be cut on the straight grain of a fabric or on the bias.

Block A single design unit that when stitched together with other blocks create the quilt top. It is most often a square, hexagon, or rectangle, but it can be any shape. It can be pieced or plain.

Border A frame of fabric stitched to the outer edges of the quilt top. Borders can be narrow or wide, pieced or plain. As well as making the quilt larger, they unify the overall design and draw attention to the central area.

Chalk pencils Available in various colours, they are used for marking lines or spots on fabric.

Cutting mat Designed for use with a rotary cutter, it is made from a special self-healing material that keeps your cutting blade sharp. Cutting mats come in various sizes and are usually marked with a grid to help you line up the edges of fabric and cut out larger pieces.

Design wall Used for laying out fabric patches before sewing. A large wall or folding board covered with flannel fabric or cotton batting in a neutral shade (dull beige or grey work well) will hold fabric in place so that an overall view can be taken of the placement.

Free-motion quilting Curved wavy quilting lines stitched in a random manner. Stitching diagrams are often given for you to follow as a loose guide.

Fussy cutting This is when a template is placed on a particular motif, or stripe, to obtain interesting effects. This method is not as efficient as strip cutting, but yields very interesting results.

Grain The direction in which the threads run in a woven fabric. In a vertical direction it is called the lengthwise grain, which has very little stretch. The horizontal direction, or crosswise grain is slightly stretchy, but diagonally the fabric has a lot of stretch. This grain is called the bias. Wherever possible the grain of a fabric should run in the same direction on a quilt block and borders.

Grain lines These are arrows printed on templates which should be aligned with the fabric grain.

Inset seams or setting-in A patchwork technique whereby one patch (or block) is stitched into a Y shape formed by the joining of two other patches (or blocks).

Patch A small shaped piece of fabric used in the making of a patchwork pattern.

Patchwork The technique of stitching small pieces of fabric (patches) together to create a larger piece of fabric, usually forming a design.

Pieced quilt A quilt composed of patches.

Quilting Traditionally done by hand with running stitches, but for speed modern quilts are often stitched by machine. The stitches are sewn through the top, wadding and backing to hold the three layers together. Quilting stitches are usually worked in some form of design, but they can be random.

Quilting hoop Consists of two wooden circular or oval rings with a screw adjuster on the outer ring. It stabilises the quilt layers, helping to create an even tension.

Reducing glass Used for viewing the complete composition of a quilt at a glance. It works like a magnifier in reverse. A useful tool for checking fabric placement before piecing a quilt.

Rotary cutter A sharp circular blade attached to a handle for quick, accurate cutting. It is a device that can be used to cut several layers of fabric at one time. It must be used in conjunction with a self-healing cutting mat and a thick plastic ruler.

Rotary ruler A thick, clear plastic ruler marked with lines in imperial or metric measurements. Sometimes they also have diagonal lines indicating 45 and 60 degree angles. A rotary ruler is used as a guide when cutting out fabric pieces using a rotary cutter.

Sashing A piece or pieced sections of fabric interspaced between blocks.

Sashing posts When blocks have sashing between them the corner squares are known as sashing posts.

Selvedges Also known as selvages, these are the firmly woven edges down each side of a fabric length. Selvedges should be trimmed off before cutting out your fabric, as they are more liable to shrink when the fabric is washed.

Stitch-in-the-ditch or Ditch quilting Also known as quilting-in-the-ditch. The quilting stitches are worked along the actual seam lines to give a pieced quilt texture.

Template A pattern piece used as a guide for marking and cutting out fabric patches, or marking a quilting, or appliqué design. Usually made from plastic or strong card that can be reused many times. Templates for cutting fabric usually have marked grain lines which should be aligned with the fabric grain.

Threads One hundred percent cotton or cotton-covered polyester is best for hand and machine piecing. Choose a colour that matches your fabric. When sewing different colours and patterns together, choose a medium to light neutral colour, such as grey or ecru. Specialist quilting threads are available for hand and machine quilting.

Walking foot or Quilting foot This is a sewing machine foot with dual feed control. It is very helpful when quilting, as the fabric layers are fed evenly from the top and below, reducing the risk of slippage and puckering.

Yo-Yos A circle of fabric double the size of the finished puff is gathered up into a rosette shape.

Y seams See Inset seams.

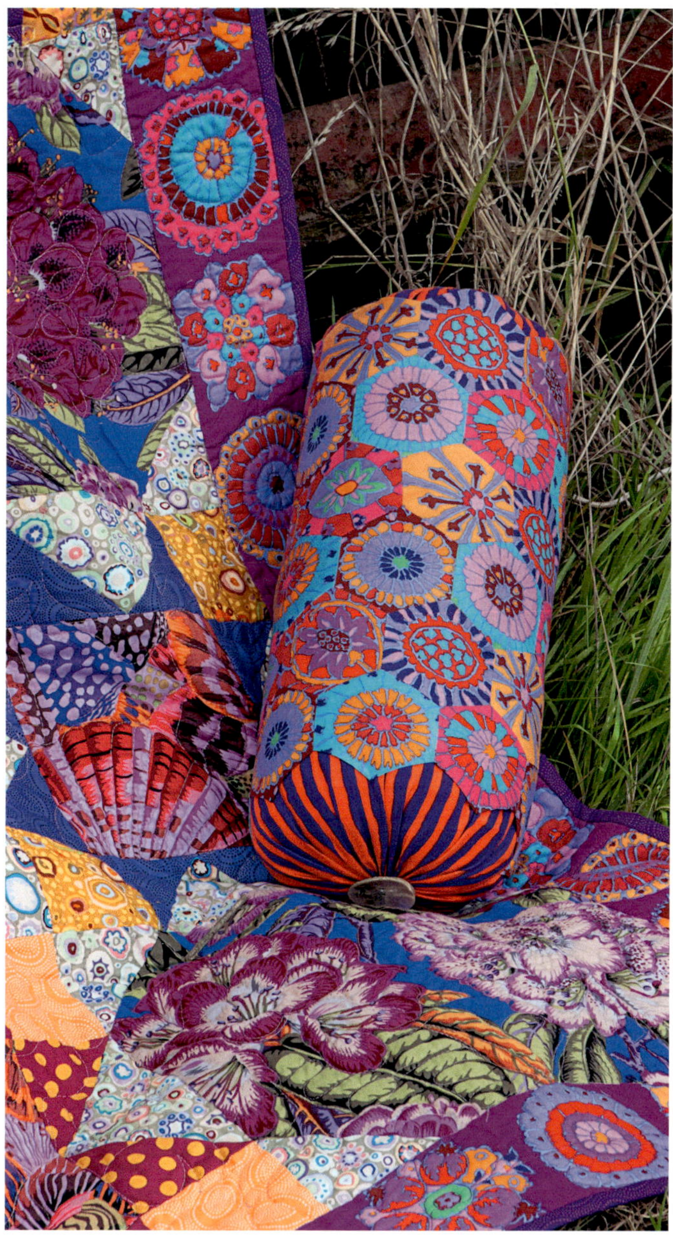

ACKNOWLEDGMENTS

I would like to thank Wakeham's Farm and Powdermill Wood for our wonderful settings for this book. Thanks to Belinda and Yvonne Mably for giving us a base to operate from and researching our farm location.

Always the deepest gratitude for a creative and joyful contribution from our quilt-making teams: Janet Haigh, with stitchers Ilaria Padovani and Julie Harvey, in the UK and Liza Lucy, with stitchers Mira Mayer, Bobbi Penniman and Emilija Gross in the USA. We are always grateful to Judy Irish and Mary-Jane Hutchinson for their quilting.

Grateful acknowledgment also to Bundle Backhouse for her detailed organising and careful checking of patterns in this book. Thanks, too, to our graphic designer, Anne Wilson, for her beautiful layouts. This book would never exist without the immensely talented eye of our photographer Debbie Patterson. Special thanks to Brandon Mably for overseeing everything at the studio from first inspiration to quilt location photography. Many thanks, too, to Susan Berry, for managing the process through to print, along with the team at Taunton.

And, for keeping our office afloat, along with a million and one invaluable jobs, and for her unquenchable enthusiasm, our deepest gratitude to Dorothy Hill, our studio assistant.

QUILT DESIGNERS, MAKERS AND QUILTERS
USA team (with Liza Prior Lucy)
Barn Doors Liza Prior Lucy: designer and maker; Judy Irish: quilter
Bean Stalks Kaffe Fassett: designer; Liza Prior Lucy: maker; Judy Irish: quilter
Faded Shuttles Kaffe Fassett: designer, Mira Mayer: maker; Judy Irish: quilter
Criss Cross Kaffe Fassett: designer; Liza Prior Lucy: maker and quilter
Rhododendron Stars Liza Prior Lucy: designer and maker; Judy Irish: quilter
Sailor's Gift Kaffe Fassett: designer; Liza Prior Lucy: maker; Judy Irish: quilter
Blooming Octagons (Dark and *Pastel)* Kaffe Fassett: designer; Emilija Mayer Gross: maker; Judy Irish: quilter
Golden Stars Kaffe Fassett: designer; Liza Prior Lucy: maker; Judy Irish: quilter
Windmills Kaffe Fassett: designer; Liza Prior Lucy: maker; Judy Irish: quilter

UK team (with Heart Space Studios: Janet Haigh)
(all UK quilts quilted by Mary-Jane Hutchinson)
Gingham Lattice Kaffe Fassett: designer; Julie Harvey: maker
Garden Bricks Kaffe Fassett: designer; Julie Harvey: maker
Gentleman's Relish Kaffe Fassett: designer; Ilaria Padovani: maker
Pearly Dream Kaffe Fassett: designer; Ilaria Padovani: maker
Lightning Strike Kaffe Fassett: designer; Ilaria Padovani: maker
Leafy Circles Kaffe Fassett: designer; Julie Harvey: maker
Blushing Nine-Patch Kaffe Fassett: designer; Ilaria Padovani: maker
Flowers and Fences Kaffe Fassett: designer; Julie Harvey: maker
Country Snowballs Kaffe Fassett: designer; Julie Harvey: maker
Deco Floral Kaffe Fassett: designer; Ilaria Padovani: maker

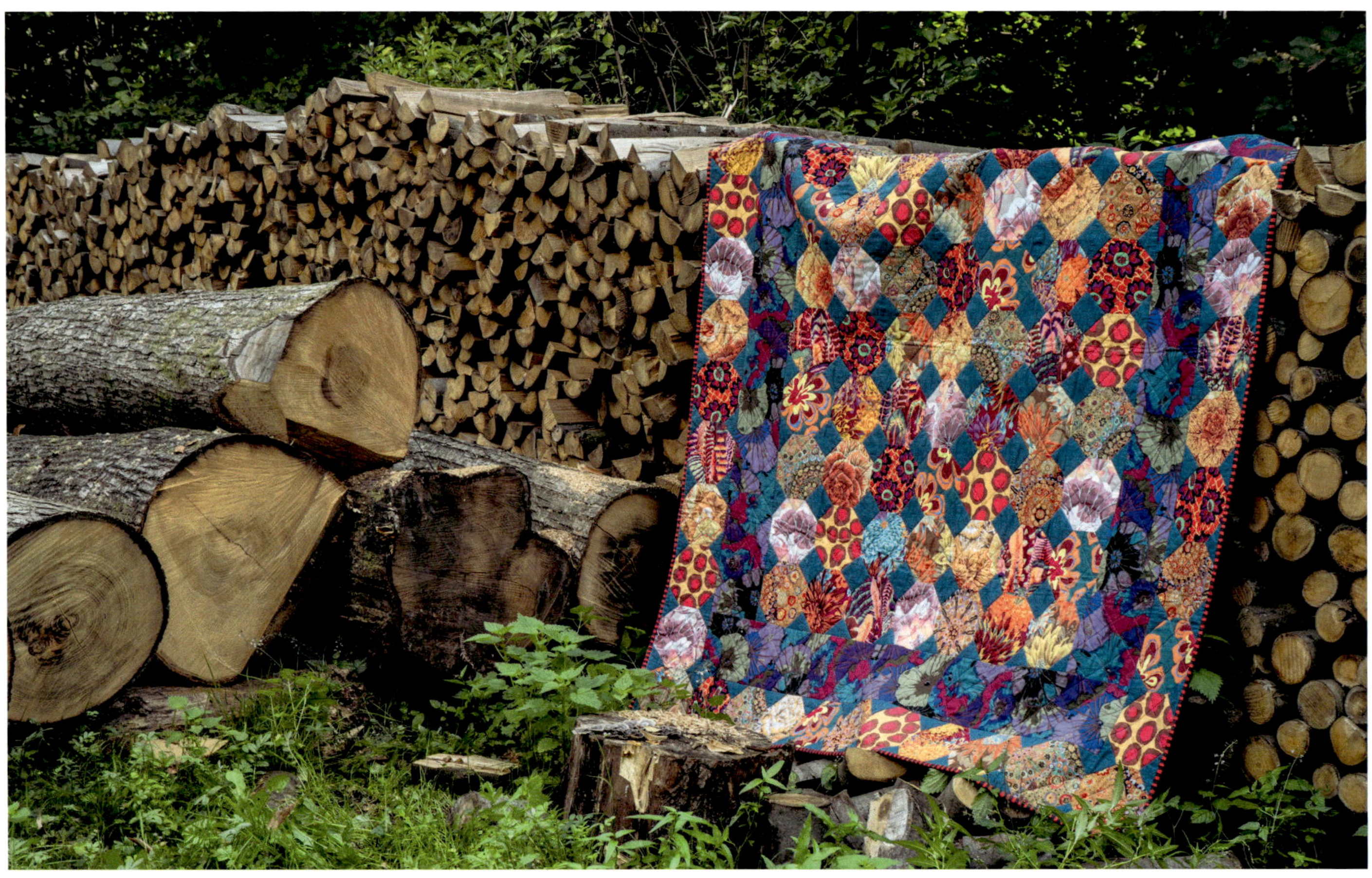